Urban Catholic Education

Tales of Twelve American Cities

CATHOLIC EDUCATION STUDIES DIVISION

Alliance for Catholic Education Press
at the University of Notre Dame

Urban Catholic Education

Tales of Twelve American Cities

Edited by
THOMAS C. HUNT
and
TIMOTHY WALCH

ALLIANCE FOR CATHOLIC EDUCATION PRESS
at the University of Notre Dame

Notre Dame, Indiana

Copyright © 2010 by

Alliance for Catholic Education Press
at the University of Notre Dame
158 IEI Building
Notre Dame, IN 46556
http://www.nd.edu/~acepress

ISBN: 978-0-9819501-8-1

Cover design by Mary Jo Adams Kocovski
Text design by Julie Wernick Dallavis

Cover photographs courtesy: (*top row*) Catholic Review Collection, Archives of the Archdiocese of Baltimore, Associated Archives of St. Mary's Seminary & University; The University of Saint Mary of the Lake/Mundelein Seminary; Archives of the Sisters of Charity of Cincinnati; (*second row*) Archives of the Sisters of Charity of the Incarnate Word, San Antonio; Archives of the Archdiocese of New York; Archives of the Archdiocese of Philadelphia; Archives of the Archdiocese of Detroit; (*third row*) Archives of the Archdiocese of Detroit; Archives of the Sisters of Charity of the Incarnate Word, San Antonio; Archives of the Archdiocese of New Orleans; Catholic Review Collection, Archives of the Archdiocese of Baltimore, Associated Archives of St. Mary's Seminary & University; (*bottom row*) Sisters of St. Joseph of Carondelet, St. Louis Province Archives; Archives of the Archdiocese of San Francisco; Boston CSJ Archives; Archives of the Archdiocese of Los Angeles.

Library of Congress Cataloging-in-Publication Data

Urban Catholic education : tales of twelve American cities / Edited by Thomas C. Hunt, Timothy Walch.
    p. cm.
  Includes bibliographical references and index.
  Summary: "Traces the history of Catholic schooling in twelve urban areas of the United States"--Provided by publisher.
  ISBN 978-0-9819501-8-1 (pbk. : alk. paper) -- ISBN 978-0-9819501-9-8 (hardcover : alk. paper)
  1. Catholic schools--United States--History--Case studies. 2. Urban education--United States--History--Case studies. I. Hunt, Thomas C., 1930- II. Walch, Timothy, 1947-
  LC501.U73 2010
  371.071'273--dc22
                        2010010767

This book was printed on acid-free paper.

Printed in the United States of America.

*For the five generations of sister-teachers
who educated tens of millions of American children,
one soul at a time. Thank you, Sister!*

Contents

PART THREE: THE BORDERLAND

Foreword

Education has been a central preoccupation of Americans from the earliest days of settlement when English dissenters recognized the need to take deliberate steps to pass on their most cherished values to their children. Far from their ancestral homeland, forming new communities on the edges of the wilderness, hopeful but anxious about the future, parents could not take it for granted that their children would understand or appreciate the momentous decisions that had brought them to the New World. They would have to be taught. This experience continued on through a long national history of immigration and community formation.

In some places parents had to do this work of education almost alone, as in frontier families, but in many places churches took shape around this need for generational transmission of the family story. Protestant, Catholic, and Jewish congregations had as a central purpose education, first among immigrants struggling to be themselves while adapting to the requirement of American society, then in each subsequent generation wrestling with problems of economic insecurity, mobility, and religious and cultural diversity. Public schools joined the project, sometimes supplementing the work of religious associations, sometimes battling with them for control of what eventually became a common project of education. Public schools made their adjustments to family and ethnic interests, while private schools acknowledged civic as well as more limited ethnic or religious responsibilities. The story of Catholic education, then, is a story about Catholics and about Americans, and the stories told here are about twelve cities and a significant portion of the people who lived there.

Catholic education is surely one of the most dramatic American education stories. In city after city Catholic churches, schools, and social service agencies were created by the people, almost all of whom were poor, many of whom were immigrants. This was a people's church, and so were these schools. In these schools, and in the parishes that supported them, "folk memories" blended with "new aspirations" as communities shared resources to make sure that traditional values were passed on: this worried some, though far from all, Protestants, native Americans, and assorted reformers, who feared these institutions would perpetuate divisions and weaken democratic institutions. Instead the contrary was true, for as several of these historians brilliantly point out, the schools were agencies of public cohesion as well as group interest.

That is in part because they were not just about memory and never were intended to be systems of social separatism. Instead they were aimed at the realization of "new aspirations," family aspirations for economic security, ethnic aspirations for social respect, ecclesiastical aspirations for organized, consistent religious practice. Toward these ends poor, working-class peoples assembled considerable economic and human resources to construct networks and institutions that helped shape American cities and helped millions of people move from the margins to the centers of American life. It is a remarkable success story.

But it is not one story. Thomas C. Hunt and Timothy Walch are two veteran scholars who have helped write the history of American Catholic education. One thing they learned was the importance of place: each local church is different, shaped by its unique combination of history, communities, cultures, and leaders. Accordingly they assembled this team of first-rate American historians to examine the history of Catholic education in sites across the country. Each of these historians has a distinguished record of research; several have already written impressive local diocesan histories. They know their local communities and each is also a respected student of American history and American Catholic history. As a result, we now have twelve extremely valuable scholarly essays that merit close attention from students of American urban and social history, educational and religious history.

The themes are many, but a few stand out as helpful in reflection on the overall story of American educational history. One is surely how local voluntary associations of bishops, priests, sisters, and lay people were able to construct educational institutions that made democracy work for millions of families. Another is the delicate balance of particular and general, denominational and public interests. In almost every chapter the reader will find well known but freshly told stories of Catholic-Protestant, nativist-immigrant conflicts. But they will also find plenty of evidence that most Catholic leaders took their public responsibilities seriously: their arguments as citizens for a positive role for religion in education still deserve respectful attention, for that question is far from resolved. And the reader will find some non-Catholic civic and educational leaders who respected what the Catholic schools achieved and found them to be assets in constructing a stable civic culture. Perhaps most interesting is the way that at least three of the essays explicitly acknowledge the irony that, in fighting to make public schools accessible to Catholic families, Catholics contributed to the very secularization that they wished to avoid for themselves and that they considered a serious civic problem. Contemporary critics of secularization might consider this experience. Here one deals with the related theme of diversity, not only as natives and immigrants fought with each other but as ethnic groups contended with each other within the Catholic community. Here one asks about the value of separate and integrated religious institutions.

Finally there is the story of race. Justin Poché adds rich background and remarkable details to the story of the desegregation of Catholic schools and parishes in New Orleans. Almost all the other essays end with the crisis of the sixties and seventies, one part of which was "white flight" and racial conflict, stories not yet fully told. One hopes that Hunt and Walch might commission a set of essays on the local post-1960 stories.

After reading this book I wanted to talk about it with the many active Catholics working so hard today to support Catholic education. Wherever serious discussions are taking place about Catholic educational ministries and shared responsibilities for public education, this book will be a valuable resource, thanks to the editors and to these talented scholars.

David O'Brien
University Professor of Faith and Culture, University of Dayton
Loyola Professor of Catholic Studies Emeritus, College of the Holy Cross

Introduction

Thomas C. Hunt

Timothy Walch

This book traces its origins to the excellent study published by the Thomas B. Fordham Institute in 2008 entitled *Who Will Save America's Urban Catholic Schools?* The study revealed that 1,300 Catholic schools, most of which were located in cities, had closed since 1990, with the result that an estimated 300,000 students had to go elsewhere to school. The report further stated that Catholic school closings in the last two decades had "likely cost taxpayers more than $20 billion to accommodate the additional students that district and charter schools have absorbed."

The Fordham report utilized case studies in addressing the issues that surrounded the plight of Catholic urban schools in the twenty-first century. That focus led directly to the structure of this book: a collection of historical case studies on the evolving history of Catholic education in twelve of the nation's largest cities.

Historically, Catholic schools were mainly located in the country's urban centers. Such a statement should not imply a common experience, however. There were substantial differences among and between the Catholic schools in these very different cities, and this book purports to show those differences. A distinguished collection of authors relate the unfolding of Catholic education in twelve major metropolitan centers in the United States from their beginnings to the middle of the twentieth century.

Each author was asked to consider the following points in presenting the development of Catholic schools in each city. First was the matter of the ethnic mix in the community and what impact demographics had on both urban and school development. Second was the interest and commitment of Catholic leaders—prelates, pastors, parents, and women religious—in the establishment of parish schools. Third were the attitudes for and against Catholicism and Catholic schools on the part of non-Catholics in these emerging communities. Fourth was the size and subsequent growth of the Catholic community in these cities. Finally, each author was asked to consider how these four factors contributed to the distinctive educational experiences for Catholics in the respective communities.

These twelve cities were selected for several reasons. First, they were chosen for their importance as centers of Catholic educational development. Second, the editors wanted to show the diversity of Catholic educational experiences in these varied cities and regions. In truth, there was no single Catholic educational experience in these United States. Third, we planned a book that presented the story of the history of Catholic schools in different geographical regions of the country from the large archdioceses of the East coast, to the burgeoning archdioceses of the industrial heartland, to the archdioceses on our southern and western borderlands.

Although the evolution of Catholic education in each of these cities was unique, a careful reading of these chapters reveals a number of common threads that are woven throughout the history of Catholic education not only in these twelve cities but also in other cities across the nation.

The first of these threads is, of course, the sheer will to survive. Beginning in the middle of the sixteenth century, Catholics struggled to sustain their religion and its few churches in a hostile land. Spanish missionaries in Texas and French missionaries in Louisiana, for example, suffered great hardship in a largely futile effort to educate the native populations. Irish-born priests in cities along the East coast struggled to sustain their small flock of colonial Catholics in the face of a hostile Protestant majority. It was not clear until the 1820s that Catholicism in general, and Catholic schools in particular, would survive in this country.

The second thread is immigration. What secured the future of Catholic education in these twelve cities was the arrival of tens of millions of immigrant Catholics during the years from 1820 to 1920. Impoverished but ambitious, concerned about the preservation of their religion and their culture in the New World, many of these immigrants embraced parish schools as the answer to their concerns. It was the determination of these immigrant Catholic parents that took parish schooling from a few dozen schools in 1820 to nearly ten thousand schools 140 years later.

The third thread is the variety of responses to the parish school movement. Contrary to the popular belief that American Catholics uniformly supported these schools, less than half of the Catholic school-age population received a Catholic education. To be sure, many immigrant Catholics were eager and enthusiastic supporters of parochial education, but most Catholic parents did not join the cause. Indeed, as these chapters clearly document, not all Catholic bishops and pastors were uniformly supportive of parish schools. In truth, there was a wide range of responses to the Catholic school movement. That variety of response is seen chapter by chapter in this book.

A fourth thread is adaptability. The success of parochial education in these twelve cities was insured by the willingness of Catholic educators over many generations to change and revise the parochial school curriculum in response to changes in the public school curriculum and the desires and aspirations of Catholic parents. Catholic educators realized that a rigid, doctrinaire curriculum would force Catholic parents to choose between their religious faith and their children's future. By incorporating many of the elements of public schooling into the parish school curriculum, Catholic educators promised to secure both the Faith and the future of her children.

The fifth thread is community. Perhaps the greatest asset of parochial schooling—even to the present day—is that the Catholic schools in these twelve cities reflected the goals, aspirations, and even the prejudices and fears of the neighborhood Catholics who supported these institutions. Public school teachers often lived outside the neighborhoods where they taught, and the curriculum was established by a school superintendent or a school committee downtown.

But parish schools were community based in every sense of the word. Each immigrant group established its own "national" parishes with their own ethnic Catholic schools. Parents had a sense of involvement in these schools. To be sure, these immigrants deferred to their pastors and to the nuns in the classrooms, but pastors and teachers alike were well aware that parental support was vital if parish schools were to thrive.

A final thread is identity. For most of its existence, the Catholic school was seen as a safe haven for a religious minority that did not feel welcome in the public schools. But after the Second Vatican Council in the 1960s, and for the next generation, the differences between Catholics and non-Catholics on educational issues seemed to fade away. The justification for maintaining a separate, very costly school system seemed less compelling. Many schools were closed and those that remained were redefined. But with this redefinition came a new vitality. Catholic schools were more willing to experiment with new ideas and respond to the diverse and changing needs of today's Catholic students. In short, Catholic schools became leaner, more cost-effective institutions than their public counterparts. Out of adversity had come a new identity.

These threads—survival, immigration, variety, adaptability, community, and identity—interweave to tell the dramatic story of a social institution in a dozen cities that ingeniously responded to almost constant change in American society without abandoning two basic goals: the preservation of the religious faith of Catholic children and the preparation of these children for productive roles in American society.

It is a story that is worth telling and a story that Catholic parents should not overlook in the day-to-day effort to support Catholic education. Just as past generations survived and even thrived, so will future generations of American Catholic schools thrive in the next century. The common threads of our past keep our future in perspective.

Any book such as this one is the product of many hands and the editors would be remiss if we failed to acknowledge our colleagues. Foremost, of course, are the authors of the chapters that follow. Even a cursory review of the biographical statements at the end of this book provides ample evidence of the stature of these authors; they are an impressive group. Just as important as their scholarship, however, are their contributions as teachers, pastors, parents, and administrators. Our contributors are "catholic" in the fullest sense of that word.

Also worthy of special commendation is the tireless staff of the Alliance for Catholic Education Press at the University of Notre Dame. Led by the Reverend Ronald J. Nuzzi with the assistance of Julie Dallavis, the newly established ACE Press promises to provide new avenues of thought for anyone interested in the contours of Catholic education in the United States.

Finally, the editors wish to acknowledge the lasting contributions of the sister-teachers and the teaching brothers and priests who educated them in the Catholics schools of Madison, Wisconsin, and Detroit, Michigan. These extraordinary men and women are fundamental to the history of urban Catholic education. We hope that we have made them proud with this book.

Part One
The Cradle of Catholic Education

"Maryland's unique status as an English colony founded by Catholics in 1634 would prove decisive for the history of the Baltimore church and its educational institutions."
— *Maria Mazzenga*

"Philadelphia's urban Catholic schools originated from a zealous missionary ideal, religious tolerance, Catholic migration from other colonies, and the laity's dedicated efforts. From this point forward, these factors would figure prominently in the founding, expansion, and systematization of the Quaker city's urban Catholic schools."
— *Richard M. Jacobs*

"Archbishop [Timothy] Dolan was under no illusions that he faced an uphill struggle to save the Catholic school system in New York and that many observers were skeptical about his prospects for success. However, as a professional Church historian, Dolan was also well aware that Clio has a habit of confounding prophets."
— *Thomas J. Shelley*

"[Bishop John Fitzpatrick of Boston] would not allow specific instances of anti-Catholicism in the schools to break his fundamental belief in the American systems of government, justice, and education. He believed that to open a parochial school system parallel to that already funded by the government was a waste of money and would perpetuate an Irish 'separateness' that he considered unhealthy."
— *John J. White*

The Cradle of Catholicism:
Catholic Education in Baltimore

Maria Mazzenga

Maryland's unique status as an English colony founded by Catholics in 1634 would prove decisive for the history of the Baltimore church and its educational institutions. To be sure, the colony's legacy of Catholic religious freedom was inconsistent, but Maryland could rightfully take credit for the origins of Catholic education in the British colonies with the arrival of Jesuit missionaries in the seventeenth century.

The City of Baltimore also could take credit for being the site of the first Catholic diocese of the United States, established in 1789, and the first archdiocese in the United States, established in 1808. The city's prominence as the "premier see" of the Catholic Church in the United States, therefore, gave added attention to its educational initiatives during the years from 1789 to 1830.[1]

Baltimore historian Thomas W. Spalding discerns two basic traditions that shaped the history of the diocese in its formative years. The "Maryland tradition" emerged during the episcopacy of John Carroll (1789-1815) and had its origins in the Calvert family and the other Catholic families who dominated the state from earliest settlement through the 1820s. This tradition "presupposed a neutral state based on the principles of religious freedom and separation of church and state."[2]

Carroll himself championed this tradition, one that emerged out of the revolutionary ferment he witnessed during that era as well as the democratic principles and missionary possibilities of the new republic. The Maryland tradition tended toward ecumenism, particularly with respect to the Protestant majority. An overarching spirit of experimentalism prevailed, as the Church adapted to its new surroundings. To be a Maryland Catholic was to fully embrace the values of the American Republic.

A second tradition—the "immigrant tradition"—emerged as millions of Catholics from Europe emigrated to Baltimore beginning with the episcopacy of Samuel Eccleston (1834-1851) and continuing at a steady pace until Michael Curley (1921-1947) served as the Baltimore archbishop. Very different historical circumstances, of course, shaped the immigrant church than had shaped the Carroll church. Industrialization, ethnic diversity, and wide-scale poverty were common among Maryland Catholics from the middle of the nineteenth to the middle of the twentieth century.

The immigrant tradition produced a "ghetto" church in Baltimore, that is, a church that developed a defensive attitude toward the broader, often anti-Catholic society as well as a separate set of institutions in which this Catholic culture could thrive. Both the Maryland and immigrant traditions shaped the history of Catholic education in Baltimore, though the immigrant church is far more prominent in the evolution of the city's parochial schools.[3]

The experimentalism exhibited by John Carroll and the Catholics of the archdiocese's early years proved useful in an era of practical challenges. John Carroll was well aware that the survival of Catholicism in the new republic demanded educational institutions to shape future generations. To that end, Carroll attempted to secure clerical leaders and religious educators to open and sustain such schools.

One such leader was Father Francis Moranville, a French immigrant priest who Carroll appointed pastor of St. Patrick's parish in 1805. Eager to establish a parish school, but lacking the funds to do so, Moranville first founded the St. Patrick's Benevolent Society to raise money for educational purposes. In 1815, Moranville finally opened the St. Patrick's Free School and enrolled fifty young female pupils within a month. A separate building was acquired for boys, and students of all faiths were admitted. Since there were no public schools in the city at the time, this was an educational first for Baltimore.[4]

St. Patrick's Free School was an example of the general pattern of Catholic parish school building in the early to mid-nineteenth century Baltimore. The city's Catholic leadership clearly placed a high priority on education, but lacked the funds to establish parish schools; this would be a problem through the nineteenth century. Additionally, if Baltimore's educational institutions were to follow the European model, which was considered ideal, the bishop and his pastors had to recruit numerous teaching sisters to staff the classrooms. This was no small challenge for Carroll and his successors.

Though Carroll worked hard to secure teaching sisters, lay teachers were essential to staff many Catholic schools. At St. Patrick's, for example, Peggy James, assisted by Bridget Connell, taught the female students, while a "Mr. O'Connor" taught the boys.[5] Decades later, the Brothers of St. Patrick, the Xaverian Brothers, and the Sisters of Holy Cross ran the school.

The challenge of staffing the schools did not slow the growth of parochial education in Baltimore in the middle years of the nineteenth century. By 1855, there were eleven Catholic parochial schools in Baltimore, and by 1865, there were four communities of teaching sisters in the city that would influence the city's Catholic schools well into the future: the School Sisters of Notre Dame, the Sisters of Mercy, the Sisters of the Holy Cross, and the Sisters of Charity. By this time, there also were two communities of teaching brothers: the Christian Brothers and the Brothers of Holy Cross. Key educational issues in the nineteenth century for nearly all of the parish schools were staffing and funds to maintain the schools; these issues were gradually addressed by the city's Catholic authorities.[6]

Securing vowed religious as teachers in the city's schools was a priority for Baltimore's early archbishops. In this regard, the influence of French Catholics on the development of the city's earliest educational system would be prominent. While the Jesuits exercised strong influence over education in the earliest years of the archdiocese, particularly outside the city of Baltimore, within the city, it was the French Sulpicians who dominated. The Sulpicians ran St. Mary's Seminary and largely focused on training for the priesthood. As a result, they were constrained by financial circumstances to educate only students who could pay tuition.[7]

Also important was the introduction of the Sisters of Charity into the city's educational history. The sisters were established by Elizabeth Bayley Seton, an American-born convert to Catholicism. Seton came to Baltimore in 1808 with assistance from the president of St. Mary's Seminary, Father William DuBourg. Although Seton's aim was to educate youth from the archdiocese's impoverished families, her order was in debt and was forced to establish academies for wealthier students to support the order and to pay for schools for the less fortunate. Seton would soon leave Baltimore for Emmitsburg, Maryland, where she established the Sisters of Charity, later named the Daughters of Charity.

The second Catholic school in Baltimore was St. Mary's Asylum and Free School, which was established in 1817 and administered by the Sisters of Charity beginning in 1821. This school, like other schools for the poor run by the sisters, trained pupils in vocational trades and was sustained by private donations. The Sisters of Charity would have a significant impact on Baltimore education, staffing many of its parish schools and educating many thousands of its children well into the twentieth century.[8]

Also founded in Baltimore through the efforts of the Sulpicians was the first successful order of black sisters, the Oblate Sisters of Providence. Father Jacques Hector Nicholas Joubert, who had served in Haiti as a government official before being ordained a Sulpician priest at St. Mary's Seminary in 1810, met two Haitian women interested in religious life and engaged in teaching in their home. Joubert worked with the women to establish the Oblate Sisters of Providence in 1828.

Simultaneous with the foundation of the order, the Oblates established the first school for black Catholics in Baltimore with an enrollment of twenty female students. The sisters taught English, French, writing, sewing, embroidery, washing, and ironing to these first students, and would, like the Sisters of Charity, serve the Catholic community well into the twentieth century. By 1944, nineteen Oblate sisters were teaching 693 black students in three Baltimore parochial schools. Unfortunately, these schools practiced racial segregation with the rest of the city's educational institutions until the initiatives of the twentieth century civil rights era challenged the practice.[9] These earliest schools fit into the Maryland tradition of experimentation, openness, and a desire to prepare functioning citizens for the new nation.

The Maryland tradition, though only initiated by Carroll, dominated Baltimore's urban Catholic educational landscape past that prelate's episcopacy well into the 1830s. Thomas Spalding asserts, however, that it survived in only an attenuated form due largely to the dramatic transformation in Baltimore Catholicism caused by the influx of immigrants to the city. The number of Catholics in Baltimore grew throughout the Carroll episcopacy, reaching four thousand by 1810 and making it the city's single largest denomination at 12 percent of the religious population.[10]

Each decade of the nineteenth century saw the acceleration in this trend of Catholic growth. The immigrant church began to emerge during the Eccleston administration with streams of Irish and German Catholics entering the city beginning in the 1830s. The number of Catholics in the archdiocese under Eccleston grew from eighty thousand to one hundred twenty thousand with most of the newcomers residing in the city itself. By 1862, sixty thousand Catholics of predominantly English, Irish, German, and African descent resided in Baltimore. Under the lengthy term of Archbishop James Gibbons (1877-1921), the older groups of immigrants became more and more American, but the Church's ethnic character also increased. One 1887 estimate put the number of German Americans in the city at one hundred thousand out of a total population of four hundred twenty-five thousand. Over a third of these Germans were Catholic and possessed a network of social, devotional, and cultural institutions. In 1913, according to Gibbons, there were twenty thousand Poles, eight thousand Bohemians, two thousand five hundred Lithuanians, and two thousand Italians in the Archdiocese of Baltimore.[11]

By the 1920s and the Curley episcopacy, there were as many as fifty thousand Polish Catholics in Baltimore, six thousand Lithuanian Catholics, and several thousand Italians. The Catholics that migrated to the United States during these years were generally less educated than their forebears and came from predominantly rural areas. They adopted a different posture toward their new surroundings than their predecessors, a posture dictated in part by the attitudes of the native population toward them. Anti-Catholicism surfaced in a variety of forms in Maryland in the 1830s, 1850s, 1890s, and the 1920s, and this animosity shaped the direction of Baltimore Catholicism.

The construction of the Baltimore and Ohio Railroad in this port city accelerated the development of its manufacturing and shipping industries. In addition to work on the docks and the railroads, immigrants and the city's working class found employment in the city's canneries and garment, textile, and steel industries, among others.[12] A network of ethnic and territorial parishes populated by a combination of working- and middle-class Catholics arose in the nineteenth century, expanding into the early twentieth.

The Third Plenary Council of Catholic Bishops, held in Baltimore in 1884, produced Catholic legislation mandating the construction of Catholic schools across the nation just as Catholic migration to the city was making the expansion of parish churches imperative. One quarter of the legislation of the council addressed the matter of Catholic schools. The assembled bishops and archbishops ordered that "within 2 years a parochial school was to be erected near each church and was to be maintained 'in perpetuum.'" Postponement required episcopal approval. Parents, moreover, were strongly urged to send their children to parochial schools.[13]

As it happened, the advocacy of Gibbons for parochial school construction was not particularly vigorous despite the apparent urgency of the Council's educational directives. Pastors went ahead and built schools alongside their churches, but Gibbons was not strict about enforcing the Council's legislation. In fact, this nationally prominent archbishop was better known for his involvement in several controversies erupting within the American Catholic community in the late nineteenth century.

One of the more well known was the Americanist controversy when Gibbons and other Catholic bishops defended efforts to find accommodation between Catholic doctrine, American pluralism, and freedom of religion. Gibbons favored adaptation and openness toward American ideals, a position that would eventually earn him a mild rebuke by Vatican authorities. Although he was an immigrant himself, his views placed him squarely in the Maryland tradition rather than the immigrant tradition of Baltimore Catholicism.[14]

Robust American values also would color the response of Gibbons to the so-called "Cahenslyism" crisis of 1891, which had implications for the U.S. parochial school system in general. In 1890, Peter Paul Cahensly, a German Catholic lay man, had drafted a petition to Pope Leo XIII outlining ways to sustain Germans' Catholic values after they immigrated to the United States. Known as the Lucerne Memorial, the petition claimed that more than ten million German souls had lost their Catholic faith in Protestant America and that separate German Catholic institutions, including parochial schools, were necessary to prevent further losses of Germans from the Faith. When the Lucerne Memorial became public, a national debate ensued, and Gibbons, who favored the rapid Americanization of immigrants, vigorously opposed separate institutions for German American Catholics. In a response to the Lucerne Memorial, the Pope appeared to agree with Gibbons.

Gibbons also defended the concept of tax-supported Catholic schools as manifested in the small towns of Faribault and Stillwater, Minnesota. Archbishop John Ireland of St. Paul, a friend of Gibbons and a fellow Americanist, favored state use of Catholic schools for public instruction during regular hours, with religious instruction after normal school hours. Ireland implemented the plan, already in existence in upstate New York, in those two Minnesota towns. The act appeared to challenge the mandate for parochial school construction passed at the Third Plenary Council and generated much controversy. In fact, there also were publicly supported parish schools in the Archdiocese of Baltimore. Gibbons appeared to lean toward creating more such schools, but the plan never came to fruition.

These two controversies were suggestive of the attitudes of Gibbons toward Americanization, ethnic Catholics, and parochial schooling. He favored a Catholic education that was more open to compromise with American institutions and ideals than several of his more conservative contemporaries, such as Bishop Bernard McQuaid of Rochester and Archbishop Michael Corrigan of New York, both of whom believed the positions of Ireland and Gibbons would amount to an abandonment of the parochial school system.[15]

Gibbons, as well as his predecessor Martin John Spalding, oversaw a substantial expansion of the Catholic school system. For example, between 1865 and 1900, twenty-seven parochial schools were established in the city, including three for African American Catholics. Staffing was always a challenge, but new religious orders arrived during these years to meet the educational needs presented by the enormous influx of Catholics into the city. The Sisters of St. Francis of Mill Hill came to minister to the black Catholic community, joining the Oblate Sisters. Reflecting the expansion of the immigrant church, the Felician Sisters, a Polish order, arrived to serve the Polish Americans in St. Stanislaus and Holy Rosary parishes, where sixteen sisters helped staff schools with 1,012 students in 1900; they would also staff St. Casimir's parish school when it opened in 1904. Others were the Sisters of St. Benedict and the Sisters of St. Joseph.[16]

Destined to have an enormous impact on Catholic education in Baltimore were the School Sisters of Notre Dame (SSND), many of whom were assigned to the newly established schools. This German order came to Baltimore at the request of the Redemptorist Fathers, who had been asked previously by Eccleston to come and minister to the burgeoning German population in the city. In 1847, the Redemptorists managed three schools connected to German parishes, and the SSND sisters taught the girls. During the Gibbons episcopacy, the sisters taught in sixteen of the new schools established in Baltimore. By 1922, just after the death of Gibbons, they were teaching in forty schools in the archdiocese, nineteen of them in Baltimore city. This number remained steady to the mid-1940s: in 1944, 220 sisters taught 8,740 students in nineteen parochial schools, making them the largest teaching order in the city.[17]

A closer look at this influential teaching order's schools, teachers, and pupils during this more recent period illuminates the ways in which the economic problems and class issues of the previous century worked out over time. Class divisions were reproduced among the Catholic school youth of Baltimore as they were in the broader society.

As noted previously, Elizabeth Seton and the Sisters of Charity were compelled to open academies for upper-class youth in order to help fund schools for less fortunate students, a fact that underscored the class divisions between the two groups of students. Indeed, this was a common practice: several orders started "paying schools" or academies that attracted elite students in order to help sustain their work among youth of less stable financial circumstances.

While many SSND taught in parochial schools requiring nominal fees, they also staffed schools that catered to vastly different constituencies as well. The SSND opened the Institute of Notre Dame in 1847, for example, as a boarding school for girls. By 1883, the school had 134 students. The school was so popular that by 1916 it was functioning as a day school only, which enabled higher enrollments. By the early 1940s, however, it offered both an academic course and a business course to its curriculum and featured a range of classes and clubs to enhance students' cultural and social literacy, including painting, drawing, music classes, dressmaking, and sodality. In 1942, there were 518 girls enrolled at the institute, and it was a source of pride to Catholic educators throughout the city. The sisters also opened Notre Dame College of Maryland in 1873, which one Catholic chronicler of the city's Catholic schools called "one of the most high-toned high schools and colleges of the country."[18]

The institute enrolled students from all over the city, but middle- and upper-class German American and Irish American youth predominated in the early 1940s. The list of 140 graduates of the 1941 class is mainly one of Irish and German names; only five Polish and five Italian names appeared on the roster that year.[19]

The experience of one student of the institute in the mid- to late-1930s, Eleanor Apicella, who had grown up in Baltimore's Little Italy, is anecdotal but suggestive of what this ethnic configuration might have looked like to an Italian American girl of a working-class background. She says of her experience at the institute, "I felt very comfortable in Little Italy until I went to high school." There was

> a lot of suburbia. They made us feel inferior when we told them we were from Little Italy because Little Italy in those days was the slums. . . . I had never been aware of that until I went there. [Mimicking girls' reactions:] "You live in Little Italy!? Oh my God, how could you stand it? Aren't you afraid that they'll come out with guns and knives?" I said, "I never saw anybody with a knife." . . . They were afraid of crime because of the slums.[20]

Apicella says that there were about ten Italian American youth that attended the Institute when she did. "We kept to ourselves. . . . We really didn't mix in too much with the girls because we just felt we weren't equal to them."[21]

Julia Poggi, also from Little Italy, attended Notre Dame College in the 1920s. She found that her Italian background caused her to be considered a "peon."[22] While this suggests, as does the Apicella memoir, a class antagonism with ethnic overtones, one need only look at the experiences of other SSND sisters in the city to grasp that not all members of the older ethnic groups had climbed into middle- or upper-class status.

SSND sisters taught schools with impoverished children of a range of ethnic groups as well. Sister Emeline Evler, for example, taught students of Irish, German, and Polish descent, among others, at Sacred Heart of Jesus in the Highlandtown section of the city in the 1940s. Her students were from economically deprived families, "all blue collar," and employed at the local canning factory or "putting boxes together." She prayed for her impoverished students constantly, even as she took pride in those of her students that had moved on to successful careers.[23] These educators, then, both altered and furthered the class system in which they operated.

Even though Baltimore's Catholic educational system contained opportunities for the education of African American girls, these were far fewer in number than those available to white girls. Guinevere Spurlock notes that St. Frances Academy, run by the Oblate Sisters, was the only secondary school open to African American Catholic girls. None of the parish schools for black Catholics went beyond the eighth grade. According to Spurlock, demand for a high-school level education peaked in the 1940s, remaining high into the 1950s.[24]

Collectively, these circumstances reflect the finding of Paula Fass that the U.S. Catholic high school social structure was an "elongated pyramid." At the top of the pyramid, writes Fass, "were those who attended elite, almost exclusively college-oriented, private schools. Below them were the students in diocesan and parish high schools" and "at the bottom, pushed out of the Catholic track entirely, were the majority of Catholic students who for one reason or another chose to attend public school or could not get into or remain at the Catholic schools."[25]

Whether or not Curley would have claimed that the social structure within the Catholic school system he inherited from Gibbons was an "elongated pyramid" is questionable. To be sure, he seemed to be aware that this was the case, and in focusing on reforming the educational system, he clearly tried to create a more inclusive Catholic high school system.

Curley is viewed as a figure nearly opposite in temperament and vision from his predecessor Gibbons. "The Curley Church," writes Spalding, "would stand at the opposite pole of American Catholicism" compared to Gibbons.[26] In this view, Curley embodied the immigrant church and facilitated the growth of ghetto Catholicism. He encouraged ethnics to maintain their traditions and was not an "Americanizer" in the style of Gibbons.

Curley's emphasis, rather, was on bolstering the Catholic faith in a world he often perceived as hostile toward the Church. To do this, Curley used all of the instruments at his disposal: his diocesan newspaper, the Baltimore *Catholic Review*, public pronouncements, lay devotional organizations, charitable organizations, and especially educational institutions. He favored a highly organized diocesan governing structure and strict adherence to rule and doctrine. Curley took strong public positions on anti-Catholicism, persecution of Catholics in the Mexican Revolution (1926-1940) and the Spanish Civil War (1936-1939), among other issues of the day. He was vociferously anti-Communist, and battled indecency, as he saw it, in film and culture.[27]

Curley's style of leadership and vision had a significant impact on Baltimore's Catholic schools, the improvement of which he made a priority during his episcopacy. Upon his installation as archbishop in 1921, Curley stated,

> The battles of the future will be fought on the fields of education. The
> Catholic Church takes her stand on the progress of the best secular train-

ing, united to or rather permeated by the teaching of the God Man. The attempt is being made to so completely secularize the education of youth that God and the things worth while are left out of the curriculum. . . . I need not tell you that if we of the Faith are to save our children to their religion, if we are to instill into their young lives moral principles that will stand in good stead in life's fight, if we are to make them worthy of their citizenship in the Church of God and in this Republic, then we must see to it that close to the church stands a Catholic School. Where there is a doubt as to which we shall erect—a stately church or a capacious school—let us have no hesitation in making our choice: The School.[28]

Curley did indeed make education his priority. In 1922, he created a central office to standardize Catholic education in the archdiocese. Overseeing the office was Father John I. Barrett who appointed supervisors from the various local teaching orders. Textbooks and curriculum materials were normalized across schools; teacher-training programs were developed and educators were urged to think in terms of broader strategic educational goals.[29]

Curley's emphasis on education dovetailed with more general trends in the field. First, since the early twentieth century there had been a general recognition that a curriculum more focused on the needs of the individual student in the context of broader society was necessary to suit the student to the increasingly industrialized, professionalized society. The Maryland State Board of Education officially recognized commercial education as part of the high school curriculum in the early twentieth century, an act that had consequences for Baltimore's parochial schools. Second, beginning in the 1930s, adolescent students were more and more likely to attend high school than to enter the workforce. By 1936, 65 percent of teenage youth nationally were high school students, the highest proportion to that date.[30]

These national trends of increased attendance in high schools with differentiated curricula reshaped Baltimore's Catholic school system. Parochial schools expanded their programs in the early twentieth century to include business arithmetic, bookkeeping, and other commercial courses. In Baltimore, eight parish schools offered business courses by 1942.[31] Secondary schools had been focused more on the academic course of study than commercial, technical, or vocational, but this began to change. Mount St. Joseph High School for boys adopted a curriculum similar to that of the public schools. Several of the girls' schools also came to adopt such curricula.

Moreover, Curley's vision for an expanded education system caused him to advocate the establishment of diocesan high schools. Seton High School, which opened in Baltimore in 1926, was the first of such schools, providing an education for twenty-five dollars per year. The site of the school was chosen because of its accessibility by bus or street car. The school offered five separate courses: Latin-science, modern-classical, academic-commercial, general-clerical, and general. Hence the school offered courses of study for those who planned to attend college as well as for those who planned to start careers after graduation. The school's enrollment at its opening in 1926 was 359; by 1942 enrollment had reached 1,116 with the school drawing students from nearly all of the sixty-one parishes in the city.

To further address the need for secondary education, there were two other parish high schools in Baltimore: St. John's and St. Martin's. Such schools brought more diverse populations and more diverse curricula into the city's Catholic educational programs. In another move toward making a Catholic education more widely available, Curley also started a scholarship fund that enabled some girls to attend the other Catholic secondary schools in the city. This program had only a limited impact—far less than the school construction projects. In short, scholarships could not be offered to every student who wanted one.[32]

The war years saw a rise in patriotism in the schools and acceleration in Americanization in the Catholic schools of the city. In 1940, there were nearly 195,000 Catholics in the city, 62,711 of these were youth and 27,121 of these youth were in parish schools.[33] Where the city's parishes had been more insulated in earlier days, the war years saw extensive Catholic engagement with the city. Schools, like other city institutions, fully mobilized for the war effort. A Catholic Americanism emerged in the city's Catholic schools through the collective activities of students and their teachers.

In addition to engaging in the usual rationing and distribution of wartime materials through the schools, students and teachers in the Catholic schools engaged in a range of patriotic activities. Students read in their *Young Catholic Messenger* that patriotism and strong faith were intertwined: "To Catholics, patriotism is a solemn religious duty.... Remember that your duty to your country comes next to your duty to God. Pray and do penance for victory and a speedy and just peace."[34]

One Sister of Mercy who taught in a city school secured geographical maps that she and her students used to track the movements of soldiers in wartime. Sister Emeline Evler's elementary school students, for example, planted a victory garden, said daily prayers for soldier relatives, and conducted letter-writing campaigns to soldiers.[35] For the most part, Catholic faith and patriotic sentiment reinforced each other during the war.

In addition to these expressions of patriotism, the city's Catholic school students experienced a new kind of Catholic Americanism in the 1940s through curriculum materials created by the Commission on American Citizenship at The Catholic University of America (CUA) in Washington, D.C. In 1938, Pope Pius XI had asked CUA to create new curriculum materials that would promote Christian democratic ideals. The result was a series of textbooks, pamphlets, and periodicals promoting distinct American Catholic values. The materials were published under the imprimatur of Curley and used in the city's Catholic schools.

The materials promoted racial inclusiveness and the Commission members consulted with leaders in the African American, Jewish, and Protestant communities to ensure that the materials did not represent minorities and non-Catholics in objectionable ways.[36] These materials were not promoting the kind of insular and triumphalist Catholicism that was normally associated with Curley, and Baltimore's wartime-era Catholic schools may have contained the seeds of post-conciliar Catholicism normally associated with the leadership of Archbishop Lawrence Shehan (1961-1974).

After World War II, the stable parish system that had existed for decades began to change due to demographics. By the end of Curley's tenure, the Catholic population of the archdiocese had increased from 276,000 to 429,517 and the number of parish grammar school students had increased from just fewer than 32,000 to well over 50,000.[37] These increases, however, were not reflected in Baltimore city's educational institutions. The episcopacy of Francis Keough (1947-1961) saw the contraction of Baltimore's population, including its Catholic population. Dundalk, Essex, Towson, Catonsville, Fullerton, Overlea, and Glen Burnie all saw an influx of Catholics of varying ethnic backgrounds, while the city parishes began to decline in numbers in the 1950s.

The suburban parishes all saw an increase in numbers during the Keough years. Of course, these demographic changes not only coincided with the desire for the suburban lifestyles they now could afford, but they were also due to whites' desires to leave a city that was forced to desegregate its neighborhoods and schools. The decline in the city's white population began in the late 1940s and continued through 1990. Whites comprised 76 percent of Baltimore's population in 1950, 53 percent in 1970, and 39 percent in 1990. Put another way, 350,000 whites left Baltimore between 1950 and 1980. While working- and middle-class white Catholics of European descent moved out, non-Catholic and non-European Americans moved in.[38]

By the late 1960s, there was an educational crisis in the archdiocese. Though parochial school enrollments rose steadily until 1964 when they reached 61,500, by 1974 enrollment had dropped to 35,000. High school enrollments increased for a longer period of time, but then also began to decline. The general crisis in the archdiocesan educational system was worse in Baltimore city than in the suburbs. By the late 1960s it was clear that some schools would have to be closed and consolidated. A group of education and clerical authorities engaged in "clustering," a process that entailed consolidating schools with low enrollments. By the 1970s several of the city's Catholic high schools were closed, others consolidated, and some of the high schools were turned into coeducational institutions.[39]

While these developments cannot be interpreted as positive for the city's Catholic educational institutions, it should be noted that some parishes found creative ways of adapting to the upheavals of the 1960s and that such adaptation served as examples for other educational institutions. As Efa Ahmed Williams shows, the St. Peter Claver community integrated parish life with the civil rights activities occurring around it.

During the 1960s, the parish's pastor adapted to the social changes occurring in the city by expanding St. Peter Claver's educational activities beyond the school level to educate priests and the broader community on matters of civil rights. For example, the pastor arranged to have Bayard Rustin, Floyd McKissick, and A. Philip Randolph participate in a workshop aimed at educating priests and vowed women religious in the mid-1960s. McKissick spoke at St. Peter Claver, and Rustin spoke at Mercy High School. This parish, as Williams suggests, sought to make sense of community change in innovative ways.

This would not change the financial situation and declining enrollment at the school: St. Peter Claver merged with St. Edward School and became Father Charles A. Hall School in 1973, in memory of an African American Josephite priest. St. Francis Xavier School in East Baltimore experienced some of the same issues as demographic and social changes caused a decline in enrollments. Working with the Oblates, St. Francis

Xavier's pastor reopened the school as a coeducational institution, St. Francis-Father Charles A. Hall upper school in 1973.[40] Baltimore's Catholic school system was altered dramatically during the 1960s, but there were always possibilities for adaptation.

NOTES

1. Thomas Spalding, *The Premier See: A History of the Archdiocese of Baltimore, 1789-1994* (Baltimore: Johns Hopkins University Press, 1995), 1-14, 21; Harold Buetow, *Of Singular Benefit; The Story of Catholic Education in the United States* (London: Macmillan, 1970), 25-26, 49.

2. Spalding, *Premier See*, 17.

3. Ibid., 17-20, quote on 17; on Carroll's role in early Maryland, see Robert J. Brugger, *Maryland, A Middle Temperament* (Baltimore: Johns Hopkins University Press, 1988), 147-148.

4. Sister Mary Leonita Buckner, O.S.F., "The History of Catholic Elementary Education in the City of Baltimore" (master's thesis, The Catholic University of America, 1948), 11-12; Buetow, *Of Singular Benefit*, 64; Vernon S. Vavrina, "The History of Public Education in the City of Baltimore, 1829-1956" (PhD diss., The Catholic University of America, 1958), *xix, xii*; Brugger, *Maryland*, 148.

5. Buckner, "History of Catholic Elementary Education," 11-12.

6. Ibid., 31.

7. Buetow, *Of Singular Benefit*, 53-57; Spalding, *Premier See*, 55; see also on the Sulpicians, Christopher J. Kauffman, *Tradition and Transformation in Catholic Culture, the Priests of St. Sulpice* (New York: Macmillan, 1988).

8. Buckner, "History of Catholic Elementary Education," 14 and passim; Buetow, *Of Singular Benefit*, 60-62; Spalding, *Premier See*, 207-208.

9. Cyprian Davis, *The History of Black Catholics in the United States* (New York: Crossroad, 1992), 99-100; Owen B. Corrigan, *The Catholic Schools of the Archdiocese of Baltimore* (Baltimore: St. Mary's Industrial School Press, 1924), 45, 54-55; Diane Batts Morrow, "The Oblate Sisters of Providence: Issues of Black and Female Agency in Their Antebellum Experience, 1828-1860," (PhD diss., University of Georgia, 1996); Buckner, "History of Catholic Elementary Education," 81; Brugger, *Maryland*, 580-581.

10. Spalding, *Premier See*, 30.

11. Ibid., 132-133, 165, 270-276, 296.

12. Ibid., 122-125, 132-133, 242, 296. Spalding notes that the numbers Gibbons provides may be too low (296), but it should be noted that Gibbons is probably talking about first generation immigrants, while the numbers for the Curley period are probably first and second generation, see Maria Mazzenga, "Inclusion, Exclusion, and the National Experience: European and African American Youth in World War Two Baltimore," (PhD diss., The Catholic University of America, 1999), 30-33. In the U.S., the Catholic population jumped from an estimated 125,000 in 1820 to nearly 13 million by 1900, see Neil McCluskey, *Catholic Viewpoint on Education* (New York: Hanover House, 1959), 27; Jay P. Dolan, *The American Catholic Experience, A History from Colonial Times to the Present* (Notre Dame: University of Notre Dame Press, 1992), chapter 8; on general patterns of migration to the U.S., see Roger Daniels, *Coming to America; A History of Immigration and Ethnicity in American Life,* 2nd ed. (New York: Harper Perennial, 2002); on the periodic bouts of anti-Catholicism, see Spalding, *Premier See*,

113, 133-134, 171-172, 285, 354; Brugger, *Maryland*, 263-264.

13. McCluskey, *Catholic Viewpoint on Education*, 32-33; Buetow, *Of Singular Benefit*, 152-153.

14. R. Scott Appleby, *"Church and Age Unite!" The Modernist Impulse in American Catholicism* (Notre Dame: University of Notre Dame Press, 1992), 80-81; Spalding, *Premier See*, 259.

15. Dolan, *American Catholic Experience*, 272-273, 298-299; James Hennesey, S.J., *American Catholics: A History of the Roman Catholic Community in the United States* (New York: Oxford University Press, 1981), 186; Spalding, *Premier See*, 262-264; Buetow, *Of Singular Benefit*, 170-171.

16. Buckner, "History of Catholic Elementary Education," 56-63; Spalding, *The Premier See*, 244.

17. Corrigan, *Catholic Schools of the Archdiocese of Baltimore*, 72-73; "Schools Conducted by the School Sisters of Notre Dame in the Archdiocese of Maryland," Baltimore Catholic school materials, St. Mary's Seminary and University Associated Archives, Baltimore, Maryland; Spalding, *Premier See*, 142; Buckner, "History of Catholic Elementary Education," 58-63, 80-81.

18. Corrigan, *Catholic Schools of the Archdiocese of Baltimore*, 74, 78-79; Sister Mary John Gerrity, O.S.F., "The Growth and Development of Catholic Secondary Education for Girls in Baltimore and Vicinity from Colonial Times to the Present" (master's thesis, The Catholic University of America, 1942), 48-51.

19. "Notre Dame Institute has 140 Graduates," *Baltimore Catholic Review*, June 20, 1941.

20. Eleanor Apicella interviewed by Doris Stern, October 31, 1979, transcript, Baltimore Neighborhood Heritage Project, Langsdale Library, University of Baltimore, Maryland.

21. Apicella interview transcript.

22. Julia Poggi interviewed by Jean Scarpaci, October 12, 1979, transcript, 35, Baltimore Neighborhood Heritage Project, Langsdale Library, University of Baltimore, Maryland.

23. Sister Emeline Evler interviewed by Maria Mazzenga, January 31, 1995, School Sisters of Notre Dame Villa, Baltimore, Maryland, in author's possession.

24. Guinevere Spurlock, "A History of St. Frances Academy" (master's thesis, Morgan State College, 1974), 33.

25. Paula Fass, "Imitation and Autonomy: Catholic Education in the Twentieth Century" in *Outside In: Minorities and the Transformation of American Education* (New York: Oxford University Press, 1989), 189-228, 203.

26. Spalding, *Premier See*, 322.

27. Ibid., 322, 321-385; Vincent de Paul Fitzpatrick, *Life of Archbishop Curley: Champion of Catholic Education* (Baltimore: Baltimore Catholic Review, 1929).

28. Quote in Fitzpatrick, *Life of Archbishop Curley*, 52. For an outline of Curley's views on education see also Archbishop Michael Curley, "Suffer the little ones to come unto me and forbid them not" undated sermon in "Curley Sermons/Talks, 1904-1920," St. Mary's Seminary and University Associated Archives.

29. Spalding, *Premier See*, 329-330; Gerrity, "Growth and Development of Catholic Secondary Education," chapter IV.

30. Grace Palladino, *Teenagers: An American History* (New York: Basic Books, 1996), 5; Gerrity, "Growth and Development of Catholic Secondary Education," 93-95; Buetow, *Of Singular Benefit*, 240-241.

31. Gerrity, "Growth and Development of Catholic Secondary Education," 93-95; Buetow, *Of Singular Benefit*, 240-241.

32. Gerrity, "Growth and Development of Catholic Secondary Education," 96, 94-101; Spalding, *Premier See*, 331; see also Maria Mazzenga, "More Democracy, More Religion: Baltimore's Schools, Religious Pluralism, and the Second World War," in *One Hundred Years of Catholic Education: Historical Essays in Honor of the Centennial of the National Catholic Educational Association*, ed. John Augenstein, Christopher Kauffman, and Robert J. Wister (Washington, DC: National Catholic Educational Association, 2003), 199-219.

33. Mazzenga, "Inclusion, Exclusion, and the National Experience," 336, 339.

34. Mazzenga, "More Democracy, More Religion," 206-207.

35. Ibid., 207.

36. Ibid., 208-210.

37. Buckner, "History of Catholic Elementary Education," 77; Spalding, *Premier See*, 385.

38. Efa Ahmed Williams, "St. Peter Claver Catholic Church: Civil Rights Activism and Surviving the Decline of a West Baltimore Community" (master's thesis, Morgan State University, 2007), 46; Spalding, *Premier See*, 391-394.

39. Williams, "St. Peter Claver Catholic Church," 50-53; Spalding, *Premier See*, 459-461.

40. Williams, "St. Peter Claver Catholic Church," 41.

Quaker City Catholicism:
Catholic Education in Philadelphia

Richard M. Jacobs, O.S.A.

Easter Sunday 2007 at Philadelphia's Cathedral Basilica of Saints Peter and Paul featured the liturgical opening of the archdiocesan bicentennial. Cardinal Justin Rigali preached, using as his theme: "Blessed are the eyes that see what you see! For I say to you, many . . . desired to see what you see, but did not see it."[1]

This essay focuses upon the origins, founding, expansion, systematization, and apex of Philadelphia's urban Catholic schools between 1681 and 1961. Woven into this history are four contributions these schools have made to the history of U.S. Catholic education: religious tolerance in the face of bigotry; the exclusion of religious education from public schools; a heritage of sometimes contentious collaboration involving laity and clergy; and, a national model for urban Catholic education. This legacy made it possible for the congregation gathered on Easter Sunday 2007 to rejoice, for they witnessed what their forebears "desired to see . . . but did not see it."

The immigration of Catholics into Pennsylvania came as a consequence of the colony's heritage of religious tolerance. On May 14, 1681, Anthony Brockholes, a Catholic, was appointed colonial governor of a territory that included Maine, New Hampshire, Massachusetts, New York, Pennsylvania, New Jersey, and Delaware.[2] Although freedom of religion had been abolished in New York, New Jersey, and Maryland, it survived in Pennsylvania and the appointment of Brockholes suggested to Catholics living in those colonies that Pennsylvania, Delaware, and the western part of New Jersey would offer religious tolerance.[3] Pope Pius VII would later designate this territory as the Diocese of Philadelphia.[4]

Many historians identify St. Mary's School, which opened in 1783, as Philadelphia's first urban Catholic school,[5] making St. Mary's "the mother-school of all the parochial schools in the English-speaking States."[6] However, this assertion overlooks the opening of two schools antedating St. Mary's opening. The first school, St. Aloysius Academy, was opened by a zealous Jesuit missionary, Theodore Schneider, in 1743, approximately forty miles north of Philadelphia.[7] Indicative of the spirit of religious tolerance, Schneider's school welcomed children of any religious tradition.[8] Lay men comprised the faculty's majority.[9] The second school, a Catholic elementary school, was opened by a lay woman, Ann Bryald, as early as 1756.[10]

Thus the earliest origins of Philadelphia's urban Catholic schools were shaped by four factors: Catholic migration from other colonies; religious tolerance; zealous missionary ideal; and, the laity's dedicated efforts. From this point forward, these factors would figure prominently—and at times, not without contention—in the founding, expansion, and systematization of the Quaker City's urban Catholic schools.

In 1732, the Jesuits founded St. Joseph's, the first parish in the City of Philadelphia.[11] But as late as the parish's silver anniversary, there were only 1,365 adult Catholics residing in Pennsylvania. Of these, 378 called Philadelphia home with 150 claiming Irish ancestry and 228 claiming German ancestry.[12] In a colony of some 300,000 inhabitants, the strong opposition accorded this tiny minority attests to pervasive anti-Catholic prejudice,[13] especially as this was enshrined in "penal laws."[14]

Even though the Protestant majority needed Catholic support for the revolutionary cause, anti-Catholic bigotry persisted during this era.[15] Following the colonists' victory over England, penal laws were rarely enforced, and in Philadelphia, Catholics and Protestants appeared to co-exist peaceably.[16] Even so, anti-Catholic bigotry always simmered just beneath the surface, sometimes boiling over onto the public square. As early as 1754, an angry mob attempted to destroy St. Joseph's.[17] Then, with Catholic immigration increasing, the "Romish" Church and its "popery" were targeted, especially during the first half of the nineteenth century.[18]

By the 1820s, Catholics in Pennsylvania numbered fifty-nine thousand, 5 percent of the state's population. Fearing this growing minority, nativists stoked the hot embers of anti-Catholic bigotry. Asserting the pope was conspiring to overthrow the government and establish the "papal states" in America by taking over the public schools,[19] the fires of anti-Catholic prejudice eventually spread into the public square in 1844.

This marked a significant moment in the origins of Philadelphia's urban Catholic schools, because the spark fanning the red hot embers of anti-Catholicism into the white hot fire of mayhem was the religious education program in Philadelphia's public schools.[20] This intolerance assists in explaining how the origins of Philadelphia's urban Catholic schools were shaped by a fifth factor: religious and racial intolerance.

Religious intolerance was codified in the rationale for founding St. Joseph's English and Classical Academy; namely, to educate boys in a place "without the fear of their being . . . insulted on account of their religion."[21] Apparently, parents and pastors believed their children needed a protective environment where they could learn. Racial intolerance was evident indirectly in the founding of schools for African Americans. For decades, Protestant denominations sponsored these schools because local schools excluded African Americans.[22] As early as 1744, the Abolition Society opened a school for African Americans as did the female members of the Society of Friends (Quakers) in 1795.[23]

This also was the case for the school Father Felix Barbelin founded in 1860.[24] Not all African Americans in Philadelphia wanted their children to attend schools where Protestant religious instruction was normative. As early as 1817, African American Catholics requested of St. Mary's School Board a tuition-free education so their children would "acquire the Knowledge of our Religion & its duties whereby they might be able to repel the incessant attacks made on them by a set of beings who can quote the Scriptures with every phrase in order to seduce the ignorant." With the economy in recession and the parish in debt, the trustees denied the request but not because St. Mary's lacked space. The denial resulted from having to build a separate school because segregation was normative.[25]

In 1858, Father Thomas Lilly founded a school for and taught by African American Catholics. When Lilly died in 1862, the school declined.[26] The next year, the Oblate Sisters of Providence opened a school "for the instruction of female children of color" and another in 1872.[27]

Both efforts failed, with prejudice and racism forcing the sisters to leave Philadelphia altogether. Six years later, the Sisters of Notre Dame de Namur opened another school for African Americans. It closed in 1882, when the law excluding African Americans from public schools was repealed.[28]

While these efforts to stem the tide of religious and racial intolerance failed, each represented a religious minority educating the children of co-religionists who were members of an ethnic minority.

Between the attack on St. Joseph's Church in 1754 and the "Bible Riots" of 1844, John Carroll became the nation's first Catholic bishop.[29] Although a separate system of schools was not part of Carroll's agenda, he quickly issued a pastoral letter in which the subject of religious education figured prominently.[30] However, national culture, anti-Catholic prejudice, and the Protestant program of religious education in the public schools conspired in these decades to frustrate Carroll's efforts to find accommodation between the values of his church and his country.[31]

In 1792, Carroll announced the opening of Georgetown College, identifying the preparation of Catholic lay teachers for service in public schools as a principal purpose for the new school.[32] The laity figured prominently in this effort, further underscoring their critical role in this history.[33]

With no "guiding local Catholic tradition or precedent" for establishing Catholic schools in Philadelphia, the need to provide Catholic youth a religious education program served as the impetus for establishing separate schools. Anti-Catholic prejudice in the common (and later, public) schools, the desire on the part of immigrant Catholic groups to transmit the faith according to their own traditions, and the willingness of religious sisters to work for low wages served as the rationale for establishing separate schools.[34]

Thus, during the colonial and post-revolutionary eras, five factors shaped the origins of Philadelphia's urban Catholic schools: religious tolerance; Catholic immigration from other colonies; a zealous missionary ideal; dedicated laity; and, religious and racial intolerance. By the mid-1800s, resolving the question about how best to provide Catholic youth a religious education would cause these factors to coalesce and, in turn, fuel the expansion of Philadelphia's urban Catholic schools.[35]

As Philadelphia's Catholics struggled to resolve these and other challenges, the founding of urban Catholic schools in the post-revolutionary, antebellum era in the nation's history between 1780 and

1860 slowed due to inadequate funding, internal and external conflict, and low pay. Schools operated independently as the diocese had neither adequate funds nor personnel to support these institutions. Perhaps for this reason, Philadelphia's bishops provided little guidance, pleased that the laity was willing to take the initiative to meet this pastoral need.[36]

As noted above, St. Mary's opened a school in 1783[37] and soon was called "Saint Mary's Free School" because as early as 1784, teachers were required to provide tuition-free instruction to six children of the congregation's poorer members. This notion of "tuition-free" Catholic schooling set a pattern that would extend in Philadelphia not only to other parishes but also to high schools with the opening in 1890 of the first central Catholic high school in the United States.[38]

Where would the money come from to fund St. Mary's? Parishioners' contributions and regular "special" collections that frequently followed a "charity sermon" at Mass helped to defray expenses.[39] Periodic bequests and donations were also received between 1788 and 1810 with the objective of building an endowment.[40] However, these sources proved insufficient and parents ultimately had to pay tuition to cover school expenses.[41] Despite this hardship, more than forty boys and girls were enrolled at St. Mary's in 1805 and the school was expanded in 1810 to accommodate increasing enrollment.[42]

Other problems emerged as internal conflicts between lay trustees and school personnel erupted periodically. St. Mary's schoolmaster, David Doyle, resigned in April 1807 because students were not achieving academically. The problem? The Act of Incorporation stipulated that the trustees would supervise admissions, preside at quarterly examinations, as well as contract and dismiss personnel. In 1807, the particular bone of contention was that the trustees were using the quarterly examinations to evaluate teachers.[43]

External conflict also abounded because the trustees did not share a common allegiance. Some sided with the clergy while other influential and wealthy Catholics who were aligned with the trustees withheld their financial support. Complicating matters were clergymen who were dismissive in their attitudes toward the trustees.[44] In many ways, this particular conflict prefigured what would be normative by the 1970s: "when all the trappings and rhetoric are set aside, the trustees mirror in many ways any viable home and school association in Philadelphia parishes today."[45]

Low pay also undercut the expansion of Philadelphia's urban Catholic schools. The trustees at St. Mary's seemingly had resolved this problem by 1833 when they hired the Sisters of Charity to staff the school.
The contract's terms stipulated: the trustees could admit students; no
boy would be admitted until he was nine years old; and, trustees would
be invited to the semi-annual examinations. The trustees would pay
the sisters' rent and other expenses associated with their maintenance
including an annual salary one-half of that paid to the lay schoolmaster two decades earlier.[46] This last stipulation foreshadowed what later
would be normative for the religious teaching in diocesan schools.

Despite these and other obstacles, many urban Catholic schools
were founded between 1780 and 1860, with most experiencing similar
challenges to those plaguing St. Mary's. Dissatisfied with the English-
speaking clergy at St. Mary's, German parishioners broke away and
formed Holy Trinity in 1788.[47] Funds for a school building were insufficient, so classes were held in the church basement. As the parish grew,
so also did the school's enrollment, which led to the construction of a
school. Strapped for cash, the congregation petitioned the legislature
to create a lottery to support the school. Approved in 1803, the lottery
made construction possible,[48] although there are no records of income
being received from the lottery.[49] Again, the laity controlled the school,
that is, until Philadelphia's third bishop, Francis Patrick Kenrick, settled the issue once and for all. Abolishing the office of trustee, Kenrick
shifted control of the schools to himself and his clergy.[50] However, Kenrick's handling of this issue set a negative precedent that would live on
in the collective memory of Philadelphia Catholics for at least the next
eighteen decades.[51]

Irish Augustinian priests founded a third school in 1811—St. Augustine's Academy—with thirty-nine students. The curriculum featured three divisions: elementary, preparatory, and collegiate studies.[52]
The effort was short lived, closing in 1815 and reopening as Villanova
College in 1852.[53] The parish reestablished the school in 1842, another
short-lived effort, as the building was destroyed during the 1844 Bible
riots.[54] The parish opened yet another school in 1854, managed by a lay
board in cooperation with the clergy. Lay teachers staffed the school
until the hiring of the Brothers and Sisters of Holy Cross (1860).[55]
Other schools founded during this era included St. Patrick's (1839),
St. Philip Neri (1841), St. Francis Xavier (1845),[56] St. Michael's (1852)
which a Catholic newspaper at the time mistakenly identified as "the

first Catholic Parochial School in the city of Philadelphia,"[57] St. Malachy and St. Alphonsus (1860), St. Ann's (1861), and St. James (1863), the last urban parish school opened before the Civil War.[58]

A number of private Catholic schools were also founded during this era. Three Alsatian immigrants opened Claremont Seminary (1806), Philadelphia's first Catholic secondary school.[59] Father Francis Brosius founded Mount Airy Seminary in Philadelphia (1807),[60] the first school in the United States featuring blackboards and chalk.[61] Father Jeremiah Keily opened an academy in a house adjoining St. Mary's Church (1829), which lasted until 1834, when Father John Hughes opened Western Academy at St. John's Church. A "Mr. Nugent" opened the "Catholic Seminary" to provide a "course of instruction [that] embraces all the branches of a sound English and Classical education" (1835). As noted above, St. Joseph's English and Classical Academy opened in 1840 and admitted girls in 1843, but closed in 1848. John D. Bryant opened St. Paul's English and Classical Academy in 1842; it closed in 1848.[62]

While most were founded for males, a number of private urban Catholic schools were founded for females. The Misses Lloyd's School for Girls opened in the early 1830s, the Young Ladies French and English Academy and Rodrigue's Academy for Young Ladies both opened in 1833, Miss Mary Kelly's School (the precursor of St. Ann's School), Mrs. Holmes Seminary for Young Ladies, and St. Mary's Classical Academy opened in 1845, and the Ladies of the Sacred Heart School for Girls opened in 1846.[63] The Sisters of St. Joseph operated academies in their convents at St. Philip Neri, St. Augustine, and St. Joseph parishes, at St. Vincent De Paul in the Germantown section, and in 1859, opened an academy on Summer Street in Philadelphia. The Immaculate Heart Sisters operated a private school at St. Joachim's in Frankford. The Sisters of Mercy sponsored an academy at St. Malachy's parish. The Notre Dame Sisters opened an academy in Assumption parish in 1856 and the Holy Child Sisters opened an academy on Spring Garden Street in 1863.

In addition, the women's religious orders and congregations operated female academies in their convents.[64] While many of these academies were conducted for the purpose of supplementing the sisters' meager salaries, some would eventually provide post-elementary education, from which diocesan secondary schools in Philadelphia originated in the late 1800s.[65] Not just in Philadelphia but throughout the nation, female academies inculcated moral and domestic virtues so that graduates one day would be the moral guardians of the home.[66]

Philadelphia's urban Catholic schools also provided for disadvantaged youth. The first of these efforts originated in 1797 in response to a yellow fever epidemic. More than four thousand Philadelphians (10 percent of the population) died, leaving many orphans. A Jesuit priest at St. Joseph's, Father Leonard Neale, founded the first Catholic orphanage.[67] Father Michael Hurley organized a campaign culminating in the incorporation in 1807 of "The Society of St. Joseph for maintaining and educating Roman Catholic orphan children of both sexes."[68]

The Sisters of Charity assumed responsibility for Hurley's orphanage in 1814[69] and entered into a formal contract one decade later which included "the economy of the house, the care of the children, their schooling, and religious instruction."[70] The sisters objected to housing both genders at St. Joseph's; thus, Hurley's initial effort blossomed in 1829 into two orphanages, St. Joseph's and St. John's Orphan Asylums, both of which quickly grew overcrowded. Then, in 1834, the pastor of Holy Trinity, Father Francis Guth, established St. Vincent's Orphan Asylum for Boys.[71] Within two years, sixteen orphans from St. Peter's Church resided at St. Vincent's,[72] resulting in St. Joseph's being designated exclusively for girls and St. John's and St. Vincent's merging into one orphanage for boys, St. John's. In 1849, the Sisters of St. Joseph assumed responsibility for both institutions.[73]

Although inadequate funding, internal and external conflict, and low pay slowed the founding of Philadelphia's urban Catholic schools, their number expanded between 1780 and 1860. The schools, academies, and orphanages did not reflect the pattern of the Jesuit schools founded in Maryland or the territory of the Commonwealth lying beyond Philadelphia which emphasized a prescribed curriculum and were "paternalistic and authoritarian."[74] In contrast, Philadelphia's schools were "rooted more in the intangibles of the past such as an intense desire on the part of the laity for Catholic schools; the interest of the financially well disposed; and the nature of the early public school system."[75] Furthermore, no real "system" existed; schools opened and closed with pastors and parents doing their best to educate Catholic youth in a hostile environment.

This history of urban Catholic education in Philadelphia would be incomplete without a brief mention of the opening of St. Charles Borromeo Seminary in 1832. Housed in the upstairs rooms of the bishop's residence at St. Mary's, this arrangement soon proved insufficient. In 1836, the seminary was moved into a house adjoining the church. Two years later, the Commonwealth incorporated the seminary as the "Philadelphia Theological Seminary of Saint Charles Borromeo" and the diocese purchased a new seminary building.[76]

In the early to mid-1800s, Philadelphia's public school board oversaw a curriculum that included a generic Protestant religious education program.[77] Because most Catholics could ill-afford separate schools and the tuition, under Kenrick's twenty-one year administration pastors and laity began to collaborate, expanding the number of urban Catholic schools.[78]

Immigration fueled much of this expansion. Between 1810 and 1880, Philadelphia's population of Catholics increased from thirty thousand to three hundred thousand (from 3 to 20 percent of the population).[79] This trend only served to rekindle nativist fear. But, whereas Bishop Carroll immersed himself in political affairs only reluctantly, some of his successor bishops were not so reluctant.[80] In the early 1840s, Kenrick rejected Carroll's apolitical stance, jumping headfirst into the political arena to defend his flock. This foray provided nativists with ammunition that "proved" a papist conspiracy.

It all transpired with the best of intentions between 1824 and 1854, the era of Jacksonian democracy.[81] First, the Commonwealth adopted a "common school" proposal in 1834 to incorporate neighborhood schools into a common system.[82] In Philadelphia, although resistance to public schools was strong, elementary schools began operating two years later and secondary schools were in the planning stage.[83] By 1838, Philadelphia Boys High School had opened and by the 1880s, Philadelphia's public schools were graded: primary schooling (grades one through four) and secondary schooling (grades five through eight), with each grade meeting for five months; grammar schooling (grades nine through twelve), with each grade meeting for ten months.[84]

Second, the Protestant majority organized to protect its interests in the public schools, especially the program of religious education. By the early 1840s, the majority captured enough seats on the school board to ensure the program would reflect nondenominational Christian faith and practice. Meanwhile, evangelical entrepreneurs produced textbooks—self-described "handbooks of the common morality, testaments to the Protestant virtues which a half-century of experience had elevated into the culture religion of the new nation"—for use in the schools.[85]

For the Protestant majority, these schoolbooks were utterly non-controversial.[86] Many Catholics vehemently disagreed, arguing the textbooks were a tool for proselytizing Catholic youth.[87] When the school board approved *Parlay's Common School History* in 1842, a correspondent for *The Catholic Herald* railed that the textbook contained "all the slanders, calumnies, and falsehoods Protestants have brought against the Catholic Church for the last three hundred years."[88] Of course, Catholics objected to the interpretation given to the incidents reported, but they were impossible to disprove.[89] However, a 1913 survey of public elementary school history and geography textbooks used between 1800 and 1840 did note: "The publications, almost without exception, speak of Catholics and Catholic countries as hopelessly ignorant, superstitious, bigoted and benighted."[90]

Pastors and laity alike reacted.[91] *The Catholic Herald* soon called for non-sectarian public schools. In November 1842, Kenrick challenged the school board to ban the source of discord, maintaining that Catholic youth deserved to be exposed to Roman Catholic faith and its practice in public schools just as Protestant youth were being exposed to the Protestant faith and practice in the public schools.[92] Policy favored Kenrick but nativist factions misrepresented Kenrick's petition, arguing it would deprive Protestant youth of a religious education.[93] This only exacerbated anti-Catholic bigotry and, over the next two years, both sides hurled charges and Protestants staged "Save the Bible" rallies.[94]

On Friday, May 3, 1844, some three hundred nativists and sympathizers gathered in Kensington, Philadelphia's Irish Catholic neighborhood.[95] Leaders declaimed how "a set of citizens, German and Irish, wanted to get the Constitution of the U.S. into their own hands and sell it to a foreign power."[96] Upon hearing this harangue, the Irish destroyed the platform and the nativists retreated.

Three days later, three thousand nativists and sympathizers regrouped. Few Catholics were present, having been warned at Sunday Mass to avoid confrontations. A downpour caused the crowd to seek shelter in the Nanny Goat Market. After one speaker jumped onto a stall to continue his invective, fighting broke out; bloody riots ensued, lasting several days. Leaving Kensington, the nativists directed their ire toward Catholics residing in Center City, setting fire to two churches, St. Augustine's and St. Michael's. Four nativists were killed and both sides sported injuries. With Catholic churches and homes being burned to the ground, Kenrick fled Philadelphia.[97]

Peace did not come quickly. Independence Day 1844 featured nativists staging a parade in Southwark, just south of Center City; the next day, they targeted St. Philip Neri Church. By July 8, the destruction was evident: religious paintings were slashed and destroyed, sacred vessels and objects were desecrated, the church building was burned to the ground, and the school was severely damaged, remaining closed until 1852.[98] The general of the militia sent to protect the church, George Cadwalader, had his own troops fired upon for complicity with the nativists.[99] When the militia left on July 10, fourteen were dead, including two militia members.[100] A commission of inquiry later blamed Cadwalader for siding with the immigrants and trampling upon the nativists' rights.[101]

In the nine years between 1834 and 1843, the school board contended with the divisive source of the mayhem by eventually forging a compromise that removed the program of religious education from Philadelphia's public schools. The result pleased neither side and it would take four more decades to rid the public schools of religious bias.[102]

In retrospect, Carroll's early admonition that clerics refrain from involvement in politics was prescient. Kenrick's foray into the political realm led to religious education being completely expunged from the public school curriculum by 1913, an outcome many Catholics and non-Catholics in the late twentieth century lamented.[103] In retrospect, one unintended and ironic consequence of this entire affair is that Kenrick, the Catholic newspaper, and many Catholics in Philadelphia bear at least some of the burden of responsibility for the origins of the secularization of the public schools.[104]

In the years following the riots, Kenrick resolved to build Catholic schools in the twenty-six parishes he had established.[105] Because most parish schools did not enroll females, Kenrick gave priority to the education of females.[106] He also encouraged the founding of private secondary schools, some of which became permanent institutions.[107] However, a major impediment blocked this expansion. "I do not know how we are to establish [the schools]," Kenrick wrote in 1847. "Teachers of a religious character are not to be had, and schoolhouses are wanting."[108]

If urban Catholic schools in Philadelphia were to continue expanding, the challenge confronting Kenrick and his successors was not simply that of building schools—presenting the perennial financial challenge—but also that of finding teachers—presenting the perennial personnel challenge. While funding the construction of schools presented its own difficulties, the latter has always presented greater difficulties in that meeting the personnel challenge requires finding qualified teachers who are also capable of infusing into their work the faith and practice of the Church. Further complicating success in meeting this challenge is finding qualified teachers who are willing to work for what the schools can afford to pay.

Appointed Archbishop of Baltimore in October 1851, Kenrick selected a Bohemian immigrant and Redemptorist missionary, John Nepomucene Neumann, as his successor and Philadelphia's fourth bishop.[109] Installed on February 1, 1852, Neumann presided over a diocese of one hundred seventy thousand Catholics (9 percent of the population) and approximately fifty parish schools, including several non-urban parish schools.[110]

With the tide of immigration showing no signs of abating, Neumann was firm that "the school, with its own building, adequate staff and proper resources, should be a major component of every parish." The bishop urged pastors to spare no effort in this regard.[111]

Less than a month after his installation, Neumann hosted a meeting to advance the cause of Catholic schools. Participants recommended the formation of a school board, with Neumann as president and the pastor and two lay men from each parish as members. Duties included general financial aid appeals and planning for the hiring of teachers; pastors alone would be responsible for hiring all faculty and administrators.[112] Due to a host of obstacles, diocesan secondary schools were out of the question, a goal that would be pursued in the future.[113]

Neumann implemented these recommendations, perhaps for three reasons. First, they assisted Neumann in resolving the trustee dispute. Second, policy would not emanate unilaterally from Neumann, but would be framed with input from those whose children would benefit. Third, financial decisions involved those who would bear the burden of those decisions, pastors and laity, and especially single persons who had expressed concern about the undue financial burden they would shoulder.[114]

Salaries for Catholic school teachers could not match those of the public schools, thus Neumann worked to enlist religious orders and congregations whose members' salaries would be lower.[115] As the religious—especially sisters who had served as nurses during the Civil War—began to staff parish schools, Neumann's tenure demarcates the gradual transition away from direct lay control of the schools.[116]

Neumann's 1854 *ad limina* report identified thirty-four urban parish schools enrolling almost nine thousand students. Three years later, there were forty-three schools, most staffed by lay teachers, predominantly females.[117] When Neumann died in 1860, Philadelphia boasted thirty-six parish schools with seventeen located in the city, marking the era when non-urban parish schools were beginning their expansion.[118] Although the population of Catholics in the Diocese of Philadelphia had increased by 1858 to 250,000, the schools enrolled only 8,710 students, a decrease directly attributable to the erection of the Diocese of Newark, Delaware, in 1853.[119]

Due to these efforts, Neumann is considered the "founder" of Philadelphia's parish schools. Although few doubted his sanctity—Neumann was declared a saint in 1976—the rapid expansion of Catholic schooling left the diocese deep in debt.[120] This frustrated Neumann's coadjutor bishop, James Frederick Wood, a native-born Philadelphian who converted from the Unitarian Church and had worked as a young adult in Cincinnati as a banker. Once installed as bishop, Wood halted most building projects.[121]

However, Wood did expand educational opportunities for disadvantaged youth, opening St. Vincent's Asylum (1860),[122] the Catholic Home for Destitute Children,[123] the Immaculate Conception Industrial School for Girls, and three night schools (all in 1867), as well as the Gonzaga Home School, an orphanage for girls (1872).[124] In 1881, Wood also invited the Sisters of St. Joseph to open a Sunday school for girls who at the time were referred to as deaf and dumb at their academy.[125] Three decades later, this initiative culminated in the founding of the Archbishop Ryan Memorial Institute for the Deaf in 1912.[126]

By the mid-1860s, Philadelphia sponsored thirty-three urban Catholic schools, including nineteen parish schools serving 9,200 students (of which 5,400 were females), twenty-three academies for females (two for males),[127] and seven orphanages caring for six hundred residents. In 1870, there were forty-two parish schools.[128] When Wood died in 1883, there were fifty-eight.[129] Despite this growth, not everyone was pleased with the process. The Catholic newspaper argued that those who lived "in more favorable circumstances in some other sections" of Philadelphia were not doing enough to promote Catholic education.[130] Furthermore, the expansion of diocesan urban Catholic schools had led to a decline in private urban Catholic schools.[131]

This postbellum expansion of Catholic schools raised anew the decades-old arguments about the threat these schools posed. In turn, some Catholics railed against the public schools and increased pressure to systematize Catholic education. Apparently, Wood condoned these criticisms, going so far as to promulgate them in the Catholic newspaper.[132] Meanwhile, public and Catholic schools vied with one another for superiority; but, the best the Catholic schools could do was to provide a basic curriculum, while the public school curriculum was being revised to reflect the requirements of industrialization.[133]

The Irish immigrant Patrick John Ryan—whose *modus operandi* was "whatever is necessary is possible"[134]—succeeded Wood in 1884. Ryan expanded urban Catholic schools in three ways. First, he dutifully implemented the *Decrees* of the Third Plenary Council of Baltimore (1884). Second, he transformed what was, in effect, a loose confederation of schools into a centralized system. And third, as a member of the newly-formed Commission for Catholic Missions among the Colored People and the Indians, Ryan worked assiduously to provide for the educational needs of marginalized children.

The Third Plenary Council of Baltimore proved instrumental in expanding parish schools throughout the United States,[135] its *Decrees* unequivocally asserting: "Two objects . . . we have in view, to multiply our schools, and to perfect them."[136] A "clarification" specified these terms: "No parish is complete till it has schools adequate to the needs of its children, and the pastor and people of such a parish should feel that they have not accomplished their entire duty until the want is supplied."[137]

How could the *Decrees* possibly be implemented in urban locales when most Catholics residing in those locales were poor immigrants? One strategy the bishops at Baltimore utilized was a two-pronged approach: first, appeal to the mind and then revisit the specter of nativism.[138] A second strategy involved coercion.[139] The antidote? Catholic schools.[140] To achieve this goal, the Council issued a dire warning: "In the great coming combat between truth and error, between faith and agnosticism, an important part of the fray must be borne by the laity, and woe to them if they are not well prepared."[141]

Even though the Baltimore Council mandated parish schools, most bishops did not or could not comply.[142] Furthermore, although the bishops had empowered themselves to coerce pastors and congregations into enrolling children in parish schools, most feared doing so and, thus, could not or did not.[143]

This was not the case in Philadelphia, however. The *Decrees* emboldened Ryan to expand urban parish schools to serve newly-arrived Irish, German, Italian, and Polish immigrants.[144] Lay Catholic groups also expanded the number of institutions for disadvantaged youth, especially orphans.[145] Incredibly,

> there were more children in Philadelphia Catholic schools in 1910 than in the public schools of all but a dozen United States cities. As many as one hundred boys and girls crowded into a single classroom, in the charge of a religious sister who more often than not had only a secondary school education herself.[146]

In an effort to systematize Catholic schooling, Ryan reinvigorated the school board in 1887, pressing farther than Neumann had when he first established the school board. For example, Ryan's board introduced a new graded system to prepare students better for admission to secondary school (1890) and uniform diocesan examinations (1892).[147] By the early 1890s, the school board was so busy that its members petitioned the archbishop to appoint a superintendent. The key issue was whether the superintendent would be a lay man or cleric. In 1894, Ryan appointed Father John W. Shanahan the first superintendent of Catholic schools in Philadelphia.[148]

With urban parish schools proliferating, Shanahan set about systematizing the schools by introducing diocesan-wide professional development. As teachers would engage in "perfecting ourselves in the science and art of teaching," Shanahan hoped the schools would become national models.[149] An educational progressive in a decidedly anti-modern era,[150] Shanahan wanted teachers to generate interest on the part of students so they would be formed rather than informed.[151] He also wanted the curriculum to include drawing, vocal music, natural science, and physical culture.[152] Additionally, Shanahan urged pastors to establish parish libraries for the schools and called upon the board of health to inspect them to ensure sanitary conditions as well as to notify pastors of needed improvements. However, because pastors possessed great autonomy, Shanahan was "a voice crying in the wilderness."[153]

During these years, the archdiocese also opened Catholic Boys' High School (1890), the first urban Catholic high school in the United

States. Made possible by a bequest from a wealthy Philadelphia Catholic businessman, Thomas Cahill, who himself had attended public schools and did not receive a Catholic religious education, students admitted to "Catholic High" would receive a tuition-free religious education. The faculty was comprised of laity.[154] That accomplished, Ryan set his sights on opening a similar school for girls.

At the turn of the twentieth century, *The Catholic Standard and Times* editorialized: "Our parochial school system will never realize its grand possibilities until we have . . . a high school [for girls]. Our girls have as good a right to a thorough and comprehensive education as our boys."[155] Despite the plea, nothing happened and "senior grades" for female students desiring one or two additional years of post-elementary school education, normally under the direction of religious sisters in their convents, expanded exponentially.

Shanahan's successor as superintendent of Catholic schools, Father Philip McDevitt, picked up in 1905 where *The Catholic Standard and Times* editorial had left off in 1900, soliciting Catholics to contribute to the building of the school to honor the archdiocesan centennial in 1908.[156] McDevitt failed to meet that goal but Catholic Girls' High School finally did open in 1912, staffed by sisters from four religious congregations—each responsible for a different branch of studies, so that "one does not encroach on the other"—and one lay teacher.[157] From the beginning, the school admitted African Americans.

With the two central high schools, students of both genders now could receive a Catholic high school education. The schools proved popular, although the quality of the educational program at Catholic Girls' High School was called into question,[158] with 61 percent of graduates of parish schools attending the two diocesan high schools. Another 10 percent attended private Catholic high schools.[159] During the next four decades, expansion of the high schools continued unabated as did elementary schools, with dozens of schools opening.[160]

Besides calling for an increase in the number of parish schools, the Third Plenary Council also decreed an annual collection for the "Black and Indian Missions" and formed a board of bishops—the Commission for Catholic Missions among the Colored People and the Indians—to supervise, collect, and distribute funds. As one of three bishops named to the Commission, Ryan immersed himself in this cause and, when the first collection was taken in 1887, Philadelphia led the nation in fundraising.[161] In Philadelphia, Ryan founded a school for African

Americans that split into two institutions including an orphanage to care for boys who were more than ten years of age, what locals called "The Colored Mission." In 1893, Ryan hosted the annual meeting of the National Congress of Colored Catholics and in his address called for the economic, social, and educational improvement of African Americans since, he noted, "the incarnation was for people of all races."[162]

Archbishop Ryan also was a member of the Bureau of Catholic Indian Missions which worked with the U.S. Bureau of Indian Affairs to supervise the care and education of Native Americans living on government-owned reservations.[163] In this role, Ryan testified before Congress in 1898, asking for Catholic representation in the supervision of the reservations and for federal money to assist Catholic schools serving Native Americans.[164] This initiative solidified the special relationship between the archdiocese and Native Americans tracing its origins as far back as 1638, when a Susquehannock Indian, Arenhouta, was baptized in Canada, becoming the first Native American of the Commonwealth to convert to Catholicism.[165]

However, this special relationship is best exemplified in the heroic witness of Katharine Mary Drexel. Born in Philadelphia into wealth and taught early in life that wealth carried a special obligation to care for the poor, she cared deeply about the extreme poverty of both Native and African Americans.[166] Early in her life, Drexel resolved to devote herself to help these disadvantaged populations and, in 1886, used a portion of her inheritance to establish a school for African Americans in Philadelphia.[167]

During a private audience in 1887, Drexel asked Pope Leo XIII to recommend a religious congregation to staff the schools she was financing. The pope suggested that she become a missionary and, two years later, she entered the Sisters of Mercy. Then in 1891, along with a few companions, "Mother" Katharine Drexel founded the Sisters of the Blessed Sacrament for Indians and Colored People.[168] Through her generosity, the Archdiocese of Philadelphia opened St. Catherine's in 1916, a parish school for African American children.[169] Drexel died on March 3, 1955, and was declared a saint in 1987, her ministry having expanded Philadelphia's heritage of educating children of minority populations within and beyond the borders of the archdiocese.[170]

Only in retrospect does the magnitude of expansion during these decades become clear. In 1830, there were three urban parish schools. As immigrants flooded into the city during the 1830s, the Catholic population swelled from 100,000 to 475,000.[171] In the mid-1800s, Philadelphia had two nascent school "systems"—public and Catholic—characterized by a lack of unity as well as the need for expansion and professionalization.[172] In 1884, there were 58 parish schools; in 1904, there were 103;[173] and, during the next seven years, at least 45 were added, with suburban schools expanding at double the rate of urban schools. Philadelphia's urban Catholic school system was quickly becoming a national model.[174] No bishop in the United States exceeded Ryan in founding parish schools.[175] But much of this success is a result of the indefatigable creativity on the part of Ryan's superintendent of Catholic schools, Father John W. Shanahan.[176]

Following Ryan's death in 1911, another Irish immigrant, Edmond Francis Prendergast, was installed as Archbishop of Philadelphia. Many of his immediate predecessor's projects required completion if the archdiocese was to boast a complete educational system. Prendergast set about doing just that.

As this concerned urban Catholic schools, Prendergast opened the aforementioned Catholic Girls' High School in 1912. To honor his predecessor's concern for disabled youth and fulfill his dream of providing a school for this need, Prendergast opened the Archbishop Ryan Memorial Institute for the Deaf in 1912.[177] Expanding this effort, Prendergast opened two special education facilities, Madonna House and L'Assunta House (both in 1914), and founded St. Edmond's Home for Children, the first urban Catholic school for severely handicapped youth in 1916.[178]

But Prendergast accomplished much more. Crucial in this regard was delegating unprecedented authority to his superintendent, Father Philip McDevitt, who became Prendergast's spokesman for all matters concerning Catholic education[179] and worked tirelessly to make the schools more efficient and to strengthen their identity.[180] McDevitt's watchword: "Excellence." This impacted pedagogy, curriculum, and mission. "We are not making our standard that of comparison with the public schools," McDevitt maintained. "The efficiency of the latter is far from being well proven, and the best educators of our country are not slow in faultfinding with its results."[181]

So dogged was McDevitt that he insisted pastors formulate plans to strengthen and correct problems in their schools.[182] He also warned religious congregations not to send unqualified or inexperienced teachers into classrooms.[183] Believing that principals "determined the character of the school," McDevitt supervised them directly.[184] He called for additional high schools and advocated a unionized faculty.[185] Lastly, McDevitt directed in 1915 that every school provide special education for students not requiring special facilities. Although this directive was not implemented uniformly, "by the time McDevitt's tenure ended, the awareness of, and momentum for special education had been implanted in the Catholic school system."[186]

McDevitt's insistence upon excellence earned him a fair share of critics, including some pastors and superiors of religious congregations. In fact, McDevitt was once charged as "out of line" and in need of "censuring." In these disputes, Prendergast always supported his superintendent; where compliance lacked, Prendergast "made it a personal matter."[187]

During McDevitt's tenure, the number of diocesan schools in Philadelphia increased from 112 to 170 and the number of teachers increased from 689 to 1,293.[188] Finding teachers to staff the system presented a daunting but not novel challenge. In 1900, sisters staffed urban Catholic schools for the most part, but continuing expansion made the goal of having a sister in each classroom impossible and, by 1905, religious communities could no longer meet the demand.[189] In response, McDevitt focused upon hiring and training Catholic lay teachers, continuing the gradual return of the laity to the schools.[190] Operating "on a shoestring," McDevitt sponsored professional development programs on Saturdays that led to teacher certification by the Commonwealth[191] and published "Educational Briefs," a quarterly pamphlet treating pedagogical topics.[192]

Between 1910 and 1920, high school enrollment increased 340 percent[193] and there were more than eighty-one thousand students attending Philadelphia's urban Catholic schools, not including those attending Catholic private schools.[194] Despite this growth and with many Catholics unconvinced of the need for Catholic schools, there still were not enough schools and most classrooms were badly overcrowded.[195] To meet demand during Prendergast's last three years, the archdiocese opened four urban parish schools, four other parishes opened new school buildings, and two more added classrooms. Within four years of Prendergast's death in 1918, six urban parishes opened schools while five others added classrooms.[196] In 1925, only twenty parishes in the city did not sponsor schools.[197]

If Prendergast was a "Master Builder" and "Real Estate Genius,"[198] his successor, Dennis Joseph Dougherty, was "God's Bricklayer."[199] An indefatigable prelate who possessed exceedingly strong convictions intensely, some alleged Dougherty authoritarian,[200] especially reluctant pastors to whom he made it clear "that failure to operate a parish school constituted cause for removal from office."[201] Dougherty's *modus operandi*? "The system first, apologetics—later."[202] Installed as archbishop in 1918, Pope Benedict XV named the Pennsylvania native the archdiocese's first cardinal in 1921. Dougherty served thirty-three years, the longest tenure to date.[203]

Dougherty's commitment to urban Catholic schools soon evidenced itself in three ways. First, expansion continued and, in particular, urban Catholic high schools. Second, tuition-free Catholic schooling was extended. Third, African Americans and other foreign nationalities were welcomed into the schools, Dougherty's goal being to eliminate racial discrimination.[204]

During the "Roaring Twenties," Dougherty established fifty-four new parishes, with most operating schools.[205] Between 1925 and 1931, the archdiocese opened twenty-eight urban parish schools, with twelve additional urban parishes improving or constructing new school facilities.[206] To avoid proliferation of parish high schools and achieve greater centralization, Dougherty divided the archdiocese into two zones: "inside" and "outside" Philadelphia. No parish could open or conduct a high school in either zone without permission; centralization being normative for the "outside" zone.[207] In light of restrictions on building during World War II, Dougherty's commitment to Catholic education proved exceptional.[208] His belief? Catholic schools, and especially Catholic high schools, were "no luxury."[209] His ambition? The archdiocese would provide an egalitarian model for the rest of the nation to emulate.[210]

But where would sufficient revenue come from? Similar to other dioceses, each Philadelphia parish subsidized its school. As for high schools, the archdiocese bore construction costs; but, once a school opened, operating costs were assessed on a per capita basis to each parish, unless other sources were available.[211] Understandably, many pastors passed these costs directly to parents; but, this practice ended in 1926 when the school board mandated "each parish itself, and not parents or guardians, shall pay for the education of its pupils in our Catholic elementary and high schools."[212]

One can only imagine the muted response this regulation elicited, particularly in rectories. Why muted? The regulation was strictly

enforced "and where complaints were received of pastors asking individual parents for their children's tuition, swift remedial action was
taken by the cardinal and the school board." As operating deficits accrued for the central high schools, pastors were required to pay a pro
rata assessment. Yet, "the desire for Catholic education on the part of
the people, as well as continued self-sacrificing service by religious and
lay teachers, provided a financial pool which enabled the diocesan system to survive." The same can be observed concerning urban Catholic
private schools.[213]

Absolutely crucial to reducing operating costs was the "army" of
religious sisters teaching in Catholic schools who generated a revenue
stream of miraculous proportions. By 1930, more than 5,130 sisters
were teaching in 228 parish schools in Philadelphia; most sisters were
young and energetic, though not well-trained.[214] Classrooms were
overcrowded, some having sixty or more students and with only rudimentary pedagogical tools, like textbooks and blackboards, available.
Some schools—like St. Bernard's in the Mayfair section—were so overcrowded that "shifts" were implemented.[215] This solution proved unsat-
isfactory and so much so that some religious community supervisors
suggested in 1943 that in those elementary schools where large classes
were the norm, poor teachers be put into the largest classes, causing
so much trouble for pastors that they "will be forced to see the light."
This suggestion contrasted to those other schools where pastors "were
willing to open more classes but complained religious communities did
not send additional teachers."[216]

Despite these conditions, Dougherty used diocesan and scholarship test results between 1927 and 1931 to crow that "in most cases
we are equal [to the public schools], and in many cases superior."[217]
Crowing he was because the only accredited school in the archdiocese in 1928 was Mount St. Joseph's Academy, a private school. That
same year, eighty-seven boys failed the entrance examination to St.
Charles Seminary. Behind the scenes at archdiocesan school board
meetings, Dougherty was questioning the efficiency of the Catholic
schools, making his superintendent, Monsignor John Bonner, the
scapegoat.[218] By the mid-1930s, however, test results improved, indi-
cating that "the accomplishment of the schools of the Archdiocese is
not below the average of public schools of the country as a whole" and
instruction in the schools "provided adequate preparation for high
school." Over the next decade, "National standardized tests given

in all the high schools on essential secondary subjects in 1944, show that in all subjects norms for Philadelphia Catholic high schools were higher than national ratings . . . despite the crowded conditions in the schools."[219]

In the end, Dougherty's mandate succeeded, many parish schools remained open and expanded, and outcomes on standardized tests improved due, in large part, to one factor: the modest stipend paid the sisters. In 1946, this amounted to four hundred dollars annually for each teaching sister.[220]

The Depression began in 1929 and continued through the outbreak of World War II in 1941. Between 1930 and 1936, the archdiocese opened no new elementary schools or facilities, but did construct five new urban high schools. However, between 1931 and 1937, enrollment in the system plummeted by nearly ten thousand, coinciding with a similar decrease in the number of infant baptisms.[221] Despite parish subsidies and the sisters' meager stipends, finances continued to beleaguer Philadelphia's Catholic urban schools, causing Dougherty to become so irate in 1934 that "he ordered the superintendent not to divulge any [financial] information . . . when replying to a questionnaire."[222] To stem declining enrollment, Dougherty mandated in 1934 that all Catholic parents send their children to Catholic schools. To ensure compliance, the Ninth Archdiocesan Synod ruled the same year that tuition not be collected, except the annual textbook fee mandated in 1926.[223] Three years later, the high schools had accrued a debt of $2.5 million.[224] Yet, tuition-free Catholic education continued in Philadelphia.

As a young priest, Dougherty was consecrated a missionary bishop for the Philippines.[225] Now a cardinal, Dougherty vociferously opposed racism and demonstrated his commitment to the poor and dispossessed by welcoming all students into Philadelphia's urban Catholic schools. He not only embraced African American children and students with special needs, but also children of foreign nationalities.[226]

Regarding African Americans, Dougherty once stated: "I do not wish to create an impression of discrimination against the poor colored race who, through no fault of their own, have been persecuted ever since they were dragged here in chains."[227] Bigotry and racism had always simmered just beneath the surface in Philadelphia, but now racism was evidencing itself on the part of ethnic, white Catholics. Dougherty tolerated none of this, requiring pastors to accept African

American Catholic children in parish schools. Any complaint alleging racism or failure to comply resulted in a personal inquiry from the cardinal.[228] Despite these efforts and with African Americans moving into Philadelphia's ethnic enclaves, whites fled to the suburbs, a phenomenon that began during the 1920s, as children of immigrants left their cultural "ghetto" behind. Racial discrimination against African and Mexican Americans as well as immigrants from Central America (especially Puerto Rico) persisted well into the 1950s.[229]

Demonstrating his commitment to African American Catholics, the cardinal appointed Father Edward Cunnie pastor of St. Elizabeth's parish in 1937. Cunnie turned the parish, which had served immigrant populations including the Germans and Irish, into "the showcase of Philadelphia's black Catholic community." Eighteen years later, the parish boasted three thousand members—90 percent of whom Cunnie had converted—and the school enrolled nine hundred students. Regarding children of foreign nationalities, besides welcoming them into the system, Dougherty opened Holy Redeemer School (1941), an urban Catholic school that provided bilingual instruction for Chinese children.[230] It was one of only four elementary schools that opened during World War II, this meager number causing Dougherty no small degree of upset.[231]

Some labeled Dougherty "abrasive," others "a genius," and still others what later would be termed "a micromanager." Yet, none doubted his "holy, almost ruthless, determination to permanently establish a complete system of Catholic education." Despite national trials, including the Depression and World War II, as well as formidable obstacles which included financing and staffing an overburdened system as well as errors in judgment, the system emerged stronger. What Dougherty desired to see but did not was a national model where every Catholic child would "obtain not only instruction in secular knowledge but also where . . . development as a true Christian will go hand in hand with physical growth."[232] Within the three years following Dougherty's death, more than 135,000 students were enrolled in 305 parish elementary schools and another 28,000 in 31 archdiocesan high schools.[233]

An educator-priest of the Congregation of Holy Cross and former president of the University of Notre Dame, John Francis O'Hara succeeded Dougherty in 1951. O'Hara had the appearance of a gentle pastor, characterized by sensitive care and appreciation for people. Yet,

O'Hara was an equally "hardheaded, realistic, exacting businessman" just as committed to Catholic schools as was his predecessor.[234] O'Hara's common piety—"one went to mass" and "one received communion"— also included "one went to Catholic school."[235]

O'Hara was fueled by his "passionate belief in the influence of Catholicism."[236] He once said: "If the bishops one hundred years ago were not afraid of the ideal of every Catholic child in a Catholic school, we today should not give way to pessimism. Had they been afraid, what would we have today?"[237] To those who suggested closing Catholic elementary schools, O'Hara wrote: "We cannot ignore our responsibility to the souls of the children entrusted to us; we are responsible to God for the wreckage we may produce through experimentation."[238] Despite his idealism, the percentage of students registered in Philadelphia Catholic schools during O'Hara's brief tenure failed to make the top twenty dioceses in the nation.[239]

Perhaps not quite the micromanager Dougherty was, O'Hara was "his own superintendent of schools," actively directing the system. In response to those who argued that "slow students" took up scarce desks, O'Hara mandated in 1956 that any student "who conscientiously gives his best to school work [would be] passed even if his scholastic attainments are small," causing some to claim the archbishop did not emphasize intellectual development.[240] In response to parents who argued that a child who had a lay teacher in Catholic school all day might just as well attend public school, O'Hara mandated in 1955 that the ratio be limited to one lay teacher for every five religious.[241] To improve academic achievement, O'Hara dictated curriculum revisions.[242] He also sought to improve achievement among African Americans attending Catholic schools.[243]

The archdiocese founded seven urban parish schools during O'Hara's tenure, although much of the expansion was now transpiring beyond the city's boundaries.[244] In addition, the archdiocese constructed three new urban Catholic high schools.[245] The archbishop also extended two traditions. The first was the tuition-free policy for diocesan high schools.[246] The second was providing welcome to immigrants and providing for orphans, children with special needs, and children of nursery school age.[247]

Concerning the second tradition, large numbers of Spanish-speaking Catholics continued to emigrate from Central and South America and the Caribbean, with many settling in the city's Spring

Garden neighborhood.[248] Each day, the archdiocese bused many of these students to Assumption School for one hour to be taught English as a second language.[249] In 1954, O'Hara dedicated Casa del Carmen Settlement Center, which provided members of the Hispanic community a full range of social and educational services.

Parents of children with special needs desired a school where their children could receive religious education as well as special education. A 1951 meeting with O'Hara resulted in the opening of St. Katherine Day School (1953).[250] O'Hara also founded St. Barbara's Day School and Our Lady of Confidence Day School (both in 1954) for mentally handicapped youth[251] as well as St. Lucy Day School for Children with Visual Impairment (1955).[252] Lastly, he sponsored an annual fundraiser to support these institutions (1956).[253] Providing educational services for children with special needs arguably was O'Hara's most substantive achievement.[254]

In 1959, the year after O'Hara was created a cardinal, Pope John XXIII called for a second Vatican Council.[255] *Aggiornamento*—"openness," "reform," and "renewal"—was in the air.[256] In Philadelphia, the post-World War II "baby boom" and exodus of white, ethnic Catholics from the city to the suburbs continued. The realities of urban life raised anew the challenge of welcoming and educating new immigrants as well as minorities representing diverse cultures and religious traditions. Even with the demonstrated success of Philadelphia's urban Catholic schools in providing for these needs since 1681, if these schools were to provide for this need beyond 1961, *aggiornamento* on the part of Philadelphia's Catholics would be needed.

O'Hara died on August 28, 1960, and John Joseph Krol was named Philadelphia's sixth archbishop on February 11, 1961.[257] The archdiocese that had once covered approximately fifty-three thousand square miles and had given birth to ten dioceses now covered a mere five thousand square miles. Despite this 90 percent decrease in territory, the original population of approximately 30,000 Catholics had grown to 4,521,801 (from 3 percent to 34 percent of the population).[258] And, what Dougherty and O'Hara desired to see but did not live to see, under Krol, had become a national model for other dioceses to emulate.[259]

In a 1956 article, the Archdiocese of Chicago's superintendent of Catholic schools, Father William McManus, wondered whether Catholic schools were moving from their "childhood" into their "adolescence."[260] Perhaps the metaphor McManus used was apt, as the adolescent years for many teenagers enrolled in Catholic schools during the 1960s and 1970s were characterized by great turbulence as these young people shaped their adult identity.

Turbulence was clearly evident by 1961 as urban Catholic schools nationally could not meet demand.[261] As was the case elsewhere, there were too many overcrowded classrooms, poorly trained teachers, and unqualified students attending Philadelphia's Catholic schools.[262] Despite this turbulence, standardized tests indicated that the system in Philadelphia was succeeding.[263]

Yet, the two challenges dating back to the origins of urban Catholic schools in the Quaker City in 1681—the financial challenge and the personnel challenge—continued to generate no small amount of turbulence in 1961. It was difficult to imagine how the schools would mature into healthy adulthood if the archdiocese failed to deal with either impediment adequately.

The decrees of the Second Vatican Council (1962-1965) also generated turbulence.[264] Inspired by the Council's spirit of *aggiornamento*, a New Hampshire housewife and religious educator, Mary Perkins Ryan, raised anew the question many had been asking for generations if not since the first parish school opened in the United States: *Are Parochial Schools the Answer?*[265] "Mrs. Ryan's little book landed like a stink bomb in the old schoolhouse," James O'Connor observed,[266] generating no small amount of turbulence nationally.[267] While Mrs. Ryan did not argue for closing Catholic schools, she raised anew the financial challenge; namely, whether the limited funds available in most parishes and dioceses would better be directed at expanding religious education programs to reach all Catholic youth in the post-Vatican II era.

For more than six decades in Philadelphia, many in the Catholic community—including Archbishops Ryan, Prendergast, Dougherty, and O'Hara in Philadelphia—had stubbornly refused to acknowledge the question Mrs. Ryan raised. But, with the exodus of the religious sisters and brothers and priests from the Catholic schools in its early stages, Krol had to acknowledge not only Mrs. Ryan's question concerning financing the system but also the personnel question that was first raised when Philadelphia's urban Catholic schools began to expand in the 1800s: Who will teach in them? For example: although the number of lay teachers in the nation's Catholic schools increased 190 percent between 1956 and 1966, 4,750 sisters left the convent in 1966 alone.[268]

What was unimaginable in Philadelphia when Dougherty died in 1951 was now the trend one decade later and not only in Philadelphia but also nationally: urban Catholic elementary and high schools had to be closed or merged.[269] The situation eventually would grow so serious that, in 1972, the nation's bishops would declare: "Today, this school system is shrinking visibly. The reasons are many and include complex sociological, demographic, and psychological factors."[270] Regarding Catholic schools, the bishops continued: "the unfinished business on the agenda of Catholic schools includes the task of providing quality education for the poor and disadvantaged of our nation."[271]

For this faith-filled heritage to be bequeathed to future generations, the history of urban Catholic schools in Philadelphia teaches that parents—as the primary educators of their children—must determine what program of intellectual and moral formation they wish their children to receive and, then, must possess the courage of their convictions to see that their children receive it. This history also teaches that future archbishops will need their predecessors' fortitude if they are to convince a broad range of constituents to understand just how vitally important urban Catholic schools are to the Church's mission in Philadelphia and why these schools deserve continued, unwavering support.

Despite what parents and future archbishops may desire to see, the future of urban Catholic schools in Philadelphia will most likely come down to dealing creatively with those two omnipresent challenges, funding and staffing. Some constituents will have to imitate "Business Leaders Organized for Catholic Schools"[272] by contributing directly to or by discovering alternative ways to secure adequate financing for urban Catholic schools. Others—especially the members of the urban and minority communities or whose children have special needs—will have to offer their lives as educators in service to the church in Philadelphia. Since as early as 1681, many have possessed the courage of their convictions and others have stepped forward to assist in overcoming those two perennial challenges. Today, two are saints: Bishop John Nepomucene Neumann and Mother Katharine Drexel.

These efforts represent what may very well be the only way future generations in Philadelphia will experience what Jesus taught his disciples: "Blessed are the eyes that see what you see! For I say to you, many . . . desired to see what you see, but did not see it."[273]

NOTES

1. Archdiocese of Philadelphia, *Our Faith-Filled Heritage: The Church of Philadelphia-Bicentennial as a Diocese, 1809-2008* (Strasbourg, France: Editions du Signe, 2007), 15-19.

2. J. A. Burns, *The Catholic School System in the United States: Its Principles, Origin, and Establishment* (New York: Benziger Brothers, 1908); John Tracy Ellis, *American Catholicism* (Chicago: University of Chicago Press, 1969), 19-34; Martin I. J. Griffin and William L. J. Griffin, eds., *The American Catholic Historical Researches* (Philadelphia: M.I.J. Griffin, 1885), 95-96; Archdiocese of Philadelphia, *Faith-Filled Heritage*, 24.

3. Burns, *Catholic School System*, 105; Ellis, *American Catholicism*, 28-34.

4. Thomas J. Donaghy, *Philadelphia's Finest: A History of Catholic Education in the Catholic Archdiocese, 1692-1970* (Philadelphia: University of Pennsylvania Press, 1972), 32; Archdiocese of Philadelphia, *Faith-Filled Heritage*, 42-43.

5. Harold A. Buetow, *Of Singular Benefit: The Story of U.S. Catholic Education* (New York: Macmillan, 1970), 34-36; Joseph L. J. Kirlin, *Catholicity in Philadelphia* (Philadelphia: University of Philadelphia Press, 1909), 110-111; Timothy Walch, *Parish School: American Catholic Parochial Education from Colonial Times to the Present* (New York: Crossroad, 1996), 17.

6. Burns, *Catholic School System*, 142.

7. Ibid., 125-131; James J. Hennesey, *American Catholics: A History of the Roman Catholic Community in the United States* (New York: Oxford University Press, 1981), 51-52.

8. Archdiocese of Philadelphia, *Faith-Filled Heritage*, 2, 41.

9. Donaghy, *Philadelphia's Finest*, 8.

10. Ellis, *American Catholicism*, 19; Donaghy, *Philadelphia's Finest*, 7.

11. Archdiocese of Philadelphia, *Faith-Filled Heritage*, 27; Hennesey, *American Catholics*, 82.

12. Donaghy, *Philadelphia's Finest*, 4.

13. John Tracy Ellis, *Catholics in Colonial America* (Baltimore: Helicon, 1965), 370-380; Archdiocese of Philadelphia, *Faith-Filled Heritage*, 30; Ellis, *American Catholicism*, 62-64.

14. Burns, *Catholic School System*, 116; Jay P. Dolan, *The American Catholic Experience: A History from Colonial Times to the Present* (Garden City, NY: Doubleday, 1985), 84-85; Hennesey, *American Catholics*, 50; Archdiocese of Philadelphia, *Faith-Filled Heritage*, 30.

15. Hennesey, *American Catholics*, 59-60.

16. Ellis, *Catholics in Colonial America*, 37-40.

17. Archdiocese of Philadelphia, *Faith-Filled Heritage*, 30.

18. David H. Bennett, *The Party of Fear* (Chapel Hill, NC: University of North Carolina Press, 1988); Ray Billington, *The Protestant Crusade, 1800-1860* (New York: Macmillan, 1938); Ira M. Leonard and Robert D. Parmet, *American Nativism, 1830-1860* (New York: Van Nostrand Reinhold Co., 1971).

19. Archdiocese of Philadelphia, *Faith-Filled Heritage*, 51.

20. Philip Gleason, "The School Question: A Centennial Retrospect," in *Keeping the Faith: American Catholicism Past and Present*, ed. Philip Gleason (Notre Dame, IN: University of Notre Dame Press, 1987), 121.

21. Archdiocese of Philadelphia, *Faith-Filled Heritage*, 59.

22. Donaghy, *Philadelphia's Finest*, 39.

23. Ibid., 21.

24. Old St. Joseph's Church; Archdiocese of Philadelphia, *Faith-Filled Heritage*, 36.

25. Donaghy, *Philadelphia's Finest*, 39.

26. Ibid., 65.

27. Ibid., 68.

28. Ibid., 90.

29. Dolan, *American Catholic Experience*, 103-107.

30. Hugh J. Nolan, ed., *Pastoral Letters of the United States Catholic Bishops* (Washington, DC: National Catholic Conference of Bishops/United States Catholic Conference of Bishops, 1984), 1:14, 16-27; Ellis, *American Catholicism*, 74-75.

31. Robert D. Cross, "Origins of the Catholic Parochial Schools in America," *American Benedictine Review* 16 (1965): 194-209; Otto F. Kraushaar, *Private Schools: From the Puritans to the Present* (Bloomington, IN: Phi Delta Kappa Educational Foundation, 1976), 27.

32. Nolan, *Pastoral Letters*, 1:18.

33. Richard M. Jacobs, "Putting First Things First: The Religious—Their Contributions to and Challenges for—U.S. Catholic Schooling," in *The Catholic Character of Catholic Schools*, ed. James Youniss, John Convey, and Jeffrey McLellan (Notre Dame, IN: University of Notre Dame Press, 2000), 82-102.

34. Ellis, *American Catholicism*, 54.

35. Dolan, *American Catholic Experience,* 276-277.

36. Donaghy, *Philadelphia's Finest*, 46.

37. Ibid., 19.

38. Archdiocese of Philadelphia, "History," http://www.catholicschools-phl.org/about/history.htm/

39. Burns, *Catholic School System*, 137, 139-140; Hennesey, *American Catholics*, 94; Donaghy, *Philadelphia's Finest*, 116.

40. Donaghy, *Philadelphia's Finest*, 28.

41. Burns, *Catholic School System*, 137.

42. Archdiocese of Philadelphia, *Faith-Filled Heritage*, 41-43; Donaghy, *Philadelphia's Finest*, 32.

43. Donaghy, *Philadelphia's Finest*, 26-27, 43.

44. Ibid., 35.

45. Ibid.

46. Archdiocese of Philadelphia, *Faith-Filled Heritage*, 43; Donaghy, *Philadelphia's Finest*, 26-27, 49-50, 198.

47. Ellis, *American Catholicism*, 45; Hennesey, *American Catholics*, 74, 83, 95-98.

48. Burns, *Catholic School System*, 142-143.

49. Donaghy, *Philadelphia's Finest*, 28.

50. Archdiocese of Philadelphia, *Faith-Filled Heritage,* 38, 47; Donaghy, *Philadelphia's Finest*, 20.

51. Donaghy, *Philadelphia's Finest*, 34.

52. Burns, *Catholic School System*, 143.

53. David R. Contasta and Dennis J. Gallagher, *Villanova University, 1842-1992: American-Catholic-Augustinian* (Pennsylvania State University Press, 1995), 10-14; Donaghy, *Philadelphia's Finest*, 69.

54. Donaghy, *Philadelphia's Finest*, 41, 44.

55. Ibid., 67.

56. Archdiocese of Philadelphia, *Faith-Filled Heritage,* 59.

57. Donaghy, *Philadelphia's Finest*, 67.

58. Ibid., 68.

59. Ibid., 23.

60. Ibid., 25; Archdiocese of Philadelphia, *Faith-Filled Heritage*, 41.

61. Donaghy, *Philadelphia's Finest*, 23.

62. Ibid., 44-46.

63. Ibid., 45-46, 64, 69; Archdiocese of Philadelphia, *Faith-Filled Heritage*, 59.

64. Donaghy, *Philadelphia's Finest*, 68-70.

65. Dolan, *American Catholic Experience*, 251.

66. Ibid., 250.

67. Old St. Joseph's Church.

68. Donaghy, *Philadelphia's Finest*, 24; Arthur J. Ennis, "The Augustinians in the United States: The Story of Michael Hurley, OSA (1780-1837)," *Augustinian Heritage* 34 (1998): 140-141.

69. Ennis, "Augustinians in the United States," 141.

70. Donaghy, *Philadelphia's Finest*, 43.

71. Ibid., 44.

72. Archdiocese of Philadelphia, *Faith-Filled Heritage*, 49-50.

73. Donaghy, *Philadelphia's Finest*, 43-44.

74. Hennesey, *American Catholics*, 186.

75. Donaghy, *Philadelphia's Finest*, 29.

76. Archdiocese of Philadelphia, *Faith-Filled Heritage*, 49.

77. Dolan, *American Catholic Experience*, 266-272; David Tyack and Elisabeth Hansot, *Managers of Virtue: Public School Leadership in America, 1820-1980* (New York: Basic Books, 1982), 72-83.

78. Archdiocese of Philadelphia, *Faith-Filled Heritage*, 46.

79. Ibid., 21.

80. Ellis, *American Catholicism*, 73.

81. Glenn Altschuler and Stuart M. Blumin, "Limits of Political Engagement in Antebellum America: A New Look at the Golden Age of Participatory Democracy," *Journal of American History* 84 (1997): 855-885; James L. Bugg, *Jacksonian Democracy: Myth or Reality?* (New York: Holt, Rinehart and Winston, 1952); Sean Wilentz, *The Rise of American Democracy: Jefferson to Lincoln* (New York: W. W. Norton, 2005).

82. Vincent P. Lannie and Bernard C. Diethorn, "For the Honor and Glory of God: The Philadelphia Bible Riots of 1840," *History of Education Quarterly* 8 (1968): 46-47.

83. Donaghy, *Philadelphia's Finest*, 50.

84. Ibid., 87, 95.

85. Timothy L. Smith, "Protestant Schooling and American Nationality, 1800-1850," *Journal of American History* 53 (1967): 695.

86. Ruth Elson, *Guardians of Tradition: American Schoolbooks of the Nineteenth Century* (Lincoln, NE: University of Nebraska Press, 1964).

87. Marie L. Fell, "The Foundations of Nativism in American Textbooks, 1783-1860" (PhD diss., The Catholic University of America, 1941); Elson, *Guardians of Tradition*.

88. Donaghy, *Philadelphia's Finest*, 51-52.

89. Fell, "Foundations of Nativism," 77-91.

90. Donaghy, *Philadelphia's Finest*, 55, fn. 76.

91. Michael Feldberg, *The Philadelphia Bible Riots of 1844: A Study of Ethnic Conflict* (Westport, CT: Greenwood Press); Lannie and Diethorn, "For the Honor and Glory of God"; John C. Schneider, "Community and Order in Philadelphia, 1834-1844," *Maryland Historian* 5 (1974): 15-26; Sam Warner, *Private City: Philadelphia in the Three Periods of its Growth* (Philadelphia: University of Pennsylvania Press, 1968), 144-152; Walch, *Parish School*, 25, 33-34, 44-48.

92. Donaghy, *Philadelphia's Finest*, 52; Hennesey, *American Catholics*, 122-124.

93. Lannie and Diethorn, "For the Honor and Glory of God," 57-65.

94. Bruce Dorsey, *Reforming Men and Women: Gender in the Antebellum City* (Ithaca, NY: Cornell University Press, 2002), 203-205; Lannie and Diethorn, "For the Honor and Glory of God," 67.

95. David Montgomery, "The Shuttle and the Cross: Weavers and Artisans in the Kensington Riots of 1844," *Journal of Social History* 5 (1972): 411-446.

96. Margaret Fitzgerald, "The Philadelphia Nativist Riots: Irish Culture Society of the Garden City Area," http://204.3.199.208/Hedgemaster%20Archives/philadelphia.htm

97. Lannie and Diethorn, "For the Honor and Glory of God," 72-81.

98. Dorsey, *Reforming Men and Women*, 206-209.

99. Fitzgerald, "Philadelphia Nativist Riots."

100. Archdiocese of Philadelphia, *Faith-Filled Heritage*, 53-54; Dorsey, *Reforming Men and Women*, 209-212; Lannie and Diethorn, "For the Honor and Glory of God," 81-87.

101. Fitzgerald, "Philadelphia Nativist Riots."

102. Lannie and Diethorn, "For the Honor and Glory of God," 69-70.

103. Donaghy, *Philadelphia's Finest*, 55, fn. 76.

104. Edgar P. McCarren, "The Origin and Early Years of the National Catholic Educational Association" (PhD diss., The Catholic University of America, 1966), 207.

105. Archdiocese of Philadelphia, "History"; Archdiocese of Philadelphia, *Faith-Filled Heritage*, 55.

106. Donaghy, *Philadelphia's Finest*, 36.

107. Ibid., 69.

108. Ibid., 60.

109. Archdiocese of Philadelphia, *Faith-Filled Heritage,* 55-56.

110. Donaghy, *Philadelphia's Finest*, 63.

111. Archdiocese of Philadelphia, *Faith-Filled Heritage,* 57.

112. Donaghy, *Philadelphia's Finest*, 61-62; Archdiocese of Philadelphia, *Faith-Filled Heritage,* 58-59; Glen Gabert, *In Hoc Signo? A Brief History of Catholic Parochial Education* (Port Washington, NY: Kennikat Press, 1973), 68.

113. Donaghy, *Philadelphia's Finest*, 63.

114. Ibid.

115. Ibid., 75.

116. Ibid., 71, 75-76; Richard M. Jacobs, "The Future Belongs to Those Who Control the Schools: Part II—Contributions in the First Six Decades of the 20th Century," *Catholic Education: A Journal of Inquiry and Practice* 2, no. 1 (1998): 4-23.

117. Archdiocese of Philadelphia, *Faith-Filled Heritage*, 59; Donaghy, *Philadelphia's Finest*, 118-119.

118. Archdiocese of Philadelphia, "History."

119. *The Catholic Encyclopedia*, "Archdiocese of Philadelphia," New Advent, http://www.newadvent.org/cathen/11793b.htm/

120. Philip Douglas, *Saint of Philadelphia: The Life of Bishop John Neumann, 1811-1860* (Still River, MA: The Ravengate Press, 1977); Jane F. Hindman, *An Ordinary Saint: The Life of John Neumann* (New York: Arena Letters, 1977); Robert H. Wilson, *St. John Neumann, 1811-1860, Fourth Bishop of Philadelphia* (Philadelphia: Archdiocese of Philadelphia Institutional Services, 1977).

121. Archdiocese of Philadelphia, *Faith-Filled Heritage*, 61-62.

122. Donaghy, *Philadelphia's Finest*, 72.

123. Ibid.

124. Ibid., 93.

125. Ibid., 94.

126. Ibid., 197.

127. Ibid., 64.

128. Archdiocese of Philadelphia, *Faith-Filled Heritage,* 64-65; Donaghy, *Philadelphia's Finest,* 88-95.

129. *The Catholic Encyclopedia,* "Archdiocese of Philadelphia."

130. Donaghy, *Philadelphia's Finest,* 82.

131. Ibid., 94.

132. Ibid., 82-88.

133. Ibid., 95-96.

134. Ibid., 161-162.

135. Thomas T. McAvoy, "Public Schools," *Review of Politics* 28 (1966): 256.

136. Nolan, *Pastoral Letters,* 1:225.

137. Ibid.; McCarren, "Origin and Early Years," 20.

138. Nolan, *Pastoral Letters,* 1:223.

139. McAvoy, "Public Schools," 260.

140. Gleason, "School Question," 117-121, 129-133.

141. Nolan, *Pastoral Letters,* 1:223.

142. Timothy H. Morrissey, "Archbishop John Ireland and the Faribault-Stillwater Plan of the 1890's: A Reappraisal" (PhD diss., University of Notre Dame, 1975); John Spalding, "Religious Instruction in State Schools," *Education Review* 2 (1891): 105-122.

143. Dolan, *American Catholic Experience,* 275-276.

144. Archdiocese of Philadelphia, *Faith-Filled Heritage,* 68; Dolan, *American Catholic Experience,* 127-157.

145. Donaghy, *Philadelphia's Finest,* 114; Archdiocese of Philadelphia, *Faith-Filled Heritage,* 69.

146. Hennesey, *American Catholics,* 209-210.

147. Donaghy, *Philadelphia's Finest,* 103-105.

148. Ibid., 101-120. Augenstein identifies Rev. Nevin F. Fischer as Philadelphia's first "Diocesan Inspector of Schools," using the term synonymously with "Superintendent. John J. Augenstein, *Lighting the Way, 1908 to 1935: The Early Years of the Catholic Schools Superintendency* (Washington, DC: National Catholic Educational Association, 1996) 1-2.

149. Donaghy, *Philadelphia's Finest,* 106, 119.

150. Dolan, *American Catholic Experience,* 317-320, 352; Darrell J. Jodock, *Catholicism Contending with Modernity: Roman Catholic Modernism and Anti-Modernism in Historical Context* (Cambridge, UK: Cambridge University Press, 2000), 1-19, 20-28.

151. Dolan, *American Catholic Experience,* 106, 115.

152. Ibid., 116-118; Donaghy, *Philadelphia's Finest,* 118.

153. Dolan, *American Catholic Experience,* 108; Donaghy, *Philadelphia's Finest,* 105.

154. Archdiocese of Philadelphia, "History"; Dolan, *American Catholic Experience,* 292; Donaghy, *Philadelphia's Finest,* 152-156; Archdiocese of Philadelphia, *Faith-Filled Heritage,* 72; Hennesey, *American Catholics,* 187.

155. Archdiocese of Philadelphia, *Faith-Filled Heritage,* 74.

156. Donaghy, *Philadelphia's Finest,* 164.

157. Ibid., 161-165.

158. Ibid., 168-169.

159. Ibid., 168.

160. Ibid., 166; Archdiocese of Philadelphia, *Faith-Filled Heritage,* 74.

161. Archdiocese of Philadelphia, *Faith-Filled Heritage,* 70.

162. Ibid., 71-72.

163. Dolan, *American Catholic Experience*, 285.

164. Archdiocese of Philadelphia, *Faith-Filled Heritage*, 25.

165. Ibid., 25.

166. Hennesey, *American Catholics*, 104.

167. Dolan, *American Catholic Experience*, 285; Donaghy, *Philadelphia's Finest*, 90, 111-112.

168. Archdiocese of Philadelphia, *Faith-Filled Heritage*, 72.

169. Donaghy, *Philadelphia's Finest*, 133, 136.

170. "Saint Katharine Drexel, Virgin & Foundress—AD 1955 Feast: March 3." *L'Osservatore Romano*, November 21, 1988, http://www.ewtn.com/library/mary/drexel.htm/

171. Buetow, *Of Singular Benefit*, 90-91; Burns, *Catholic School System*, 142-143; Archdiocese of Philadelphia, *Faith-Filled Heritage*, 21; Walch, *Parish School*, 17-18.

172. Donaghy, *Philadelphia's Finest*, 109-111.

173. Archdiocese of Philadelphia, "History."

174. Donaghy, *Philadelphia's Finest*, 132-133.

175. Archdiocese of Philadelphia, "History."

176. Donaghy, *Philadelphia's Finest*, 120.

177. Ibid., 145; Archdiocese of Philadelphia, *Faith-Filled Heritage*, 78.

178. Dolan, *American Catholic Experience*, 145, 188; Archdiocese of Philadelphia, *Faith-Filled Heritage*, 78.

179. Dolan, *American Catholic Experience*, 124-128, 131.

180. Ibid., 138.

181. Ibid.

182. Ibid., 128.

183. Ibid., 140.

184. Ibid., 129.

185. Ibid., 158-159, 163-164.

186. Ibid., 145.

187. Ibid., 130.

188. Ibid., 132.

189. Ibid., 140-141.

190. Ibid., 181.

191. Ibid., 182-183.

192. Ibid., 143.

193. Ibid., 173.

194. Ibid., 186.

195. Ibid.

196. Ibid., 187.

197. Ibid., 188.

198. Donaghy, *Philadelphia's Finest*, 123-124, 174; Wikipedia, "Edmond Francis Prendergast," http://en.wikipedia.org/wiki/Edmond_Pendergast/

199. James Connelly, ed., *A History of the Archdiocese of Philadelphia* (Philadelphia: Archdiocese of Philadelphia, 1976), 380; Hennesey, *American Catholics*, 241; Dolan, *American Catholic Experience*, 350.

200. Donaghy, *Philadelphia's Finest*, 174, 178-179.

201. Hennesey, *American Catholics*, 237.

202. Donaghy, *Philadelphia's Finest*, 176.

203. Archdiocese of Philadelphia, *Faith-Filled Heritage*, 82-84.

204. Hennesey, *American Catholics*, 241.

205. Ibid., 237.

206. Donaghy, *Philadelphia's Finest*, 188.

207. Ibid., 193-194.

208. Ibid., 215-216.

209. Ibid., 175.

210. Ibid., 225 fn.

211. Ibid., 198.

212. Ibid., 198-199.

213. Ibid., 199.

214. Madeleva Wolff, *My First Seventy Years* (New York: Macmillan, 1959); Donaghy, *Philadelphia's Finest*, 140; Harold A. Buetow, *A History of United States Catholic Schooling, NCEA Keynote Series 2* (New York: Macmillan, 1985), 33-34; Hennesey, *American Catholics*, 211.

215. Archdiocese of Philadelphia, *Faith-Filled Heritage*, 92.

216. Donaghy, *Philadelphia's Finest*, 217.

217. Ibid., 191.

218. Ibid., 196.

219. Ibid., 216-217, 224.

220. Ibid., 227; Dolan, *American Catholic Experience*, 277.

221. Archdiocese of Philadelphia, *Faith-Filled Heritage*, 86; Donaghy, *Philadelphia's Finest*, 206-207.

222. Donaghy, *Philadelphia's Finest*, 208.

223. Archdiocese of Philadelphia, *Faith-Filled Heritage*, 86.

224. Donaghy, *Philadelphia's Finest*, 208, 210.

225. Archdiocese of Philadelphia, *Faith-Filled Heritage*, 83.

226. Donaghy, *Philadelphia's Finest,* 175; Archdiocese of Philadelphia, *Faith-Filled Heritage*, 97.

227. Archdiocese of Philadelphia, *Faith-Filled Heritage,* 90.

228. Ibid., 90.

229. Dolan, *American Catholic Experience*, 357-383.

230. Ibid, 367; Donaghy, *Philadelphia's Finest*, 215.

231. Donaghy, *Philadelphia's Finest*, 241.

232. Ibid., 233-234.

233. Archdiocese of Philadelphia, *Faith-Filled Heritage,* 84, 97-98; Donaghy, *Philadelphia's Finest*, 149-150, 218-221.

234. Donaghy, *Philadelphia's Finest*, 239.

235. Hennesey, *American Catholics*, 266.

236. Dolan, *American Catholic Experience*, 391.

237. Donaghy, *Philadelphia's Finest*, 236.

238. Ibid.

239. Ibid., 237, 260.

240. Ibid., 238-239, 246.

241. Ibid., 252.

242. Ibid., 247.

243. Ibid., 248-249.

244. Ibid., 242; Archdiocese of Philadelphia, *Faith-Filled Heritage*, 74.

245. Archdiocese of Philadelphia, *Faith-Filled Heritage*, 74, 97-98; Donaghy, *Philadelphia's Finest*, 245.

246. Donaghy, *Philadelphia's Finest*, 256.

247. Archdiocese of Philadelphia, *Faith-Filled Heritage*, 97-99.

248. Ibid., 97-98.

249. Donaghy, *Philadelphia's Finest*, 243.

250. Archdiocese of Philadelphia: Office of Catholic Education, "History," http://www.catholicschools-phl.org/about-oce/history/

251. Donaghy, *Philadelphia's Finest*, 253.

252. Ibid., 254; St. Lucy Day School, "St. Lucy Day School—History," http://www.slds.org/History.html/

253. Archdiocese of Philadelphia, *Faith-Filled Heritage*, 99.

254. Donaghy, *Philadelphia's Finest*, 260.

255. Dolan, *American Catholic Experience*, 424-428.

256. Ibid., 417.

257. Archdiocese of Philadelphia, *Faith-Filled Heritage*, 100.

258. Ibid., 21.

259. Donaghy, *Philadelphia's Finest*, 266.

260. William E. McManus, "How Good are Catholic Schools?" *America* 95 (1956): 522-527; Hennesey, *American Catholics*, 297.

261. John P. Sullivan, "The Growth of Catholic Schools," *America* (1957): 205; William E. McManus, "Ten Points for Catholic Education," *The Catholic Mind* 52 (1954): 710-717.

262. Dolan, *American Catholic Experience*, 286-288.

263. Donaghy, *Philadelphia's Finest*, 280-281.

264. Ellis, *American Catholicism*, 237-254.

265. Mary Perkins Ryan, *Are Parochial Schools the Answer? Catholic Education in the Light of the Council* (New York: Guild Publishers, 1964).

266. James A. O'Conner, "The Modest Proposal of Mary Perkins Ryan," *Catholic World* (1974): 220.

267. Thomas C. Hunt and Norlene M. Kunkel, "Catholic Schools: The Nation's Largest Alternative School System," in *Religious Schooling in America,* ed. James C. Carper and Thomas C. Hunt (Birmingham, AL: Religious Education Press, 1984), 1-34.

268. Ellis, *American Catholicism*, 193.

269. Archdiocese of Philadelphia, *Faith-Filled Heritage,* 115-116.

270. Nolan, *Pastoral Letters,* 3:330.

271. Ibid., 3:332.

272. Business Leaders Organized for Catholic Schools, "History and Mission," http://www.blocs.org/

273. Archdiocese of Philadelphia, *Faith-Filled Heritage*, 15.

Empire City Catholicism:
Catholic Education in New York

Thomas J. Shelley

New York City is the only city in the United States where ecclesiastical jurisdiction is shared by two dioceses, the Archdiocese of New York and the Diocese of Brooklyn. This has been the situation since 1898 with the creation of Greater New York City which is composed of the five boroughs or counties of Manhattan (New York County), Bronx, Queens, Brooklyn (Kings County), and Staten Island (Richmond County). Prior to that date Brooklyn was a separate city. When the Brooklyn Bridge was opened in 1883, it connected the first and third largest cities in the United States.

Today, Manhattan, Bronx, and Staten Island fall within the jurisdiction of the Archdiocese of New York; Brooklyn and Queens comprise the Diocese of Brooklyn. A further geographical specification is in order. New York City was coterminous with the twenty-two square miles of the island of Manhattan until 1874 when the state legislature allowed the city to annex territory on the mainland that was then part of Westchester County and later became part of Bronx County.

The Archdiocese of New York dates from 1808 when it was one of four new dioceses carved out of the original American diocese of Baltimore. It included all of New York state and the northern half of New Jersey (approximately fifty-five thousand square miles) until 1847 when new dioceses were established in Buffalo and Albany for upstate New York. Six years later, two additional dioceses were established in

Newark and Brooklyn, reducing the boundaries of the diocese to one tenth of its original size.

Nonetheless, despite its diminished size, New York was made an archdiocese in 1850 in recognition of its burgeoning Catholic population, which accounted for as many as half of the city's total population of approximately 725,000 by the end of the Civil War. The Archdiocese of New York is unique among major American dioceses because its boundaries have not been altered since 1853, except for a minor border adjustment with the Diocese of Albany in 1861.

The Diocese of Brooklyn, created in 1853, originally included all of Long Island. As a result of the flight of many Catholics from the inner city to the suburbs after World War II, the new Diocese of Rockville Centre was established in 1957 for the two eastern counties on Long Island—Nassau and Suffolk—which reduced the Diocese of Brooklyn to the boroughs of Brooklyn and Queens. Today, Brooklyn is a totally urban diocese (179.25 square miles), the smallest in area in the United States, but the fifth largest in population.

The first Catholic school in New York City was the short-lived Latin School established by three English Jesuits—Thomas Harvey, Henry Harrison and Charles Gage—during the governorship of Thomas Dongan (1683-1687). It was probably opened in 1684 and probably closed in 1687 after Dongan was removed from office. It is certain that it did not survive the revolution of 1688 in England, which toppled the Catholic King James II from the throne and brought to an end this brief period of religious toleration in colonial New York. Nothing is known about the curriculum or enrollment, although it is said to have attracted the sons of wealthy Dutch and English residents.

Not until the 1780s did New York Catholics again have the freedom to practice their faith publicly or to conduct schools. In 1785, when the Catholic community numbered no more than two hundred, they laid the cornerstone for the city's first Catholic church, St. Peter's on Barclay Street. Fifteen years later they established the city's first permanent Catholic school, when the trustees of the church unanimously passed a resolution that "a free school for the education of the children be and is hereby established, and that a proper master be chosen to superintend such school."[1]

The school continued with an entirely lay staff until 1830 when the Sisters of Charity took charge of the girls' department. By 1806, St. Peter's was the largest denominational school in New York City.

"The applications for admission having been so numerous of late, we have established another school in the Bowery," the pastor told Bishop John Carroll. "The entire number of scholars is about two hundred and twenty and will in a short time exceed three hundred."[2] The average attendance soon reached nearly 450.

In 1808, the Jesuits made their second appearance in the diocese and their second contribution to Catholic education when Anthony Kohlmann, an Alsatian Jesuit, was appointed vicar general in the absence of the first bishop, Richard Luke Concanen, an Irish Dominican, who never reached New York and died in Europe in 1810. Kohlmann opened the New York Literary Institute, an embryonic Jesuit college that lasted from 1808 until 1813, when, much to Kohlmann's chagrin, he and his fellow Jesuits were reassigned to Georgetown College. Kohlmann was virtually the founder of the Diocese of New York and was also responsible for the establishment of the first St. Patrick's Cathedral (now known as St. Patrick's Old Cathedral), which was dedicated in 1815. By that date the Catholic population of the city numbered about fifteen thousand. That same year a free school was opened in the basement of the old cathedral. The oldest Catholic school in continuous operation in New York City, it was slated to close in June 2010 due to declining enrollment.

The year 1817 witnessed the arrival in New York City of the first three Sisters of Charity from their motherhouse in Emmitsburg, Maryland, at the invitation of several lay men and Bishop John Connolly. One diocesan historian considered it the most important decision made by Connolly, New York's second bishop (1815-1825), because of the contribution that the Sisters of Charity would make to Catholic education and social services in future years.[3] Although the original mission of the Sisters of Charity in New York was to administer the Roman Catholic Orphan Asylum, in 1822 they took charge of the girls' department of the free school in the basement of the cathedral and opened a tuition-based academy or "select school," the first of many schools that they would eventually staff in the Archdiocese of New York.[4]

Reflecting on his early days in New York twenty years later, John Hughes gave a bleak but not altogether accurate assessment of the state of Catholic education in the diocese in 1838. "There were no really Catholic schools in existence," he said, "except two, kept by the Sisters of Charity, who had charge of orphan children at the cathedral and at St. Peter's. One or two other churches had schools under a hired male teacher for the instruction of poor boys."[5]

In fact, there were eight parochial schools in New York City by 1840 and one select school. All but one of the parochial schools were located south of 14th Street; two were connected with German parishes, the others with Irish parishes; every one of them was located in a church basement.[6] Except for a few schools where the Sisters of Charity were in charge of the girls' department, the schools were managed by lay men of varying abilities. As the historian John Talbot Smith observed tartly, "Such teachers as had the necessary qualities and virtues ran their own schools, in which they made money, enjoyed a fine patronage, and lived on the surface of the earth, not under it."[7] The select school at the cathedral was closed in 1825 after only three years, but in 1835 the Sisters of Charity opened another academy that prospered, St. Mary's Select School for Young Ladies on Grand Street.

In his recollections of his early years in New York, Hughes seems to have forgotten that Brooklyn and Long Island were part of his diocese until 1853. Brooklyn Catholics got their first parish church when Bishop Connolly dedicated St. James Church (today St. James pro-Cathedral) on August 28, 1823, at the corner of Chapel and Jay Streets. It was the sixth Catholic church in New York State and the third oldest Catholic church within the confines of present-day New York City. Brooklyn was then a village of 8,800 residents. The initiative for the church came from a devout lay man, Peter Turner, an Irish immigrant who worked in the Brooklyn Navy Yard. Turner circulated a petition among his fellow Catholics, saying, "We want our children instructed in the principles of our Holy Religion, we want more convenience in hearing the word of God ourselves."[8]

That September, a school was opened in the basement of St. James Church with a single male teacher who also served as the sexton of the church and caretaker of the cemetery. As in Manhattan, the first women religious in Brooklyn were the Sisters of Charity. Three of them came to Brooklyn in 1831 at the invitation of the pastor of St. James Church, where they soon took charge of the parish orphan asylum, taught in the parochial school, and opened a boarding academy. In 1839, they also started an orphanage at St. Paul's Church in Court Street, Brooklyn's second oldest Catholic church. In the meantime, in 1834, Brooklyn was incorporated as a city.[9]

In 1840, Father Sylvester Malone became pastor of St. Mary's Church in Williamsburg, then a village in the town of Bushwick, where he remained as pastor for the next fifty-five years. In 1844, Malone commissioned the Irish-born architect Patrick Keely to build a new Gothic church which he dedicated to Saints Peter and Paul. It was the first of some seven hundred churches built by Keely in the United States. Malone started a parochial school in 1851 which was staffed by the Sisters of St. Joseph after 1856. It was their first foundation in the Diocese of Brooklyn. As a diocesan community, known as the Sisters of St. Joseph of Brentwood, they were to become one of the two largest communities of women religious in the Dioceses of Brooklyn and Rockville Centre.

In 1841, Williamsburg got a second Catholic church when Father John Raffeiner, the pioneer German priest in New York State, founded Most Holy Trinity Church for the German Catholics. It was the first of eighteen German parishes to be established in the diocese by 1891. Like every German pastor, Raffeiner soon added a school in the basement of the church.

In 1853, Raffeiner had an unexpected windfall when four Dominican Sisters from Bavaria, who were on their way to Latrobe, Pennsylvania, found themselves stranded in New York. Raffeiner offered them temporary shelter at Most Holy Trinity where they decided to remain as teachers in the parochial school. In subsequent years these Dominican Sisters established their motherhouse in Amityville on Long Island. They and the Sisters of St. Joseph became the two largest communities of women religious in the Diocese of Brooklyn. Together they made an indispensable contribution to Catholic education in Brooklyn and on Long Island.[10]

The physical facilities of the antebellum Catholic schools in both Brooklyn and Manhattan left much to be desired. After conducting an inspection in 1842, the deputy superintendent of the public schools in New York City reported that he "found them full to overflowing." He added that "in many instances schools were so full that every bench and seat was occupied; the scholars being so closely packed together that they had hardly room to move."[11]

The curriculum consisted largely of basic subjects such as reading, writing, arithmetic, and religion. Other subjects such as history and geography were sometimes available at extra cost. The content and quality of instruction varied from one school to another, although there was a heavy emphasis on religious instruction in all the schools. Boys and girls were taught in separate classrooms or at least in separate parts of the same room. As in the public schools, teachers used the so-called

Lancasterian system which enabled them to teach large classes by using older students to teach the younger students. Discipline was strict, but there was also a lavish use of prizes and awards to motivate students. There was no supervision or even coordination of education at the diocesan level, but in most parishes committees of the trustees visited the schools regularly, not only to check on the quality of the teaching, but also to evaluate the moral character of the teachers. Religion was often taught by the parish priests themselves.[12]

New York was a diocese adrift until the appointment in 1837 of John Hughes as coadjutor to New York's third bishop, the aging French-born John Dubois (1826-1842). After surveying the local scene upon his arrival, Hughes told his friend, Bishop John Purcell of Cincinnati, "I feel that I have been appointed in punishment for my sins."[13] Appointed apostolic administrator in 1839, Hughes succeeded Dubois as bishop in 1842, became the first archbishop of New York in 1850, and ran the archdiocese with an iron fist until his death in 1864. A born autocrat, Hughes remains the most significant figure in the history of the archdiocese to this day. For better or worse, he shaped New York Catholicism to a degree unmatched by any other archbishop of New York.

"The subject that of all others he had nearest his heart," said his biographer and former secretary, John Hassard, "was education."[14] The involvement of Hughes in Catholic education had monumental consequences not only in his own archdiocese but throughout the United States as he became the foremost episcopal advocate of parochial schools. Two developments in the 1840s reshaped Catholic education in New York and Hughes was at the center of both of them.

His first contribution to Catholic education in his own diocese was his epic confrontation with the Public School Society, a private organization dominated by the city's Protestant elite that had enjoyed a monopoly of public education in New York City since 1825.[15] Each year the state legislature allotted a lump sum to the Public School Society to administer the city's "common schools." Many Catholic parents refused to send their children to these schools because they found the atmosphere biased and prejudicial to their religion. Since the city's Catholic schools could only accommodate a small proportion of Catholic children, Hughes estimated that as many as half of the city's Catholic children, perhaps as many as twenty thousand, received no education at all.

The situation was not only a matter of concern to Catholics, but also to the Governor of New York State, William H. Seward. In an address to the state legislature on January 7, 1840, Seward called for the establishment of schools for the children of immigrants "in which they may be instructed by teachers speaking the same language and professing the same faith."[16] New York Catholics interpreted this address as an invitation to ask for a proportionate share of the funds allotted to the Public School Society every year by the state legislature. It was not an unreasonable request, since Catholic schools had received government funding prior to 1825.[17] In the absence of Hughes—who was in Europe soliciting funds for two other educational projects, a college and a seminary—New York Catholics organized a campaign to secure public funding for their schools.

Upon his return from Europe in July 1840, Hughes put himself at the head of the Catholic campaign. "On my return," said Hughes, "I found my diocese and especially the city of New York in a ferment."[18] Over the course of the next twenty-one months, from July 1840 until April 1842, the bishop waged a spirited battle that saw him argue his case for eight hours before the Common Council of the City of New York without the benefit of legal counsel, create his own short-lived political party, and appeal to the state legislature for redress. It was an amazing tour of force on the part of Hughes. In his own words, he "kneaded up" New York Catholics into a potent political bloc that forced a reluctant Democratic party to endorse the educational agenda of a Whig governor whose own party deserted him on the issue. The result was the destruction of the hated Public School Society.[19]

Hughes achieved this goal in 1842 when the state legislature enacted the Maclay Bill which replaced the Public School Society with elected school boards. However, it was a pyrrhic victory for Hughes because the state senate amended the Maclay Bill to prohibit sectarian religious instruction in the common schools. With that provision of the Maclay Bill, the bishop's dream of religious instruction for Catholic students in the common schools or public funding for his own schools went up in smoke.

Moreover, the Maclay Bill led eventually to the complete elimination of religion from the public school system in New York, a result that Hughes had never intended or wanted. "It is paradoxical," wrote the leading authority on the struggle of Hughes with the Public School Society, "that the father of American Catholic education should unwittingly have become a leading light in the ultimate secularization of the public school."[20]

As a result of his failure to secure state financial aid, Hughes decided to build a system of parochial schools financed entirely by the voluntary contributions of the laity. "The time is almost come," he announced in a pastoral letter in 1850, "when it will be necessary to build the school-house first and the church afterwards."[21] It was a battle cry that would be taken up by many other American bishops in the later nineteenth century and led to the decree of the Third Plenary Council of Baltimore in 1884 that every pastor should establish a parochial school within two years.

The bold venture of Hughes to start his own school system would never have gotten off the ground except for the increasing availability of large numbers of women and men who were members of religious orders and whose donated services made the Catholic school system financially viable. It was in this area that Hughes made his second great contribution to Catholic education in New York. He became involved in a protracted conflict with the superiors of the Sisters of Charity in Emmitsburg, which led to the establishment of a new diocesan community in 1846, the Sisters of Charity of St. Vincent de Paul. Beginning with only 33 sisters in 1846, this new community grew at a prodigious rate. According to James McMaster, the editor of the *Freeman's Journal*, by 1871 they numbered 430 sisters and they were operating fourteen academies and thirty free parochial schools.[22] Like the Sisters of St. Joseph and the Amityville Dominicans in the Diocese of Brooklyn, in the Archdiocese of New York the Sisters of Charity became the backbone of the Catholic school system, eventually staffing over one hundred schools in the course of the following century.

Hughes made impressive strides in his effort to create a Catholic school system in New York. The city itself experienced unparalleled growth during the years of the Hughes administration. When Hughes arrived in New York in 1838, only 33,000 people lived north of 14th Street, and a third of them listed their occupation as agricultural. Between 1840 and 1865 a whole new city sprang up between 14th Street and 42nd Street with over 190,000 people. The total population of the city more than doubled from 312,710 in 1840 to 726,386 in 1865, giving New York City more people than twenty of the thirty-three states. Much of the increase was due to massive immigration from Ireland and Germany. By 1865 one of every four New Yorkers had been born in

Ireland and one of every six New Yorkers had been born in Germany.[23]

In 1840 there were only nine Catholic schools in the diocese, eight free schools and one select school for girls. Hughes established twenty-five new parochial schools, bringing the total number of Catholic schools to fifty: thirty-three free parochial schools and seventeen select schools or academies. Sixteen of the new parochial schools were in Manhattan. In a break with the past, they were located not only downtown, but also in Midtown, and as far north on the island as Yorkville, Manhattanville, and Harlem. All but three of the seventeen select schools and academies were also located in Manhattan. Hughes also established the first parochial schools in the Bronx and on Staten Island as well as in Yonkers and Port Chester and in the upstate cities of Newburgh, Beacon, and Poughkeepsie.[24]

The physical facilities of the new schools still left much to be desired. In that era, pastors of new parishes usually erected a cheap wooden church as soon as possible, hoping to replace it later with a more substantial structure. They followed the same practice with schools. In 1847, at the new German church of St. Alphonsus on the Lower West Side, the pastor built a wooden church in three months at a cost of five thousand dollars, and then spent an additional one thousand dollars to outfit a five-classroom school in the basement. In 1854 at St. Lawrence O'Toole in Yorkville, the pastor opened a one-room school in the wooden building that had served as the first church. At St. Gabriel's Church in Midtown, Father William Clowry did the opposite. Taking to heart the injunction about building the school first, he opened a school building in 1859 with a chapel that served as the parish church until the permanent church was built six years later.

The classroom furnishings were spartan, if not primitive. In the words of one historian of New York's Catholic schools, "[They] had the crudest equipment: globes of parchment stretched over willow frames, parchment maps, and blackboards of planed wood, painted and fastened to the wall. Libraries were a thing of the future." The curriculum continued to place heavy emphasis on religion and basic subjects such as reading, writing, and arithmetic with a smattering of instruction in history and geography. Each school still set its own standards with little or no supervision or coordination by the archdiocese.[25]

A major change occurred in Catholic education with the increased numbers of teaching sisters and brothers. The Sisters of Charity alone staffed the girls' department in seventeen of the parochial schools in 1864, and by that year Hughes could also count on the services of the Religious of the Sacred Heart, the Ursulines, the Sisters of Mercy, and the School Sisters of Notre Dame. Although there were still lay teachers in virtually every school, the majority of the girls were taught by sisters.

The situation was quite different with the boys. The Brothers of the Christian Schools arrived in New York from France in 1848 to take charge of the parochial school at the Church of St. Vincent de Paul, New York's only French parish. By 1864 they staffed the boys' department in nine of the parochial schools, but the majority of the boys were still taught by lay teachers.

By 1870 two thirds of the churches had parochial schools, and the number of students in Catholic schools had increased from 5,000 in 1840 to 22,215 in 1870. Nonetheless, as the historian Jay Dolan has pointed out, despite the best efforts of Hughes, the enrollment in the Catholic schools could not keep pace with the growth of the Catholic population. The percentage of children in Catholic schools actually declined from 20 percent of the total school population in 1840 to 19 percent in 1870. Contemporary Catholic estimates of the percentage of Catholic children in Catholic schools varied between 17 percent and 33 percent.[26] Although New York was the largest, most prestigious, and reputedly the wealthiest archdiocese in the country, it simply did not have the resources in money or personnel to provide a place in a Catholic school for every Catholic child.

Hughes was also responsible for the third coming of the Society of Jesus to the Archdiocese of New York. In 1846, he invited a group of exiled French Jesuits to leave a faltering college in Kentucky to take charge of St. John's College at Rose Hill in Fordham, an institution that he had established as a diocesan college in 1841 with six students and a faculty of one. He paid the bargain price of $29,750 for 103 acres. However, he admitted years later, "I had not, when I purchased the site of this new college . . . so much as a penny wherewith to commence the payment for it."[27]

In 1847, the Jesuits opened a second college in the archdiocese, the College of St. Francis Xavier, which finally found a permanent home in the heart of Manhattan on West 15th Street. It soon overshadowed St. John's College and by 1900 it was the largest of the twenty-one Jesuit colleges in the United States and Canada with over five hundred students. Primarily a day school with an initial tuition of sixty dollars per year, St. Francis Xavier placed a college education within reach of lower middle class Catholics and trained a whole generation of Catholic lawyers, doctors, businessmen, and priests. The alumni formed the nucleus of the New York Catholic Club, the premier Catholic social organization in New York for half-a-century. The prominence of the organization was symbolized by an impressive club house on Central Park South.[28] By 1863, when the Christian Brothers incorporated their Manhattan Academy as Manhattan College, the Archdiocese of New York could boast of three Catholic colleges.

In 1866, a writer in the *Catholic World* estimated that the Catholic population of New York City was growing at the rate of twenty thousand per year, and he claimed that "New York is now about the fourth city in the world in Catholic population." Whatever the accuracy of that claim, for several decades in the late nineteenth century, the majority of the city's population was probably Catholic. As early as 1871, James Raymond, the editor of the *New York Times*, expressed his outrage that "there is an established church and a ruling class in New York, but the church is not Protestant and the ruling class is not American."[29]

Nonetheless, Father John Talbot Smith, a well-informed diocesan priest, complained about the timidity of Catholic politicians in protecting and promoting Catholic interests. As a case in point, he mentioned the composition of the Board of Education, which never numbered more than two or three Catholics among its twenty-two members. His comment may explain the reaction of Archbishop John Farley in 1904 when the newly elected Mayor George McClellan asked him if he had any candidates to recommend as city commissioners. Farley replied that he would prefer to see fair-minded non-Catholics in those positions rather than Catholics who would bend over backwards to avoid the impression that they were favoring their own church.[30]

In this atmosphere it is not surprising, therefore, that the two immediate successors to Hughes, Cardinal John McCloskey (1864-1885) and Archbishop Michael Augustine Corrigan (1885-1902), continued his policy of expanding the Catholic school system. This was especially true of Corrigan, who, like Hughes, became one of the foremost proponents of parochial schools in the American hierarchy.

It was a policy that was generally welcomed by the Catholic clergy and laity in New York as the public schools became increasingly secular. One senior New York priest, Father James McGean, the pastor of

St. Peter's Church, expressed the feelings of many New York Catholics about the shortcomings of the public schools at the dedication of the new St. Joseph's parochial school in Greenwich Village in 1897. "I remember," he declared, "when in the common schools the name of God was mentioned on every page of the reading book." "Unfortunately for ourselves," he added, "there was a positive opposition in many of the lessons that were given inside the old schools to what we claim to be the religion of Almighty God." "On this account," he said, "there were those who were willing that their children should be from day to day in the basement of this old church that they might receive the religious instruction that they could not have in the common school."[31]

McCloskey, the successor to Hughes and the first American cardinal, was a quiet, self-effacing man, who modestly said that he reaped what others had sown. He continued the policy of expanding the Catholic school system, adding nineteen new parochial schools, nine in Manhattan, one in the Bronx, one on Staten Island and the rest in Westchester County or upstate. By the time of his death in 1885, the Catholic school population of the archdiocese had almost doubled in two decades to 43,699 students (33,000 in the parochial schools) in thirty-three academies, sixty parochial schools, eight orphanage schools, and thirteen industrial and reform schools.[32]

Corrigan (1885-1902) was the coadjutor to the ailing McCloskey from 1880 to 1885. Even more than McCloskey, Corrigan shared the commitment of Hughes to parochial schools and enthusiastically endorsed the decrees of the Third Plenary Council of Baltimore in 1884 that every parish should establish a school within two years. He founded forty new parochial schools, seventeen of them in Manhattan, during his seventeen years as archbishop. By 1902 there were forty academies for boys and girls, and ninety-six parochial schools, sixty of them in New York City (which now included the Bronx and Staten Island as well as Manhattan) and thirty-six upstate. The total number of students, including those in colleges and academies for boys as well as those in the orphan asylums and industrial schools and reform schools, came to 71,620.[33]

Corrigan also gave New York Catholics a centralized system of parochial schools for the first time in the history of the archdiocese by setting up two boards to centralize Catholic education on the elementary level. The first was the New York Diocesan Board of Examiners of Teachers with eleven members, all priests, headed by Monsignor John

M. Farley, the senior vicar general. One of their major responsibilities was to formulate a standardized curriculum. In 1887, they produced "The Directory and Course of Instruction" which contained a syllabus for the teaching of religion, reading, arithmetic, history, and geography, which was closely modeled on the course of instruction in the public schools, except of course for religion. The second board was the New York Diocesan Board of School Examiners, which had the more difficult task of inspecting the schools. It consisted of eighteen members, all priests, headed by Monsignor Joseph Mooney, the junior vicar general.[34]

In 1888, to coordinate the work of the two boards, Corrigan appointed Father William E. Degnan the first inspector of parochial schools. In effect it was the beginning of the office of superintendent of schools, the first in any diocese in the United States. Degnan resigned within a year because of ill health and was replaced by Father Michael J. Considine, who served as inspector of parochial schools for the next fourteen years and made the board of school examiners, the first such board in any diocese in the United States, an efficient and effective agency for setting uniform standards for Catholic schools. Considine inspected the physical condition of the buildings, investigated the qualifications of the teachers, evaluated the effectiveness of teaching methods, and prepared new manuals for both the teachers and the pastors.

The boys and girls were still taught in separate classrooms, although it became more common for the sisters to teach not only the girls but also the boys, at least in the lower grades. The number of teaching sisters and brothers continued to increase, with the arrival in the archdiocese of the Sisters of St. Agnes, the Sisters of the Congregation of Notre Dame, Mother Cabrini's Missionary Sisters of the Sacred Heart and the Marist Brothers. By 1902, only 15 percent of the parochial schools had exclusively lay staffs. By 1908, there were twenty-eight religious communities engaged in teaching in the archdiocese, four communities of men and twenty-four communities of women. Another new feature was the introduction of the first kindergartens in Catholic schools, while at the other end of the educational spectrum, some schools in poorer neighborhoods conducted night classes for children who had to work to support their family.[35]

Some of the parochial schools in Manhattan had huge enrollments. In 1900, at St. Patrick's Old Cathedral, there were 2,018 students but only twenty-seven teachers, which meant an average class size of about seventy-five students. In 1908, Sacred Heart School on the West Side of Manhattan had an enrollment of 2,780. The salaries of teachers were not a major concern for pastors when most of the teachers were sisters and brothers assisted by a few poorly paid lay teachers, who numbered about three hundred in 1900. Corrigan thought that many of them were happy to work for "pin money" (his phrase). The situation in the city of Yonkers illustrated the cost effectiveness of Catholic education. In 1900, there were three parochial schools in the city with a total enrollment of 2,171. There were only thirty-one teachers. The total cost for salaries was $10,556.96 or $4.86 per pupil.[36]

Nonetheless, in Manhattan, Father Henry Brann, the pastor of St. Agnes Church in Midtown, wanted to reduce the salaries of the nine Sisters of Charity who staffed his school, even though they received a stipend of only three hundred dollars per year, less than a dollar a day. The Board of Diocesan Consultors unanimously rejected the request, pointing out that the sisters were already underpaid. Shortly thereafter, their stipend was raised to four hundred dollars per year.[37]

Like Hughes fifty years earlier, Corrigan became a national figure when he emerged as a leader of the conservative bloc in the American hierarchy during the last two decades of the nineteenth century. A staunch supporter of parochial schools, he vigorously opposed the efforts of Archbishop John Ireland of St. Paul to work out a *modus vivendi* with the public schools for fear that it would undermine the efforts of the American bishops to create their own parochial school system. In an address to the National Educational Association in 1890, Ireland described the public schools as "our pride and glory" and declared with characteristic bravado, "Withered be the hand raised in sign of its destruction."

The following year, Ireland approved the arrangements made by the pastors of two parishes in his archdiocese—one in Stillwater and the other in Faribault—whereby they rented the parochial school to the local school board, which paid all the expenses of operating the school, including the salaries of the teaching sisters. Only secular subjects were taught during the school day, but religious instruction was provided before and after regular school hours.

Corrigan feared that the spread of the Stillwater-Faribault experiment to other dioceses would be a fatal blow to the parochial school system and persuaded six other archbishops to join him in 1892 in a protest to Rome against the Stillwater-Faribault arrangement. None-theless, despite this maneuver, Ireland was successful in obtaining Roman sanction or at least temporary toleration for the experiment. Corrigan's continued opposition in the face of Roman approval led to an angry confrontation with Archbishop Francisco Satolli, the first Apostolic Delegate to the United States, and earned Corrigan a rebuke from the pope himself.

While the outcome of the battle between Corrigan and Ireland was still in doubt, Father Michael Considine, the inspector of the parochial schools, told Monsignor John Farley, the president of the Catholic School Board, that the controversy had led to widespread demoralization in the parochial schools of the archdiocese with many sisters and brothers wondering if they should look for work in Catholic charitable institutions. "Well-disposed parents wondered, ill-disposed parents became jubilant," Considine reported. "Some pastors who had worked hard and long for the schools became discouraged; some who had never done anything for the schools were ready with their 'I told you so's.'" Ironically, the whole Stillwater-Faribault experiment collapsed within a year because of opposition from local Protestants, and Leo XIII sent a letter to Cardinal Gibbons reaffirming his support for the legislation of the Third Plenary Council of Baltimore.[38]

It was even more ironic that in Corrigan's own archdiocese a successful version of the Stillwater-Faribault plan was in operation for a quarter century in the city of Poughkeepsie. It began in 1873 when Father Patrick McSweeny, the pastor of St. Peter's Church, obtained approval from McCloskey to rent his two parochial school buildings to the city for an annual fee of one dollar each. He agreed to accept non-Catholic students, to refrain from religious exercises or instruction during school hours, and to allow the city to inspect the schools and to examine both the teachers and the students. In return the city agreed to pay the fuel bills and to permit him to use the buildings for religious instruction outside of class hours. The arrangement only came to an end in 1898 when the state superintendent of public instruction declared it illegal on the grounds that the religious habits worn by the sisters violated the new state constitution.[39]

It was a further irony that one of the most vociferous Catholic critics of the parochial school system was one of Corrigan's own priests, Father Edward McGlynn, the pastor of St. Stephen's Church. Although St. Stephen's was the largest parish in the archdiocese with twenty thousand parishioners, McGlynn, who was a product of the local public schools, adamantly refused to build a parochial school on the grounds that the Church should concentrate its financial resources on charitable institutions such as orphanages. Anticipating Ireland by twenty years, McGlynn hailed the public schools as the "pride and glory of the Americans" in 1870, provoking widespread criticism from the New York diocesan clergy. In 1886, a confrontation between Corrigan and McGlynn over McGlynn's involvement in municipal politics led to his removal as pastor of St. Stephen's and his excommunication for five years.[40]

Three of the first four bishops of Brooklyn (whose combined administrations spanned more than a century) were priests of the Archdiocese of New York. Brooklyn's first bishop, John Loughlin (1853-1891), had been vicar-general to John Hughes, and the second bishop of Brooklyn, Charles McDonnell (1892-1921), had been the chancellor and secretary to Corrigan. Both of them shared the commitment of Hughes and Corrigan to parochial schools. At the time of Loughlin's appointment as the first bishop of Brooklyn there were only eleven Catholic schools in the diocese. At his death in 1891, there were sixty-six parochial schools (all except one, St. Andrew's in Sag Harbor, located in Brooklyn and Queens), twenty academies or select schools, three industrial schools, and sixteen other specialized schools with a total of 34,270 students. The Sisters of St. Joseph and the Dominican Sisters of Amityville staffed twenty-eight of the parochial schools, while the Franciscan Brothers, who came to the diocese from Ireland in 1858, staffed the boys' department in fourteen of the parochial schools. There were also two Catholic colleges, St. Francis College, established as an academy by the Franciscan Brothers of Brooklyn in 1858, and St. John's College, established by the Vincentian Fathers in 1870.[41]

During the administration of McDonnell the Catholic population of the diocese almost tripled from 280,000 in 1892 to 819,217 in 1921. The number of parochial schools almost doubled from 66 to 124 with an enrollment of 72,398. There were another 9,400 children in 14 academies, 4 high schools, 3 industrial schools, and 11 orphanages. All but 13 of the 124 parochial schools were located in Brooklyn and Queens.[42]

Although there were seventeen communities of teaching sisters in the diocese, the Sisters of St. Joseph and the Dominican Sisters of Amityville still staffed the bulk of the parochial schools. Three new communities of brothers also came to the diocese, the Marianists,

Xaverian Brothers, and the Brothers of the Sacred Heart, but the Franciscan Brothers remained the largest male community engaged in teaching in sixteen schools and St. Francis College. On the other hand, unlike their experience in the Archdiocese of New York, the Jesuits had little success in the Diocese of Brooklyn. They opened Brooklyn College in 1908 but were forced to close it in 1921 because of financial difficulties, although the high school department, Brooklyn Preparatory School, continued to exist for another half-century.

Like Corrigan in New York, McDonnell was responsible for giving Brooklyn a centralized parochial school system with uniform educational standards when he appointed Father John L. Belford the first superintendent of schools in 1893. His successor, Father Thomas J. O'Brien, devised the first standard curriculum to be used in all the parochial schools, while the legendary Monsignor Joseph V. S. McClancy served both as pastor of a Brooklyn parish and as superintendent of schools from 1915 to 1954 during a period when the Diocese of Brooklyn created the second largest system of Catholic elementary schools in the entire nation.[43]

The first half of the twentieth century was the golden age of Big City Catholicism in the United States when the bulk of the Catholic population was concentrated in the major cities of the Northeast and the Midwest. In cities like Boston and Philadelphia, Cleveland and Chicago, there were many solidly working-class Catholic neighborhoods where the local Catholic parish church was the dominant social institution and even non-Catholics often identified their neighborhood by the name of the nearest Catholic church. Charles Morris said memorably that "an alien anthropologist landing in a working-class Philadelphia parish in the 1930s or 1940s would know instantly the centrality of religion to the lives of the inhabitants."[44]

In the Diocese of Brooklyn, the zenith of this golden age coincided with the administration of Bishop Thomas E. Molloy (1922-1956) and leveled off under Bishop Bryan J. McEntegart (1957-1968). The first priest of the diocese to be named the bishop of Brooklyn, Molloy inherited an almost perfectly balanced diocese demographically with many solidly middle-class neighborhoods in Brooklyn and Queens, attractive suburbs in Nassau County, and unspoiled rural areas in Suffolk County. During his thirty-four years as bishop the Catholic population almost doubled from 819,217 to 1,497,598, making the Catholic population of the Diocese of Brooklyn slightly larger than that of the

Archdiocese of New York which had 1,491,019 Catholics in 1957.

The growth of the Catholic school system under Molloy was even more impressive than the growth of the Catholic population. The number of elementary schools more than doubled from 124 to 259 with 209,174 students and another 28,713 students in 50 high schools for a total enrollment of 237,887. The comparable figures for the Archdiocese of New York were 42,604 students in 98 high schools and 156,494 students in 311 elementary schools for a total school population of 199,098.[45]

Even more remarkable was the fact that in 1967, ten years after the creation of the Diocese of Rockville Centre, which had reduced the Diocese of Brooklyn to Brooklyn and Queens, the Diocese of Brooklyn still had almost as many students in Catholic high schools and elementary schools as the Archdiocese of New York (222,417 in Brooklyn and 223,001 in New York).[46]

During the first half of the twentieth century the situation in the Archdiocese of New York was somewhat different from that in Brooklyn. In New York it was not so much a golden age as an Indian summer, the last hurrah of the traditional Irish parishes that had defined New York Catholicism for over a century. While the Catholic population of the United States (and the Diocese of Brooklyn) continued to grow, in the Archdiocese of New York the Catholic population declined for the first time in history, from 1.2 million in 1902 to only 1 million in 1938. "Brooklyn and [New] Jersey have taken away our industrious middle class," complained Father James H. McGean, the pastor of St. Peter's Church, as far back as 1898.[47]

Despite the decline in the Catholic population, there was a surprising increase in the number of Catholic schools, especially in the Bronx, Staten Island, and Westchester, where pastors sought to provide parochial schools for middle-class Catholic families who were fleeing the tenements of lower Manhattan. Although Hughes and Corrigan are generally credited with the development of the Catholic school system in New York, the greatest growth actually took place during the administration of Cardinal John Farley (1902-1918), who presided over the establishment of eighty-one schools, almost the equivalent of all the parochial schools founded during the previous century. The first three Catholic women's colleges were opened during Farley's administration: the College of New Rochelle in 1904, the College of Mount St. Vincent in 1910, and the Manhattanville College of the Sacred Heart in 1917. Cardinal Patrick Hayes (1918-1938) followed in Farley's footsteps, opening fifty-six new schools, almost all of them before the onset of the Depression in 1929.

The demographic breakdown of the new schools built between 1902 and 1938 reflected the shifting population patterns in the archdiocese. Of the new schools, 32 of 137 were in Manhattan, but there were 49 new schools in the Bronx, 16 on Staten Island, 21 in Westchester and the rest upstate. Even as new parochial schools were being built in Manhattan, others were being closed and many suffered a decline in enrollment. Between 1924 and 1934 parochial schools in Manhattan lost almost one third of their enrollment (31 percent). There was an even steeper decline in the public elementary schools in Manhattan, which lost 40.5 percent of their enrollment in those years. The increase in enrollment in the other parts of the archdiocese was not sufficient to offset an overall decline in the Catholic elementary school population from 95,592 in 1924 to 91,773 in 1938.[48]

The centralization and professionalization of the school system made steady progress under the direction of Father Thomas A. Thornton and Father Joseph F. Smith, who succeeded Considine as the *de facto* superintendents of schools in 1903. Smith was an especially significant figure who remained in that post until his death in 1927. He supervised the construction of over one hundred new parochial schools, many of them impressive buildings that were comparable to the best public schools erected in that era. In addition, he was regularly elected to top positions in the newly-founded Catholic Educational Association. "I can say without hesitation," declared Monsignor Joseph McClancy, the longtime superintendent of schools in the Diocese of Brooklyn, "that Monsignor Smith was the outstanding schoolman of our time."[49]

By the end of the administration of Farley in 1918, if not earlier, the two school boards established by Corrigan had been effectively combined into one Catholic school board that was the major policymaking agency for the archdiocese in the field of education. In 1911, the school board produced a new 400-page "Course of Study," which contained detailed syllabi for most of the courses taught in the parochial schools that adhered closely to the syllabi in the public schools. It even contained detailed directions for allotting specific amounts of time to each subject from grade one through grade eight. Both English and mathematics were allotted more classroom time than religion. In fact English was given almost four times as much classroom time as religion (4,230 minutes and 1,200 minutes respectively).

The "Course of Study" contained many surprisingly progressive features. The religion curriculum was not limited to catechetical instruction, but also included Bible history and Church history. Mathematics included not only arithmetic, but also algebra and bookkeeping in the eighth grade. Instruction in science began in the first grade with nature study and physiology and included three hours of physics in the seventh and eighth grades.

The curriculum for American history also included a three-page supplement on Irish history. The school board was unapologetic about this addition. "As the majority of the children attending the parochial schools of this diocese are of Irish birth or descent," they declared, "it is only fair that they should not be left in ignorance of the glorious deeds of their brave forefathers."[50]

Teachers were reminded of their responsibility for the health and physical well-being of their students. They were urged to relieve the classroom tedium by physical exercise, even if it only consisted of having the children march around the classroom with the windows open. Teachers were also told to be alert for signs of malnutrition in the children as well as symptoms of eye and ear problems. Lengthy detention after school hours was discouraged on the grounds that it was harmful to the physical welfare of the children.[51]

As far back as 1908, the school board urged Catholic schools to introduce the New York State Regents exams that were a standard feature of the curriculum in the public schools. By the 1930s, virtually all Catholic schools had done so, and the high scores achieved by the students in Catholic schools did much to enhance their academic reputation. The Regents Exams were supplemented by diocesan exams in grades three through eight in religion, English, spelling, arithmetic, history, and geography that were introduced in 1931. A revised course of studies was issued for each subject between 1931 and 1935, and a comprehensive examination in religion was added to the eighth-grade curriculum.

A constant concern was the educational background of teachers in the parochial schools in an era when young sisters were sometimes rushed off to the classroom fresh from the novitiate. To address this problem, the school board convened a meeting of representatives of the six largest communities of teaching sisters in the archdiocese. They unanimously agreed that all teachers should have completed at least two years of college and should be certified by the archdiocese. The new rules were to take effect in September 1939, although there was a grandfather clause for men and women vowed religious who had been teaching for fifteen years.

As part of this same effort to improve the educational standards of teachers in the parochial schools, the School of Education of Fordham University devised a series of teacher-training courses. By 1939, more than a thousand brothers and sisters were enrolled in these courses and several hundred others were taking extension courses at Manhattan College, the College of New Rochelle, the College of Mount St. Vincent, Ladycliff College, and Good Counsel College.[52]

The Catholic educational system in the Archdiocese of New York reached its apogee during the twenty-eight year administration of Cardinal Francis Spellman, the longest on record, which stretched from the beginning of World War II in 1939 to the post-Vatican II era in 1967. Spellman was the last of the great brick-and-mortar archbishops of New York. A national figure like Hughes, Spellman was the most influential American Catholic prelate since the death of Cardinal James Gibbons in 1921. His close personal friendship with Pope Pius XII gave him an unrivaled position in the U.S. hierarchy.

Immediately after World War II, Spellman embarked on a massive building campaign. In a memorandum prepared in the spring of 1952, Monsignor John J. Voight, the superintendent of schools, listed 134 elementary and high schools that had either been built or expanded between 1939 and 1952. Spellman's building campaign intensified in the late 1950s. Between 1953 and 1959 the Archdiocese of New York erected or expanded fifteen churches, ninety-four schools, twenty-two rectories, sixty convents, and thirty other institutions at a cost of $139.7 million. Spellman also expanded the diocesan high school system from one school to ten schools. The press release issued by the Chancery Office to commemorate his twenty-fifth anniversary in New York in 1964 required twenty-four pages to list his accomplishments.[53]

Spellman practically doubled the enrollment in the elementary and high schools from 117,907 in 1939 to 223,001 in 1967. They were also boom years for religious vocations, which made it relatively easy to staff the schools with teaching sisters and brothers. In 1967, the Sisters of Charity alone had 710 sisters teaching 46,971 students in eighty-eight schools. There were a total of 4,130 sisters, 634 brothers, and 506 priests teaching in the schools of the archdiocese.

As was already mentioned, in addition to the 223,001 students in Catholic elementary and high schools in the Archdiocese of New York in 1967, there were another 222,417 students in Catholic elementary and high schools in the Diocese of Brooklyn, making a grand total of 444,418 students. Monsignor George A. Kelly, who was the secretary of education for the archdiocese, claimed that the Catholic schools in New York and Brooklyn together had a larger enrollment than any public school system in the United States except New York and Chicago.[54]

The late 1960s and the 1970s were a tumultuous period in American history as a result of the resistance to the civil rights movement and the Vietnam War. American Catholics had the added burden of contending with the ferment in the Church after Vatican II. It was also a critical period for Catholic education in the United States when for the first time in history there was a precipitous drop in the enrollment in Catholic schools throughout the nation.

The causes for the decline in Catholic schools were varied and included the flight to the suburbs from the old urban Catholic neighborhoods, the steep decline in the number of teaching sisters and brothers with a corresponding increase in the cost of tuition, and a more critical attitude toward Catholic schools on the part of many parents. Both the Archdiocese of New York and the Diocese of Brooklyn were deeply affected by these changes.

In New York, Cardinal Terence Cooke (1968-1983), the last native New Yorker to become archbishop, made a determined effort to preserve the Catholic school system. He employed such innovative strategies as establishing in 1970 the Commission for Inter-Parish Financing, which levied a tax of 6 or 7 percent on all parishes and used the proceeds to aid financially ailing parishes. During its first year the commission distributed almost $3 million to fifty-three needy parishes. Much of the money went to subsidize parochial schools. Cooke also established the Inner-City Scholarship Fund, which was soon providing over $1 million a year to minority students (two thirds of them non-Catholic) in parochial schools in New York City. The fund attracted generous contributions from corporations and non-Catholic benefactors who appreciated the contribution of Catholic schools to the city's economy.

Thanks to such innovative financial strategies, only 20 of the 294 Catholic elementary schools were closed during the Cooke administration.

It was especially noteworthy that during the devastation of the South Bronx by crime, arson, and abandonment of buildings in the 1970s, not a single Catholic school was closed.

Nonetheless, despite this effort to keep every Catholic school open, there was a massive decline in enrollment from 213,476 in 1968 to 131,238 in 1983. The decline was especially severe in the parish elementary schools where the numbers shrank from 157,435 to 88,753.[55]

The last two archbishops of New York, Cardinal John O'Connor (1984-2000) and Cardinal Edward Egan (2000-2009) remained committed to preserving the Catholic school system, giving pastors permission to close parochial schools only when it became financially impossible to maintain them. As a result of such policies, in 2008 the Archdiocese of New York had one of the largest Catholic school systems in the nation with 29,624 students in 55 high schools and 63,001 students in 231 elementary schools for a total Catholic school population of 92,625.[56]

Under Bishop Francis J. Mugavero (1968-1990), the first native of Brooklyn to become the bishop of the diocese, Brooklyn experienced the same dramatic decline in the Catholic school population as the Archdiocese of New York. The total enrollment shrank from 217,103 in 1968 to 85,383 in 1990. As in New York the steepest decline occurred in the parish elementary schools. Thirty-eight parish elementary schools were closed and the enrollment decreased from 176,439 in 1968 to 62,504 in 1990. The same trend continued under Bishop Thomas V. Daily (1990-2003) and accelerated under Bishop Nicholas A. Dimarzio (2003-). In 2008 there were 16,974 students in 20 high schools and 37,741 students in 116 elementary schools for total enrollment of 54,715. In January 2009, the diocese announced plans to close 14 more elementary schools.[57]

Both the Archdiocese of New York and the Diocese of Brooklyn have suffered massive losses in the size of their Catholic educational systems over the past forty years. In 2008, New York had less than half as many students as it did in 1967. It continues to have one of the largest Catholic school systems in the nation, but only because many other dioceses have suffered even greater losses such as Brooklyn, which had only one quarter as many students in 2008 as it had in 1967. In both dioceses the Catholic school population in 2008 was approximately the size that it was ninety years ago when the Catholic population was half the size that it was in 2008.

Patricia Byrne has reminded us recently that "Catholic education in the United States is the largest private educational enterprise known to history."[58] However, it is an enterprise that would never have succeeded without the dedication and self-sacrifice of many thousands of vowed women religious. The virtual disappearance of the teaching sisters (and also the brothers and priests) from the classrooms is not the only reason for the decline in the Catholic school system in the United States, but it is so closely related to it that it cannot be ignored or minimized. In 1967, there were 7,314 sisters teaching in the Catholic schools in the Archdiocese of New York and the Diocese of Brooklyn. In 2008 there were only 368 teaching sisters left in the two dioceses, 253 in New York and 115 in Brooklyn. In fact, there were only 5,718 teaching sisters in the entire United States.[59]

Archbishop Timothy M. Dolan, who was installed as the tenth archbishop of New York on April 15, 2009, quickly announced his determination to preserve the Catholic school system in the Archdiocese of New York: "[Catholic schools] are worth something not only internally for us as a church as we pass on the faith for our kids and grandkids," he said, "but it is also a highly regarded public service that we do for the wider community."[60] Dolan was under no illusions that he faced an uphill struggle to save the Catholic school system in New York and that many observers were skeptical about his prospects for success. However, as a professional Church historian, Dolan was also well aware that Clio has a habit of confounding prophets.

NOTES

1. William R. Kelly and John J. Voight, "Parish Schools in New York, 1800-1939," *Catholic News,* June 17, 1939.

2. Leo R. Ryan, *Old St. Peter's: The Mother Church of Catholic New York* (New York: U.S. Catholic Historical Society, 1935), 237-238.

3. Florence D. Cohalan, *A Popular History of the Archdiocese of New York* (New York: U.S. Catholic Historical Society, 1983), 34.

4. On the history of the Sisters of Charity in New York, see Sister Marie de Lourdes Walsh, S.C., *The Sisters of Charity in New York, 1809-1959,* 3 vols (New York: Fordham University Press, 1960); and Sister Mary Elizabeth Earley, S.C., *The Sisters of Charity of New York, 1960-1996,* 2 vols (New York: The Sisters of Charity of New York Press, 1997).

5. "The Archdiocese of New York a Century Ago: A Memoir of Archbishop John Hughes," ed. Henry J. Browne, *Historical Records and Studies* 39-40 (1952): 134.

6. The parochial schools were located at St. Peter's (1800), St. Patrick's Cathedral (1815), St. Mary's (1827), St. Joseph's (1834), St. Nicholas (1836), Transfiguration (1836), St. James (1838), and St. John the Baptist (1839). St. Nicholas and St. John

the Baptist were German parishes. In addition, there was a parochial school at Christ Church on Ann Street from c.1827 to 1833 when the church was closed and replaced by St. James and Transfiguration. St. Peter's School occupied a free-standing building from 1803 until 1838 when it was relocated to the basement of the new church. Not until 1873 was it again housed in a separate building. Kelly and Voight, "Parish Schools," *Catholic News*, June 17, 1939.

7. John Talbot Smith, *The Catholic Church in New York* (New York: Hall and Locke, 1905), 1:186.

8. John K. Sharp, *History of the Diocese of Brooklyn, 1853-1953* (New York: Fordham University Press, 1954), 1:39.

9. Ibid., 1:45-46.

10. Ibid., 1:107-110.

11. *Truth Teller*, July 2, 1842.

12. Harriette A. Martirè, "A History of Catholic Parochial Elementary Education in the Archdiocese of New York," (PhD diss., Fordham University, 1955), 83-87.

13. Hughes to Purcell, February 24, 1838, Archives of the University of Notre Dame.

14. John Hassard, *Life of the Most Reverend John Hughes* (New York: D. Appleton and Company, 1866), 189.

15. The standard history of the Public School Society, with full documentation of the controversy with Hughes, is William Oland Bourne, *History of the Public School Society of the City of New York* (New York: William Wood and Company, 1870).

16. *The Works of William Seward*, ed. George Baker (New York: J.S. Redfield, 1853), 2:215.

17. Between 1805 and 1823 St. Peter's Free School received $13,209.37 in public money and St. Patrick's Free School received $5,748.61 between 1817 and 1823. The trustees of the two parishes reported to the Superintendent of the Common Schools that the cost per pupil at St. Peter's was $3.70 ½ and at St. Patrick's $3.01 ¼. Ryan, *Old St. Peter's*, 242-243.

18. "The Archdiocese of New York A Century Ago," 149.

19. Thomas J. Shelley, *The Bicentennial History of the Archdiocese of New York, 1808-2008* (Strasbourg: Editions du Signe), 112-126.

20. Vincent P. Lannie, "Archbishop Hughes and the Common School Controversy, 1840-1842," (PhD diss., Teachers College, Columbia University, 1963), 571.

21. Kehoe, *Works of John Hughes*, 2:715

22. *New York Freeman's Journal and Catholic Register*, February 18, 1871.

23. Jay P. Dolan, *The Immigrant Church: New York's Irish and German Catholics, 1815-1865* (Baltimore: The Johns Hopkins University Press, 1975), 14-15.

24. *Sadlier's Catholic Almanac and Ordo* (New York: D & J. Sadlier, 1864), 89-90.

25. Martirè, "History of Catholic Parochial Elementary Education," 124.

26. Dolan, *The Immigrant Church*, 105-106.

27. "The Archdiocese of New York a Century Ago," 144.

28. Charles G. Herbermann, J.E. Cohalan, and J.J. Wynne, S.J., eds., *The College of St. Francis Xavier: A Memorial and a Retrospect, 1847-1897* (New York: College of St. Francis Xavier Alumni Association, 1897), 9.

29. *Catholic World* 3 (1866): 387; *New York Times*, January 7, 1871.

30. Smith, *Catholic Church in New York*, 2:446; George B. McClellan, Jr., *The Gentleman and the Tiger*, ed. Harold C. Syrett (Philadelphia: J. B. Lippincott, 1956), 237-238.

31. *Catholic News*, March 10, 1897.

32. *Sadlier's Catholic Directory, Almanac and Ordo* (New York: D. & J. Sadlier, 1885), 116.

33. *Catholic Directory, Almanac* (Milwaukee: M.H. Wiltzius, 1902), 117.

34. Michael J. Considine, *A Brief Chronological Account of Catholic Educational Institutions in the Archdiocese of New York* (New York: Benziger Brothers, 1894).

35. Martirè, "History of Catholic Parochial Elementary Education," 162-163, 194-195.

36. Annual Financial Reports of St. Mary's, St. Joseph's and Sacred Heart Church, 1900, Archives of the Archdiocese of New York (AANY).

37. Corrigan to Brann, November 9, 1899, AANY, G-16.

38. Considine to Farley and the School Board, July 10, 1893, AANY, G-29; Gerald P. Fogarty, S.J., *The Vatican and the American Hierarchy from 1870 to 1965* (Wilmington: Michael Glazier, 1985), 65-85.

39. Edward M. Connors, *Church-State Relationships in Education in the State of New York* (Washington, DC: The Catholic University of America Press, 1951), 109-123.

40. Ibid., 107-109. Fifty-five New York priests signed a petition to Archbishop McCloskey protesting McGlynn's stand on parochial schools.

41. *Sadliers' Catholic Directory, Almanac and Ordo for the Year of Our Lord 1892* (New York: D. & J. Sadlier, 1892), 198-204; Sharp, *Diocese of Brooklyn*, 2:203-204.

42. Sharp, *Diocese of Brooklyn*, 2:104, 204.

43. Joseph W. Coen, Patrick J. McNamara, and Peter I. Vaccari, *Diocese of Immigrants: The Brooklyn Catholic Experience, 1853-2003* (Strasbourg: Editions du Signe, 2004), 71-74.

44. Charles Morris, *American Catholic* (New York: Times Books, 1996), 174

45. *The Official Catholic Directory, 1957* (New Providence, NJ: P.J. Kenedy & Sons, 1957), 180, 321.

46. *The Official Catholic Directory, 1967*, 218, 381.

47. Minutes of the Meetings of the Board of Diocesan Consultors, December 2, 1898, AANY.

48. Kelly and Voight, "Parish Schools," *Catholic News*, June 17, 1939.

49. Ibid.

50. *Course of Study and Syllabus for the Elementary Schools of the Archdiocese of New York* (New York: New York Catholic School Board, 1911), 53.

51. Ibid., passim.

52. The religious communities were the Sisters of Charity, the Dominican Sisters of Blauvelt, the Dominican Sisters of Sparkill, the Dominican Sisters of Newburgh, the Presentation Sisters of Newburgh, the Presentation Sisters of Staten Island and the Missionary Sisters of St. Francis. Kelly and Voight, "Parish Schools."

53. Voight, memorandum, April 3, 1952; Eugene Holt to Leonard Hunt, April 30, 1959, AANY.

54. Earley, *Sisters of Charity of New York*, 5:336. *The Official Catholic Directory, 1967.* If one adds the students in Catholic colleges, the combined total for the two dioceses in 1967 was 486,617 students.

55. *The Official Catholic Directory, 1968*, 554; *1983*, 626.

56. *The Official Catholic Directory, 1983*, 626; *2008*, 877.

57. *The Official Catholic Directory, 1968*, 115; *1990*, 134; *2008*, 167. *New York Times*, January 13, 2009.

58. Patricia Byrne, C.S.J., in *Creative Fidelity: American Catholic Intellectual Traditions*, eds. R. Scott Appleby, Patricia Byrne, and William L. Portier (Maryknoll: Orbis Books, 2004), 55.

59. *The Official Catholic Directory, 2008*, 167, 877.

60. *Wall Street Journal*, May 9, 2009.

Puritan City Catholicism:
Catholic Education in Boston

John J. White

Henry M. Rogers, Class of 1858, was the oldest alumnus to attend the convocation commemorating the 1935 tercentenary of the Boston Latin School.[1] He had attended Boston Latin in a decade when most Bostonians were concerned about the waves of Irish Catholics who were taking refuge in the city. City fathers had passed laws to compel Catholic children to attend the common public schools, but to little avail. These dirty, illiterate immigrants were a blight on the "Athens of America."

At the time Rogers was a student, Boston Latin was above the fray—a public school attended by the sons of the city's privileged class. At the ceremony, a memorial from George Santayana, Class of 1882, noted that there were schools older than Boston Latin, but all of them had "suffered a complete change of spirit and have only endured by ceasing to be themselves." Even Harvard College, one year younger than the Latin School, "has undergone radical transformations, losing its original directive mission, and becoming a complex mirror of the complex society which it serves. But the Latin School, in its simpler sphere, has remained faithfully Latin."[2]

Santayana was addressing himself to the unchanging curriculum at the Latin School; certainly he was not referring to the composition of the contemporary student body or the extended Latin School family of 1935. Featured speakers at the ceremony were Boston Mayor James Michael Curley, school committee chairman Charles E. Mackey,

Boston schools superintendent Patrick T. Campbell '89, and Boston Latin headmaster Joseph L. Powers '96, all of whom were Irish Catholics.

Long after the descendants of the Puritans had abandoned the public schools in the wake of Irish immigration, they continued to insist that public schools were essential in order to create a common identity, and they would go to great lengths to encourage Catholic children to attend those schools.

Campbell had been the first Catholic to serve as headmaster, and he was succeeded in 1929 by Powers, who had taken degrees from Boston College prior to beginning his teaching career. The majority of the teaching masters in 1935 were no longer Harvard men but graduates of Boston College, a Jesuit school founded five years after Rogers had graduated from the Latin School.

Rabbi J. Solomon Shubow '16 delivered the Invocation at the ceremony, while another Jewish alumnus, Arthur Fiedler '14, conducted the Boston Symphony Orchestra in works by Wagner, Brahms, and Handel. The Glee Club sang a Victoria motet, "Jesu Dulcis," after which Father Michael Cuddihy '91 pronounced the Benediction.[3]

The only Yankees on stage were A. Lawrence Lowell, president emeritus of Harvard, and Payson Smith of the state board of education. In a very human way, the Latin School had become a mirror of the complex society that it served, far removed from the original purposes of the city fathers who designed the school's classical curriculum.

That evening, the school administration hosted a dinner at the Copley Plaza Hotel. The keynote speaker was Joseph P. Kennedy '08 chairman of the newly established Securities and Exchange Commission. Kennedy praised "those stern Puritans [who] had the rare wisdom to sense that enlightened society could evolve in the spirit of democracy only through the generous offer of education to all." He captured the hope, but not the reality of public education in Boston. The Latin School was the original model of equal opportunity in America. It was a school "where the boy is judged on merit, where race or creed plays no part."[4]

Kennedy then spoke about his work in Washington and made an allusion to another Bostonian on the Commission, Judge John J. Burns, whom Kennedy had brought to D.C. to serve as the Commission's first general counsel. A graduate of St. Paul's parochial school, Boston College High School, and Boston College, Burns had taken a different route to success for an Irish Catholic. The only "out" about Judge Burns, Kennedy remarked, "is that he didn't prepare for college at Latin School."[5]

The parallel childhoods and intersecting careers of Kennedy and Burns are a reflection of the Catholic educational experience in Boston, where parents often made a choice between school systems, and where there was no stigma in the decision to choose the public schools.

Several elements made the Catholic educational experience in Boston unique. Unlike other American cities, the ethnic composition of Boston in 1830 was essentially the same as it had been in 1630; most of Boston's elites could trace their ancestry back to the seventeenth century Puritans. The city also had a large Catholic population prior to 1875 that was virtually all Irish. The lack of diversity between the Protestant elites and the Catholic underclass created an often antagonistic relationship between the two groups.

The second distinguishing factor in the history of Catholic education in Boston is the leadership of the Boston diocese. Except for Jean Cheverus, who became the first bishop of Boston in 1808, and Humberto Medeiros, who became archbishop in 1970, all of Boston's bishops were born in the United States. This meant that the Catholic Church in Boston was, in many ways, the Catholic Church of Boston, taking its cues from social and educational developments within "the Athens of America," and not from either the broader American church or from the Vatican.

In 1825, Bishop Benedict Fenwick inherited a small, poor diocese. The only Catholic school in Boston at that time was a day school staffed by Ursuline nuns who had come to Boston from Quebec. That school closed when the sisters crossed the harbor to Charlestown to open an ill-fated boarding school in 1826. Fenwick then opened small schools in two rooms in the basement of the cathedral; the boys' room was staffed by "house seminarians" he was preparing for the priesthood. The girls' school was eventually staffed by Sisters of Charity, who came from Emmitsburg, Maryland. Both schools struggled and closed in 1839.

Fenwick encouraged the Ursulines to build a convent school in Charlestown. The students at the convent school were predominantly daughters of middle-class Unitarians trying to escape what they believed to be the suffocating Protestantism found in the Boston public schools. Charlestown was a working-class community comprised of people from northern New England who had migrated to the Boston area for work in the brickyards and the small manufacturing concerns in Charlestown.

On August 10, 1834, the Reverend Lyman Beecher, a Presbyterian preacher who had left his church in Boston to found Lane Theological

Seminary in Cincinnati gave a series of sermons in Boston denouncing the presence of the nuns in Charlestown and chastising the community for tolerating them. The next night, a mob burned the convent to the ground. The Ursulines and the boarders escaped and took refuge in the home of a sympathetic Protestant family.

There was no violent retaliation by the small Catholic community after the arson, despite the fact that none of those charged with the burning of the convent were ever convicted, nor were any of Fenwick's several attempts at seeking restitution successful. The Ursulines left Boston, some returning to Quebec while others migrated to New Orleans.[6]

None of Fenwick's future educational activities were directed at the development of parochial schools. He focused on specific, narrow and somewhat affluent constituencies. In need of priests and seeking a personal retreat, he sponsored Mt. St. James Seminary in Worcester. By the time the school opened in 1843, it was not a seminary but a boarding school staffed by the Jesuits and named "The College of the Holy Cross."[7]

Boston had one of the nation's oldest and best systems of public schools. In 1789, the legislature passed a comprehensive state law requiring each town in the Commonwealth to support an elementary school at least six months out of the year. Larger towns like Boston were required to have year-round elementary schools as well as grammar schools. Boston created its first school committee in 1789.[8]

By the 1830s, the religious solidarity of the Puritan Commonwealth had disintegrated. The Congregational Church had been disestablished in 1833, and many congregants left that denomination for other denominations such as the Baptists or the Unitarians. Lack of agreement on religious fundamentals led to a significant dilution of the role that religion played in the public schools. Recitation of the Decalogue or the chanting of psalms and the Lord's Prayer and occasional reading of portions of Scripture were all that remained of the religious rigor of the original Puritan schools.

Named the first secretary of the Massachusetts Board of Education in 1837, Horace Mann envisioned the common school as an engine of social reform. He believed that the public school alone could check uncontrolled passions and make children temperate, frugal, industrious, and willing to do their public and civic duties. Because there no longer was a unified church to compel citizens to behave morally, the old Puritan concept of innate total depravity slowly gave way to an environmental perspective on social ills and evils. Rather than remediating poor behavior through prisons, the public school became the agent of instruction for proper social behavior, an antidote and a preventative to society's problems.[9]

In 1825, the population of Boston was less than 10 percent Catholic. By 1846, the year just before the Famine would bring thousands each month from Ireland to Boston, that figure had jumped to 26 percent, and by 1850, the city was 40 percent Irish.[10] Although nothing could have prepared Boston for the waves of impoverished Irish that arrived between 1846 and 1855 and beyond, the people of Boston looked to the schools to deal with the problems associated with the assimilation of a large and foreign element in what had been America's most homogenous city.

Senator Daniel Webster, Massachusetts' most prominent politician and statesman, one-time governor and Harvard president Edward Everett, and the textile magnate Abbot Lawrence all believed the common school could bring the Irish into American society. Ralph Waldo Emerson went further, claiming that once immigrants were successfully assimilated and Americanized they would create a new race, more vigorous than anything that had ever been seen in the past.[11]

The son of an Irish tailor, John Bernard Fitzpatrick became the third bishop of Boston in 1846. Fitzpatrick had attended the Boylston Grammar School and then graduated from the Latin School in 1829. While at the Latin School, Fitzpatrick made lifelong friends from among Boston's elite families and moved in those social circles throughout his episcopate. It seems he shared many of their beliefs about the public schools and assimilation. His sister was one of the very first Catholics to teach at the Boylston school they had attended as children.[12]

Fitzpatrick stands at the head of the long list of Boston Irish who earned the respect of the Boston establishment by reason of their wits and were welcomed into the "aristocracy of brains."[13] Fitzpatrick insisted that the Irish enter the educational, cultural, and intellectual life of mainstream Boston whenever possible. Frustrated at times at the narrowness and religious intolerance that he observed among individual Protestants in power, Fitzpatrick refused to abandon his belief in American constitutional law and in religious freedom, and he would not allow specific instances of anti-Catholicism in the schools to break his fundamental belief in the American systems of government, justice, and education. He believed that to open a parochial school system parallel to that already funded by the government was a waste of money and would perpetuate an Irish "separateness" that he considered unhealthy.[14]

Catholics soon had to respond to an organized political reaction to their presence. Alienated from the centers of power since the rise of Unitarianism, the common people of Boston found themselves threatened by the waves of Irish immigrants pouring into the city. By the 1850s, what had begun as a series of small and splintered groups coalesced into a political organization controlling the state house and city hall.

Known commonly as the "Know Nothings," these citizens saw church schools as a battleground to prevent the Irish from becoming American. A "Nunnery Commission" was created by the legislature in 1855 to investigate conditions in Catholic institutions of learning. They visited Holy Cross in Worcester and the convent academies run by the Sisters of Notre Dame at Lowell and at Roxbury. Arriving unannounced in Roxbury, the commissioners intimidated sisters and schoolchildren, searched the cellars, and entered the sisters' bedchambers, opening closets and other doors without asking permission.[15]

There were no parochial schools in Boston in the 1850s, but fearing that Catholics might one day seek state funding for parochial schools, the Know Nothings in the state legislature passed a constitutional amendment prohibiting state monies being directed to sectarian schools. In 1855, that same legislature passed a law mandating the reading of the Bible in schools. A second law, one to require priests and religious to receive teaching licenses from the state, was narrowly defeated.

Fitzpatrick reacted to the attempt to require Bible reading in the schools by calling for calm, and by appealing to the Commonwealth to acknowledge that religious pluralism in the schools was protected by the state and the U.S. Constitution. "We have a constitutional right," the *Boston Pilot* editorialized, "to demand that all sectarian matter shall be banished from the schools, and that the faith of Catholic children shall not be either openly or covertly assailed."[16] By 1857, to mollify Catholic objections, the law had been modified so that the teacher alone would read the Scriptures aloud and the students could only be called upon to recite the Ten Commandments.[17]

St. Mary's Church was near the Eliot Grammar School in the North End, an area crowded with poor Irish. Of the eight hundred boys in the school in 1859, approximately six hundred were Catholics whose families were parishioners at St. Mary's. Citywide, over one half of the ten thousand children in the Boston Public Schools at that time were

Catholic.[18] Jesuit fathers John McElroy and Bernard Wiget were serving the parish. In 1849, McElroy convinced the Sisters of Notre Dame to come from Cincinnati to Boston, where they opened the first free parochial school for girls at St. Mary's. By Rule, the sisters could not teach any but the youngest boys, so the parish and the diocese still had no recognizable parochial school for boys, who attended the Eliot Grammar School.[19]

In March of 1859, Thomas Whall, a Catholic student at the Eliot School refused to recite the Ten Commandments when asked to do so, and was beaten by the master of the school until his hands bled. His father brought suit against the teacher and the master for malicious assault. Wiget announced from the pulpit that any boy who recited the "Protestant" Ten Commandments would be denounced from the altar. The next week, between three and four hundred boys walked out of the school rather than recite the Protestant version of the Commandments. The boys were now in danger of falling afoul of yet another Know-Nothing law, a compulsory school law which called for truant boys to be sent to a reform school where they could be kept until age twenty-one with no hope of Catholic instruction.[20]

The bishop, who had attempted to keep the peace by remaining quiet on the school issue, had to act publicly. In his *Memoranda* he wrote that the cost of pulling Catholic students out of the public schools *en masse* would be prohibitive, as there were insufficient funds and properties in which to place children immediately. He also recognized that the state was ruled by "a vast majority of persecuting bigots who, a few years ago, were bound by oath, as members of the Know-Nothing party, to oppress Catholics. The very laws alluded to were framed, no doubt, for the express purpose of corrupting the faith of Catholic children." Fitzpatrick concluded that the children should "under open protest, submit to the tyranny exercised over them, but at the same time to loathe and detest its enactments." The unjust oppression might "with God's grace, strengthen them in their attachment to their faith."[21]

Fitzpatrick wrote a measured open letter to the school committee explaining the Catholic position in light of constitutional protections of religious liberty. Assuming that his readers believed in the individual's right to be free from religious compulsion, he wrote that Catholics had "serious and solid objections, based on individual conscience and individual faith" which precluded them from accepting the King James Bible. Yet "the law, as administered, says 'you must, or else you must be scourged, and finally banished from the school." He explained that the King James Version of the Decalogue was "offensive to Catholics, and had been used by adversaries as a means to attack" the tenets and the practices of the Church. He then demonstrated how the system then in place in the schools violated Catholic students' right to religious freedom. "The chanting of the Lord's Prayer, psalms, or hymns, addressed to God, performed by many persons in unison, being neither a scholastic exercise, nor a recreation, can only be regarded as an act of public worship." Protestants could do this together without qualms, but Catholics could not. It would be a violation of conscience to worship with Protestants, or it would be a "merely simulated union of prayer and adoration." He carried the insistence on religious liberty the furthest when he pledged not to entertain any argument that might appear after his letter. "Any discussion or show of argument to prove the reasonableness of such belief and of such conscience," Fitzpatrick wrote, would be "out of place; inasmuch as the question to be solved is not why people believe, but what they believe."[22]

The teacher and the master were found not guilty, but Fitzpatrick could consider the case a small victory nonetheless. The regulations were again revised so that only the teacher would have to read or recite the Decalogue. Within a year, Father George Harkins, a convert from the Episcopal Church, was named to the Boston School Committee. The Eliot case established a relationship between Catholics and the Protestant dominated school committee that was to last for nearly fifty years. Liberal Protestants were committed to the Boston Public Schools as agents of assimilation and as a solution to the city's social problems, they pressured the more rigid, evangelical hardliners to relent in the fear that the Catholics, if provoked, might withdraw from the public schools and create a viable parochial system. As a result, the Catholic presence contributed greatly to the slow but steady process of the secularization of the public schools. Each time a crisis was brought on by the evangelicals, the moderate mainline Protestants and Unitarians urged greater sensitivity to the Catholic position, and the schools slowly became more secularized.[23]

After the crisis passed, Catholics continued to attend the Eliot School without incident; Mayor John "Honey Fitz" Fitzgerald graduated in 1877. Rather than seeing the school as oppressive or detrimental to his faith, Fitzgerald remembered his years at the Eliot as the happiest of his childhood, and thirty years after graduating he assumed the responsibility for organizing the school's bicentenary celebrations.[24]

At the time of Fitzpatrick's death in 1866, the city had only two academies and two parochial schools for girls, St. Mary's and another in East Boston. The one German parish in the city, Holy Trinity, had a school since 1844, staffed by the Sisters of Notre Dame since 1859. On occasion, lay men could be found to teach the boys.[25] The Sisters of Notre Dame had agreed to teach very small boys, but older boys who wished to attend school had no choice but to attend the public schools. By age eleven or twelve, they could attend Boston College, which was McElroy and Fitzpatrick's institutional answer to the Eliot crisis.[26] The ambivalence of Boston Catholics toward Catholic schools was already evident, for despite the alleged indignities to which Catholic boys were being subjected, when Father Robert Fulton, S.J., opened the gates of the Boston College in 1864, he was "dismayed to find that instead of an army of students that he had expected to see thronging through the gates . . . there were only 22 boys."[27]

Historian James Sanders refutes the argument that the diocese was too poor to build schools. In 1847, Fitzpatrick quickly collected $150,000 for famine relief in Ireland; in the mid-1850s he rebuilt and enlarged Holy Cross after a fire and by 1863 he had built Boston College. A $120,000 orphanage was built in 1858, and several parishes within the city built large stone churches. Sanders maintains that these funds could have been directed to educational purposes. The schools that Fitzpatrick supported were schools that could do what the public schools were incapable of doing, like the girls' academies and the Jesuit preparatory school.[28]

John Williams succeeded Fitzpatrick as bishop in 1866, and became the first archbishop of Boston in 1875. Williams learned to read and write in Fenwick's short-lived school at the Cathedral and was sent to seminaries in Montreal and France. The Williams years were decades of institutional growth, but schools did not become a diocesan priority, despite the fact that the Third Plenary Council of Baltimore in 1884 had mandated the construction of parish schools. Like Fitzpatrick, Williams had a *laissez faire* approach to schools. During his first ten years as bishop, not a single parochial school was opened in the city.[29]

Because the decision to build schools rested with parish priests, the erection of parochial schools between 1866 and 1907 was not related to any centralized diocesan initiative, but to the efforts of individual clerics. The benefice system persisted in the archdiocese until 1952. It provided parish priests with tremendous power over how parish funds could be used. In addition to an annual salary, the pastor was entitled to all of the income generated by the free will offerings of his parishioners except for a few collections a year that were earmarked for specific purposes. The pastor was responsible for paying debts on the church and other parish structures, maintaining the property, and the salaries of curates, housekeepers, janitors, and other parish employees.

Whatever funds remained became the property of the pastor. Some saved this often substantial amount of money and bequeathed it to a family member while others chose to spend the money building parish complexes that might include a school, convent, rectory, and church. The priest was under no obligation to build a school, and even in later decades, when pastors were occasionally challenged by Cardinal William O'Connell to build schools, they were still free to rebuff his commands.[30]

In 1869, Father Thomas Scully of St. Mary of the Annunciation in Cambridge opened a school for girls and extended it through high school in 1875. A school for boys was opened that same year, staffed by lay men and women. In 1881, a two-year college for men was opened, graduates of which could continue at Boston College or at St. John's Seminary. In 1905, the boys sections of the high school and the college would be transferred to Boston College and to Boston College High, and the high school remained open for girls. Scully sponsored baseball teams, a rowing club, summer camps, a uniformed brass band, and separate state of the art gymnasia for boys and girls that he personally donated to the parish. The parish had a large library and meeting hall and debating and dramatic societies.[31]

At the adjacent parish, Sacred Heart, Father John O'Brien was philosophically opposed to parochial schools and believed that the separation they fostered was neither good for the Church nor the country. Elected to the Cambridge School Committee in 1880, O'Brien believed that Catholics had the right to attend the public schools. To his thinking, public schools were the best hope for improved social relations between Catholics and Protestants. He further believed that separate schools would only prolong the current state of misapprehension and misunderstanding that led to prejudice. He developed a dynamic parish, with an impressive complex of buildings, a rich devotional life, and a top notch Sunday school program with "advanced" classes in theology that produced the *Sacred Heart Messenger*, a weekly magazine.

The parish boasted secular activities ranging from a debating society to a parish bowling league. But he would not build a school.[32]

Some of O'Brien's critics claimed that he was a "Protestant priest," while others called Scully a tyrant. In 1879, Scully began to denounce from the altar those families who were sending their children to the public schools and even denying them the sacraments. Denunciations flew back and forth, until Rome told Williams to remedy the situation and address the larger school issue. In the meantime, the Unitarian minister J. P. Bland and O'Brien were engaged in a heated exchange over O'Brien's suggestion during a school committee meeting that the Cambridge public schools provide funding for both Catholic and Protestant teachers in the common schools. At another hearing, O'Brien said "I hope the time will never come when I shall be obliged to build a Catholic school" as he believed that "the time was fast approaching when our present system would be so changed as to render the establishment of a parochial school unnecessary."[33]

Williams finally declared his position in the *Boston Pilot,* the diocesan newspaper, in December 1879. He wrote that while Catholic schools were "preferable" for Catholic children, if there were none, parents should send children to the public schools. Schools should be built, but not at the price of causing "serious financial embarrassment" to the parish. If parents took "precautions against the dangers" of the public schools and provided for the religious instruction of their children, no priest could deny them the sacraments.[34] The determination as to what constituted practicality and serious financial embarrassment continued to lie with the individual pastors, whose priorities were to erect large churches and to avoid putting the parish in debt any longer than necessary.

Clearing the debt on his new church was a pastor's first priority. Father Dennis O'Callaghan, for example, was the pastor of St. Augustine's in South Boston where parishioners worshiped in a small cemetery chapel. A new church was completed in 1874 and for the next ten years O'Callaghan "set to work to remove the burden of debt incurred from the shoulders of his loyal parishioners." By 1884, the parish was debt free. Writing in 1899, W. A. Leahy praised O'Callaghan, because "By postponing the project of a parish school for a few years, Fr. O'Callaghan was enabled the more securely to carry out his plans for Catholic education."[35]

Similarly, St. Patrick's paid off its mortgage before building a school. Encompassing much of Roxbury, St. Patrick's was relocated from the

South End to Dudley Street in 1874 after the new Holy Cross Cathedral parish had been erected within the old parish boundaries. Father Joseph Gallagher quickly built a new brick church, which was paid off by 1880. Only then did he introduce the Sisters of Charity, Halifax to the diocese to staff a school, and by 1899 the sisters also had a high school for girls.[36]

Independence of action is reflected in the actions of pastors who were given large geographical parishes on the outskirts of the city. Parochial schools sometimes developed in several parishes in an area of the city because the pastor of the original parish that was divided into new parishes insisted upon it. This was the case in East Boston, where Father James Fitton was sent in 1857 to finish the construction of Most Holy Redeemer Church after the pastor died. Within twelve years, two mission churches that Fitton built were erected as parishes. By 1859 he established a community of Sisters of Notre Dame and these sisters opened a girls' school. In 1867 the sisters opened a secondary school for girls. Assumption parish opened its church and school together in 1869. Adolescent boys could not attend parochial school until the introduction of the Xaverian Brothers to each of the three parishes in 1889. By 1900, 1,461 boys and 1,736 girls were attending schools in parishes founded by Fitton; small wonder that East Boston was referred to as "Fitton's Island Diocese."[37]

Other pastors might fund several missions in their large parishes before a school was built. St. Gregory's, founded in 1844 in Dorchester, did not have a school until 1915. The church was rebuilt after a fire in 1863 and a new rectory was built and paid for by 1890; in 1894, the church was expanded and two large towers were added. Land had been purchased for a school in 1890, but the school would not be built for another twenty-five years.[38] Between 1875 and 1894, the pastor, Father William Fitzpatrick purchased pieces of property on which he maintained mission churches until they were ready to become parishes. In the Neponset section, he built St. Ann's, erected as a parish in 1889; in 1890 he established a mission on Norfolk Street that became St. Matthew's in 1900, and in 1899 he bought a piece of land on Dorchester Avenue one mile from St. Gregory's that became St. Mark's in 1905. None of these parishes had a school before 1915.[39]

In 1872, the northern end of Dorchester was taken from St. Gregory's to create St. Peter's parish. St. Peter's is at one end of a small park that was the original town Common, also the site of the town's 1639

Latin grammar school. Rejecting the plan of Williams for a modest brick church, the young pastor, Peter Ronan engaged Patrick Keely to design one of the largest churches in New England. Dorchester was changing from a large town with several village centers into a "streetcar suburb" of Boston. Although Dorchester would later become famous for its working-class Irish community and its rows of inexpensive, distinctive "three deckers," at the time that St. Peter's was built, Dorchester was the center of Irish middle-class respectability. Irish-born mayor Patrick Collins built a home just up the street from St. Peter's, while Mayor John "Honey Fitz" Fitzgerald lived on Melville Avenue, near the Dorchester Avenue mission church that was to become St. Mark's.[40]

Ronan also purchased pieces of property in his parish and created missions. Between 1893 and 1914, five parishes were carved out of St. Peter's.[41] When the debt on St. Peter's Church was discharged in 1884, Ronan engaged Keely to design a three-story rectory, and in 1898, he opened the first Catholic school in Dorchester. When school opened that September, very few parishioners chose to send their children to the new school because they were satisfied with the public schools. Ronan decided on a course of attraction rather than coercion. "Very wisely," the Sisters of Charity annalist wrote, "Fr. Ronan did not try to force his people to send their children to the Sisters' school; and the fact that they had a choice in the matter did more than anything else to overcome prejudice." Ronan opened classes to inspection for the first three weeks of school, and although the sisters found the daily crowd of visitors "somewhat trying at the time, at the end it produced much good. Little by little prejudice against parochial schools weakened, and finally disappeared. Soon, those who had been most opposed to St. Peter's School became its most zealous supporters."[42]

St. Peter's was not alone in seeing middle-class hostility to parish schools; lay people also expressed opposition to the opening of a parochial school in 1888 when St. Paul's opened in the shadow of Harvard.[43] By 1915, when the new parishes in Dorchester finally began to open parish schools, the neighborhood had changed. There were still pockets of large, middle-class homes, but much of the community had been developed with multi-unit "three decker" houses designed for the working class. It was only after Dorchester was transformed from a middle-class Catholic community to a working-class community that parochial schools were built. By 1928, all but one of the Dorchester parishes carved out of the St. Gregory's parish had built schools.

Working-class and poor Catholics in Boston embraced parochial schools more readily than the middle class. In Roxbury, the Redemptorist parish of Our Lady of Perpetual Help (the "Mission Church") and St. Joseph's opened schools in 1889. St. Joseph's, the oldest parish in Roxbury (1845) underwent an enlargement of the church in the 1860s, and architect Patrick Keely was brought in for further renovations in 1883. It was only after "the people had contributed enough money to pay for these improvements and rid the property of debt" that the pastor, Father Hugh Smith, took up the school problem. Smith opened a large new school because the Sisters of Notre Dame could no longer tend to the numbers of children seeking instruction in the day school that they had operated at their nearby academy, and he finally could afford the "risk" of a new school. The Mission Church School opened in September with 914 pupils; one month later, there were over 1,000. By 1896, over 1,500 children were attending the primary and grammar school there.[44]

The Catholic middle class understood that the public schools offered an excellent secular education. Although they were reminded that the support of the Catholic schools was a duty, there was a great ambivalence about them. Many parents who were being pressured to support parochial schools had been educated in the public schools themselves and were not convinced of the quality of the parochial schools. Mayor John Fitzgerald, for example, had attended the Latin School, as had his son-in-law, Joseph P. Kennedy. Most of the native born priests in Boston were the products of the public schools before they entered Boston College or St. John's Seminary.[45]

In the last decades of the nineteenth century, the Irish middle class were sending their sons to the public grammar schools and then to the Latin School in increasing numbers, and by 1910 they were by far the largest group in the school.[46] Redemptorist Father Joseph Manton liked to tell the story of the future John Cardinal Wright, who joined the line of scholars walking from the Latin School to the Mission Church on Wednesday afternoons for the Perpetual Help Novena in the 1920s.[47]

Politics was considered the route to middle-class respectability for Irish Catholics. In the Massachusetts House and Senate, twenty-six American educated Irish Catholics represented Suffolk County (Boston) in 1908. Of that number, only five attended parochial schools. Two attended Boston College High School. Ten years later, thirty-one Irish Catholics represented Suffolk County in the State House and Senate, with only three having attended parochial schools. Again, two members attended Boston College High. The Catholicity of these men was not in doubt; most reported that they were members of the Knights of Columbus, the Foresters, the St. Vincent DePaul Society, the Holy Name Society, or a neighborhood Catholic club; several reported that they were ushers in their parish churches, and many belonged to at least one temperance society.[48]

The gender issue also contributed to parents' ambivalence; until the Sisters of St. Joseph opened their first school in 1873, the options for boys in parochial schools were very limited. Even when a pastor wanted to open a school for boys, the lack of willing teachers made it difficult. When Father James Chittick became pastor of Most Precious Blood parish in Hyde Park in 1882, he expanded the parish school and brought in the Sisters of Charity of Nazareth, who also opened a high school for girls. Chittick spent four hours a day teaching the high school boys himself in a room the sisters provided in the convent. Chittick built two mission schools rather than chapels in distant sections of his parish; the school in the Readville section eventually became St. Pius X parish. Lack of staffing and ever increasing enrollment in the primary and grammar schools led to the closing of the high school after eleven years.[49] By 1900, there were 4,957 boys and 8,113 girls enrolled in parochial schools within the city. Over two thirds of those boys were in the primary grades; the higher the grade, the higher the percentage of girls because the boys left school to work. Apart from the Jesuits at Boston College High, there were no orders dedicated to teaching Catholic boys in Boston until 1888, when the Xaverian Brothers came to Holy Redeemer in East Boston.[50]

The Mission Church School was an exception when it came to the education of boys. The School Sisters of Notre Dame welcomed boys into their classrooms, so that by 1917, there were more boys graduating than girls, 117 to 100. The quality of the school is also reflected in the Mission's domination of the Boston College High School scholarship program for parochial school graduates. Between 1902 and 1920, boys from Mission earned twenty-one out of a possible seventy-six scholarships. In 1914, all four scholarships awarded that year went to Mission boys.[51]

Because there was so little ethnic diversity in Boston, the Irish leadership felt no threat from other ethnic Catholics and tended to accommodate them in whatever way they needed. There were few ethnic parishes in the city. By 1907, most of the French-Canadian parishes in the archdiocese were located in the mill cities and towns to Boston's west and north. There was one French school in Cambridge at Notre Dame de Pitie, and one French parish in Boston itself. By the time Williams died in 1907, there were six French schools in the immediate Boston suburbs, but none in the city itself.

As Italians moved into the North End and East Boston in the decades around 1900, they took over the older Irish parishes, and in some cases established ethnic Italian parishes. By 1930, only four of the ten Italian parishes in Boston and its immediate suburbs had schools. The Italians in Boston were never avid supporters of Catholic schools; when the Franciscan Friars opened Columbus High in the North End in 1945, many of the students came from Charlestown, South Boston, or Dorchester, the three Irish centers of the city, where no boys' high schools existed. Of the two Polish parishes in the city, Our Lady of Czestochowa in South Boston maintained a school while St. Adalbert's in Hyde Park never finished building their church and the parish eventually became Irish.[52]

The one German parish, Holy Trinity, had operated a school since 1844, with the School Sisters of Notre Dame coming in 1859 and lay men teaching the older boys. As the German American population moved to other parts of the city, the parish opened schools in those areas as well. By 1870, the parish was educating 440 students at its main school and another 500 in South Boston. A third school was opened in Roxbury in 1891. A larger school was built in South Boston in 1895, which operated until 1927. A request by members of the parish to erect a second German parish on its Roxbury property was denied by Williams on the advice of the Jesuits at Holy Trinity because they argued that there were not enough Germans to support two parishes.[53]

Boston saw its last outbreak of anti-Catholicism in the late 1880s and 1890s. In 1888, the legislature debated a bill to require all private schools in the state to be under control of local school committees or the state board of education. Acrimonious hearings were held at the state house, and many Protestants joined the archdiocese in opposing the bill. President Charles Eliot of Harvard testified that every school committee election in the Commonwealth would become a sectarian struggle and that the bill could backfire and cause the Catholics to become more determined to build parochial schools. The fear of losing Catholic children won the day, and the bill was defeated.[54]

Shortly thereafter, another anti-Catholic incident occurred when a teacher at the English High School made theologically incorrect statements regarding indulgences in a history class on the Reformation. When corrected by a Catholic student, he persisted in his assertion that an indulgence was a "license to sin." The student complained to his pastor, who wrote a letter of protest to the school committee. Unlike the Eliot case forty years earlier, by the 1890s there were several Catholics on the school committee, and the situation was handled wisely by removing the teacher and giving him a comparable assignment elsewhere and by changing the offensive textbook that had provided erroneous information.

Very quickly, however, a "Committee of One Hundred" organized protests because of a rumor that Catholics were about to take over the Boston schools and were being instructed by the Jesuits to kill all of the city's Protestants with an arsenal hidden in the basement at Boston College. Speeches and rallies were held at the Tremont Temple, the center of Baptist revivalism in the city. As women were entitled to vote in school board elections, evangelicals convinced twenty-five thousand women to register to vote in order to redeem the schools from the Catholics and to see to it that the ever-rising percentage of Catholic teachers in the public schools be ended and the Catholics removed from the school committee.[55]

Lay Catholics responded in a more vocal and militant fashion than they ever had before. Knowing that they now constituted an overwhelming majority of the public school population and having the slow but steady increase in the numbers of parochial schools as evidence that they could create a large and viable parochial school system, they threatened to do so. For the first time ever, the *Pilot* called for the full-scale development of a diocesan school system, and Mary Elizabeth Blake, a long-time teacher and one-time school committee candidate whose husband was on the school committee and who had sent five children through the Boston schools, wrote a pamphlet that addressed the issues. Blake was bluffing the school committee. Knowing that moderate Protestants and those with vested professional interests in the public schools could not bear the loss of tens of thousands of Catholic children, she threatened that Catholics might do just that, writing that "the parochial school is no longer a question of feasibility but of necessity" and that this "new departure" can be made a success "if it should be agreed upon."[56]

Moderate Protestants responded to Catholic threats by assuring Catholics that their rights would be protected in the schools. A Citizens'

Public Schools Union (CPSU) was founded by the moderates to ensure that the evangelicals would not take control of the schools and drive the Catholics out. William T. Harris, the U.S. Commissioner of Education entered the fray and argued that the separation of church and state necessitated the separation of religious and secular instruction, pointing out that the almost complete secularization of the Boston public schools had led to their general adoption by Catholic parents, who had nothing to fear in the way of Protestant proselytism.[57]

Historian Francis Parkman also weighed in. He wrote that the common schools were "crucibles, in which races, nationalities, and creeds are fused together until all alike become Americans." Parkman understood the divisions within the Catholic community in Boston on the issue of the schools, and he wrote that "many Catholics prefer the public school, and will do so as long as public schools maintain their present superiority of secular instruction and avoid offending the sensibilities of reasonable Catholics." The public and parochial schools were increasingly in competition with one another, and the most effective defense of the public schools would be "the increasing of their teaching efficiency and the maintenance and growth of their superiority over the parochial school." While believing that the Catholic clergy "will never be content until education is under their control," Parkman also pointed out that "the interests of the Catholic laity are not always the same as those of the Catholic clergy."[58]

The two poles of Catholic thought on the school issue appear in the ideas of the city's two most renowned Catholic journalists. John Boyle O'Reilly, publisher of the *Boston Pilot* and the most widely respected Catholic lay man in New England, was in favor of secularized public schools. He believed that there was agreement among informed Protestants and Catholics on the role of religion in the schools. "Most Bostonians," he wrote in 1885, "want no religious questions raised in the schools or in politics" and he saw genuine progress and a reason for optimism, as Catholics and Protestants came to share the work of the school committee: "Every year added to the good feeling and the liberality of the school board."[59] His former partner, Patrick Donahoe, disagreed, believing that Parkman and the CPSU wanted the public schools to be "superior to the parochial schools" so that Catholic children could be weaned from their attachment to their priests and their church in order to fuse "all sects and creeds into one homogenous mass-yes, of Agnostic skepticism."[60]

The crisis of the 1890s was the last attempt by evangelicals to "save" the schools from the Catholics, and it failed. The Puritan ideal of education as an important component of the city as a *Corpus Christianum* had slowly evolved into a system where students learned a common set of values and where mutual respect for differences became the highest good. Throughout the nineteenth century, Catholics were successful in challenging the city to an acceptance of pluralism and to create a school system free of proselytism. This might have happened in Boston without the Catholic presence, but the threat of removing Catholic children from the public schools ensured that it would happen.

There is an irony, therefore, to the Catholic position in that as soon as the schools were made "godless" to satisfy those Catholics opposed to proselytism, other Catholics rebelled against the belief that teaching a common civic morality required no specific creed.[61] While many lay Catholics and a significant proportion of the city's pastors were happy with the quality of education in the Boston public schools in 1900, there were others who believed that Catholic children were in greatest danger in schools where morality was taught without religion.

This was the position of William Cardinal O'Connell, successor to Williams and Boston's first "Romanizing" bishop. He was thoroughly Roman in discipline, liturgy, and organization, and the need to build Catholic schools was one aspect of the effort to Romanize the archdiocese. Boston's elites had abandoned their patrimony, O'Connell believed, and it was the Catholics who must pick up their lamp and ensure that Boston remain the city set on a hill. O'Connell also took issue with what he perceived as the insidious evils in Progressivism. He loathed the centralizing authority of the godless State and its manifestations in progressive education, particularly its child-centeredness. He railed against the "inspection of schools, the physical treatment of children, food for indigent pupils," all evidence of "machine centralization and control," which reflected the "false and undemocratic principle that the state should be the only educator of the nation."[62] Meanwhile, the young are "sacrificed to the Moloch of destructive formulas; teachers, instead of using the wisdom and experience of their years, deliberately encourage little ones to say or do whatever fancy or chance puts into their small heads." While the Christian should learn to have confidence in God alone, progressive educators believed that "the most sublime purpose of training is the attainment of self confidence."[63]

O'Connell transformed parochial schools within the city. When he died in 1944, seven out of ten parishes in the city had schools. Most of this growth occurred between 1907 and 1930, when the Great Depression nearly halted the construction of new schools.[64] By 1944 the archdiocese could boast of sixty-six high schools, although all of these were small parish high schools that were in essence extensions of the parochial grammar school. Many offered a two- or three-year commercial course, while others offered a full, four-year "college prep" course. Boston College High School adopted more of a high school curriculum, although through the 1920s it was still not unusual for men in their twenties who wished to matriculate at Boston College or the seminary to spend three or four years at Boston College High studying Latin and Greek. At 1,200 students in grades nine through twelve, it became the largest classical school in the country, over twice the size of the Latin School, which reported 594 students in grades seven through twelve in 1905.[65]

The notion that "higher" education was reserved for the elite continued to inform the archdiocesan approach to secondary education. After personally inheriting $3 million from the estate of Mr. and Mrs. Benjamin Franklin Keith, O'Connell founded Keith Academy for boys and Keith Hall for girls in his hometown of Lowell, and in 1941 he founded St. Sebastian's School, a day school for boys that sold itself as the Catholic version of the fashionable prep school. St. John's, the normal school developed by the Xaverian Brothers in Danvers became a day school for boys. A system of Catholic central high schools did not appear until 1963, when Cardinal Cushing incorporated many of the parish high schools into an archdiocesan system.[66]

O'Connell tried to centralize parochial schools through the diocesan schools office, but he really only possessed power to try to persuade pastors to build schools. He had no power to coerce. He required that the Chancery be made aware of any expenditure over one hundred dollars, and he frequently responded to these requests by suggesting that a school be built. He wrote to one pastor that he "should keep in mind the need for planning for a parochial school," while to another, who had an extremely large balance on hand, he "wanted to know whether or not you have considered the erecting of a high school." The decision to build, however, remained the pastor's alone. "A few years ago you told me to build a school as soon as I thought it well to do so. Hence these plans," Father John Daly of St. Mark's in Dorchester wrote to O'Connell in 1926, twenty-one years after the parish was erected. Two years later, the school was built.[67] Father Richard Neagle's plans to build a high school at Immaculate Conception in Malden came to O'Connell in his morning newspaper in May 1931. When O'Connell wrote to ask where the money would come from, as the parish showed only $6,061.49 in the parish treasury, Neagle responded that financing the $100,000 needed to construct the school would not be a problem, as "The money is in my hand, to be used as needed." His plans were approved without comment.[68]

Despite the cardinal's rhetoric regarding the evils of progressive education, the Catholic schools had a good working relationship with the city's schools. The two systems were aware that they were in competition for students, and it was still necessary to prove that the parochial schools were every bit as good as the public schools. Writing in 1899, W. A. Leahy praised the Sisters of St. Joseph's methods of teaching, as their schools were graded on the public school system, and public school texts were used, "so that pupils can pass readily from one [school system] to the other." The Sisters of Charity, Halifax did much the same thing, and they incorporated visiting days in public schools soon after they arrived in Boston in 1887.[69] When Father Augustine Hickey, supervisor of archdiocesan schools, petitioned O'Connell to approve annual school visitation days for all of the sisters in the archdiocese, he pointed out that "this is not an innovation—all of the public schools do it."[70]

Beginning in 1910, the archdiocesan school supervisor began to sponsor an annual summer teacher's institute at Boston College High. The system's tacit recognition that the public schools were better can be seen in the rosters of speakers at the institutes. By the late 1920s, over one thousand sisters were attending these week-long professional development workshops in content, child development, and pedagogy each August. Between 1910 and 1945, not a single vowed religious from any of the archdiocesan schools was ever on the faculty. For religious topics, or topics dealing with morality or child development the instructors were almost all either Jesuits or priests on the faculty of The Catholic University of America in Washington. Nearly all of the content and pedagogy courses were taught by public school teachers. Boston Public Schools faculty worked with the sisters over the years on teaching methods in geography and history, assisting sisters in reading and mathematics instruction for the elementary education and training others in the skills needed to prepare high school students for the College Entrance

Examination Board tests. It was also customary most years for one of the physicians associated with the Boston Public Schools to come and speak with the sisters on issues of public health in the schools.[71]

The public schools' administration was one of the last places from which Boston Protestants had managed to exclude Catholics by ensuring that Catholics never gained a majority on the school committee. Catholics had come to dominate the corps of teachers in the classrooms of the city's schools by the early twentieth century, despite the efforts of Protestants to hire teachers from out of town and to limit the number of Catholics in graduating classes at the city's normal school.[72] By 1915, the school committee was finally controlled by Catholics, and beginning with the appointment of Frank Thompson as superintendent in 1918, Catholics served as superintendent of schools until the Cushing years. Equally important was the fact that by 1930, four of the six assistant superintendents were Catholic, as was the headmaster at the Latin School, and the deans of the Boston Teachers' College. Eight of the ten most important jobs in public education were held by Catholics, five of whom were Boston College graduates.[73]

The connections between the two school systems grew as Catholics assumed positions of power in the city's schools. The Boston College Graduate School of Education was founded in 1919 at the request of superintendent Jeremiah E. Burke in order to increase the number of male teachers in the city's high schools. Until the city's normal school was given the right to confer degrees in 1924-25, the city paid the tuition of all candidates for the Boston College master of education degree.[74] The connection between Boston College and the public system deepened throughout the 1920s, as James Mellyn, S.J., was dean of the Graduate School of Education, and his sister Mary was assistant superintendent of teacher development in the Boston schools.[75]

Boston College also began offering Saturday extension and summer classes to sisters in the archdiocese. These classes were taught by Boston College faculty or by Boston Public Schools faculty hired by Boston College as adjuncts, including Mary Mellyn, Patrick J. Campbell of the Latin School, and teachers and masters from schools around the city. O'Connell never objected to any of the public school faculty or administrators invited to teach the sisters of the archdiocese either in the summer institute or through the Boston College extension program. Although it took up to ten years for a sister to get a degree studying part time, between 1927 and 1941, 21 sisters earned the doctoral degree, 226 earned either the master of arts or the master of education degree, and 284 were granted either a bachelor of arts or a bachelor of science in education degree through Boston College.[76]

The high point of cooperation between the two school systems was in the area of character education. In 1923, lay Catholics within the public schools created a model character education program that sought to approximate the character education that was embedded in the archdiocesan course of studies that had been released earlier that year. In the early planning stages, they approached the archdiocese for advice on how to proceed. O'Connell essentially directed Hickey, diocesan schools supervisor not to say no, and to continue the discussion, but he did not suggest that Hickey volunteer the resources available to him in order to help. As the public schools could only teach natural virtue, O'Connell seemed somewhat wary, and he expressed little personal interest in seizing this opportunity for apostolate and collaboration.[77]

The faculty at Boston College and at the city's teachers' college collaborated on several courses that could be taken for credit at either institution, including one series of lectures that O'Connell endorsed at the Boston Public Library. The public schools' curriculum that emerged in 1926 was heavily influenced by Aristotle and Aquinas and carried natural virtue as far as it could go without becoming theological, even providing readings on several saints as models of virtue.[78] One senses that this was as much due to the *Ratio Studiorum* that the public school teachers received as undergraduates at Boston College as it was due to encouragement from the archdiocese.

When O'Connell died in 1944, he left his successor Richard Cushing with a mixed record of growth and consolidation, most of which had taken place between 1907 and 1930. In the entire archdiocese, O'Connell inherited 76 parish schools and 22 high schools, and by 1942 there were 158 parochial schools and 67 high schools. Over ninety thousand children attended parochial schools by 1942, and 70 percent of parishes in the city itself had schools.[79] O'Connell's desire for separateness not only went against the Catholic experience in Boston prior to his arrival but it also caused the archdiocese to fail to capitalize on the rich opportunities for collaboration with public schools.

While speeches claiming that "the hour of the Puritan is passed" made for fine rhetoric, O'Connell's separatist and triumphal attitude toward a vanquished Protestant foe discouraged the type of intellectual and cultural fusion of Yankee and Irishman that had characterized the best vision of what Boston might become. Bostonians might not have been evolving into the new race that Daniel Webster and Emerson had predicted two generations earlier, but the stumbling process of accommodation that Fitzpatrick and Williams had followed was creating a new Boston that was nourished by several traditions, including the Puritan, Irish, and Catholic traditions. In his effort to insulate Boston Catholics and to foster loyalty to the hierarchical Church, O'Connell insisted on a Catholicism that was more Roman in tone. Sadly, in order to become more Roman, it had to be less Bostonian.

Born in South Boston of Irish parents, Richard Cushing was a public school and Boston College High School product. He attended Boston College for two years before entering the seminary. Scheduled to study in Rome, he was not sent because of the First World War. As a result, Cushing never developed the "Roman" outlook of his predecessor. He reached out to his co-religionists and spoke in dozens of Protestant churches and synagogues while he was archbishop. He served for many years as the director of the Society for the Propagation of the Faith, which supported missionary efforts around the world. It was in this capacity that his remarkable fundraising abilities first surfaced.[80]

Between 1945 and 1960 the Catholic population of the archdiocese was increasing at a rate between 250,000 and 300,000 every five years. Returning veterans chose to send their children to parochial schools at a sizable rate. Even though he created seventy-one new parishes between 1944 and 1960, it was not enough to meet the demand, as many were taking advantage of G.I. Bill financing and moving to the suburbs. Between 1944 and 1959, the number of elementary schools in the archdiocese went from 158 to 169; by 1960, there were 211 parochial schools. Most of these were in the suburbs, with many in new parishes.[81]

Cushing encouraged the development of multi-parish diocesan high schools. This represented a significant break with what had been the earlier practice of small, parish high schools. He helped the Salesians purchase a former Boston high school building for the archdiocese's first vocational-technical school. The Franciscan Friars purchased a Boston school building in the city's North End and opened Christopher Columbus High School for boys, which they shared with a girls' school operated by the Sisters of Notre Dame. Monsignor Charles Donahue of St. Teresa's parish in West Roxbury donated a school building to the Christian Brothers, who opened the Catholic Memorial High School in 1957. High schools were also opened in North Cambridge, Arlington, and South Boston.

Most of Cushing's construction was in the suburbs. Outside the city, Cushing built several high schools that he named after his predecessors: Archbishop Williams High School in 1949 and Bishop Fenwick High School in 1959. In 1958, he built Cardinal Spellman High School near the New York prelate's home parish. Cushing helped existing academies that catered to the upper and middle classes move out of the city to more spacious and convenient settings for suburban families. He helped Boston College High to move from the South End to a new campus on a former landfill on the harbor in Dorchester, close by the new expressway that connected the school with the largely Irish suburbs on the South Shore; then he built them a new academic building with a gymnasium. In 1962, the boys' school at the Mission Church in Roxbury moved to suburban Westwood, where it was renamed Xaverian Brothers High School. In 1954, he assisted the Sisters of St. Joseph in establishing Fontbonne Academy, a girls' day school in affluent Milton, and in 1965 he helped the Sisters of Notre Dame relocate their academy from Roxbury to Hingham. When the Sisters of Charity, Halifax expressed a desire to open a girls' central high school on the campus of their Academy of the Assumption in Wellesley in 1962, Cushing offered the Sisters $500,000, spread over five monthly payments of $100,000. The Elizabeth Seton High School opened in September 1965.[82]

Within the city, the old disputes with Protestants over the role of Catholic schools and the position of Catholics in the public schools had largely been put to rest. Cushing had a brief exchange with Harvard president James Bryant Conant over comments Conant made in a speech to the American Association of School Administrators. Conant called the private and Catholic high school a divisive element in American life. Cushing replied by suggesting that Harvard put its charter and its endowment under state control. In general, there were none of the old sectarian squabbles. Race, rather than religion, would prove to be the next challenge to public and parochial schools.[83]

By the early 1960s, Cushing knew that the school system was headed for some sort of cataclysm. He once stated that he needed to raise $30,000 a day in order to pay for the building that he had been financing—about $11 million per year.[84] Unlike O'Connell, who urged prudence, in his haste to see schools built in the suburbs Cushing often lent tremendous sums to pastors for a school and then forgave the note. By 1967, the archdiocesan debt was over $80 million.[85] As early as 1962 he was speaking of his "dilemma of increased enrollments" and that a "noiseless revolution" was underway in the faculty structure of the diocesan schools, as in some places there was one lay teacher for every four priests or religious. He predicted that if the Catholic school population remained constant, by 1971 "there will be more lay teachers than sisters in the parochial school system" and that "the enrollment in the Catholic elementary schools is growing almost four times as fast as the number of teaching sisters who thus far have been the mainstay of Catholic schools."[86] Little did Cushing know that by 1970 he would be witnessing a mass exodus of sisters from the classroom as many religious fled the convent for secular life. Underestimating the resourcefulness of the laity, just before he died in 1970 he made the gloomy prediction that Catholic schools would cease to exist by 1980.[87]

NOTES

1. "Glee Club to Sing in Tercentenary of Boston Latin," *The Harvard Crimson*, April 23, 1935, http://www.thecrimson.com/article.aspx?ref=453427

2. Quoted in Pauline Holmes, *A Tercentenary History of the Boston Public Latin School, 1635-1935* (Westport, CT: Greenwood, 1935), 1-2.

3. "The Tercentenary Celebration of the Boston Latin School: Order of Exercises," in Holmes, *A Tercentenary History*, 522-523.

4. "Address of the Honorable Joseph P. Kennedy at the Tercentenary Dinner, Boston Latin School, April 23, 1935, The Copley Plaza, Boston," http://www.sechistorical.org/collection/papers/1930/1935_04_23_Latin_School_Spee.pdf

5. Ibid.

6. While virtually every historian who has written on the history of nineteenth century Catholicism in Boston has written on the burning of the convent, the most readable and up-to-date scholarly treatment is Nancy Lusignan Schultz, *Fire and Roses: The Burning of the Charlestown Convent, 1834* (New York: Simon and Schuster, 1999). See also Robert H. Lord, John E. Sexton, and Edward T. Harrington, *History of the Archdiocese of Boston in the Various Stages of Its Development* (New York: Sheed and Ward, 1944), 2:205-237.

7. Lord, Sexton, and Harrington, *History of the Archdiocese of Boston*, 2:326-329.

8. Stanley K. Schultz, *The Culture Factory: Boston Public Schools, 1789-1860* (New York: Oxford, 1973), 14-20.

9. Ibid., 14-66, 242.

10. Figures taken from James W. Sanders, "Boston Catholics and the School Question, 1825-1907," in *From Common School to Magnet School: Selected Essays in the History of Boston's Schools*, ed. James W. Fraser, Henry L. Allen, and Sam Barnes (Boston: Trustees of the Public Library of the City of Boston, 1979).

11. Thomas H. O'Connor, *Fitzpatrick's Boston, 1846-1866* (Boston: Northeastern University Press, 1984), 89-90.

12. William A. Leahy, "Archdiocese of Boston," in Very Rev. William Byrne, D.D. et al., *History of the Catholic Church in the New England States* (Boston: Hurd and Everts, 1899), 71-72.

13. Polly Welts Kaufman, *Boston Women and City School Politics, 1872-1905* (New York: Garland, 1995), 115.

14. O'Connor, *Fitzpatrick's Boston*, 101.

15. Lord, Sexton, and Harrington, *History of the Archdiocese of Boston*, 2:686-699; O'Connor, *Fitzpatrick's Boston*, 153-158.

16. *Boston Pilot*, November 26, 1852.

17. Lord, Sexton, and Harrington, *History of the Archdiocese of Boston*, 2:587-589.

18. O'Connor, *Fitzpatrick's Boston*, 112.

19. Lord, Sexton, and Harrington, *History of the Archdiocese of Boston*, 2:614-616.

20. Ibid., 592-595. Bishop Fitzpatrick's *Memoranda*, March 15, 1859, Archives of the Archdioceses of Boston (AAB). The problem with the Decalogue as it appears in the King James Version is that the Commandments are split so that the Second Commandment prohibits graven images, which Catholics believed was a direct assault on the use of images in their churches and devotional life.

21. Fitzpatrick's *Memoranda*, March 15, 1859, AAB.

22. Quoted in Lord, Sexton, and Harrington, *History of the Archdiocese of Boston*, 2:595-598.

23. Kaufman, *Boston Women and City School Politics*, 140; John T. McGreevy, *Catholicism and American Freedom: A History* (New York: W.W. Norton, 2003), 24-41. McGreevy adds an interesting and enlightening twist to previous interpretations of the Eliot School case. He sees the case not only resulting from the feud between Unitarians and evangelicals over the role of religion in the schools, but also as one of the first American rounds in the battle over control of the Church between ultramontanes and Gallicans. McGreevy illustrates how John McElroy was one of the last American Jesuits who was not trained as an ultramontane, while Father Wiget was a Swiss Jesuit who wished to bring a Romanizing influence to Boston. He founded a boys' sodality at St. Mary's to which all of the boys in the protest belonged, including Thomas Whall. Wiget viewed the Church's willingness to seek accommodation with Protestants with dismay, and thought that the sodality was the best available means to wean the boys from the influence of what he saw as lax American Catholics, including McElroy. The incident at the Eliot School was only possible because McElroy was away and Wiget seized on an opportunity to make a loud and public Catholic stance over something that McElroy most likely would not have protested.

24. Doris Kearns Goodwin, *The Fitzgeralds and the Kennedys: An American Saga* (New York: St. Martin's Press, 1991), 35-37.

25. Louis S. Walsh, *Historical Sketch of the Growth of Catholic Parochial Schools in the Archdiocese of Boston* (Newton Highlands: St. John's Industrial School, 1901), 3-4; Robert J. Sauer, *Holy Trinity German Church, 1844-1994* (Dallas: Taylor, 1994), 38.

26. Lord, Sexton, and Harrington, *History of the Archdiocese of Boston*, 2:608-609; W.E. Murphy, S.J., "The Story of Boston College," in *Catholic Builders of the Nation: A Symposium on the Catholic Contribution to the Civilization of the United States*, ed. C.E. McGuire (Boston: Continental, 1923), 248-259; Charles F. Donovan, S.J., David R. Dunigan, S.J., and Paul A. Fitzgerald, S.J., *History of Boston College, from the Beginnings to 1990* (Chestnut Hill: University Press of Boston College, 1990), 42; David Loftus, *Boston College High School, 1863-1983* (Boston: Getchell and Son, 1984), 1-11.

27. Edward I. Devitt, S.J., "History of the Maryland-New York Province," *Woodstock Letters*, 64:405 (1935); Robert Fulton, S.J., *Diary*, entry for 1864; Manuscript volume, "Register of Students" (n.d.), Archives of Boston College; all quoted in Donovan, Dunigan, and Fitzgerald, *History of Boston College*, 42-44.

28. Sanders, "Boston Catholics and the School Question, 1825-1907," 52-54.

29. Ibid.

30. Robert E. Sullivan, "Beneficial Relations: Toward a Social History of the Diocesan Priests of Boston, 1875-1944," in *Catholic Boston: Studies in Religion and Community, 1870-1970*, ed. Robert E. Sullivan and James M. O'Toole (Boston: Roman Catholic Archbishop of Boston, 1985), 225-231; James W. Sanders, "Catholics and the School Question in Boston: The Cardinal O'Connell Years" in Sullivan and O'Toole, *Catholic Boston*, 137-138.

31. Lord, Sexton, and Harrington, *History of the Archdiocese of Boston*, 3:81-82; Sister Mary Xaviera Sullivan, "The History of Catholic Secondary Education in the Archdiocese of Boston" (PhD diss., The Catholic University of America, 1946); Thomas H. O'Connor, *Boston Catholics: A History of the Church and Its People* (Boston: Northeastern University, 1998), 136-137.

32. Lord, Sexton, and Harrington, *History of the Archdiocese of Boston*, 3:80-85.

33. *The Catholic Church in Its Relation to Civil and Religious Liberty: The Complete Discussion Between Rev. J.P. Bland and Rev. John O'Brien of Cambridge Massachusetts. Reprinted from the Boston Herald* (Boston: Duffy, Cashman and Co., 1880); *Boston Pilot*, October 9, 1880.

34. *Boston Pilot*, December 6, 1879.

35. William A. Leahy, "Archdiocese of Boston," 138-147.

36. Ibid.

37. James Fitton, *Sketches of the Establishment of the Church in New England* (Boston: Patrick Donahoe, 1872), 152-155; Leahy, "Archdiocese of Boston," 166-171; M. Sullivan, "History of Catholic Secondary Education," 20-22, 46-47; Walsh, *Growth of Parochial Schools*, 6-9.

38. Leahy, "Archdiocese of Boston," 156-158; Michael Parise, *The History of St. Gregory's Parish, Lower Mills, Dorchester, and Milton, 1862-1987* (Dorchester, MA: St. Gregory's Parish, 1987).

39. Parise, "History of St. Gregory's"; Lord, Sexton, and Harrington, *History of the Archdiocese of Boston*, 3:247.

40. M.P. Curran, *Life of Patrick A. Collins, With Some of His Most Memorable Public Addresses* (Norwood, MA: Norwood Press, 1906), 81; Goodwin, *The Fitzgeralds and the Kennedys*, 105; Sam Bass Warner, *Streetcar Suburbs: The Process of Growth in Boston, 1870-1900* (Cambridge: Harvard University Press, 1962), esp. chapter five, 67-116.

41. S.L. Emery, *A Catholic Stronghold: A History of St. Peter's Parish, Dorchester, and of Its First Rector the Reverend Peter Ronan* (Boston: George H. Ellis, 1910); Sister Maura Power, *The Sisters of Charity, Halifax* (Toronto: Ryerson, 1956), 171-195.

42. Quoted in Power, *The Sisters of Charity, Halifax*, 199-200.

43. Mary J. Oates, "Organized Voluntarism: The Catholic Sisters in Massachusetts, 1870-1940," *American Quarterly* 30, no. 5 (Winter 1978): 652-680.

44. Rev. John F. Byrne, C.Ss.R., *The Glories of Mary in Boston. A Memorial History of the Church of Our Lady of Perpetual Help (Mission Church), Roxbury, MA, 1871-1921* (Boston: Mission Church, 1921), 391; Leahy, "Archdiocese of Boston," 138-147; Walsh, *Growth of Schools*, 11.

45. R. Sullivan, "Beneficial Relations," 210.

46. Phillip Marson, *Breeder of Democracy* (Cambridge, MA: Schenckman, 1963), 148.

47. Joseph Manton, *A View from the Steeple* (Huntington, IN: Our Sunday Visitor, 1985), 9.

48. *Who's Who in State Politics* (Boston: Practical Politics, 1908); *Who's Who in State Politics* (Boston: Practical Politics, 1918).

49. M. Sullivan, "History of Catholic Secondary Education," 30-31, 46; Walsh, *Historical Sketch*, Appendix I.

50. Oates, "Organized Voluntarism," 672-673; Walsh, *Historical Sketch*, Appendices I, II, IV; Walsh, *Growth of Schools*, 10-11.

51. Byrne, *The Glories of Mary*, 391-396; Loftus, *Boston College High School*, 5.

52. James M. O'Toole, *Militant and Triumphant: William Henry O'Connell and the Catholic Church in Boston, 1895-1944* (Notre Dame: University of Notre Dame Press, 1992), 143-172; Sanders, "Catholics and the School Question in Boston," 164-168.

53. O'Toole, *Militant and Triumphant*, 144-154; Sauer, *Holy Trinity German Church*, 38-41; Holy Trinity, Boston, School Corporation Records, AAB, IV, 5.2; Board of Advisors, Holy Trinity Parish to Williams; Petition for establishment of a new parish, AAB, V, 2:43

54. Lord, Sexton, and Harrington, *History of the Archdiocese of Boston*, 3:111-128; Kaufman, *Boston Women and City School Politics*, 143-155; Dennis P. Ryan, *Beyond the Ballot Box: A Social History of the Boston Irish, 1845-1917* (Amherst: University of Massachusetts Press, 1983), 63-65.

55. Lord, Sexton, and Harrington, *History of the Archdiocese of Boston*, 3:100-159; Kaufman, *Boston Women and City School Politics*, 139-163.

56. *Boston Pilot*, April 5, 1890; Mary Elizabeth Blake, "The Trouble in the Boston Schools," *Catholic World*, January 1889, 501-510.

57. Kaufman, *Boston Women and City School Politics*, 154-158; William T. Harris, *Morality in the Schools* (Boston: Christian Register Association, 1889); Kurt F. Leidecker, *Yankee Teacher: The Life of William Torrey Harris* (New York: Philosophical Library, 1946); William J. Reese, *America's Public Schools: From the Common School to No Child Left Behind* (Baltimore: Johns Hopkins University, 2005), 63-65.

58. Francis Parkman, *Our Common Schools* (Boston: Citizens' Public School Union, 1890).

59. *Boston Pilot*, September 19, 1885.

60. *Donahoe's Magazine*, May 1890; quoted in Kaufman, *Boston Women and City School Politics*, 157.

61. McGreevy, *Catholicism and American Freedom*, 39-40.

62. William Cardinal O'Connell, "The Growth of Atheistic Stateism," *Sermons and Addresses of His Eminence William Cardinal O'Connell, Archbishop of Boston* (Boston: Pilot, 1922), 7:26.

63. O'Connell, "The Child's Training," in *Sermons and Addresses*, 5:36, 39.

64. Sanders, "Catholics and the School Question in Boston," 134-135.

65. Ibid., 134-141; Loftus, *Boston College High School*, 35-60; M. Sullivan, "History of Catholic Secondary Education," 48-82; James Tunstead Burtchaell, *The Dying of the Light: The Disengagement of Colleges and Universities from their Christian Churches*, (Grand Rapids, MI: Eerdmans, 1998), 574-575 provides a succinct discussion of the separation of Boston College High from the college and how the high school became a large, successful classical high school. To contrast this with the public Latin school, see *Documents of the School Committee of the City of Boston for the year 1905* (Boston: City of Boston, 1905), doc. no. 5, p. 7.

66. O'Connor, *Boston Catholics*, 252-272; O'Toole, *Militant and Triumphant*, 210-211; Sanders, "Catholics and the School Question in Boston," 138-141.

67. See correspondence between Riordan and O'Connell, and Riordan and Sullivan, July-December, 1915; Haberlin to Flannery, October 29, 1926; Daly to O'Connell, May 5, 1926, AAB Parish Files.

68. See correspondence between Neagle and O'Connell, May 15-November 2,

1931, AAB Parish Files; O'Toole, *Militant and Triumphant*, 212-218.

69. Leahy, "Archdiocese of Boston," 180-181; Power, *The Sisters of Charity, Halifax*, 173; Mary J. Oates, "Learning to Teach: The Professional Preparation of Massachusetts Parochial School Faculty, 1870-1940," *Working Papers Series* 10, no. 2 (Fall 1981).

70. Hickey to O'Connell, AAB Department of Education (DOE) Files, 1917-1918.

71. See the "Annual Report(s) of the Diocesan Supervisor of Schools, 1910-1944," AAB DOE Files.

72. The best recent account of the systematic Protestant effort to exclude Irish Catholic women from coming to dominate the Boston Public Schools is in Janet Nolan, *Servants of the Poor: Teachers and Mobility in Ireland and Irish America* (Notre Dame, IN: University of Notre Dame Press, 2004), especially her chapter entitled "Boston Schools for Boston Girls!" pp. 43-64; also, Polly Welts Kaufman, "Julia Harrington Duff and the Political Awakening of Irish American Women in Boston, 1888-1905," in *Women of the Commonwealth: Work, Family, and Social Change in Nineteenth-Century Massachusetts*, ed. Susan L. Porter (Amherst: University of Massachusetts Press, 1996), 165-182; and Kaufman, *Boston Women and City School Politics*, 217-269.

73. Sanders, "Catholics and the School Question in Boston," 142.

74. Donovan, Dunigan, and Fitzgerald, *History of Boston College*, 162-163.

75. Ibid.; Sanders, "Catholics and the School Question in Boston: The O'Connell Years," 147-148.

76. Lists of potential instructors to be approved by O'Connell for the Extension classes, and data on sisters granted degrees at Boston College were collected from the "Annual Report(s) of the Diocesan Supervisor of Schools," 1921-1941, AAB DOE Files.

77. Hickey to O'Connell, January 8, 1923; Haberlin to Hickey, January 10, 1923, AAB DOE Files.

78. Sanders, "Catholics and the School Question in Boston," 150-157.

79. O'Connor, *Boston Catholics*, 273; Richard J. Quinlan, "Growth and Development of Catholic Education in the Archdiocese of Boston," *The Catholic Historical Review* 22, no. 1 (April 1936): 27-41. By 1935, there were 147 parishes that had schools, which means that between 1935 and 1944 only eleven new schools were opened.

80. Cushing still awaits his first academic biographer. Several rather pious biographies were written toward the end of his life: John Henry Cutler, *Cardinal Cushing of Boston* (New York: Hawthorn Books, 1970); M.C. Devine, *The World's Cardinal* (Boston: St. Paul, 1964); John H. Fenton, *Salt of the Earth: An Informal Portrait of Richard Cardinal Cushing* (New York: Coward-McCann, 1965).

81. O'Connor, *Boston Catholics*, 249-251.

82. Sister Mary Olga McKenna, *Charity Alive: Sisters of Charity of St. Vincent de Paul, Halifax, 1950-1980* (Lanham, MD: University Press, 1998), 130-131.

83. Cutler, *Cardinal Cushing of Boston*, 118-119.

84. O'Connor, *Boston Catholics*, 272.

85. J. Anthony Lukas, *Common Ground: A Turbulent Decade in the Lives of Three American Families* (New York: Knopf, 1985), 381-382.

86. Richard Cardinal Cushing, "The Challenge of Christian Education," in *The Mission of the Teacher* (Boston: St. Paul, 1962), 119.

87. John Deedy, "News and Views," *Commonweal*, December 6, 1974; quoted in James E. Glinski, "The Catholic Church and the Desegregation of Boston's Schools," *Boston's Histories: Essays in Honor of Thomas H. O'Connor*, ed. James M. O'Toole and David Quigley (Boston: Northeastern University Press, 2004), 249.

Part Two
Catholic Education in the Heartland

"Through personal sacrifice and commitment, the clergy, religious, and laity built numerous Catholic churches, schools, and other organizations in Cincinnati. The initiative taken by the immigrants, especially the Irish and Germans, is a testimonial to the significant influence that ordinary people exerted on the development of the diocese." *— Roger A. Fortin*

"The Archdiocese of St. Louis has a strong and rich tradition of Catholic education. This tradition was built upon a vision of mission-driven leaders who proactively went to the frontiers and supplied Catholic education to populations in need even in the face of extreme difficulties." *— John T. James*

"Immigrants opted for schools that taught children their parents' faith and heritage; the more assimilated second and third generation Catholics developed schools they deemed superior to any other, public or private. . . . In Detroit, these schools continually attracted a more impressive share of Catholic children than nearly any other city in America."
— JoEllen McNergney Vinyard

"While there never had been a golden age of Chicago Catholicism with sufficient funds to ensure that all children could attend parochial schools, by the 1950s nearly every parish in the city supported an elementary school. . . . [In] the experience of thousands of Chicago families, it was the parochial school, as much as the parish church, that provided structure and continuity in neighborhoods."
— Ellen Skerrett

Queen City Catholicism:
Catholic Education in Cincinnati

Roger A. Fortin

From the founding of the Diocese of Cincinnati in 1821 to the late 1870s, the diocese experienced significant growth under the leadership of its first two prelates, Edward Dominic Fenwick (1821-1832) and John Baptist Purcell (1833-1883). This growth was particularly evident in the number of educational enterprises.

Early in his administration, Fenwick went to Europe to find funds and personnel for his struggling diocese. During that visit, he secured the services of three priests and a French Sister of Mercy who was the first vowed woman religious to minister in Cincinnati. In 1825, a year after her arrival, Sister St. Paul opened a private school for girls, the first Catholic school in Ohio and the beginning of the parochial system in Cincinnati. Encouraged by his initial success, Fenwick requested to the superior of the Sisters of Mercy that two or three additional sisters be sent to assist Sister St. Paul.[1]

In 1826, when other French Sisters of Mercy were not forthcoming, Fenwick granted two French Collettine Poor Clare Sisters permission to establish their order in Cincinnati. In the fall these two sisters joined Sister St. Paul. By January of 1827 the three nuns were instructing approximately seventy students in the school as well as conducting a large class of poor children on Sundays. However, with the untimely death of Sister St. Paul and the departure of the two Poor Clare Sisters due to their inability to recruit more sisters, the school closed in the spring of 1828.[2]

In mid-October 1829, Fenwick was pleased to learn that the Sisters of Charity would finally establish a foundation in Cincinnati. Later that fall, twenty years after Mother Seton had founded the community at Emmitsburg, Maryland, the sisters reopened the girls' school. Named St. Peter's School, it was the first permanently established tuition-free school in Ohio and marked the beginning of enduring Catholic education in Cincinnati.[3]

The new diocese was vast—then consisting of the state of Ohio, parts of Michigan, and the Northwest Territory—and the challenges were substantial. Fenwick noted early on that the Protestant sects in Cincinnati were "united against the Catholics." In fact, the Protestant and sectarian press in the Midwest charged that the young country was endangered by the growth of the Catholic Church. Intensifying the spirit of anti-Catholicism was the fact that by 1830 there were more Protestant pupils at St. Peter's School than Catholics. Protestant ministers expressed concerns about Catholics possibly influencing Protestant children.[4]

In 1830, while some Protestants criticized the growth of the Catholic Church in Cincinnati, Fenwick developed plans for the establishment of a college and seminary. Funds obtained from European Catholics enabled him to buy property and on October 17, 1831, he opened a new college named the Athenaeum. Catholic secondary and higher education had their beginning in Cincinnati with the founding of the Athenaeum. A six-year course of studies was established, as there was no formal division then of high school and college.[5]

Throughout his eleven-year tenure, Fenwick helped found those institutions essential to a new diocese. He established the first parochial school in the diocese, built a cathedral, seminary, and college, and founded the *Catholic Telegraph*, the first Catholic newspaper west of the Alleghenies and only the second Catholic paper in the country. Like other Catholic newspapers founded in pre-Civil War America, the *Catholic Telegraph* served as a primary publication for the defense of Catholicism.[6]

From the 1830s to the 1870s, the Catholic Church in the United States grew at an astonishing rate to become a major force in American religious life. For nearly a half century, the Irish-born John Baptist Purcell worked tirelessly for the advancement of the Church and proved to be one of the most successful leaders in the American hierarchy in the nineteenth century. The growth of the Cincinnati church during his administration was astonishing.

In 1839, to help relieve the diocesan clergy of the responsibility of operating the Athenaeum, Purcell offered the college to the Society of Jesus. Renamed St. Xavier College, the renovated college reopened on November 3, 1840. Before the end of the year there were 76 students enrolled. Two years later, 217 students attended the school.[7]

Through personal sacrifice and commitment, the clergy, vowed religious, and laity built numerous Catholic churches, schools, and other organizations in Cincinnati. The initiative taken by the immigrants, especially the Irish and Germans, is a testimonial to the significant influence that ordinary people exerted on the development of the diocese. The first Mass in Cincinnati was offered in 1811 in the home of the Irishman, Michael Scott. Eight years later he and other Irish colleagues built the first Catholic church, commonly known as Christ Church, in Cincinnati. In 1822, a year after the diocese was established, the church was renamed St. Peter in Chains Cathedral.[8]

From the 1830s to the 1860s, thousands of German and Irish Catholic immigrants made their way to Cincinnati. As the diocese increasingly became a church of immigrants, German Catholics came to dominate. As in some other urban centers in the nineteenth century, German and Irish Catholics refused to worship together. When the German and Irish Catholics temporarily shared St. Peter in Chains Cathedral in the early 1830s, a German parishioner commented that the Germans endured "arrogant treatment" from the Irish. Both immigrant groups wished to worship separately. As a consequence, Purcell allowed the establishment of national parishes and did his best to recruit German-speaking as well as English-speaking clergy.[9]

Both the German and Irish Catholics established organizations and institutions that helped them sustain their respective traditions and beliefs as they adjusted to their new home. In 1834, Purcell consecrated Holy Trinity Church, the second Catholic church in the city and the first parish for German Catholics west of the Alleghenies. By 1847, Cincinnati had six German parishes. In 1850, while the Irish continued to worship at St. Peter in Chains Cathedral, they also opened St. Patrick Church in the city. During the next twenty years, the Irish built two more churches. By mid-century, both the Germans and the Irish, with Purcell's approval, were building schools in tandem with their churches.[10]

With the arrival of waves of immigrants, Cincinnati's population nearly doubled every ten years in the first half of the nineteenth century.

Well into the second half of the century, the Irish and German Catholics continued to have the most visible impact in the local church.

With the erection of the dioceses of Cleveland and Columbus in 1847 and 1868 respectively, the Diocese of Cincinnati was reduced to twenty-eight counties. By the time of Purcell's death in 1883, the diocese had 157 churches and eighty-eight parochial schools with an enrollment of twenty thousand students. In leading the local church with firmness and control Purcell set the tone for his episcopal predecessors in the diocese for the next century.[11]

An important concern of the Catholic community in Cincinnati in the nineteenth century was public education. Because public education at that time reflected Protestant teachings and values, Catholic leaders committed themselves to Catholic education. Purcell took the leadership role. In the fall of 1836 he criticized Reverend Benjamin P. Aydelott's address on the study of the Bible in the public schools. Aydelott, a local physician and Episcopalian minister, recommended that the Bible be the textbook used in the public schools.

As a consequence, the Western Literary Institute, a local voluntary organization of teachers, put Purcell and Aydelott on a committee to report on the matter the following year. This was the first time that the issue of Bible usage in Cincinnati's public schools entered public discourse. In the summer of 1837, Purcell asked Bishop John Hughes of New York, a strong spokesman nationally for Catholic rights, to join him in a collaborative effort to determine the best use of the Bible in the public schools. Though Purcell was hopeful that a compromise could be reached, Hughes was not.[12]

At the October 1837 meeting of the Institute, Purcell argued that Protestant Bibles should not be placed in the hands of the Catholic youth and that the teachers in the public schools should not influence the pupils with their "sectarian bias." After much discussion, the Institute unanimously recommended that the Bible be read in all the schools as part of "a religious exercise, without denominational or sectarian comment." While Purcell continued to express concern over the policy of Bible reading as part of the curriculum in the public schools, he was pleased overall with the working relationship with public school authorities in Cincinnati.[13]

During this period, Purcell and Hughes were the most vocal national church advocates for Catholic schools. Not surprisingly, therefore, New York and Cincinnati far outdistanced the other American dioceses in the percentage of children attending parochial schools. But unlike Hughes, Purcell had a much more conciliatory policy toward public schools. To be sure, the Cincinnati public schools had a Protestant bias, but Purcell continued to work with their officials. He argued that it was better for the Catholic children to receive an education in the public schools than to not receive any education at all. "Half a loaf," the *Catholic Telegraph* wrote, "is better than no bread." Purcell was also motivated by the desire to make Catholicism more acceptable to non-Catholics. In 1840, he informed Hughes that the Cincinnati School Board "employed a Catholic Schoolmistress, the first, in one of the . . . [Public] Schools."[14]

Purcell's diplomacy and conciliatory position eventually reaped rewards. In the summer of 1852, Dr. Jerome Mudd, a Catholic who also was a school board member, raised the issue of Bible use in the public schools for a second time. After consulting with local church authorities, Mudd proposed that the Catholic children be allowed to use the Catholic version of the Bible in the schools. In November, the board settled on a compromise and instituted a new policy for Cincinnati's public schools. Though the King James Bible was still the norm, Catholics could now use their own edition of the Bible.[15]

By mid-century, anti-Catholicism had spilled over into education and politics. In 1853, the Ohio legislature considered a bill to require all school-age children to attend the public schools for a minimum of three months of the year. It threatened the existence of Catholic schools. Purcell presented the Ohio legislature with a petition, signed by eight hundred Catholics, arguing that the parents had the right to send their children to any school they chose. "The school question is thickening on us," Purcell wrote to Archbishop Antoine Blanc of New Orleans. "We are in the midst of all manner of threats from all manner of Sects & infidels." The efforts by Catholics in the diocese proved successful. The bill was defeated.[16]

Committed to transmitting the faith to the next generation, Catholics in the diocese invested heavily in their own religious and social institutions. The formation of the Catholic school system during Purcell's tenure is one of the great success stories of Cincinnati Catholicism. By the middle of the century, 80 percent of the parishes in the diocese had Catholic schools. Most of these schools were in the cities. By building a separate school system, Catholics sustained a doctrinal bond in a pluralistic society. By 1860, there were 61 schools in the diocese. Ten years later the number had risen to 103. The local parish, not just the parents, bore the cost of education. As Catholic children attended Catholic schools they segregated themselves socially and religiously from the rest of the community. Moreover, most English- and German-speaking children were segregated from each other.[17]

In 1848, the six German schools and two English language Catholic schools in the city had a combined enrollment of 2,527 pupils. Three years later, the number of parochial schools had increased by five with a total enrollment of 4,494 students at all eight schools. In 1864, the parochial schools enrolled 9,544 students who constituted 41 percent of all the pupils enrolled in the city. By 1870, between 12,000 and 15,000 children attended the German and English Catholic schools, equivalent to one third of the city's total school population. It is estimated that four-fifths of the Catholic children of school age attended parochial schools. Wherever Catholic parishes and churches were established, Catholic parochial schools were soon to follow. The diocesan paper proudly boasted "that there is not a city in the whole country where, in proportion to the Catholic population, there are so many parochial and select Catholic schools."[18]

By 1850, Purcell had emerged as a national champion of parochial schools. The elevation of the diocese to an archdiocese that year further increased the confidence of the local church and helped intensify its school policy. Through provincial councils in 1855, 1858, and 1861, Purcell, his suffragan bishops, and the superiors of three priest orders further solidified parochial school education. In the process, they generated interest in the national movement toward parochial education.[19]

At the 1855 and 1858 councils, the delegates passed a number of decrees on education. Wanting to see a parochial school connected with every Catholic church in the province, they obligated the pastors, "under pain of mortal sin," to establish parochial schools whenever possible. This legislation was more rigorous than any previously passed by other dioceses in the country. Some pastors in Cincinnati also began to deny the sacraments to parents who did not send their children to parochial schools, without prior approval by the bishop. "The Catholic school," Purcell wrote in one of his Lenten pastorals, "is the nursery of the Catholic congregation." Nevertheless, efforts to prevent Catholic children from attending the public schools were an uphill battle in a number of parishes.[20]

Though the Second Plenary Council at Baltimore in 1866 benefited from the deliberations of the Cincinnati provincial councils, the Plenary Council's statement on parochial education was less stringent than the one issued by Cincinnati's 1858 council. The Baltimore council merely recommended that in every diocese a school be built next to every church. The majority of American bishops were not yet prepared, as were Purcell and Hughes, to launch a major campaign for parochial schools. That initiative came at the Third Plenary Council of Baltimore in 1884.[21]

Purcell saw the increase of public schools' programs as a threat to the parochial school system. He wanted the Catholic schools to be as thorough and extensive in their curriculum as the public schools. In particular, Purcell was very concerned over the deplorable student-teacher ratio in the parochial schools. Whereas in 1850 the ratio of students to teachers in the public schools of Cincinnati was 88 to 1, dropping to 62 to 1 in 1858, the ratio in the Catholic schools was 94 to 1 and 100 to 1 respectively. To help bring uniformity in Catholic education in the archdiocese, Purcell founded a school board in 1863 and empowered it to improve academic standards in the schools, review credentials of teachers, and supervise the selection of textbooks. Under the leadership of the school board, the archdiocese began teacher certification. To attract more competent teachers, the diocesan school board recommended higher salaries for teachers. However, the school board was short lived, as there are no records of its existence by the mid-1860s.[22]

Moreover, in 1869 the Bible controversy in Cincinnati reemerged. A coalition of Jews, Catholics, and a few Protestants argued that because of the religious diversity in the city, religion had no place in the public schools. They attempted to make Cincinnati's public schools more acceptable by "de-Protestantizing" its curriculum. That year, Cincinnati's board of education excluded Bible reading, religious instruction, and hymn singing from the public schools. At the time one fourth of the members of the board were Catholics, a clear sign that Catholic influence had grown considerably in the city. The Cincinnati school board's decision fueled a nationwide debate. The Supreme Court of Ohio upheld the constitutionality of the board's decision. While the Bible controversy further strained relations between Protestants and Catholics, it helped hasten the secularization of public education.[23]

Under the leadership of various vowed women religious communities, Catholic education expanded in the diocese during the Purcell years. By 1850, the Sisters of Charity had over three hundred children in St. Peter's. Three years later, they opened Mt. St. Vincent Academy in Cincinnati as well as St. Mary Academy, a select boarding and day school. In 1855, St. Mary's was closed in order to open a pay and free school in the city. It was common in the pre-Civil War period for a free school to be conducted side-by-side with the select school. The select or "pay school" often provided the funds that made possible the free school.[24]

The diocese saw an increase in female academies in the 1840s, 1850s, and 1860s. The Sisters of Charity were soon joined by other vowed women religious orders who regarded the moral and religious education of the girls as future mothers as essential to the sanctity of the home. Shortly after Purcell returned from a trip to Europe in 1839, he appealed to the Sisters of Notre Dame de Namur in Belgium. The sisters accepted the bishop's invitation.[25]

On October 31, 1840, eight sisters from the order arrived in Cincinnati. In mid-January 1841, the German-speaking Sisters of Notre Dame opened the Young Ladies Literary Institute and Boarding School, later known as Notre Dame Academy. Schools for indigent students were opened by the sisters at the same time as the boarding school. A month later, there were thirty pupils in the day school, between thirty and forty in the free school, and one boarder. Catholics were "mightily pleased," the *Catholic Telegraph* editorialized in 1841, with the Sisters of Notre Dame that "grace our Queenly City." Before the end of the decade the order erected its first school building and taught girls in the German parish schools. Shortly after the Civil War, the Sisters of Notre Dame opened an academy for young girls in the western part of Cincinnati. For the next half century it became the alma mater of hundreds of Catholic, Protestant, and Jewish girls.[26]

In 1845 the Ursuline Sisters arrived in the diocese. Purcell had first established relations with the Ursulines on his trip to France seven years earlier. A year after their arrival they established "The St. Ursula Literary Institute" in Cincinnati.[27]

During Purcell's tenure Mrs. Sarah Worthington King Peter helped procure the Sisters of Mercy for the diocese. Daughter of Thomas Worthington, one of Ohio's first senators and governors, she eventually became fascinated by the Christian traditions, converted to Catholicism, and began a long career of service to the Catholic Church in Cincinnati. Eleven Sisters of Mercy arrived in Cincinnati in August 1858.

Consistent with the mission of their society, they taught young girls in the useful branches of education. In October, they opened a night school for uneducated adult Irish immigrants as well as an infant boys' school in the same quarters. Within a month, approximately two hundred working girls attended night school and eighty infant boys were registered in the day school. In the fall of 1860, the sisters opened a second school just for girls.[28]

By the second half of the nineteenth century, the various sisterhoods became the backbone of the educational work of the Archdiocese of Cincinnati. As teachers and social service providers, vowed women religious helped pioneer the growth of the Catholic Church, contributing to the religious and intellectual life of Cincinnati.

As the Cincinnati church became more centralized at the end of the nineteenth and early twentieth centuries, it built upon Purcell's educational legacy. When the bishops of the Cincinnati Province, which consisted of ten suffragan dioceses assigned to the archdiocese, convened a council in Cincinnati in 1882, they spent most of the time emphasizing the importance of Catholic education. It was their wish "that the Church and school go hand in hand; that where the one is, there also shall the other be." The bishops exhorted Catholic school parents, under serious moral obligation, not to send their children to public schools. Poverty was no excuse. Parishes assumed the cost of books for families in financial need. Whereas Catholics in the early years of the diocese were primarily concerned with the influence of Protestantism in public education, in the latter part of the nineteenth century they worried over secularism.[29]

When the Third Plenary Council convened in Baltimore in November 1884, it declared more strongly than ever the necessity of Catholic education. The seventy-two bishops required the establishment of a parochial school near each church and mandated the attendance of Catholic children at these schools. Moreover, the Council fathers established the famous uniform national catechism known to generations of Catholics thereafter as the *Baltimore Catechism*.[30]

Episcopal and clerical authority continued to grow during the administrations of Archbishops William Henry Elder (1883-1904) and Henry Moeller (1904-1925). During Elder's twenty-four year tenure in Cincinnati, he systematized the inner workings of the archdiocese and collected annual reports from all the pastors and administrators. These reports covered such items as the number of teachers and pupils in the parochial schools. Both Elder and Moeller underscored the importance of parochial education. They argued that religion should be a part of a child's education. Thinking that it was not enough to teach reading, writing, grammar, geography, and arithmetic, many Catholics argued there had to be "the careful training and development of the *moral*, as well as the intellectual, faculties."[31]

When the bishops of the Cincinnati Province met in the fall of 1892 they passed a resolution, stipulating that the Catholic children not attending parochial schools should receive catechetical instruction. They declared that it was imperative that Catholic parents send their children to parochial schools. If unable to send them to Catholic schools, they were expected to enroll them in Sunday schools, generally taught by vowed women religious and lay women volunteers. During Moeller's term, Pope Pius X promoted the Confraternity of Christian Doctrine, which helped standardize religious education programs nationally. In the spring of 1921 the Cincinnati ordinary established the Catholic Instruction League, which gave religious instruction to Catholic children attending the public schools.[32]

Though many Catholics preferred to send their children to Catholic schools for religious reasons, the local church hierarchy acknowledged the state's right to sponsor public schools. Moeller argued that the "chief objection to the public school system is that it is essentially defective. True education must be based on, directed and guided by religion." As a consequence, Catholics increasingly sponsored their own separate schools. They were generally pleased with the powerful religious and cultural influence of the environment in the parochial schools. In addition to the morning Mass, the opening and closing prayers, the recitations in Christian Doctrine, the presence of sacred images and pictures, and an appropriate curriculum, there was the influence of religious teachers.[33]

While promoting Catholic education, local church officials improved the efficiency and effectiveness of Catholic schools. Moeller urged the pastor of a local parish to replace its "unhealthy" school, so that parents "will have no . . . reason for sending their children to the public school." By the early twentieth century, the Cincinnati church approached the organization of Catholic schools in much the same manner as did administrators of the public schools. In the summer of 1904, consistent with the decrees of the Third Plenary Council of Baltimore, Elder appointed a board of examiners with the authority to hold an examination annually and issue credentials to qualified teachers in the eighteen counties of the archdiocese. Vowed women religious, who did the bulk of the teaching in the parochial schools, were now required to upgrade themselves professionally. Because of their many other duties and religious obligations, many had slighted their formal education. In time more and more vowed women religious took college-level courses and some even received their college degrees.[34]

In 1906, to provide greater efficiency in the administration of the parochial schools, Moeller appointed Father Otto B. Auer as the archdiocesan superintendent of schools. The cultural trends of centralization and professionalization, so evident in society at the turn of the century, influenced Catholic educators. The larger urban archdioceses of New York, Philadelphia, and Cincinnati paved the way. Whereas throughout much of the second half of the nineteenth century Catholic schools in Cincinnati were independent of one another, they now had a school board consisting of clergymen and a superintendent to oversee the administration of all the Catholic schools. The *First Annual Report of the Superintendent of the Parish Schools of the Cincinnati Archdiocese*, issued in 1908, showed that there were 110 parochial schools, with an enrollment of 27,233 students. Over 90 percent of the parishes in Cincinnati and over 70 percent of the parishes outside the city had their own elementary schools. Twelve years later there were 123 schools attended by 33,900 students.[35]

In the early 1900s, the cost to educate a student attending parochial school was estimated to be from twelve to seventeen dollars a year, as compared to twenty-four to forty-five dollars in the public school system. The main reasons for the difference in cost were the facts that the sisters, who did the bulk of the teaching, had low salaries and that the few lay teachers were paid less than those in public schools. Moreover, the pastors, who served as principals of their respective parochial schools, received no compensation.[36]

During this period, Auer and the school board also expressed concern over overcrowding in the classroom, which was a common complaint. Inadequate facilities and large class size, which ranged from seventy to one hundred students, supported the perception that the parochial schools were inferior to their public counterparts. They recommended that the class size of any room not exceed fifty.[37]

By the fall of 1908, notwithstanding concerns over facilities and class size, the Cincinnati archdiocese had nevertheless made significant progress in education. It became one of the first dioceses in the country to establish a centralized school system. The archbishop had appointed a diocesan superintendent and a school board and had implemented a system of teacher examinations. In addition, he constructed many new buildings and a number of the schools were tuition free. By the summer of 1920, Moeller ordered that all the parochial schools in the diocese were to open without charge. As a consequence, some people were hopeful that over time there would no longer be Catholic children in public schools.[38]

Because they had their own parochial school system, the local church hierarchy regarded it as "unjust" that Catholics were forced to support the public school system. In fact, Moeller argued that Catholics should receive a share of the Ohio funds for the support of their schools. "The State," he wrote in January 1910, "should give us our share per capita for the children in our schools for their secular education and that we look after the religious part of their education ourselves."[39]

While Catholics demanded a share of Ohio's school fund, there were several attempts by members of the Ohio legislature to impede Catholic education. When, in the spring of 1915, a recommendation was made to provide for the compulsory reading of the Bible in Ohio's public schools, Moeller and his episcopal colleagues in the state opposed the idea. The local church was doubtless pleased with Ohio Governor A. Victor Donahey's veto of the bill. Four years later an Ohio legislator presented a bill requiring parochial schools to conduct all religious instruction outside of the regular school hours, the Catholic hierarchy countered with the argument that there was no evidence religious instruction in the parochial schools interfered with the general education of the pupils. The bill was defeated. In 1923, the U.S. Congress debated bills that would create a federal department of education and grant aid to public schools, Moeller and other church leaders opposed the legislation. They argued that by excluding religious or privately owned schools, the proposed federal aid would only strengthen the public schools.[40]

At the turn of the twentieth century, Catholic secondary education in Cincinnati was still in its infancy. Although the Jesuits, the Sisters of Charity, and the Notre Dame Sisters had secondary schools, the majority of Catholic families did not send their children to school beyond the eighth grade. This was about to change. In response to the need for greater education for a larger number of students, about a dozen parishes in Cincinnati began adding secondary courses to the curriculum of their parochial schools. At the same time, the nineteenth-century pattern of combining secondary and collegiate training in one school, like at St. Xavier College, gradually disappeared. From 1900 to 1950 the modern Catholic high school, though not as extensive as the elementary school, became an integral part of the local church's mission.[41]

Arguing that parochial high schools which served only one parish were impractical, Moeller proposed that Catholics from several parishes pool their resources and build more modern high schools. In the summer of 1909 the pastors and lay Catholics of six parishes in Hamilton, Ohio, northwest of Cincinnati, helped organize a Catholic high school for boys, which became the first central Catholic high school in the archdiocese and in Ohio. For twenty years Notre Dame Academy in Hamilton had been offering secondary education for girls. Until the establishment of the new Catholic high school, placed under the charge of the Brothers of Mary, there were no such opportunities for Catholic boys in the city. The Catholic central high school concept, first established in Philadelphia in 1890, was so successful in Hamilton that the Cincinnati chancery urged Catholics elsewhere in the archdiocese to consider the same.[42]

Intending the central high school to become a model for the diocese, Moeller decreed in 1920 that Catholics in the larger cities should build a central high school for several parishes. At the time, there were over a dozen central Catholic high schools in the country. The following year, pastors representing eleven parishes on the west side of Cincinnati met to plan for a central high school in their area. The new school, dedicated to Archbishop Elder, began its operations a year later. By the middle of the decade there was a second central high school, dedicated to Archbishop Purcell on the east side of Cincinnati.[43]

Elder and Purcell High Schools became free schools in the sense that the expense was paid *pro rata* by the parishes assigned to them. No tuition was collected from the students. Although many Catholic parents did not feel the same sense of urgency to send their children to Catholic high schools as they did to the primary grades, Moeller maintained that they were "even more necessary for the preservation of the faith" of the children than the elementary schools. Both he and Elder also urged Catholic young men and women to attend Catholic colleges, arguing that religion should permeate the education of the children from kindergarten up to the university.[44]

During the episcopates of John Timothy McNicholas (1925-1950) and Karl Joseph Alter (1950-1969) the Cincinnati church attained a new level of institutional growth and became more assertive on social issues and confident of its own Americanism. Both prelates along with other American Catholic leaders from the 1920s through the 1960s attempted to develop a specific Catholic culture and hoped to influence society with their moral values. While promoting Catholicism, McNicholas and Alter also demonstrated great interest in education. They fought against increasing secularization of education from the primary to the university levels, consistently arguing that secularization undermined the moral ends of education.

McNicholas was one of the more influential and preeminent American churchmen of his time, achieving national prominence as spokesperson for such causes as labor and education. He was also regarded as one of the ablest minds among the American hierarchy. McNicholas's leadership and activities in education were widely recognized and resulted in his election as chairman of the Department of Education of the National Catholic Welfare Conference (NCWC) from 1930 to 1935, 1943 to 1945, and as president general of the National Catholic Educational Association (NCEA). He was very much interested in the NCEA, which he headed five times beginning in 1946.[45]

When McNicholas broke ground for a new high school for girls in Dayton, Ohio, in 1926, he emphasized the importance of imparting "a specific moral discipline" that was "spiritualized." As head of the Department of Education of the NCWC in the early 1940s, McNicholas spoke often on the moral bankruptcy of state-supported schools, arguing that their school boards drove religion from the curriculum and prevented the spiritual formation of children. When Ohio extended compulsory education to the high school level in the 1920s, McNicholas, the clergy, vowed religious, and laity responded to the challenge. Catholics demanded that their children be given the same benefits of a religious education on the secondary level as their nineteenth-century counterparts had demanded for elementary schools. To McNicholas and other local church officials, education without religion was unthinkable.[46]

During the second quarter of the twentieth century, Cincinnati Catholics became steadily better educated and more prosperous. This growth was reflected in the increasing number of suburban parishes. While underscoring the importance of religious instruction both at the primary and secondary levels, McNicholas thought that the time was right for the closing of most of the small, mostly two-year parish high schools and for revising Moeller's concept of a centralized school system. After several meetings with the area priests, he inaugurated a plan for a regional Catholic high school system. Instead of two big high schools in Cincinnati, one on the western side and the other on the eastern side, providing for three thousand students each, it was decided to have smaller high schools that would each handle between five hundred and eight hundred students. Each school was to serve a number of parishes and all students of a given parish were to be assigned to a given school. In this manner parishes would have more identification with the respective high schools.

During McNicholas's term, Catholic educators in the Archdiocese of Cincinnati and in other big dioceses encouraged greater professionalization and state certification of Catholic school teachers in order to improve the quality of instruction. In 1927, Ohio imposed more rigid requirements in teacher training. That same year McNicholas urged various teaching orders to discuss the establishment of a teachers' college. Until then, the religious communities and St. Xavier College largely undertook the training of teachers in the Catholic schools. In the spring of 1928, however, the archbishop organized a teachers' college, which provided a teacher preparation program for the teaching communities of sisters, lay teachers, priests, and seminarians. As the archdiocese reorganized and expanded the high school system, the teachers' college focused on the preparation of teachers in the schools.[47]

Continuing a rich local tradition of support for Catholic education, many sacrifices and contributions were made by the vowed religious and the laity in the cause of Catholic secondary education. While the laity expended millions of dollars in the building of the high schools, the religious orders, by teaching in the various schools, relieved the archdiocese of a great financial obligation. McNicholas publicly acknowledged the "extraordinary outlay" made by religious communities, especially by the vowed women religious. Complementing the work of the religious, the parishes largely supported the system of the new free high schools. They assured a high school education to every capable Catholic student. Each parish paid a certain amount for each student from the parish attending one of the high schools. The system for financing and supporting the regional Catholic high schools in the Cincinnati archdiocese attracted national attention.[48]

For over half a century, separate high schools for men and women became the pattern. Women religious taught in the female academies and high schools, and religious brothers and clergy generally taught in the schools for young men. Initially opposed to coeducation at the high school level, McNicholas helped establish separate high schools, with the single exception of the establishment in 1927 of Madonna High School in Cincinnati for black students of both sexes. Shortly before he died in 1950, McNicholas wrote that he had "lost all the inhibitions [he] had about high schools that are coeducational."[49]

During his episcopate, McNicholas anticipated the impossibility of long maintaining the growing Catholic school system without some form of government aid. At the time free to all students, Catholic schools were hurting financially during the economic depression of the 1930s. Fearing that some of the schools might have to be closed, McNicholas asked state legislators for a share of tax revenues.[50]

The local church hierarchy often pointed out that the Catholic parochial school system provided local and state taxpayers an enormous financial saving. One sixth of the children of Ohio were educated in Catholic schools. In 1933, it was estimated that the church in Cincinnati saved taxpayers over $4 million a year for education in Cincinnati alone. It was further argued that if the Catholic and other denominational schools were forced to close because of the Depression, the public schools would be responsible for educating those students. Surely, McNicholas thought, it was in the state's interest to provide "some help." When proposals for tax-based state aid failed in 1935, the archbishop, who by that time had become a national leader in the field of education, proposed a system in which parents would be given money in the form of vouchers that "they could give to the school of their choice for the education of their children."[51]

As resources became scarce during the Depression, the church in Cincinnati was forced to abandon the idea of free Catholic high schools. It required students attending the schools to pay part of the tuition. Due to the continued sacrifices made by parents, parishioners, and the teaching orders, the parochial schools survived the economic crisis. But not all Catholic families could afford to pay tuition. As a consequence, many more students began attending public high schools.[52]

During and after World War II there arose a strong possibility of federal aid to Catholic or religious education. Though American bishops had long opposed federal aid to education, positive experience with government economic relief programs in the 1930s and 1940s helped diminish some of their concerns regarding federal assistance to education. "Federal aid to public schools," McNicholas wrote in the fall of 1944, "is, I think, inevitable." A few months later McNicholas sent a telegram to Ohio U.S. Senator and Cincinnati native Robert Taft, who was a sponsor of a federal education bill that came to be associated with his name. The archbishop thought the aid should be equitable to all children, regardless of color, origin, or creed. Wanting to avoid any conflict between church and state, he urged Catholics and his episcopal colleagues to ask for assistance to all children and not for direct aid for their schools.[53]

During the remainder of his tenure in the 1940s, McNicholas, as head of the NCWC, launched a powerful campaign for public aid to parochial schools. In his lobbying efforts he had several visits with President Harry Truman, whose "friendship he valued highly." The Cincinnati archbishop consistently argued that it was the duty of the federal, state, and local governments to assure the rights of all parents to educate their children in the schools of their choice.[54]

Archbishop Karl Alter carried on McNicholas's fight for Catholic students. In full agreement with his predecessor's July 1947 pastoral that the "Catholic and public schools are partners in American education," a decade later, Alter added that the public and private schools were "parallel and not opposed to each other." Like McNicholas, Alter thought that the best way to secure fair play for all children without violating the First Amendment was not to subsidize the school, "but to provide instead a subsidy for all school children" by means of vouchers. Expressing the sentiments of most Catholics, Alter argued that such social services as bus transportation, health services, lunches, textbooks, and vouchers should be regarded as "civic benefits" and be made available to all children.[55]

When Alter became archbishop in 1950, the church in Cincinnati had twenty-six high schools. The archdiocese had a larger proportion of its Catholic children attending Catholic high schools than any other of the larger dioceses in the United States. Only the dioceses of Nashville and Lansing, both much smaller than that of the Cincinnati archdiocese, had a larger proportion in the schools. Most students from the 150 parochial schools in the archdiocese enrolled in Catholic high schools. While in some areas 30 or 40 percent of grade schoolers were in the parochial schools, more than four of every five children who graduated from them enrolled in a Catholic high school.[56]

One of the early decisions of Alter's administration was the establishment of a thirteen-member board of education to help shape policies for the parish elementary and diocesan high schools. Until 1959, all members of the school board were clergy. In 1959 the board was reorganized and, for the first time, lay persons were added to it. Moreover, by the 1950s, lay teachers in Catholic schools became the norm rather than the exception. Like many Catholic school systems in the country at the time, enrollment in the archdiocesan system grew every year. In 1958, there were over ninety-three thousand students in attendance in the Catholic schools of the archdiocese, from kindergarten to the university level. There were over twenty-nine hundred teachers and of these almost one fourth were lay teachers. "How long," Alter argued, "can we continue to operate our Catholic school system under such conditions?" He pointed out that the financial burden on a parish of the employment of one lay teacher was equivalent to "the services of four sisters."[57]

A study made by the archdiocesan school office in the 1950s projected enrollments of Catholic high schools in the Cincinnati area to increase by about two thirds by the mid-1960s. However, by the year 1955 parish reserves for investment in the high school building program had been exhausted. In a confidential report to the pastors in January 1957, Alter emphasized the need for a fund campaign to expand Catholic high school facilities in Greater Cincinnati. A few days later, the archbishop called upon the faithful to continue the rich tradition of support for education. Though the construction of Catholic elementary schools was the responsibility of the individual parishes, and over five hundred parochial elementary classrooms had been built in the archdiocese in the period 1947 to 1956, building and maintaining high schools was the responsibility, Alter argued, "of the entire Catholic community."

The Cincinnati prelate reminded the parishes, as had Moeller and McNicholas before him, that no one parish had adequate resources to operate a high school. As a consequence, the 1957 campaign collected over $8 million dollars, making it possible for the archdiocese to build three new high schools as well as make substantial additions to three others. By the early 1960s the Archdiocese of Cincinnati was only second to Philadelphia in the number of high school students in ratio to the Catholic population.[58]

In 1962, there were in the Archdiocese of Cincinnati 152 parish elementary schools, 12 private elementary schools, 29 central high schools, and 7 private high schools, for a total enrollment of 94,589 students. Among the teaching staff in the archdiocese, 695 were sisters and members of vowed religious societies; 446 were lay teachers. Over a five-year period, the elementary school enrollment had increased by 14,000, a 23 percent increase. In the fall of 1961, the Chancery Office set a maximum limit of fifty children to a classroom in parochial elementary schools. The average class size the following year was forty-one pupils per class.

In 1963, the total enrollment in the elementary and high schools of the archdiocese went over one hundred thousand students for the first time. It took about 130 years for the diocese to attain an enrollment of fifty thousand students, and only twelve years for the next fifty thousand. "Obviously," Alter argued, "any further growth will have to depend upon some new sources of revenue as well as some new sources of staff recruitment."[59]

In the face of growing school expenses, the archdiocese was in need of more revenue and restructuring. In 1961, the tuition fee in Catholic high schools was raised from $120 to $160 a year. While the parishes continued to pay the high schools $60 a year for each of their students attending the schools, the parents paid the difference. Three years later the members of the Catholic school board, with Alter's approval, established a new program to strengthen the school system. They dropped the first grade in the elementary schools, increased lay teachers' salaries by an annual increment of $100, raised sisters' salaries from $1,000 to $1,500, and increased high school tuition to $200 a year. The elimination of the first grade underscored "the burden we've been carrying all these years," Alter said, "in operating our schools without outside help." Total enrollment in the elementary schools of the archdiocese in 1964 was 68,332 or 8,644 less than in 1963, which was the peak enrollment in the history of the archdiocese.[60]

Whereas in 1964 the national average of Catholic children in parish schools was approximately 50 percent, the ratio in the archdiocese was approximately 75 percent. The percentage in the Catholic high schools was higher than in any other diocese of the country except one.

Notwithstanding the high ratio, more and more Catholic children in Cincinnati attended public schools. In the fall of 1956 the local church had helped organize a Confraternity of Christian Doctrine (CCD) program for Catholic students in the public schools.[61]

In the 1960s, parishes expended 70 percent of all their revenues for education. What made the financial problem in the archdiocese particularly acute were the rising costs of salaries and operation expenses. Whereas at the beginning of Alter's tenure in 1950 lay teachers in the elementary schools comprised less than 12 percent of the total number of teachers, seventeen years later they outnumbered vowed religious in the Cincinnati archdiocese for the first time.[62]

During Alter's nineteen-year episcopacy there were forty-one elementary schools and fourteen high schools built and over fifty elementary schools were enlarged. Parochial school enrollment rose significantly during his tenure, growing from forty-eight thousand in 1950 to over one hundred thousand students in 1963, increasing more than 100 percent. But in the face of an increasing shortage of vowed women and men religious teachers, declining vocations, increasing number of lay teachers, and growing expenses, the school system by the mid-1960s faced substantial financial problems as well as declining enrollment. This posed a significant challenge to the church in Cincinnati. Shortly before the end of his term in 1969, Alter expressed concern over the future of Catholic education. "Only an extraordinarily optimistic person," he said, "would assume that we can grow in the future as we have in the past and solve the problems of meeting the educational needs and demands of our Catholic population."[63]

For about a century and a half, from the time of the founding of the Archdiocese of Cincinnati in 1821 to 1970, vowed religious and lay people worked hard for the betterment of the local church and the community at large. In the process, each generation of Catholics emphasized the importance of Catholic education and invested heavily in it. Committed to transmitting the faith and providing a solid education to each new generation, the Catholic school system is one of the great success stories in the diocese. While that commitment to Catholic education was a source of strength for the local church in the past, it may very well prove to be a continuing source of vitality in the future.

NOTES

1. Roger Fortin, *Faith and Action: A History of the Catholic Archdiocese of Cincinnati, 1821-1996* (Columbus: The Ohio State University Press, 2002), 20, 22.

2. *U.S. Catholic Miscellany* 6:246; *Catholic Telegraph*, March 22, 1883; Sister M. Francoise Vindervoghel to Fenwick, April 28, 1828, Archives of the University of Notre Dame (AUND).

3. Sister Mary Agnes McCann, *The History of Mother Seton's Daughters* (New York: Longmans, Green, 1917), 1:162; Judith Metz, "150 Years of Caring: The Sisters of Charity in Cincinnati," *The Cincinnati Historical Society Bulletin* 37 (1979): 151.

4. Fenwick to P. Pallovicini, March 29, 1825, printed in *Catholic Telegraph*, April 2, 1891; Judith Metz, "The Sisters of Charity in Cincinnati 1829-1852," *Vincentian Heritage* 17 (1996), 208-209.

5. Roger A. Fortin, *To See Great Wonders: A History of Xavier University, 1831-2006* (Scranton, PA: University of Scranton Press, 2006), 7-10. The Athenaeum became the first Catholic institution of higher learning in the Northwest Territory.

6. *Catholic Telegraph*, October 22, 1831; October 26, 1833; July 30, 1885.

7. Fortin, *To See Great Wonders*, 22-24. In 1930 St. Xavier College became known as Xavier University.

8. *Western Spy*, September 5, 1817; *Catholic Telegraph*, February 26, 1891; Fortin, *Faith and Action*, 14-15.

9. Quoted in Joseph M. White, "Religion and Community: Cincinnati Germans 1814-1870" (PhD diss., University of Notre Dame, 1980), 159-160; Jay P. Dolan, *The American Catholic Experience: A History from Colonial Times to the Present* (New York: Doubleday, 1985), 294.

10. *Catholic Telegraph*, April 18, October 3, 10, 1834; October 10, 1840; June 3, 1868; Charles Cist, *Cincinnati in 1841* (Cincinnati, 1841), 37-38; Fortin, *Faith and Action*, 86-90; White, "Religion and Community," 162, 169.

11. *Catholic Directory* (New York, 1883).

12. Anthony H. Deye, "Archbishop John Baptist Purcell, Pre-Civil War Years" (PhD diss., University of Notre Dame, 1959), 189, 191-192; Hughes to Purcell, June 27, 1837, AUND.

13. Quoted in Deye, "Archbishop John Baptist Purcell," 193-198.

14. *Catholic Telegraph*, September 5, December 12, 1840; May 4, 1844; quoted in Deye, "Archbishop John Baptist Purcell," 243-246, 442.

15. *Catholic Telegraph*, November 13, 1852; F. Michael Perko, *A Time to Favor Zion: The Ecology of Religion and School Development on the Urban Frontier, Cincinnati, 1830-1870* (DeKalb, IL: Educational Studies Press, Northern Illinois University, 1988), 129-136.

16. Purcell to Blanc, March 10, 22, 1853, AUND; *Catholic Telegraph*, March 5, 12, 26, 1853; Perko, *A Time to Favor Zion*, 141.

17. Pastoral Letter of the First Provincial Council of Cincinnati to the Clergy and Laity, 1855, Archives of the Archdiocese of Cincinnati (AAC); White, "Religion and Community," 298; Timothy Walch, *Parish School: American Catholic Parochial Education from Colonial Times to the Present* (New York: Crossroad, 1996), 50; Dolan, *The American Catholic Experience*, 264-265, 282; David O'Brien, *Public Catholicism* (New York: Macmillan, 1989), 49, 103.

18. *Catholic Telegraph*, September 28, 1848; February 16, 1856; December 3, 1861; August 24, 1871; Dolan, *The American Catholic Experience*, 264, 282; White, "Religion and Community," 292-293; Charles Cist, *Cincinnati in 1841*, 58-59; Edward A. Connaughton, *A History of Educational Legislation and Administration in the Archdiocese*

of Cincinnati (Washington, DC: The Catholic University of America Press, 1946), 27; Robert S. Michaelsen, *Piety in the Public School* (New York: Macmillan, 1970), 93.

19. *Catholic Telegraph*, April 14, May 19, 1855; April 13, 1861; Connaughton, *A History of Educational Legislation and Administration in the Archdiocese of Cincinnati*, 46, 77; Joseph M. White, *The Diocesan Seminary in the United States: A History from the 1780s to the Present* (Notre Dame, IN: University of Notre Dame Press, 1989), 68; Michaelsen, *Piety in the Public School*, 91.

20. *Catholic Telegraph*, July 2, 1853; May 26, 1855; September 5, 1857; April 24, May 8, June 5, 1858; March 12, 29, 1859; April 13, 27, May 4, 11, 1861; August 16, 1865; February 1, 1872; May 23, 1889; Connaughton, *A History of Educational Legislation and Administration in the Archdiocese of Cincinnati*, 56, 64, 91; White, "Religion and Community," 295-298.

21. Dolan, *The American Catholic Experience*, 268-269; Thomas W. Spalding, *The Premier See: A History of the Archdiocese of Baltimore, 1789-1989* (Baltimore, MD: Johns Hopkins University Press, 1989), 191; White, "Religion and Community," 295-298.

22. *Catholic Telegraph*, November 23, 1837; March 12, May 22, 1859; October 20, 1860; Connaughton, *A History of Educational Legislation and Administration in the Archdiocese of Cincinnati*, 63, 80-87; White, "Religion and Community," 318, 325.

23. Michaelsen, *Piety in the Public School*, 89-97; Perko, *A Time to Favor Zion*, 154-191.

24. Metz, "Sisters of Charity," 231-241; Metz, "150 Years of Caring," 157-161, 163; Mary Ewens, *The Role of the Nun in Nineteenth Century America* (New York, Arno Press, 1978), 105, 120, 123-24, 128-30, 134. Like their sister counterparts in New York, in 1852 the Sisters of Charity of Cincinnati withdrew from the Emmitsburg community in Maryland and formed their own separate community.

25. Brassac to Purcell, February 22, March 10, July 12, 1840, AAC; Nicholas Joseph, Bishop of Namur, to Vicar-General of Cincinnati, April 24, 1840, AUND; *Catholic Almanac* (1840): 95, 98.

26. *Catholic Telegraph*, January 16, 1841; December 9, 1886; October 23, 1890; Connaughton, *A History of Educational Legislation and Administration in the Archdiocese of Cincinnati*, 22; Ewens, *The Role of the Nun in Nineteenth Century America*, 98, 120, 123-124, 134; White, "Religion and Community," 302.

27. Machebeuf to Purcell, September 5, 1844; April 29, 1845, AUND; George C. Stewart, Jr., *Marvels of Charity: History of American Sisters and Nuns* (Huntington, IN: Our Sunday Visitor, 1994), 143; *Catholic Telegraph*, May 23, 1895; July 9, 1931.

28. *Catholic Telegraph*, August 28, November 20, 1858; March 7, 1889; April 9, 1891; July 9, 1931; Margaret R. King, *Memoirs of the Life of Mrs. Sarah Peter* (Cincinnati: R. Clarke & Co., 1889), 2:344-346; Mary Ellen Evans, *The Spirit is Mercy: The Sisters of Mercy in the Archdiocese of Cincinnati, 1858-1958* (Westminster, MD: Newman Press, 1959), 60, 65, 70, 79-82; Ewens, *The Role of the Nun in Nineteenth Century America*, 102; Eileen Mary Brewer, *Nuns and the Education of American Catholic Women, 1860-1920* (Chicago: Loyola University Press, 1987), 27. After the arrivals of the Sisters of Mercy, Cincinnati obtained the services of two other orders of sisters to run parish schools. At Purcell's request Sisters of the Sacred Heart from Paris came to the city in 1869 and opened an academy. In the mid-1870s the Sisters of the Third Order Regular of St. Francis, located in Oldenburg, Indiana, came to teach in a parish school.

29. *Catholic Telegraph*, March 23, 30, 1882.

30. *Catholic Telegraph*, February 16, 23, March 9, 16, 23, 30, 1882; Philip Gleason, *Keeping the Faith: American Catholicism Past and Present* (Notre Dame, IN: University of Notre Dame Press, 1987), 125; Evans, *The Role of the Nun in Nineteenth Century*

America, 253, 259; Gerald P. Fogarty, *The Vatican and the American Hierarchy From 1870 to 1965* (Wilmington, DE: Michael Glazier, 1985), 14, 27; Walch, *Parish School*, 58-59.

31. *Catholic Telegraph*, March 23, 30, August 31, 1882; September 9, 1886; September 8, 1887, August 3, 1893; March 3, 1898; December 24, 1908; June 17, 1915; August 10, 1916; June 5, 1924.

32. *Catholic Telegraph*, January 1, 1885; February 6, 1890; December 1, 1892; August 10, 1893; Elder to McCloskey, November 25, 1892; copy of Meeting of Cincinnati Province, August 31, 1892; Report on Parochial Schools [1892]; copy of Meeting of the Archbishops in New York, November 16, 1892; Moeller to Pastors, September 20, 1923, AAC; Leslie Woodcock Tentler, *Seasons of Grace: A History of the Catholic Archdiocese of Detroit* (Detroit, MI: Wayne State University Press, 1990), 38.

33. *Catholic Telegraph*, March 23, 30, August 31, 1882; September 9, 1886; September 8, 1887; August 3, 1893; March 3, 1898; December 24, 1908; June 17, 1915; August 10, 1916; June 5, 1924; Moeller to Anna Laws, September 4, 1912; Moeller to Mary Frances Dillon, April 5, 1911, AAC; Patrick W. Carey, *The Roman Catholics* (Westport, CT: Greenwood Press, 1993), 51-52.

34. *Catholic Telegraph*, September 10, 1903; July 28, August 25, September 5, 1904; August 29, 1907; January 8, 1925; Moeller to John Hickey, July 10, 1904; Moeller to Rev. J. Cotter, August 14, 1880, AAC; Mary J. Oates, "Organized Volunteerism: The Catholic Sisters in Massachusetts, 1870-1940" in *Women in American Religion*, ed. Janet Wilson James (Philadelphia: University of Pennsylvania Press, 1978), 160; Walch, *Parish School*, 62, 100, 137; Carol K. Coburn and Martha Smith, *Spirited Lives: How Nuns Shaped Catholic Culture and American Life, 1836-1920* (Chapel Hill: University of North Carolina Press, 1999), 9, 151-152.

35. *First Annual Report of Superintendent of Parish Schools in the Archdiocese of Cincinnati, 1907-08*, AAC; *Catholic Directory*, 1920; Connaughton, *A History of Educational Legislation and Administration in the Archdiocese of Cincinnati*, 29; Walch, *Parish School*, 100-101.

36. *Catholic Telegraph*, August 29, 1907; August 27, 1908; June 10, 1909; March 3, 1910; January 4, 1912; July 9, 1914; August 12, 1915; August 1, 1918; *Catholic Directory*, 1920; Moeller's Secretary to W. C. Culkins, December 29, 1914, AAC; Hugh J. Nolan, ed., *Pastoral Letters of the American Hierarchy, 1776-1970* (Huntington, IN: Our Sunday Visitor, 1971), 227; Dolan, *The American Catholic Experience*, 289.

37. *First Annual Report of Superintendent of Parish Schools of the Archdiocese of Cincinnati, 1907-08; Second Report of Superintendent of Parish Schools of the Archdiocese of Cincinnati, 1908-09*, AAC.

38. *Catholic Telegraph*, September 3, 10, 1908; July 9, 1931; Moeller to Rev. J. Cotter, August 14, 1908, AAC.

39. *Catholic Telegraph*, March 30, 1882; November 27, 1884; February 5, 12, October 1, 1885; February 17, 1887; February 4, 1892; April 6, August 3, 1889; June 14, 1900; December 24, 1908; August 1, 1918; Gilmour to Elder, March 21, 26, 1885; Moeller to R. W. Rives, January 29, 1910, AAC.

40. *Catholic Telegraph*, April 8, 30, May 7, 1925; January 30, March 6, 1919; Moeller to Bishop John Farrelly of Cleveland, April 1, 1915; Moeller to Henry Ott, March 15, 1915; Moeller to William R. Collins, April 28, 1915, AAC; John Tracy Ellis, *The Life of James Cardinal Gibbons, Archbishop of Baltimore, 1834-1921* (Milwaukee, WI: Bruce, 1952), 2:543-544.

41. Connaughton, *A History of Educational Legislation and Administration in the Archdiocese of Cincinnati*, 129-130; Tentler, *Seasons of Grace*, 94.

42. Moeller to Rev. G. Meyer, August 3, 1909, AAC; Connaughton, *A History of Educational Legislation and Administration in the Archdiocese of Cincinnati*, 133-134; Tentler, *Seasons of Grace*, 250.

43. Moeller to Rev. J. H. Schengber, December 21, 1921, AAC; *Catholic Telegraph*, October 25, 1923; August 28, 1942; Connaughton, *A History of Educational Legislation and Administration in the Archdiocese of Cincinnati*, 126, 135-136. In 1924 the diocese established St. Rita School for the Deaf, which was the first Catholic high school for the deaf in the United States.

44. Moeller to Joseph Berning, May 22, 1913; Moeller to Rev. William P. O'Connor, December 30, 1921; Moeller to Rev. D. A. Buckley, September 2, 1923; Moeller to Rev. George J. Mayerhoefer, January 6, 1924; Moeller to Rev. P. J. Hunes, July 19, 1924; Moeller to Rev. Henry Brinkmeyer, December 26, 1924, AAC; *Catholic Telegraph*, March 21, 1895; September 12, 1907; November 7, 1912; July 17, November 20, 1924; Connaughton, *A History of Educational Legislation and Administration in the Archdiocese of Cincinnati*, 138; James H. Campbell, "New Parochialism: Change and Conflict in the Archdiocese of Cincinnati, 1878-1925" (PhD diss., University of Cincinnati, 1981), 320-321; Tentler, *Seasons of Grace*, 257.

45. *Cincinnati Times-Star*, April 24, 1950; Fogarty, *The Vatican and the American Hierarchy*, 348; Carey, *The Roman Catholics*, 83; Dolan, *The American Catholic Experience*, 52.

46. *Catholic Telegraph*, September 10, 1925; September 2, 1926; August 18, 1937; June 9, 1944; July 10, 1953; Gleason, *Keeping the Faith*, 168-69.

47. *Catholic Telegraph*, June 17, November 18, 1920; August 2, 1928; July 9, 1931; June 22, 1933; August 28, 1942; Minutes of Meeting on Central Normal School Problems, March 31, 1927; McNicholas to Pastors, July 30, 1928; McNicholas to Hubert Brockman, S.J., July 9, 1927; *NCEA Bulletin*, February 1931; Agreement between Archbishop Moeller and the Society of Jesus (n.d.); Moeller to James McCabe, S.J., June 1, 1920, AAC; Walch, *Parish School*, 142-145.

48. McNicholas to Archbishop Ritter, September 7, 1946, AAC; *Catholic Telegraph*, September 20, 1928; June 16, 1950; January 19, 1951; January 13, October 5, 1956; *Cincinnati Enquirer*, April 23, 1950.

49. *Catholic Telegraph*, September 29, 1927; June 16, 1950; January 19, 1951; January 13, October 5, 1956; *Cincinnati Enquirer*, April 23, 1950. In 1951, St. Joseph's Academy, founded in 1915 by the Sisters of St. Joseph, became McNicholas High School, then the only coeducational high school in the archdiocese.

50. *Catholic Telegraph*, May 8, 1930.

51. Ibid., February 4, June 6, November 21, 1935.

52. McNicholas, "School and Tax Reform," August 31, 1937, AAC. The parents or guardians of each student now had to pay forty dollars a year and the parish to which the student belonged paid an additional forty dollars.

53. McNicholas to Cicognani, October 30, 1944; McNicholas to Taft, June 28, 1946; McNicholas to Spellman, August 14, 1947, AAC; *Catholic Telegraph*, April 6, February 16, 1945; July 5, 1946; March 26, 1948; March 24, November 24, 1961; *Cincinnati Enquirer*, July 8, 1946; July 6, 1947; Robert Wuthnow, *The Restructuring of American Religion: Society and Faith Since World War II* (Princeton, NJ: Princeton University Press, 1988), 73; Fogarty, *The Vatican and the American Hierarchy*, 368.

54. McNicholas to Cicognani, September 2, 1945; McNicholas Radio Broadcast, July 7, 1946; McNicholas to President Truman, January 2, 1948, AAC; *Cincinnati Enquirer*, June 8, July 8, 1946.

55. *Catholic Telegraph*, July 11, 1946; April 13, 1956; September 26, October 5,

1958; *Cincinnati Enquirer*, May 24, 1954; May 14, 1957; February 9, 1962; *Cincinnati Times-Star*, September 22, 1950; December 19, 1952; July 6, 1950.

56. McNicholas to Ritter, September 7, 1946, AAC; *Catholic Telegraph*, June 16, 1950; January 19, 1951; January 13, October 5, 1956; *Cincinnati Times-Star*, April 24, 1950.

57. Alter to Mother Mary Anselm, January 26, 1959; Alter Pastoral, September 9, 1959; Clergy Bulletin, September 9, 1958, AAC; *Catholic Telegraph*, February 21, 1958; August 14, November 13, 1959.

58. Alter to Clergy, September 14, 1955; Confidential Report to Pastors, January 7, 1957; Alter Pastoral, April 3, 1957; Alter to Mother Helen, O.S.U., February 4, 1960, AAC; *Catholic Telegraph*, January 13, October 5, 1956; April 12, 26, 1957; January 24, 1958; January 8, December 7, 1965.

59. Profile 1962—Catholic Education in the Archdiocese of Cincinnati; Alter to Ryan, December 13, 1963, AAC; *Cincinnati Enquirer*, February 9, 1962.

60. Alter to Rev. John A. Elbert, November 18, 1957; Alter to Rev. James M. Darby, May 19, 1960; Clergy Bulletin, April 1, 1964, AAC; *Catholic Telegraph*, May 19, July 20, 1951; March 6, 13, December 11, 1964; March 26, 1966.

61. *Catholic Telegraph*, February 21, 1941. In 1938 McNicholas had appointed a priest to organize and direct such a religious program, but it was short lived. Three years later, however, the first regular religious instruction in school hours for Catholics in public high schools in Cincinnati began at one of the schools.

62. *Catholic Telegraph*, December 2, 1966; January 20, February 3, October 19, 1967.

63. *The Cincinnati Post & Times-Star*, July 23, 1969; *Catholic Telegraph*, October 5, 1967.

Gateway City Catholicism:
Catholic Education in St. Louis

John T. James

Catholic education in St. Louis was not a response to the cultural hostility to the Catholic faith that was so common in New York, Boston, and Philadelphia. In St. Louis, Catholic education arose as the fruit of visionary and missionary-minded European clerics whose work made possible settlements along the Mississippi River that in turn made possible the foundation of the city. St. Louis emerged as a community of African Americans, French, Native Americans, Spanish, Irish, and later Germans who found their way to the city that served as the gateway to the West.

Jesuit missionaries played a significant role in the exploration of the region and the foundation of the first settlements that became the City of St. Louis. The first Europeans known to have set foot in Missouri included trader Louis Jolliet and Jesuit priest Jacques Marquette in 1673.[1] Father Jean Francois Buisson de St. Cosme, another Jesuit missionary, said the first Mass on the site that would become St. Louis in 1698.[2]

In the Fall of 1700, Jesuit Father Gabriel Marest, accompanied a band of Kaskaskia Indians, crossed the Mississippi River just within the present southern city limits of St. Louis, and founded the Des Peres settlement. That settlement included several cabins, a chapel, and a primitive fort, but was abandoned in 1703 when Marest and the Kaskaskians moved to the east bank of the Mississippi and founded the settlement of Kaskaskia. It was the Kaskaskians who later crossed the Mississippi and founded Ste. Genevieve, the first permanent settlement in Missouri.[3]

The establishment of St. Louis was the last great act of the King of France in North America. In an attempt to revive a sagging post-war economy, French officials in Louisiana granted Gilbert Antoine Maxent, a New Orleans merchant, the exclusive right to trade with the Indians west of the Mississippi.[4] In 1763, Pierre Laclede, a junior partner of Maxent, agreed to establish and supervise a trading post in Upper Louisiana.

The Treaty of Paris (1763) gave the territory east of the Mississippi to England, while the secret Treaty of Fontainebleau (1762) gave the land west of the Mississippi to the Spanish. The former played heavily in the decision of Laclede to choose a site for the post on the west bank of the Mississippi. Laclede was successful in inducing many French families, cognizant of the ill-treatment of the French Acadians in Nova Scotia at the hands of the British, to cross from their villages on the east bank to the new village named "Saint Louis."[5]

In its early days, St. Louis was a frontier village without the continuous presence of a resident pastor. Priests were in short supply because of the suppression of the Jesuits by the pope in 1763 and the juridical conflict and confusion resulting from the ceding of the Louisiana territory from France, to Spain, and then to the United States.

This conflict and confusion significantly impeded the development of Catholicism in St. Louis. In 1766, Father Sebastian Meurin (a former Jesuit) visited St. Louis and performed four baptisms "in a tent for want of a church."[6] Father Pierre Gibault, a Canadian priest residing in Illinois territory, dedicated a church that was finally built in 1770 on the plot laid out by Laclede. Father Valentine, the chaplain of the small Spanish garrison, performed priestly duties in St. Louis from 1772 until 1775, before Father Bernard de Limpach, a German-born Capuchin, became the first pastor of St. Louis in 1776.

As a testament to the multicultural milieu of St. Louis at that time, de Limpach baptized "410 white people, 106 Negroes, and 92 Indians." A number of priests served the St. Louis area after 1788 including Father Pierre Joseph Didier, Father Joseph Dunand, and Father James Maxwell, the pastor of Ste. Genevieve. Maxwell reported on the church in St. Louis in 1796: "Not only is it too small for the village, but its timbers are rotted and it cannot be kept from falling into ruins."[7]

The Louisiana territory was transferred back to France at the turn of the nineteenth century and then sold to the United States in 1803. After the sale, parishes no longer received governmental support for their churches and pastors. The sorry state of the church in St. Louis was confirmed in 1814 by Bishop Benedict Flaget, the bishop of Bardstown, who reported in his journal, "This congregation is in a state of extreme indifferentism: my sojourn here will be almost useless."[8]

Flaget's assessment of St. Louis was not all bad; he also saw great potential. In a letter to Archbishop Leonard Neale in 1816, he reported: "If the Holy Father were to send a Jesuit as a bishop and give him five or six companions, I do not entertain the least doubt, but in less than twenty years it would be the most flourishing diocese in the United States."[9]

The fifty-five-year period from the foundation of St. Louis in 1763 to the arrival of its first bishop in 1818 was not without attempts at Catholic education. "Although an occasional priest conducted classes for parish children, the few schools were private and generally in operation for only short periods of time."[10] It is probable that Didier taught the young during his five years in St. Louis (1794-1799).

A group of St. Louis merchants petitioned Governor Francisco Luis Hector Carondelet in 1792 to have Didier assigned to St. Louis for among other reasons: "the accommodation which we would have of instructing our children under our very eyes without sending them abroad for that purpose which would always be costly to us." While there is no reference to him having taught in St. Louis, "among the books in the inventory of his property in 1799 was an unidentified quantity of 'livros de Escuela.'"[11]

Three nuns who had accompanied the Delassus de Luzieres family to Ste. Genevieve in 1794 had plans for opening a school for girls, but were dissuaded from doing so by Carondelet in view of the uncertain times. In 1796, a priest in New Madrid asked the government to build and help support a school, but there is no record of any action taken on this initiative. Jean Baptiste Truteau operated a school in St. Louis intermittently between 1774 and 1827, but he left it for the more financially rewarding fur trade business.[12]

The greatest Catholic educational accomplishment of this fifty-five-year period by a religious was that of Maxwell, the pastor of Ste. Genevieve from 1796-1814. Born in Ireland, Maxwell studied at the Irish College of the University of Salamanca in Spain and spoke both English and Spanish. He had grand plans for building settlements in the Louisiana territory as a refuge for Irish Catholics "from the British tyranny and persecution to which they [were] exposed on account of their religion."[13]

In July 1807, he organized a corporate board and compiled a list of subscribers to fund what was to become the Ste. Genevieve Academy. The academy offered instruction in French and English, and secured a charter from the territorial legislature. Maxwell intended to educate indigent and Native American children at no charge; unfortunately, the academy closed in 1814 due to Maxwell's untimely death and the growing debt of the school.[14]

The arrival of Bishop Louis W. DuBourg in 1818 marked the substantive beginning of Catholic education in St. Louis. DuBourg, an educator himself, recognized the importance of Catholic education and had ample experience in opening and running schools. He had been the first president of Georgetown College in 1796, founded St. Mary's College in 1799, and persuaded Elizabeth Seton to open a school for young girls in Emmitsburg.[15] Archbishop John Carroll appointed DuBourg administrator apostolic of the Province of Louisiana in 1812, and after DuBourg set things in order in New Orleans, he traveled to Rome where he was consecrated in 1815.

While in Europe, DuBourg recruited missionary workers for his new diocese:

> Posters were placed throughout the dioceses of France with this unlikely promise: "We offer you: no salary, no recompense, no holidays, no pension. But hard work, a poor dwelling, few consolations, many disappointments, frequent sickness, a violent or lonely death, an unknown grave." And they came. They came because Jesus Christ was at the heart of it and was alive in them.[16]

He recruited over fifty priests, vowed religious, and lay assistants, including Father Felix de Andreis and Father Joseph Rosati (Vincentians), Sister (later Saint) Phillipine Duchesne and four Sisters of the Sacred Heart, and three Christian Brothers (Brothers Antonin, Aubin, and Fulgence), all of whom initiated the educational ministry of their respective orders in the United States.[17]

Among the first actions taken by DuBourg were educational initiatives. Duchesne and her companions arrived in St. Louis in August 1818 and were directed by DuBourg to open a school for girls in St. Charles, Missouri.[18] Among their enterprises were a tuition-based school and the first free girls' school west of the Mississippi.[19] The schools were later moved to Florissant, Missouri.

On November 16, 1818, Father Francois Niel and three other priests opened a boys' academy that would become Saint Louis University. The academy offered classes in Latin, English, French, arithmetic, mathematics, and geography all for twelve dollars a quarter, payable in advance.[20]

A seminary was opened in two places, one in St. Louis in conjunction with Saint Louis Academy under the direction of de Andreis, and the other was established in Perryville under the direction of Rosati. The early settlers of Perryville were English-speaking Catholics who had fled the religious persecutions in Maryland. Their religious fervor and promise of support moved DuBourg to establish a portion of the seminary there.[21] After finishing their study of the English language in 1819, the three Christian Brothers were dispatched to teach at Ste. Genevieve Academy.[22]

When Saint Louis Academy opened in 1818, it accepted students of all faiths. This was a continuation of a policy that DuBourg had instituted when he opened St. Mary's College in Baltimore, but was nevertheless a truly ecumenical concept for the times. Niel took over the leadership of Saint Louis College in 1820 upon the death of de Andreis, and in 1823 hired the first prominent educator of another faith to teach at the college. In 1823, the population of St. Louis was approaching four thousand, and its citizens voted to incorporate as a city. Since there was no public school or library, the city agreed to pay Niel to educate poor boys at Saint Louis College. The school was turned over to Father Edmund Saulnier in 1824, enabling Niel to travel to Europe to solicit funds.[23]

In 1820, DuBourg was visited by a number of chiefs of the Osage Indians who requested that he send a "black robe" to their villages. In 1823, DuBourg, with the help of some funds from the War Department, enticed two Jesuit priests, three brothers, and seven novices (including Pierre Jean DeSmet) to come to St. Louis to work among the Indians. The Jesuits opened St. Regis Indian Seminary in May 1824 in Florissant, Missouri; it would become a training ground for Jesuit missionary activities throughout the entire Louisiana territory. DuBourg had large plans for the Jesuits; he wanted them to not only carry out missionary work, but to staff Saint Louis College, and administer a parish in St. Louis as well.[24]

In 1823, Pope Pius VII named Rosati, then the director of the Seminary, as the coadjutor bishop for DuBourg. Rosati served as coadjutor for three years until the diocese was split and Rosati took hold of the portion of the original diocese not selected by DuBourg. Later that year, DuBourg invited thirteen Sisters of Loretto to begin a school for girls in Perryville.[25] They eventually opened schools in Ste. Genevieve, Fredericktown, Cape Girardeau, and Perryville.[26] DuBourg returned to France in 1826 and submitted his resignation, leaving the entire diocese to Rosati.

Clearly, DuBourg left an educational legacy in St. Louis. As one biographer put it: "He was endowed with an invincible gift for setting things in motion."[27] He was responsible for starting the first Vincentian mission and educational initiatives in the United States (the seminary and college in Perryville); the first educational enterprise of the Christian Brothers in the United States (Ste. Genevieve Academy), and the foundations of the Sisters of the Sacred Heart (St. Charles) and the Sisters of Loretto (Perryville). He reenlisted the Jesuits to perform missionary work throughout the vast territory and saw the foundation of a Jesuit seminary in Florissant. He began an institution (Saint Louis Academy) that was eventually handed over to the Jesuits to run that would become Saint Louis University, the first institution of higher learning west of the Mississippi.

Rosati saw the rapid growth of the state of Missouri. The Land Act of 1820 offered settlers eighty-acre tracts at $1.75 per acre, a program that resulted in a doubling of the population in Missouri between 1820 and 1830.[28] In 1825, the upper portion of the Louisiana diocese had fifteen parishes or missions with only half having a resident priest; the remainder received a priest two, three, or four times a year.[29] Undaunted, Rosati enticed the Sisters of Charity to open the first hospital west of the Mississippi and brought Mother Duchesne and the Sisters of the Sacred Heart to open an orphanage and school for orphans along with a school for wealthy girls that collectively educated nearly one hundred students.[30]

In 1832, Rosati invited the Sisters of the Visitation to open a school in Kaskaskia, Illinois, on the eastern side of the Mississippi. Mother Agnes Brent and her eight companions arrived on May 3, 1833. Rosati arranged for the workmen at Perryville to build permanent quarters for the sisters, and two prominent citizens—William Morrison and Pierre Menard—provided funds to pay for their lodging and furniture.[31] The Sisters of the Visitation opened their academy in the Fall of 1833 and by 1837 had fifty-seven girl boarders, twelve day students and eleven orphans.[32] In 1844, the Mississippi overflowed its banks and destroyed the school, which led the sisters to move their convent and educational endeavors to St. Louis.

Rosati successfully persuaded the Sisters of Saint Joseph (Josephites) to begin their educational enterprise in the United States. In 1835, Rosati requested that a "Father Cholleton," a member of the Society for the Propagation of the Faith, secure for him some sisters willing to direct an institute for the deaf that Rosati had hoped to establish in conjunction with the United States government.[33] Cholleton convinced Mother Saint John Fontbonne to assign several Sisters of Saint Joseph to come to St. Louis and for two sisters to learn the methods of deaf education.

He likewise secured funding from Countess de la Rochejacquelin for their journey to St. Louis. Six Sisters of Saint Joseph arrived in St. Louis in March 1836 along with their spiritual advisor, Father James Fontbonne. Three sisters traveled to Cahokia, Illinois, and established a school there with an enrollment of thirty students,[34] while three others went to Carondelet in September of 1836 and opened a school in a small log cabin that by October included two orphan students.[35] The city of Carondelet subsidized the education of local girls until the opening of a public school in 1851.[36] The two sisters trained in deaf education, Sisters Celestine Pommerel and Julie Fournier, arrived in St. Louis in 1837 and began classes for four deaf girls. In February 1839, the Missouri legislature granted funds for the annual tuition of the students in the school which lasted until the opening of a state school eleven years later.[37]

By 1840, St. Louis had a population of 16,469 which was three times the total in the city just ten years earlier. One half, if not more of this population, was Catholic and mostly of French and Irish descent; "very few German Catholics having thus far reached the city of which they were afterwards destined to form so very large and creditable a portion of the population."[38]

The growth of the diocese led to the false impression that it had no need for continued support from the missionary societies; consequently, Rosati left for Europe in 1840 to address this false impression. He was greeted amiably by Pope Gregory XVI and was appointed to succeed Bishop John England in negotiations with Haiti. Rosati accepted the pontiff's appointment on the condition that he also appoint Father Peter Kenrick, the vicar-general of Philadelphia, as his co-adjutor bishop.[39]

Easter 1843 marked the opening of St. Francis Xavier Church by the Jesuits who delivered their sermons entirely in English. The Sisters of Charity conducted a school for girls called St. Vincent DePaul's Free School which was the first parish school for girls in St. Louis. Although opened in 1843 with only 130 students,[40] the school had 280 students by 1845. In addition to the free school, the sisters opened a tuition school that helped defray the cost of the free school. Four Jesuit scholastics also began a school for boys in 1843 in the basement of St. Francis Xavier Church. The Jesuits also opened a school a year later exclusively for boys of German descent.[41]

Three significant observations regarding Catholic education in St. Louis could be drawn to this point. The first observation is that Catholic education began literally and figuratively on the frontiers of St. Louis. Catholic schools, Catholic education for Native Americans, the deaf, and the poor and orphans preceded the public school by several years. In subsequent years, Catholic education for African Americans, immigrants, and students with special needs moved ahead of the establishment and found itself again on the frontiers.

The second observation is the consequent reliance of all three levels of government (city, state, and federal) on Catholic educators to assist in educational initiatives: the federal government's subsidizing of Native American education by the Jesuits at Florissant, the city government's funding of education for poor boys at Saint Louis College and of girls in Carondelet, and the state government's funding of deaf education delivered by the Sisters of Saint Joseph are evidence of this dependence by the state on the educational initiatives of the Church.[42]

The third observation is the desire for universal access to Catholic education for people of all means. "Thus from the beginning of parochial education in Saint Louis, the better-off assisted the schooling of the poorer families on a within-the-parish level."[43]

Our Lady of Victories Church (southeast) and St. Patrick's Church (northeast) were opened in 1843, while the cornerstones of St. Vincent DePaul's Church (southwest) and St. Joseph's Church (northwest) were laid in 1844. By 1844, Kenrick had eliminated all debt except for sixteen thousand dollars, and he appealed to the Leopoldine Association for help with concentration on the German-speaking Catholics. On May 25, 1845, Kenrick announced the division of the city into four parishes: the Cathedral, St. Francis Xavier, St. Patrick's, and St. Vincent's. The two churches serving German populations, Our Lady of Victories and St. Joseph's, were to be subsidiary churches of the Cathedral parish and of the St. Patrick's and St. Vincent's parishes respectively.[44] The surrounding St. Louis County had five churches.

The Sisters of Saint Joseph, like the Visitation Sisters, left their educational ministry in Illinois after the flood of 1844 and concentrated their efforts in St. Louis. Three sisters opened a parish school at the new St. Vincent DePaul parish at the request of the pastor.

Under the direction of Fr. Augustus Paris, three Sisters of Saint Joseph also opened a school for African American girls in a brick building on February 5, 1845. While most of the girls were free, some were slave children whose masters wanted them to be able to read and write. "The curriculum included the 'three R's', French, sewing, and catechism lessons from Fr. Benedict Roux twice a week. Paris showed continued interest by regular visits to the school, and took a personal concern in the improvement of 'his children.'"[45]

The school soon enrolled over one hundred students.[46] Bishop Edward Barron, the vicar apostolic of the American Negro Colony of Liberia in West Africa, in the company of Bishop Kenrick, visited the school in 1845. A mob threatened the school, and the school was closed in 1846 under pressure from civil authorities. In 1847, the state legislature outlawed the teaching of reading and writing to African Americans.[47] Undeterred, the Sisters of Saint Joseph opened a school for African American girls at St. Vincent's in 1853 that lasted until the third year of the Civil War.[48]

Two events in the late 1840s in Europe had a profound impact on the growth of St. Louis. The potato famine in Ireland in the late 1840s led to a surge in Irish immigration to St. Louis. The other event was the civil unrest in Germany that led to the immigration of a large number of northern, anti-clerical, liberal-minded Germans to America, the so-called "Forty-Eighters."

The German Catholics faced hostility from their fellow "free-thinking countrymen because they were Catholic, and from Irish and French immigrants because they were German."[49] Consequently, the St. Louis German Catholics adopted a defensive position:

> They built their own schools, kept their own language, and started their own mutual benefit associations such as the "Saint Louis Society." Alone in a strange world, they withdrew into a citadel of German Catholicism in the heart of the American Midwest.[50]

In 1847, the St. Louis diocese was raised to the level of an archdiocese. By 1850, the city population approached eighty thousand, nearly five times the population just ten years earlier, and boasted of ten Catholic churches all within eighteen blocks of the river.[51] At the invitation of Kenrick, three Christian Brothers arrived in St. Louis in 1849 and took charge of the Cathedral school. They were joined a few months later by nine more Christian Brothers.

The Christian Brothers established a branch academy on the north side called St. Patrick's, and over the years were to take on parochial schools in a number of predominantly English-speaking parishes populated by people of Irish descent: St. Francis Xavier's (1850-1854), St. Patrick's (1851-1853), Saints Mary and Joseph (1858-1888), St. John's (1862-1892), St. Lawrence O'Toole's (1863-1899), Saints Peter and Paul (1866-1870), Annunciation (1868-1893), St. Bridget's (1868-1911), St. Michael's (1870-1872), and St. Malachy's. "With these establishments, the Christian Brothers merited the distinction of being the founders of the parochial school system in the St. Louis Irish community."[52]

Father Joseph Melcher, a native of Vienna, was named vicar-general for the German-speaking Catholics and after his appointment, he returned to Europe to secure priests and religious for the rapidly growing German population. Melcher welcomed a small group of Austrian Ursuline sisters to St. Louis on September 25, 1848, and they opened a school on November 2. Six more Ursuline sisters arrived in May 1849 along with nearly one thousand dollars in donations; additional funds over the next seventeen years would come from the King of Bavaria and the Ludwigs-Verein Association of Munich.[53] A convent southwest of the cathedral was built for them and they opened an academy and boarding school.

The Ursulines were so successful in the next ten years that St. Louis became their base as they established other communities throughout the Midwest and even New York.[54] Melcher also successfully recruited two priests of particular note: Father Francis Goller and Father Henry Muehlsiepen.

Jesuit Father Arnold Damen, the pastor of St. Francis Xavier, requested Sisters of Mercy from the convent in New York City, and at the invitation of Kenrick, six Mercy Sisters arrived in St. Louis on June 27, 1856. In August 1856, they opened St. Patrick's parish free school. They lived in near destitution, taking in laundry and sewing to support themselves, but with the support of Kenrick and local

Catholics, they were able to move into St. Joseph's Convent of Mercy and devote their full energy to their mission activities.[55]

At the request of Jesuit Father Joseph Patschowski, the School Sisters of Notre Dame arrived in St. Louis in 1858 to conduct parish schools in place of the Sisters of Charity whose services were needed elsewhere.[56] On May 1, 1858, the School Sisters of Notre Dame opened St. Joseph's parochial school.[57] The following year they opened schools at Saints Peter and Paul, St. Liborius, and St. Lawrence O'Toole.[58] Goller, the pastor of Saints Peter and Paul, who had persuaded three sisters to teach three hundred pupils at the parish school,[59] also tried to establish a German-speaking order of religious brothers called Jesu Schulbruder to teach in the parochial schools.[60] The School Sisters of Notre Dame taught a large number of the German-speaking students in the parish schools, just as the Christian Brothers taught the English-speaking Irish in their parish schools.

> In a few years, the Notre Dames, along with lay teachers, taught four hundred pupils at St. Mary's parish school, one thousand pupils at Sts. Peter and Paul's parochial school, one thousand at St. Joseph's school, four hundred at St. Liborius school, and about the same number at Holy Trinity. St. John Nepomuk's school [Bohemian] had two hundred pupils. The total number of pupils under the direction of the School Sisters of Notre Dame and their lay associates in the German and Bohemian schools went over three thousand—two thirds of the children in parochial schools in the city.[61]

St. Louis doubled in population every decade between 1820 and 1870.[62] By 1870, St. Louis was the fourth largest city in the United States with a population of 310,864, surpassed only by New York, Philadelphia, and Brooklyn. Once again, a significant event in Europe would shape the growth of St. Louis and its Catholic schools. The *Kulturkampf*—the political struggle for the rights and self-government of the Catholic Church in Germany—raged in the 1870s and for some time afterwards between the Catholic populace and the Church on the one side and an alliance of liberals and conservative Protestants on the other. This conflict fueled further emigration to the United States including several hundreds of thousands of German-speaking immigrants to the Midwest.

Increasing German immigration necessitated more parishes, more parish schools, and more religious to staff them. St. Boniface serves as an example of the foundation of many German Catholic parishes in the city:

The basic features of Saint Boniface's establishment and development characterized many other parishes: A small group of immigrants formed a congregation, often splitting off from a larger community for ethnic reasons; added to their own meager resources the contributions of sympathetic parties; imported professional help from newly established seminaries or even from the homeland; and established a school either concurrent with the erection of a church or, quite often, preceding it. The motto ... was "The school first, then the Church."[63]

This motto represents a consistent theme found in about forty parish histories written to commemorate the fiftieth, seventy-fifth, or one-hundredth anniversaries of St. Louis parishes.[64]

The pioneer German churches soon spawned three new churches: St. Nicholas, St. Francis de Sales, and St. Agatha. Melcher, the vicar-general for the German-speaking Catholics, was appointed the bishop of Green Bay in 1868 and was replaced by Muehlsiepen, who supported the development of more German-speaking churches that would open in the ensuing years: Perpetual Help, St. Augustine, St. Bernard, and Holy Ghost.

In 1870, twenty-one Sisters of the Most Precious Blood accepted the school at St. Agatha in St. Louis and two other out-of-state parish schools.[65] Three years later, forty-nine sisters fleeing the *Kulturkampf,* came to St. Louis through the action of Muehlsiepen. A group of German Franciscan Sisters came to St. Louis in the Fall of 1872 at the invitation of Father Ernst A. Schindel, the pastor of St. Boniface's Church to take charge of a hospital that subsequently burnt down.[66] By 1891, Franciscan Sisters had charge of several parish schools.

Some of the religious orders that had been in St. Louis since the early days were expanding and moving west. In 1862 the Sisters of Loretto opened St. Mary's Academy and in 1874 they opened Loretto Academy. In 1873, the Christian Brothers moved their college from the Rider Mansion to a new campus that offered boarding facilities. In 1887, the Visitation Sisters moved their convent and academy that they had staffed since 1858 further west.[67] While other vowed religious orders were moving further west, the Sisters of Saint Joseph, who had earlier begun a school for African American girls in 1845, expanded their efforts in the city.

During the last quarter of the nineteenth century, under the leadership of Mother Agatha, the Sisters of St. Joseph staffed 16 more schools in St.

Louis. Sister Adele Hennessey, Supervisor of Schools for the Josephites, directed the preparation of a School Manual that prescribed a course of study, introduced new teachers to classroom techniques, set methods of teaching various disciplines and formulated a general plan for conducting schools.[68]

The Sisters of Saint Joseph continued to staff numerous parish schools throughout the city, and by 1891 were the most numerous in the archdiocese.[69]

In 1873, Saint Elizabeth's Church was dedicated as the city-wide parish for African Americans. In 1880, the Oblate Sisters of Providence, an African American order of religious sisters, came to St. Louis from Baltimore and taught fifty African American children in the parish school. When St. Elizabeth's Church moved west, the sisters remained and were joined in 1914 by the Sisters of the Blessed Sacrament—founded by Mother Katharine Drexel—who opened a two-room school in the old rectory enrolling 125 children.[70]

The Reverend William Greenleaf Eliot, a leading social reformer and minister at The Messiah Unitarian Church, was elected as president of the public school board in 1848. He found the public schools to be in poor condition and subsequently determined to improve them by hiring better teachers from New England and by securing additional funding by changing Missouri laws so that local public school districts could levy a tax on property.[71] Prior sources of revenue came from tuition and leases on land owned by the district.

This plan unleashed a bitter exchange over the legitimacy of the tax, the sectarian nature of the public schools, and the method of disbursement of funds. "A Friend of Untrammeled Education" argued that if money be raised, Catholic schools must receive a substantial share since they were educating more children than the public schools. He argued that "Catholic children attending the public schools, at present, are obliged to do so from necessity, and not from choice, and are therefore trammeled in their religious beliefs."[72] He further contended that Catholic schoolchildren were exposed to false prejudices and ideas taught by Protestant teachers under a sectarian hue, a natural consequence of the inability to separate religion and education.

Eliot responded with a series of lengthy letters noting that the schools were not prejudicial toward Catholics, that about a third of the board, "several" teachers, and many students (including a majority in some schools) were Catholics. He argued that the presence of Catholics at all these levels along with the presence of Mormons, Jews, Protestants, and even unbelievers precluded anti-Catholic bias and ensured a vigorous non-sectarian education.[73]

> Eliot's celebration of the neutrality of the schools showed that he did not appreciate a crucial aspect of the criticism. Because he was committed to the principle that public schools could foster social amalgamation, he readily accepted the absence of any formal religious teaching. This was a plausible position for a Unitarian minister; it was impossible for parents concerned with protecting their cultural and religious traditions.[74]

Prior to 1850, Catholic schools educated more students in St. Louis than the public schools. From 1850 onward, both public and Catholic school systems grew, but the public school system grew at a faster rate aided significantly by state and local funding. In 1850, Catholic schools educated 49.1 percent of the student population; by 1860 it had dropped to 36.5 percent, by 1870 to 27.7 percent, and in 1880 to 19.4 percent. Eliot proudly commented, "there is scarcely any place left in the school room, where God, or Christ, or the soul's responsibility is required to be spoken of."[75]

In 1870, Dr. Charles Smythe, a Catholic physician and state legislator, proposed a voucher plan that would provide ten dollars per child to be applied to any school that the state approved. The bill passed its first reading in the legislature before an opposing delegation of St. Louis legislators "pointed out how the bill would destroy public education" under slogans such as "A State without a Bishop and a Church without a King." Consequently, "the legislators from the largely Protestant areas outside Saint Louis joined with those city representatives sympathetic to the board in defeating Smythe's proposal."[76]

Catholic schools were also operating much more inexpensively than their public school counterparts. For example, the per pupil cost of education for Saints Peter and Paul parish school in 1908 was $8.64 per student. The school contained 1,203 pupils, with two Brothers of Mary at a salary of $375 each, and twenty-three Sisters of Notre Dame at $300 each. By contrast, the per pupil cost to educate students in the St. Louis public schools that same year was $22.76.[77]

As in other cities, the public schools in St. Louis were criticized by Catholics as being partial to Protestantism, discriminating against Catholics in hiring practices, and teaching a morality not in accord with Catholic beliefs. The vast differences between Catholic and public schools were quite evident in the profile of the teachers that worked in the respective systems. A child in public school was almost certain to have a native-born teacher who had completed normal school training, while students in the Catholic parochial schools were very likely to have foreign-born teachers who were professed members of religious orders. In 1880, 45.4 percent of the teachers in Catholic schools were foreign born in contrast to only 10.5 percent in the public schools. Furthermore, 36.4 percent of the teachers in Catholic schools came from Ireland or Germany, while only 7.3 percent of the teachers in public schools came from those two countries.[78]

The "foreign" character of Catholic education, the growth of German-speaking churches, the presence of a vicar-general for German-speaking parishes (Muehlsiepen), and his leadership role in the German American priests' society all fueled a larger controversy for the American episcopacy at the end of the nineteenth century over the purpose of Catholic schools and the identity of Catholicism in America. It is noteworthy that during this period, and against extreme challenges from within and from without, the Catholic schools forged ahead going "on the frontiers" in serving the poor, the immigrants, and African Americans without state funding.

The year 1904 was of seminal importance for St. Louis. In addition to hosting a world's fair and the Olympics, St. Louis also hosted the birth of the Catholic Educational Association. At the July meeting, Father James Burns presented the findings of the joint committee on high schools. The report found that there were two high schools for every one Catholic college; this stood in stark contrast to twelve public high schools for every college. Burns suggested that a Catholic high school ought to be built in every city to which all parishes would contribute both financially and morally under the leadership of the bishop. "Finally he advised that these be free schools, that parishes rather than individuals of the parish should support them, and that it would be desirable to engage a teaching community of religious to ease the financial problem."[79]

Archbishop John J. Glennon was at the meeting, took an active role in the discussion, and pointed out the necessity of the bishop's leadership: "Except the Bishop takes the lead, the priests would hardly come together of their own 'proprio motu' and build a high school."[80] Glennon, who had succeeded Archbishop John Joseph Kain a year earlier, felt the need for Catholic high schools quite acutely. St. Louis public high school enrollment had skyrocketed from 1,993 in 1900 to 4,487 in 1904, assisted largely through the construction of two new high schools: Yeatman and McKinley.[81]

The Catholic high schools in St. Louis at the time were either extensions of the grade school (a year or two at most), were tuition-driven academies, or were appendages of Catholic colleges with no distinct separation. In 1910, Glennon named Father Aloysius Garthoeffner to the newly created office of superintendent of schools and appointed a committee including Garthoeffner to investigate the need for high schools.[82]

The committee's report published in October 1911 found that while the lower grades of the parochial schools were well attended, the upper grades were not; a result of an exodus in the seventh and eighth grade in preparation for the free public high schools. Garthoeffner concluded: "If we can not finish the work once begun in our Catholic schools, our system is, in great measure, a failure." On September 5, 1911, a total of 125 ninth graders began high school at three centers: Kenrick High, taught by the Marianists at Saints Peter and Paul; Kain High, taught by the Sisters of Saint Joseph at St. Teresa School; and Rosati High, taught by the Sisters of Notre Dame at St. Francis De Sales.[83] Glennon was quite pleased with the development of the Catholic high schools and letters of congratulations came in from around the country.

The development of the Catholic high school was not without its detractors, both lay and religious. The primary source of the concern was financial. An anonymous priest was quoted as saying,

> Most of the Catholic churches of Saint Louis have large debts, and the support of the parish schools weigh heavily on them. If Catholics give to the high schools, they will have just so much less to give to their own parish needs.[122]

Other concerns included a fear of socialism, the high-handed manner of implementation of the plan, the need for trade schools rather than high schools, and the thought that Catholic education was a reckless extravagance.[85]

The Catholic high schools were created as tuition-free schools and were therefore funded through contributions and donated equipment. However, in February 1914, Glennon effectively levied a 2 percent tax on parish revenue to support the Catholic high schools:

It has been said that two percent of the net revenue of the parishes would be ample to continue these Catholic high schools. As you have given and are expected to give your care and the support of the parish to the parish school, it is not, I think asking too much that you should give a modicum to the High Schools, which are in reality a part and complement of your parish school.[86]

A letter from Garthoeffner, also in 1914, insisted that the schools were not free, nor should they be called "free" schools since the parents were making contributions. By 1939, the funding of the high schools came equally from the parents and parishes. The March minutes of the High School Association announced that each student would be required to pay twenty dollars annually and that each parish would be assessed twenty dollars for each student.[87]

Glennon expressed continued support of the high schools and acknowledged the need for new buildings. A campaign was initiated on the occasion of the archbishop's silver episcopal anniversary in 1921 that raised $250,000 to be used for educational purposes. An additional $250,000 was donated by Mrs. Katherine McBride from the estate of her late husband.[88] These gifts funded the construction of Rosati-Kain High School and McBride High School, formerly known as Kenrick High School and later to be known as South Side Catholic, respectively.

In 1937, Saint Joseph High School was established for African American students in a building formerly used as an orphanage for African American children. It was the first coeducational Catholic high school in St. Louis, and the first accredited four-year African American high school in Missouri.[89] North Side Catholic High School was opened in 1942.

By 1944, it was clear that additional high schools were necessary. Glennon invited every pastor and two laymen from every parish to a meeting on September 20, 1944, in the Cathedral School Auditorium. He pledged one million dollars that had accumulated from bequests and the generosity of the priests and people of St. Louis over the years, and that an additional million dollars was to be raised in a capital campaign to build three or four Catholic high schools after the war.[90] By October, plans were made for a house-by-house canvass in solicitation of pledges to kick off the full campaign on November 1.

The need for schools was real; only 989 of the 3,493 children who had graduated from Catholic grade schools the previous year went on to inter-parochial Catholic high schools. Even if half the students had entered the private Catholic high schools, at least 45 percent of the Catholic school graduates were attending public schools.[91] A full 628 students in the Fall of 1944 were denied admission due to a lack of space.[92]

The archbishop spoke on the radio, issued a pastoral letter in support of the campaign, and 128 parishes enlisted seven thousand parish workers for the actual door-to-door canvassing campaign.[93] While the campaign was a success, Glennon did not see the building of the high schools. On Christmas Eve 1945, Glennon was raised to the rank of cardinal and died on March 9, 1946 en route back from the consistory. Instead of celebrating his triumphant return, St. Louis prepared for the death of their shepherd.

While some archdiocesan parochial high schools in St. Louis had been admitting both African American and white students since 1937, integrated Catholic education was not the norm. For a number of years prior, St. Joseph's teams had played teams from McBride, Saint Louis University High, and the Christian Brothers high school, even though the Missouri State Athletic Association did not sanction such games. In 1943, the Catholic league invited St. Joseph to join, and since the Missouri High School Athletic Association presumably was unaware of the racial status of St. Joseph, approved the application and unwittingly sanctioned integrated athletics in Missouri.[94] In 1944, Saint Louis University became the first university in a former slave state to admit African Americans.

These events had obvious ripple effects on the Catholic grade schools. St. Bernadette's diocesan school had opened in 1942 in the old St. Elizabeth's property and soon was overcrowded. Father John Smith, the assistant at Visitation parish and head of the parish school, moved St. Bernadette's into unoccupied classrooms at the Visitation parish school. As a result, the Sisters of Loretto taught white students on the south side of the building, the Maryknoll sisters taught African American students on the north side of the building, and Father Patrick Malloy oversaw an integrated free lunch and recreation program. In 1946, plans were underway to integrate the seventh and eighth grades. Next, the directors gave the African American children in grades one through six the choice to attend either St. Bernadette's school or Visitation. Only one white family protested, and Glennon expressed satisfaction with what Smith had done when he celebrated the Sacrament of Confirmation in the Spring of 1945.[95]

Joseph E. Ritter became archbishop of St. Louis in 1946 after the death of Glennon. In the early part of the summer of 1947, the archdiocesan director of high schools, confronting the overcrowded conditions at St. Joseph's High School, asked whether these African American students might be admitted to other existing high schools. Ritter responded that he had no right to refuse admittance to any diocesan high school student provided the applicant was able to fulfill the scholastic requirements. Independent of this, the pastor of the largest parochial grade school in St. Louis, where integration had been the practice, suggested that pupils living outside the parish boundaries return to their own respective parish schools.[96]

Ritter's approval of these proposals raised questions about the integration of Catholic schools across the archdiocese. As bishop of Indianapolis, Ritter had previously issued a ruling that African American Catholics be admitted to schools on the same basis as whites; he implemented the same policy in St. Louis on August 25, 1947.[97] After the issuance of the letter, Ritter conveniently made himself unavailable to those who wished to discuss the policy with him.[98]

The decision did not receive universal approval. A meeting to discuss the issue was held on September 14.[99] The *Saint Louis Star Times* reported that "a group estimated at more than 700 persons voted last night to retain legal counsel and, if necessary, bring legal action to remove those Negro children now in the schools and to prevent the enrollment of others."[100] The meeting had representation from forty-three parishes.

Ritter responded with a letter that was read at all Masses the following Sunday. He acknowledged that "a small group of individuals have signified their purpose of taking civil action to restrain us from carrying out a policy which we consider our right and duty as chief pastor of the faithful of this Archdiocese." He then reminded the faithful of "the equality of every soul before almighty God" and threatened to excommunicate any individual or group of individuals who "presume (that is, after full knowledge) to interfere in the administrative office of their Bishop by having recourse to any authority outside the Church."[101] The letter, for all practical purposes, ended the debate. The full integration of Catholic schools in St. Louis preceded the *Brown v. Board of Education* decision by seven years.

The Department of Special Education was born out of the vision of Monsignor Elmer Behrmann who, in the pursuit of his doctoral studies at Saint Louis University, recognized that the needs of exceptional children were not being adequately met in either Catholic or public schools. In June 1950, Behrmann pitched his concept of providing special education for mentally handicapped students in archdiocesan facilities to Ritter. "The Archbishop asked why the archdiocese should do this and Behrmann immediately replied, 'On the basis of social justice'; The Archbishop walked away without a word."[102]

At 8:00 a.m., Behrmann received a personal call from the archbishop, summoning him to the chancery. Behrmann feared the worst when Ritter stated in a stern voice: "Young man, you kept me awake all night. When you used the words, 'social justice' yesterday afternoon, I wrestled all night with my conscience and could not wait for morning to come so I could talk to you."[103]

The archbishop pledged his full support to the endeavor. News quickly spread among parents and friends that special education was to become available and many requests for evaluations ensued.[104] This led to the rapid growth of classes for students with special needs in a large number of parish schools. Behrmann's vision of appropriate education for all children in Catholic schools preceded PL 94-142 that mandated free appropriate public education for all children by twenty-five years.

In 1959, inspired by the writings of Father Virgil Blum of Marquette University, a group of St. Louisians consisting of Martin and Mae Duggan, Vincent Corley, James Bick, and others formed the Citizens for Educational Freedom. Within three years, one hundred fifty chapters of Citizens for Educational Freedom existed in twenty states. David LaDriere, a St. Louis lawyer who served as the full-time executive secretary stated in 1963:

> Unless the current trend is halted, all except the children of the wealthy will end up in state institutions. This will be done in the name of democracy and in the name of church-state separation. We will have accomplished by economic means what the Supreme Court has prohibited.[105]

Much progress has been made in other states on this issue through the use of vouchers and tax-credits that have made parental choice in education more of a reality. This sadly is not the case in Missouri, a state shackled with the Blaine Amendment whose pedigree is tied deeply to the larger anti-Catholic bigotry of the nineteenth century.

On December 16, 1960, Ritter became a cardinal. He opened three new churches every year of his tenure in St. Louis. Forty-five new parish schools were opened during these years, and the Catholic school population doubled.[106] This rapid growth put so much strain on the system that in 1962 Ritter placed a moratorium on building schools until pastors could organize schools with forty-nine or fewer students per classroom and a ratio of three vowed religious for every one lay teacher.[107] By then the seventh largest archdiocesan Catholic school enrollment in the nation, the Archdiocese of St. Louis led the nation in the percentage of Catholics with children in Catholic schools.

The Archdiocese of St. Louis has a strong and rich tradition of Catholic education. This tradition was built upon a vision of mission-driven leaders who proactively went to the frontiers and supplied Catholic education to populations in need, even in the face of extreme difficulties. This tradition was fueled and sustained by the efforts of countless leaders who solicited funds and human capital from multiple sources and represented a proactive response to the growing needs of the community, and particularly the dire needs of the poor, the orphaned, Native Americans, the deaf, the immigrants, African Americans, and those children with special needs.

Finally, it is this success, proactive response, and contribution to the common good that drew government aid from the city, state, and federal levels in the early years. Even today Catholic education in St. Louis engages and serves Catholics and the wider community, cognizant that its mission lies on the frontiers but at the heart of the Church's evangelical mission.

NOTES

1. William E. Foley, *The Genesis of Missouri: From Wilderness Outpost to Statehood* (Columbia: University of Missouri Press, 1989), 1.

2. L.P. Kellogg, *Early Narratives of the Northwest, 1634-1699* (New York: Charles Scribner's Sons, 1917), 337-361, http://www.americanjourneys.org/aj-055/summary/index.asp

3. Foley, *The Genesis of Missouri*, 6-7, 25.

4. Ibid., 26.

5. William Barnaby Faherty, S.J., *Dream by the River: Two Centuries of Saint Louis Catholicism 1766-1997* (St. Louis: Archdiocese of St. Louis, 1997), 2.

6. Ibid., 3.

7. Ibid., 4, 7.

8. Ibid., 15.

9. Ibid., 17.

10. Foley, *The Genesis of Missouri*, 111.

11. John Francis McDermott, S.J., "Education in St. Louis before 1818," in *Philip-*

pine Duchesne and Her Times, ed. Harriet Lane Cates Hardaway and Dorothy Garesche Holland (St. Louis: Maryville College, 1968), 47.

12. Foley, *The Genesis of Missouri,* 112, 111.

13. W. A. Schroeder, *Opening of the Ozarks: A Historical Geography of Missouri's Ste. Genevieve District 1760-1830* (Columbia: University of Missouri Press, 2002), 351.

14. Foley, *The Genesis of Missouri,* 279-280.

15. Annabelle M. Melville, *Louis William DuBourg: Bishop of Louisiana and the Floridas, Bishop of Montauban, and Archbishop of Besancon 1766-1833* (Chicago: Loyola University Press, 1986), 174-175.

16. Archbishop Edwin O'Brien, "Undaunted Missionary Spirit," homily delivered on April 13, 2008, commemorating the bicentennial of the Archdiocese of Baltimore, http://www.archbalt.org/archbishop/homilies-talks/homilies-talks-item.cfm?customel_datapageid_2039=35983

17. Faherty, *Dream by the River,* 16-32.

18. Ibid., 21-22.

19. George R. Brooks, "St. Louis in 1818," in *Philippine Duchesne and Her Times,* ed. Harriet Lane Cates Hardaway and Dorothy Garesche Holland (St. Louis: Maryville College, 1968), 14.

20. Faherty, *Dream by the River,* 22.

21. Joseph Gummersbach, *The Life of Felix De Andreis, C.M.* (St. Louis: Becktold Printing, 1900), 208-209.

22. Faherty, *Dream by the River,* 22.

23. Ibid., 23, 26.

24. Ibid., 23, 27, 27-79.

25. Ibid., 28.

26. William Barnaby Faherty S.J., Sr. Elizabeth Kolmer A.P.S., Sr. Dolorita Marie Dougherty C.S.J, and Rev. Edward J. Sudekum, *From One Generation to the Next—160 years of Catholic Education in Saint Louis* (St. Louis: Archdiocese of St. Louis Catholic School Office, 1978), 3-4.

27. Melville, *Louis William DuBourg,* 165.

28. Faherty, *Dream by the River,* 34.

29. Frederick John Easterly, *The Life of Right Reverend Joseph Rosati, C.M.: First Bishop of Saint Louis, 1789-1843* (Washington, DC: The Catholic University of America, 1942), 80.

30. Faherty, *Dream by the River,* 36-38.

31. Ibid., 42.

32. Easterly, *The Life of Right Reverend Joseph Rosati, C.M.,* 149-150.

33. Faherty, *Dream by the River,* 51.

34. Ibid, 51-52.

35. William Walsh, *Life of Most Reverend Peter Richard Kenrick D.D., Archbishop of Saint Louis* (St. Louis: Catholic Publishing Company, 1891), 44.

36. Faherty et al., *From One Generation to the Next,* 4-5.

37. Faherty, *Dream by the River,* 52.

38. Walsh, *Life of Most Reverend Peter Richard Kenrick* (St. Louis: Catholic Publishing Company, 1891), 13.

39. Easterly, *The Life of Right Reverend Joseph Rosati,* 161, 164-166.

40. Faherty et al., *From One Generation to the Next,* 10.

41. Faherty, *Dream by the River,* 69.

42. Faherty et al., *From One Generation to the Next,* 5.

43. Ibid.

44. Faherty, *Dream by the River*, 70.

45. Ibid., 71.

46. Faherty et al., *From One Generation to the Next*, 10.

47. Faherty, *Dream by the River*, 71.

48. Faherty et al., *From One Generation to the Next*, 10.

49. Faherty, *Dream by the River*, 76.

50. Ibid.

51. Ibid., 80.

52. Ibid., 79.

53. Ibid, 72, 77.

54. Selwyn K. Troen, *The Public and the Schools: Shaping the St. Louis System, 1838-1920* (Columbia: University of Missouri Press, 1975), 37-38.

55. Faherty, *Dream by the River*, 84.

56. Ibid.

57. Walsh, *Life of Most Reverend Peter Richard Kenrick*, 46.

58. Ibid.

59. Faherty, *Dream by the River*, 84.

60. Faherty et al., *From One Generation to the Next*, 10.

61. Faherty, *Dream by the River*, 84-85.

62. Troen, *The Public and the Schools*, 48.

63. Ibid., 37.

64. Ibid.

65. Faherty et al., *From One Generation to the Next*, 12.

66. Faherty, *Dream by the River*, 106.

67. Ibid., 104.

68. Faherty et al., *From One Generation to the Next*, 15.

69. Walsh, *Life of Most Reverend Peter Richard Kenrick*, 44.

70. Faherty, *Dream by the River*, 106, 155.

71. Troen, *The Public and the Schools*, 41.

72. Ibid.

73. Ibid., 42.

74. Ibid.

75. Ibid., 34, 44.

76. Ibid., 45.

77. James A. Burns, *Growth and Development of the Catholic School System in the United States* (New York: Benzinger Brothers, 1912), 291.

78. Troen, *The Public and the Schools*, 40, 38, 39.

79. Mary Arthur Kolmer, "Cardinal Glennon: His Contribution to Catholic Secondary School Education in Saint Louis" (master's thesis, Saint Louis University, 1962), 26, 27.

80. Ibid.

81. Ibid., 17.

82. Faherty, *Dream by the River*, 150.

83. Kolmer, "Cardinal Glennon," 30, 34, 42.

84. Ibid., 38-39.

85. Ibid., 38-40.

86. Ibid., 58.

87. Ibid., 59, 60.

88. Ibid., 62, 64.

89. Faherty, *Dream by the River*, 176.

90. Ibid., 181.

91. Ibid.

92. Kolmer, "Cardinal Glennon," 76.

93. Ibid., 71-75.

94. Faherty, *Dream by the River*, 176-177.

95. Ibid., 180-181.

96. "St. Louis Chancery Reviews History of School Controversy," *Denver Register,* September 25, 1947, Archives of the Archdiocese of St. Louis (AASL), RG1F15.1a.

97. Ibid.

98. "Go Write Your Little Letters," *Saint Louis Post Dispatch*, June 22, 1997, 3c.

99. "No Discrimination," *The New York Times,* September 28, 1947, AASL, RG1F15.1a.

100. "Catholic Group Votes To Retain Counsel in Row Over Negroes," *Saint Louis Star Times,* September 5, 1947, AASL, RG1F15.1a.

101. Archbishop Joseph E. Ritter, "Pastoral Letter," September 20, 1947, AASL, RG1F15.1a.

102. Elmer H. Behrmann, *The History of the Department of Special Education, Archdiocese of Saint Louis* (St. Louis: Archdiocese of St. Louis, 2001), 2-3.

103. Ibid., 3.

104. Ibid., 10.

105. Faherty, *Dream by the River*, 200-201.

106. Ibid., 213, 201.

107. Timothy Walch, *Parish School: American Parochial Education from Colonial Times to the Present* (New York: Crossroad, 1996), 176.

Shrine of Sacred Heart School, Baltimore, 1955
*(Courtesy: Catholic Review Collection, Archives of the Archdiocese of Baltimore,
Associated Archives at St. Mary's Seminary & University)*

Upper Grades, St. Philip of Jesus School, San Antonio, circa 1940
(Courtesy: Archives of the Sisters of Charity of the Incarnate Word, San Antonio)

St. Patrick's Academy, San Antonio, 1942-43

(Courtesy: Archives of the Sisters of Charity of the Incarnate Word, San Antonio)

Summer School Class, St. Benedict the Moor School, Detroit, circa 1940 (*Courtesy: Archives of the Archdiocese of Detroit*)

Saint Paul's High School, Santa Fe Springs, California, circa 1958
(Courtesy: Archives of the Archdiocese of Los Angeles)

St. Cajetan School, Chicago, 1957 *(Courtesy: John C. O'Malley)*

Graduation Class, Our Lady of the Angels School, Bronx, 1944
(Courtesy: Archives of the Archdiocese of New York)

Academy Mt. St. Joseph, Cincinnati, 1920
(Courtesy: Archives of the Sisters of Charity of Cincinnati)

Commercial Typing Room, St. Monica's School, Philadelphia, 1947
(Courtesy: Archives of the Archdiocese of Philadelphia.
Reprinted by permission of Our Sunday Visitor)

St. Luke's Combination Church and School, Thibodaux, Louisiana, 1924
(Courtesy: Archives of the Archdiocese of New Orleans)

Monsignor James Brown, Superintendent of Catholic Education, blesses
courtyard statue at Archbishop Riordan High School in San Francisco
(Courtesy: Archives of the Archdiocese of San Francisco)

Graduation Class, Transfiguration School, New York City, 1892
(Courtesy: Archives of the Archdiocese of New York)

St. Peter Claver School, Baltimore, 1947

(*Courtesy: Catholic Review Collection, Archives of the Archdiocese of Baltimore, Associated Archives at St. Mary's Seminary & University*)

Second Grade, St. Joseph Orphanage, Cincinnati, 1922
(Courtesy: *Archives of the Sisters of Charity of Cincinnati*)

St. Roch School, St. Louis, circa early 1900s
(Courtesy: Sisters of St. Joseph of Carondelet, St. Louis Province Archives)

St. Francis Xavier School for the Deaf, Baltimore, 1937
*(Courtesy: Catholic Review Collection, Archives of the Archdiocese of Baltimore,
Associated Archives at St. Mary's Seminary & University)*

Grade One with Sister Simeon Kinsella, St. Andrew Parish School,
Forest Hills (Boston), 1952-53 *(Courtesy: Boston CSJ Archives)*

Eucharistic Congress, Mass of the Angels at Soldier Field, Chicago, 1926
(Courtesy: The University of Saint Mary of the Lake/Mundelein Seminary)

St. Anthony School for Girls, St. Louis, 1900
(Courtesy: Sisters of St. Joseph of Carondelet, St. Louis Province Archives)

Sister of Mercy Sister Mary St. John leads the kindergarten singers at
Our Lady of the Angels Parish, Burlingame, California, 1955
(Courtesy: Archives of the Archdiocese of San Francisco)

Motor City Catholicism:
Catholic Education in Detroit

JoEllen McNergney Vinyard

Detroit Catholics decided that public education was not the place for their children just a few years after the first school buildings opened. Once the board of education announced it would hire Protestant teachers who would use the King James Bible in their classrooms, all hope for common ground in common schools was abandoned. Age-old religious conflicts were magnified by mid-nineteenth century disagreements about the role of education in a democracy. A local Catholic newspaper editor made his people's case. Think, he begged, of the Irish immigrant who had left his native land with "heart, half broken" yet comforted that "In America I shall be free! and my children will grow up free to practice their faith, and prosecute their fortune!"[1] That immigrant knew the importance of education when it came to prosecuting one's fortune in America. He also believed that in America his children would not be subjected to Protestants or their Bible. But Catholics soon learned it was not a time for compromise; there was no chance their children's religion might receive equal treatment. Irish, German, and French Catholics went their separate ways—away from the public schools and apart from each other, too. They went despite a dire Protestant prediction that such action would cause "the young Irish and the young Germans, to be set apart . . . an outside and alien element."[2] The generations of Catholics who followed in their wake neither turned back nor regretted decisions made in the pivotal years of the 1850s.

Over the following decades as wave after wave of new Catholic immigrants arrived, realistic bishops permitted established patterns to be replicated. Bible reading in public schools faded as an issue but the role education played became ever more significant and more "Americanizing." Catholics persevered. Immigrants opted for schools that taught children their parents' faith and heritage; the more assimilated second and third generation Catholics developed schools they deemed superior to any other, public or private. This translated into dozens upon dozens of separate ethnic parishes with grade schools, many topped by high schools. In Detroit, these schools continually attracted a more impressive share of Catholic children than nearly any other city in America.

Catholics first staked claim to Detroit when Antoine Cadillac and his party of French settlers arrived on the Detroit River banks in July 1701, and the earliest base for local education was in their Ste. Anne's Church. As Yankee migrants began to trickle in after the American Revolution, Protestant and Catholic children sometimes studied together with a hired tutor, in a dame school, or in an elite-at-the-time academy. The first scheme to systematize education in Detroit reflected the peculiar mix of people who collected in this little frontier community after the War of 1812. To encourage settlement, the Territorial Legislature approved Catholepistemiad, a plan for education from the lowest grade through college. It was remarkable not only for its vision but because it was the collaborative dream of a handful of respected leaders that included Father Gabriel Richard, priest at Ste. Anne's, Reverend John Monteith, pastor of the First Protestant Society, and Lewis Cass, territorial governor and a staunch Mason. The original act made no mention at all of religion, but a subsequent act declared that no person, from president to professor to pupil, was to be refused "for his conscientious persuasion in matter of religion."[3] Only a rudimentary version of the plan materialized but the capstone University of Michigan took form in 1817 in Detroit. The president was Monteith and the vice president was Richard.

Cheap land and improved transportation made Michigan the fastest growing place in the country in the 1830s and with the influx of settlers from New York and New England, residents began to sort their children into schools with a religious foundation. A public system of education continued to enjoy the intellectual support of leaders, Catholics and Protestants, Democrats and Whigs. They all favored schools like the Irish immigrant anticipated when he set sail, schools that offered Michigan children of whatever religion the chance to grow up economically competitive, to emerge steeped in an appreciation for the democratic institutions of the nation. The chance came when Michigan became a state in 1837 with a constitution that emphasized public education and laid out innovative plans for promoting it.

The country's founding fathers provided that profits from the sale of one section of land in each township in the Northwest Territory should go toward funding public education there. More innovative than neighboring states, Michigan's first constitution established a pooled primary school fund that would be under state control. Money would be parceled out to school districts based on their number of students. It also introduced the position of superintendent of public instruction, an official charged with overseeing education statewide. Without dwelling too much on the future, most Detroiters seemed to expect private school initiatives to continue alongside tax-funded common schools, anticipating some democratic compromise to accommodate religious differences. When the Detroit Board of Education organized in 1842, its members sensibly agreed that the Bible would be excluded as a school book because the Protestant and Catholic population, "nearly equal in numbers," could not otherwise be brought "to unite in the same system and place their children under the same regulations."[4] Even as they launched this hopeful public school venture, population changes were making easy compromises less likely than before.

The population of Detroit more than doubled between 1840 and 1850, reaching 21,019 residents. Irish and German immigrants arrived alongside the Protestants who flooded in from New England and New York, all of them staking out a place in this new home and intending to preserve the values they came with. Many of the Yankee Protestants who arrived during this 1840s wave were ardent evangelicals with enthusiasm for all manner of reforms from abolition to temperance to Sunday schools. They regarded public education as the means to safeguard democracy and transmit moral precepts. Most of the Irish and about 40 percent of the Germans were Catholic and their ethnic parishes and schools began to multiply just at the same time the board of education began building neighborhood public schools. Catholics were paying less attention to school board elections than their Protestant neighbors since many of their children were studying in parish classrooms or Catholic-taught free schools. Before the decade ended, zealous Protestants had elected board members who established Bible reading in public schools.[5]

A new state constitution adopted in 1850 gave more power to voters, by then concerned about bonded indebtedness for internal improvements and spending in general. The state superintendent of public instruction was one of several positions now to be filled by election rather than appointed by the governor. Given the growing political influence of towns and farms where Protestants dominated, from 1850 to 1881 every superintendent was a Protestant, born either in New England or New York.[6] Superintendent Ira Mayhew, one of the first, set the tone for his successors. Public schools, Mayhew explained to the state legislature, were the province of Protestants and rightly so; children educated in "Romanist" schools clung to the "superstitions and absurdities of their fathers." Bible reading in public schools was necessary and proper because, after all, Papists, Jews, and Mohammedans taught their religion to their children, so "why should not Protestants do the same?"[7] The state legislature, an overwhelmingly Protestant body, heartily agreed.

Such aims for public education were championed from the pulpit by Reverend George Duffield, minister of Detroit's Presbyterian Church from 1836 to 1868, and his son, D. Bethune Duffield, a lawyer and school board member. On the other side of the religious divide was Bishop Peter Paul Lefevere, a Belgian immigrant who arrived to head the Detroit diocese just a few months before the first public schools opened. Lefevere's personality, conception of duty, and concern to exercise authority made him less cooperative in local affairs than his predecessors who had worked alongside Protestant leaders. One of the bishops who came for Lefevere's consecration in the fall of 1842 was John Hughes, at the time engaged in the highly publicized struggle over control and financing of education in New York. Lefevere agreed with Hughes's notions that public schools presented dangers and would lead to loss of faith among Catholics. He proceeded to promote the separate Catholic schools already underway and he cast about for the financial means to add more. Like Hughes, he was certain that tax support for Catholic schools was fair and just.

The school board was pressing for more tax dollars for public schools, schools already staffed with Protestant teachers who used the King James Bible. Ordinary Catholics were not necessarily attentive to the words of state superintendents or to debates over theology's finer points, but they understood the warning signs of state control and un-just taxation. Many had come across the ocean to avoid it. Now, in this new homeland, they found themselves paying taxes for schools that chose not to teach their language, appreciate their culture, acknowl-edge their religion, or hire their daughters. Surely, part of the promise of America was fair treatment. Education became the lightning rod in a volatile climate already charged with emotion over abolition, temper-ance, immigration, taxes, and power struggles.

The "school question" exploded in the public arena in January 1853 when a vocal contingent of Catholics joined Lefevere to petition the state legislature. They asked to change the Michigan school law so that tax money equivalent to that used in free public primary schools could be given to qualified teachers in any Catholic primary school taught in English. They pointed especially to Article IV, Section 31 of the state constitution: "The Legislature shall not diminish or enlarge the civil or political rights, privileges and capacities of any person, on account of his opinion or belief concerning matters of religion."[8] Reverend Duffield immediately articulated a position that would resurface in every subse-quent effort to fund Catholic schools: Such a plan to promote Catholic schools was designed by a "Romish priesthood" acting "in obedience to . . . a foreign despotic sovereign," with the object of "subversion of the free system of schools" where children gained "independence of mind" in keeping with a Republic.[9]

With an almost naïve faith in the justice of their cause, the bishop and allies in his cause paid no attention to political reality. Detroit in-deed had a sizable Catholic population, almost equal in number to the Protestants, but in the legislature only about three or four of the 104 members were Catholics. Legislators acted within two weeks, refus-ing to change school financing because to do so "would interrupt the prosperity and progress of primary schools . . . and would introduce confusion and discord in place of harmony and peace, and materi-ally affect the interests of the rising generation."[10] Determined to be vindicated, the bishop and the most ardent of his supporters immedi-ately turned their efforts toward electing "friendly" Democrats to the Detroit city council and school board with the expectation that they would divide—or divert—tax dollars so parochial schools would have their due share.

The bishop's intrusion into Detroit ward politics was not only fool-hardy but ill-timed. In the 1853 spring ward caucuses, the Democratic

Party's fragile Yankee-ethnic coalition cracked when some disgusted Democrats split from the Regular ticket with its Catholic slate; they put together an Independent slate. Nativists were energized; delighted Whigs threw their support to the Independent ticket. The "Regular" Democrats won only in the Irish-dominated eighth ward. Once the "school question" unleashed religious concerns, virulent anti-Catholics pulled along enough moderates to give them disproportionate power. Over the next two years, Catholics learned firsthand what a hostile city council and school board meant; the city charter was changed to provide for taxing the Catholic hospital, orphan asylum, and church lots along paving routes. Favoritism toward Protestants grew apace. A quiet agreement among parents in the eighth ward public school had enabled Catholic children to study upstairs with a Catholic teacher and Protestants downstairs with a Protestant teacher. Now, however, the school board president demanded twenty-five Catholic children be sent down, a number of Protestant students up, and the Catholic teacher was forced to resign.

Throughout this troubled time, conditions that contributed to nativists' popularity and Catholics' fears in other cities did not have the same chronic grip in Detroit. Given the long Catholic presence, many families were among the "better off" and established residents. In this small city, the rate of immigration was moderate, jobs were plentiful, and land was available; even newcomers and working-class residents could often afford single family homes. Protestants and Catholics had their separate churches but they lived and worked among one another. "Irish need not apply" signs were uncommon and local Protestants had been recently generous in sending relief to Irish potato famine victims. Between 1853 and 1856 when the issue of tax dollars for parochial schools impacted every local election, there were alarmist warnings but no riots in the streets, no houses stoned. The "school question" rather than the "school war" was an appropriate term for the dispute in Detroit, bitter as feelings were.

Lefevere veered to a new course and by 1856 was insisting that the Church must remain above politics. Astute Catholics recognized the damage their bishop had done by "his lack of knowledge of people, customs, laws, and institutions of this country" and that his "unpopular course" had hurt the laity.[11] Catholics had come to realize the need for Protestant allies and Protestant Democrats recognized the formidable threat the new Republican Party posed, stronger in its Michigan birthplace than anywhere else. Catholic demands for tax dollars quieted and to hang on to power in Detroit, Democrats necessarily patched their coalition back together. The school question was answered. Tax dollars would go to public schools. Catholics would continue on their own path, resolved to make personal and financial sacrifices for parish schools "rather than run any risk of their young minds being tampered with, by a non-Catholic teacher."[12]

During the controversy, their opponents threatened Catholics that separate schools would cause "the young Irish and the young Germans, to be set apart." So educated, such children could expect to be considered "an outside and alien element, disturbing and disturbed, a pest in politics, and a thing of Bigotry."[13] The school question had, in fact, helped advance immigrants' pride of nationality and affirmed their determination to control the schools their children attended. Dating from the 1850s, they would accelerate a pattern of separate parish schools, contradicting Lefevere's intention to rally and thereby unite immigrants as Catholics. As the city grew in size and diversity, Catholic ethnic groups could separate their children from each other, parish by parish. Protestants might regard parochial schools as all of a piece but Catholic parents knew better and preferred otherwise. Thwarting any bishop or church spokesman who aimed for one Catholic system, each parochial school in Detroit was in fact the province of parishioners who supported it, the parish priest who presided over it, and the particular congregation of sisters who taught there.

In the thirty years following the failed campaign for tax support, the number of parish schools in Detroit increased from three to fifteen and enrollment jumped from six hundred to more than six thousand. More than a third of all Detroit children in school were attending Catholic schools by the mid-1880s, a figure closely approximating the percentage of Catholics in the population.[14] This remarkable embrace of parochial education came about through a combination of effort, sacrifice, and fortunate circumstances. Detroit Catholics, most of them Irish and German immigrants or second generation, found themselves managing to build new parishes and schools because it was a time when immigrants did not come in such a rush or in such uniform poverty as to undermine their own chances in the local economy. A diversified commercial base in Detroit provided jobs for newcomers, upward mobility for people who stayed in the city for a time, and professional ranks open to anyone with the training and ability. Catholics also found themselves able to afford their schools because congregations of vowed religious women were willing and anxious to teach. The sisters made parochial schools desirable not only because of their religious emphasis but also because the women shared and appreciated the immigrant origins of pastor and parents, taught immigrant children the skills they needed as Americans, and labored for bare subsistence wages—sums they often helped parishioners come up with by one means or another.

When Lefevere turned from his political foray to advocate an independent course, he was already confident in his ability to staff the schools. He had encouraged two religious women from the Oblate Sisters of Providence, a faltering Baltimore community "of color," to establish a new religious community and school in Michigan. They arrived in 1845, opened their motherhouse in Monroe, forty miles from Detroit, and soon took the official name Sisters, Servants of the Immaculate Heart of Mary (IHMs). After a power struggle with the bishop in the late 1850s, IHM foundress Mother Theresa Maxis and about half the sisters left to teach in Pennsylvania. The bishop accused Mother Theresa of sexual misconduct and threatened to expose that she was a mulatto, a fact that would remain long buried in the community's history.[15] The women who remained in Monroe acquiesced to his demand that they teach only in the Detroit diocese and set about earning a reputation as its premier teachers. In the 1860s, through happenstance of personal connections, the IHMs embraced what became their "Dupanloup" or "St. Andre System." The underlying philosophy was that of the liberal humanist Felix Antoine Dupanloup, a French bishop-educator, coupled with principles of methodology and school administration brought from the St. Andre Normal School in Belgium. In practice, however, the IHM curriculum and methods were an amalgam that included mainstream American thinkers, a blend they deliberately crafted for children who would be making their way in America.

Set apart by their royal blue habits and energized by opportunity, the IHM community attracted many of its members from Michigan's French, Irish, German, and Belgian families. Most of the first to come were in their twenties; a few had experience as teachers. All were attracted by the congregation's teaching mission. The IHMs did not accept applicants to the congregation until they had completed a high school course and starting in 1876, the women were systematically trained at their motherhouse normal school where St. Mary's Academy served as a laboratory school. The teacher-training program focused not only on mastery of subject material but on their uniform curriculum and pedagogy that emphasized the dignity of the child, the child's right to participate in learning, character formation, and the Catholic religion.[16]

By making shrewd or perhaps instinctive use of their ethnic diversity, the IHMs were especially attractive to priests and parishioners because the mother superior and her assistants often matched principals and teachers to the ethnic background of pupils. When the first diocesan school board took a systematic count in 1887, the five distinctively Irish parishes, enrolling 2,239 children, were all taught by IHMs—most of them Irish sisters; nearly half the 2,750 German children attended IHM schools—where their teachers were often Germans.[17] More usual was the situation in Chicago, where several separate Irish congregations taught in the various Irish parishes and several German communities divided German immigrant parishes and their children among them.[18]

Initially the IHMs were given charge of boys only until they reached the age of twelve, but Detroit's Irish and German Catholic parents sent their sons to school as commonly as their daughters and the age rule was abandoned by the 1880s. Boys who stayed on in the upper grades inherited a curriculum designed by strong women for the benefit of girls expected to make full use of their talents and abilities; they could grow up to become teachers, perhaps IHMs, or it would make them better wives and mothers. Classes in music, penmanship, Christian doctrine, and proper manners were ever-present but once they added high schools on top of their parish grade schools, boys and girls proceeded through rigorous courses in composition and history, algebra, rhetoric, chemistry, natural philosophy [physics], astronomy, botany, zoology, and geography. Their work was frequently praised by the Catholic press and, in succession, proud and friendly Detroit bishops allowed the congregation of women to choose where, who, and how they would teach. So far as generations of satisfied parents and pupils saw it, IHM schools set the standard for Catholic education.

Detroit's German Catholics were not as uniform in their approval of the IHMs as were the Irish. German parents and priests who feared that children in IHM parish schools were at risk of becoming too Americanized, too "worldly," opted for sisters more to their liking—the School Sisters of Notre Dame. The School Sisters, a Milwaukee-based German-speaking community, were first introduced to Detroiters in the early 1850s when they arrived at the German "mother church," St. Mary's. They took charge of the girls and the smaller boys; initially, Christian Brothers taught the older boys. Over the following decades, nearly half the city's German Catholic children attended classrooms staffed by the School Sisters and, in keeping with the pattern common in Detroit, these women played a significant role in setting the course of education for the children who grew up under their tutelage.

The original core of School Sisters came from Bavaria in 1847 to establish their motherhouse in Milwaukee. Their superior, Mother Caroline Friess, guided the educational philosophy of the American branch until she died in 1892. Throughout the nineteenth century, these "German nuns," as Detroiters called them, came mostly from German families, immigrants, or second generation. Like the IHMs, teaching was their sole mission and although they did not have a comprehensive curricular plan until the late nineteenth century, at the motherhouse postulants and novices absorbed a certain basic philosophy centering on religion, character formation, and mastery of skills "in the secular branches."[19] As they saw it, their mission was to the poor and immigrant Catholics and when the IHMs began adding upper grades and high school courses to their schools in the 1880s, the "German nuns" operated elementary schools only. The School Sisters had come to America to keep German immigrants faithful to the Church; that was their priority.

They hoped to hold the faithful and win back lapsed or lukewarm parents through their children. For this reason, they emphasized the German language and culture as a tie between generations. From the writing on the blackboards to the decorations and saints' pictures on the walls, their elementary schools were unmistakably German. Many children arrived speaking only their parents' language and although the School Sisters also emphasized the need to read, write, and speak in English, they selected books in German for many of their classes, and boys and girls who studied with them spent a significant portion of their day studying in German. When the diocesan school board began its school visits in 1887, member-priests expressed displeasure that children taught by the School Sisters were less proficient in English. The School Sisters' loyal constituency was not swayed by the school board's assessment, however, and by the end of the century, the School Sisters were instructing nearly 18 percent of the city's parochial school children.[20]

Detroit bishops commanded little national notice within the Church but, like the rest of the American hierarchy, they agreed that parochial education must be promoted. Bishop Caspar Borgess (1870-1887) stood with the "Americanists" in his desire for the Church to avoid any stigma as "foreign" and was opposed to ethnic self-interest. Unable to resolve problems within the comparatively new Polish community, however, Borgess made no attempt to meddle with the Germans or Irish. Instead, he emphasized building schools, improving the quality of education, and demanding attendance. Among the hard-liners in the Church, he told fellow bishops that they should deny the sacraments to parents who sent their children to public schools without good reasons.[21] His successor John Foley (1888-1918) actively promoted the IHM curriculum that emphasized Americanization but recognized he could neither order nor persuade Detroit Catholics to accept territorial parishes and centralized parochial schools. Realists, the Detroit bishops agreeably went along with a habit that measured faith, in part, by bricks and mortar. For their part, priests together with sisters, parents, and pupils worked tirelessly to piece together the means to operate their schools. Such efforts meant that Most Holy Trinity parents, for example, had to pay tuition averaging eight cents per year in 1880 and still less than $1.70 a year in 1894.[22] With Catholic education affordable as well as preferable, public schools had little lure.

By 1884 when the Third Plenary Council met in Baltimore and decreed that Catholics must attend Catholic schools, Detroiters were already set on the course without any prodding. Of the sixteen city parishes, fourteen conducted schools, compared with a rate of merely 40 percent of all Catholic churches nationwide. The various statistical reports taken together suggest that 25 to 30 percent of all Detroit children enrolled in school in the 1880s were in Catholic schools, approximately the proportion of Catholics then in the total Detroit population. Satisfaction with their parish schools had become at least as important as their mistrust of Protestant-dominated public schools.

A flood of Polish immigrants began by the 1880s, dramatically changing the scope of parochial education in Detroit. St. Albertus, the first Polish parish and school had been dedicated in 1872, established by the then-small community of three hundred Prussian Polish families.[23] By the turn of the century, there would be six Polish Catholic schools with a total enrollment of nearly five thousand. This meant that even before the auto industry brought a quick rush of newcomers, almost 40 percent of the children in Catholic schools were Polish.[24] So, too, were most of their teachers.

Denied autonomy and "Germanized" in the old country, it did not take long for parents to search out sisters who appreciated and could teach the Polish language and culture. Four Felician Sisters had emigrated at the request of a Polish priest, Father Joseph Dabrowski, who asked their help in his mission to keep the Polish culture and religion alive in America.[25] Properly known as the Congregation of St. Felix of Cantalicio, Third Order of Francis, the Felicians were the first European congregation of sisters to establish a province in the United States. When Dabrowski decided upon Detroit as the appropriate site for his work, the Felicians followed him. In January 1880, they established their American motherhouse and academy across the street from St. Albertus Church and School. Soon they added a Polish orphanage. From the time they arrived at St. Albertus, the Felicians attained an early lead as the major educators of Detroit's Polish Catholics and, for many years, they would be the largest group of Polish nuns in the country. Two blocks north of their motherhouse was the Seminary of Saints Cyril and Methodius which Dabrowski opened in 1886 to train Polish-American priests.[26] Borgess, no advocate of ethnic rights or separatism, pragmatically endorsed Dabrowski's projects. These institutions offered a permanence that encouraged incoming immigrants to settle in the neighborhood and gave Detroit a nationwide reputation as the center for Polish education. In turn, the growing Polish population provided a ready supply of applicants for the seminary and convent. In the midst of such impressive accomplishments, however, trouble within the community further shaped the direction that parochial education would take.

From December 1885 through the spring of 1887, Polish Detroiters fought publicly with each other, their priests, their sisters, and their bishop. The precipitating issues were matters of parish finances, parish autonomy, and the bishop's right to hold title to church property. The trouble was exacerbated by class and regional animosities festering within the Polish community; and, too, these were immigrants strained by financing huge church building projects while supporting their own large families. Sides lined up. On one side were those behind Dabrowski who represented "better off" Poles and supported the bishop's demand for control over parish finances. More newcomers were on the other side backing Father Dominic Kolasinski who defied the bishop. The local press, including the *Michigan Catholic*, regularly ridiculed these "Polish Wars" that killed two men in the course of street riots and the Detroit police were constantly in the "Polak Quarter." In one episode, a group of women stormed into St. Albertus School and chased "Dabrowski's nuns" and their students from the building.

Borgess exiled Kolasinski to the Dakota territory but the priest's loyalists "won" by going their own way. They bought land a few blocks from St. Albertus, opened their own school, built the magnificent Sweetest Heart of Mary Church, and operated it as a schismatic parish with Kolasinski as pastor. Discouraged and exhausted, Borgess resigned. New to the scene, Foley managed an uneasy reconciliation and in 1894, dedicated Sweetest Heart for the sake of peace and the salvation of renegade parishioners' eternal souls.[27] Americanists in the Church saw this experience in Detroit as all the more reason to hasten assimilation in parochial schools. Detroiters saw it differently. Irish and German Catholics, on their way now into a rising middle class, were confirmed in their distaste for the "Polish rabble" and were pleased, indeed, to be off in their own parish schools. Public school administrators felt no obligation to reach out to this horde. Polish parents responded in kind. They would have their own parish schools, taught by sisters who were on their side.

Successive generations of Poles chose one community of sisters over another depending upon allegiances forged in these formative years, long after the old issues were forgotten. Because the Felicians were so closely tied to Dabrowski, his friends were their champions and his enemies became theirs. Priest and parishioners at Sweetest Heart of Mary and the westside Polish parish, Saint Francis of Assisi, opted for the School Sisters of St. Francis from Milwaukee. The School Sisters of St. Francis were predominantly German, but Polish girls were beginning to join their ranks so Polish principals and some Polish teachers were assigned to Detroit. By 1901, several Sisters of St. Francis teaching in the Detroit parishes were instrumental in seceding to form a new Polish sisterhood, the Sisters of St. Joseph with a motherhouse in Stevens Point, Wisconsin.[28] Detroit's Sweetest Heart of Mary and St. Francis of Assisi parishes now opted to replace the Sisters of St. Francis in favor of the new "exclusively Polish religious congregation."[29] By 1925 the Felicians and IHMs taught almost half the city's Catholic students; the Sisters of St. Joseph and their parent community, the Sisters of St. Francis, instructed another quarter of the children.

In the first three decades of the twentieth century, the auto industry transformed Detroit. The population soared from 285,704 in 1900 to 1,568,662 by 1930, and the 56,624 Polish immigrants were the largest single group in the city. Polish teachers and their parish schools continually struggled to cope with circumstances Detroit's Irish and German parishes had not faced. Year after year, the need for teachers outstripped the supply of sisters ready to teach. As many as one hundred pupils crowded into a classroom—triple the number in IHM classes; strict, even harsh discipline was deemed necessary to keep order. The number of girls arriving at the Detroit motherhouse to become Felicians did climb along with the influx of new residents but most were young—fourteen or fifteen and a few as young as nine. The daughters of poor or working-class immigrants, they generally had only a rudimentary reading and speaking ability in the Polish language and none at all in English. Felician sister superiors agreed that they must provide these "aspirants" to the sisterhood with an elementary education before proceeding to a secondary program; still, most girls started teaching before they had completed even two years of high school. Their academy high school was not able to add a fourth year until 1914. The St. Joseph Sisters, similarly, could not keep up with the demand for their services and they too struggled to educate the young Polish immigrant girls who joined their convent. Further complicating their task, the Felicians and St. Joseph Sisters were not diocesan congregations and their leaders took on many requests from Polish parishes in other states out of a sense of duty.

Regardless of their particular community of sister-teachers, Polish parish schools shared common purposes. Priests, sisters, and parents agreed that their parish schools must preserve the Polish heritage and language, provide solid grounding in Catholicism, and equip Polish youth to make a living in America. Accordingly, the course of study was a mix of conservative Catholic European influences and American educational expectations with most classes conducted in Polish. As late as World War I, children generally arrived in schoolrooms able to speak only Polish, and many sisters remained more fluent in Polish than in English. Unable to find appropriate texts in Polish, one of the Felicians and Dabrowski wrote and printed their own books for many years. Polish students were expected to read and write in English in certain classes and especially in English class, but according to the Felician plan, only by grade eight was all instruction to be in English.[30] Still, St.

Albertus was the first of their schools to graduate an eighth-grade class in 1908 and most Polish parish schools did not extend beyond grade six until after World War I. For Polish children, their course of study preserved the language and culture their elders valued, but it inevitably set them farther apart from parochial and public school children who were learning from English texts. Yet, at great personal sacrifice and against overwhelming odds, their "Polish nuns" educated thousands of children who would have been unwelcome and neglected elsewhere.

All the while Polish immigrants were establishing their place within Catholic Detroit, other ethnic groups were joining the mix, weighing their options, and making their choices accordingly. Detroit became a magnet for Hungarian immigrants who began to collect around westside riverfront iron and steel factories in or near the enclave of Delray in the late nineteenth century. By the 1930s, Detroit boasted more Hungarians than any city but Budapest. The majority of the Hungarians were Catholic and in 1906, they opened their own church and school, Holy Cross. Foley allowed the Dominicans from their motherhouse in Adrian, Michigan, to take on this small, "foreign" place on the outskirts of the city. The Dominicans were mostly second generation German and Irish women but the bishop had diverted them to Chicago or Grand Rapids out of his favoritism for the IHMs. Despite their best efforts at Holy Cross, the sisters met opposition from strong-willed Hungarian priests and indifferent or even hostile parents. Determined to preserve the Hungarian culture, the priest dismissed the Dominicans in the 1920s and brought in the Daughters of Divine Charity who were staffing Hungarian schools in other states. Nonetheless, Hungarian immigrant parents saw no reason for advanced schooling since jobs were so plentiful. Their sons especially found the strict, crowded, and unattractive classrooms to be a "most humdrum life compared to working at the Michigan Sprocket Chain . . . and getting paid for it to boot."[31] The school struggled along and only a few Holy Cross children completed the eighth grade until compulsory school laws were in place and enforced.

Italian Catholics slightly outnumbered the Hungarians by the 1920s. They dedicated their first church, San Francesco, in 1898, a second in 1910, and two more small parishes by the mid-1920s—one of them in the enclave of Highland Park where many Italians worked at the huge Ford factory. San Francesco operated the one Italian parochial school within the city of Detroit. Parents regarded it as "the

finest Italian school in the United States" according to the School Sisters
of Notre Dame who taught there. Nonetheless, it grew slowly compared
to the immigrant population and had only five hundred students by the
mid-1920s.[32] In the 1930s, the Highland Park parish students became
the first and only Italians to study with teachers who were also Italian.[33]
That Italians lagged behind other immigrant groups when it came to
providing parish schools was a common enough pattern in other cities. In Detroit, several factors contributed. Italian men did not often
go into the industrial structure and their wages were lower than even
unskilled Hungarian factory workers. They sought housing wherever
they could best afford it and did not cluster in such tight communities
as the Poles and Hungarians. This meant their ethnic parishes gathered
members from distant corners of the now spread-out city and children
would have a longer walk to attend a parish school of their own. Other
closer parish schools were not welcoming; so as far as many Catholics
saw it, the Italians were possibly the children of racketeers or radicals.
For whatever private reasons, a majority of Italian parents persistently
opted for public school when, by law or by choice, they sent their children to school.

By the time the auto industry arrived to alter wages, work, and
upward mobility, some observant Catholics had already recognized the
advantages of extended schooling and each year hundreds of students
were funneling into parish high schools. Organized efforts to introduce Catholic secondary instruction followed in the wake of public initiatives. Detroit's first tax-supported high school opened in 1858, but
enrollment lagged and not until 1876 were all four secondary grades
finally under one roof.[34] By the early 1880s, Irish parishes and their
IHM sisters were pioneering the idea of adding a secondary program
for girls to their grade schools, one year at a time. The first students
graduated from an abbreviated program at Most Holy Trinity in 1881
and soon the nearby but more middle-class St. Vincent's had all four
years in place. These two schools became the prototype for the others
and established the local image of parochial secondary education at
its best—small with classes almost like tutorials, tailored to fit individual needs, and charging low tuition. Offering four years of Latin,
Greek, French, and German, advanced chemistry, physics, and math,
the curriculum was almost as rigorous as the one for boys who studied with the Jesuits. Yet the IHMs managed to merge the usual two
types of Catholic girls' schools, the school that aimed at "womanly

accomplishments" and the school that aimed at teaching a girl to earn a living. Even the reluctant *Michigan Catholic* began to see the advantages of secondary education for girls. To hold "their boys" who might otherwise have gone to public high schools, the IHM high schools soon became coeducational. By 1915 when the IHM sisters staffed eight of the nine parish high schools in Detroit, all but two admitted boys although the coeducational schools still attracted nearly four or five times more girls than boys.[35]

The Felicians and St. Joseph Sisters stretched their thin resources and, like the IHMs and Dominicans, began sending a succession of sisters to college and normal training programs to prepare for high school teaching. In 1920, when the Felicians opened available spaces in their convent academy to include day students, it became the first four-year Polish Catholic high school in Detroit for girls. All of the women's congregations arranged outside accreditation for their four-year programs, the IHMs with the University of Michigan and the Felicians with Catholic University. Accreditation meant that graduates could be admitted to many colleges, including Detroit Teachers, without college entrance examinations.[36]

Certain schools were gaining an elite status even beyond the Catholic community. Chief among them was the Jesuit's Detroit College, later called University of Detroit High School, which began as a preparatory school for boys in 1877. If boys were capable and motivated, parents, pastor, and sisters encouraged them to go to "The High." Tuition, book costs, and a demanding classical education meant that Detroit College attracted an elite corps; with 515 students in 1925, the school was at capacity and turning boys away.[37] Those who graduated were prepared for college and went on to become part of a widening Catholic middle and upper class.

For boys interested in a business curriculum, there was St. Joseph's Commercial started in 1889, even before the Detroit High School of Commerce opened. Operated by Christian Brothers on top of the St. Joseph's grade school, "St. Joe's Commercial" was never as large as Detroit College but it attracted students from parishes across the city, nearly all of them the sons of Irish or German immigrants. Even though the parish had come to include Italians, Hungarians, and Poles before World War I, few boys from those families were on the St. Joe's Commercial roster. Its graduates, usually between the ages of seventeen and nineteen, were positioned for the city's white-collar job market that exploded alongside the auto industry.[38] Nonetheless, the well-paying factory jobs beckoned Detroit youth. Grade school or a few years beyond would still be the limit of education for many working-class children when World War II ended.

Those Catholics who paid attention understood the gulf that separated their schools; they appreciated what the various parishes had accomplished and understood there was much yet to be done. More commonly, Catholics congratulated themselves for their own particular institutions and cared little about the others. Then, just in the middle of parish building programs and boom times in Detroit, the heterogeneous Catholic community necessarily joined forces to defend its schools as a whole against opponents trying to outlaw all church-related or private schools. In 1920, Michigan voters were presented with a ballot amendment that, if passed, would require all students between the ages of five and sixteen to attend public schools through the eighth grade. In the 1850s, the "school question" was whether Catholics had a right to claim tax support for their schools. In the 1920s, the issue took a very different and more threatening direction: did Catholics and other denominations have a right to maintain schools? Their critics' efforts were, in part, a response to the gains Catholics were making.

With its dizzying physical expansion, radically altered economy, and explosion of Central and Southeastern European newcomers alongside a rush of African Americans, Detroit was a place certain to stir nativists' fears even before World War I brought new demands and patriotic slogans insisting upon "100% Americanism." The growing number of immigrant churches and schools convinced working-class Protestants that foreigners might soon grab the better jobs. Rural Michigan was overwhelmingly native-born and Protestant, long mistrustful of an alien Detroit. Fuel was added to the fire during the Justice Department's "Red Raids" in 1919 when more than eight hundred possible "enemy aliens" were rounded up in Detroit.[39] Xenophobic proponents of what became known on all sides as the "anti-parochial school amendment" regarded Catholic schools as hotbeds of Bolshevism because they answered to a foreign head, tolerated no democratic thought, and refused to teach the lessons or language of democracy.

Although Catholic schools were the acknowledged target, the amendment swept in all private and church schools and so a coalition of odd bedfellows joined forces to fight it. Catholics formed the

Educational Liberty Lobby and the Missouri Synod Lutherans mounted
a parallel campaign with the slogan "Whose Is the Child?"[40] Respected
Republicans from the party's progressive reform wing spoke forcefully
against the amendment and they were joined by the Episcopal bishop,
a prominent rabbi, and both Detroit newspapers. Leaders on each side
urged women to use their vote, now allowed for the first time; Polish Catholics who had been otherwise preoccupied hurried to register.
On election day, an unprecedented 90 percent of the registered voters
turned out in Detroit where 63 percent voted against the amendment.
Statewide, the tally was 610,669 against to 353,818 for the proposition.[41] Catholics, although only about 20 percent of the state's voters,
had achieved impressive support.

Opponents did not fade away. The amendment was back on the
ballot in 1924 with the backing of the revived Ku Klux Klan. Prejudice
against Catholics and fear over their un-American schools accounted
for most of the support behind the KKK in Michigan, especially among
rural and outstate residents where Catholics loomed larger than the
Klan's other targets—blacks and Jews. In this election, school financing
proved the most decisive argument against requiring all children to
attend public schools. A group of leading citizens, all "non-Catholics,"
made speeches and issued statements to publicize an important but
overlooked reality. By state law every public school district received
a per-capita payment from the Primary School Interest Fund for all
children of school age in the district whether those children attended
public, private, or parochial school.[42] This meant that Detroit public
schools received money for the 125,000 children that Catholic, Lutheran, and private schools absorbed but which those parents paid for—in
addition to their taxes.[43] Detroit taxpayers were already struggling with
heavy bonded indebtedness caused by public school building projects.
This was no time to require public school attendance. The 1924 amendment went down to defeat almost two to one, a bigger margin than four
years before.[44]

Catholics came away from this political experience frightened by
the number of their enemies but grateful for the measure of support
from outsiders and more aware of the protections coalition-building
offered. Proud of the praise recent allies heaped on their schools and
their "well-behaved" children, they were more determined than ever to
polish that reputation. In the course of the campaigns, Catholic school
proponents embraced a new state law—put forth by an Irish Catholic

legislator educated in parochial schools and at the University of Detroit—which provided for state accreditation of private and parochial
schools including the qualifications of teachers. The act took effect in
1925. Those within the Catholic hierarchy and community who had
worried over the quality of some of their parochial schools privately
welcomed this newly important reason to improve standards; strong
schools welcomed this external validation.

On the last day of 1929, Pope Pius XI issued the encyclical *Divini
Illius Magistri* (Christian Education of Youth), telling Catholics they
were bound in conscience to attend Catholic schools. He also pronounced that Catholic schools had the right to state support. By then,
Detroit was sinking into the Great Depression which hit earlier and
harder than most anywhere else in the nation. The pontiff's words were
almost irrelevant to local Catholics. Detroiters preferred their parochial schools; they understood, too, that the pontiff had little knowledge
of the political or financial reality as they knew it. Hard times were, in
fact, not so hard on parochial schools as on the now-devastated Detroit public system which soon went to half-day shifts and teacher lay-
offs. Accustomed to mending their own shoestrings, parochial school
teachers knew how to make do at a time when parents could not pay
the tuition and Sunday collections fell off.

The city's population leveled off in the 1930s but parochial school
enrollments climbed. The high school population tripled in the diocese
between the Depression and the outbreak of World War II, in part a
reflection of new compulsory school laws and a dismal job market but
also the result of a growing grade school population in the parishes
that experienced a burst of newcomers during the booming 1920s. In
1934, Bishop Gallagher appointed Monsignor Carroll Deady as school
superintendent, a post he would hold until 1957. Gallagher's successor,
Archbishop Edward Mooney (1937-1958) was a more determined cen-
tralizer. With Mooney's approval, Deady forced the Catholic schools
into one centralized system—at least into one bureaucracy—but he
struggled always with internal, competing forces. On one hand were
the weaker schools that needed to be quickly improved in quality;
on the other were the more assimilated Catholics and their teachers
who regarded the central office bureaucrats as interference and their
rules as unnecessary limitations. Just as they had worked around bishops for generations now, vowed religious congregations of women
collaborated with priests and parents and long-standing patterns held

firm; the sisters remained mostly in charge of what went on in their classrooms and differences from one Catholic school to another persisted. Two Catholic central high schools had finally opened in Detroit, one for girls in 1927 and one for boys in 1928. They served parishes where grade schools had not proven able to develop their own secondary programs but never replaced the dominant pattern of coeducational parish high schools.

Detroit continued to extend its boundaries until the late 1920s when the last annexations put the sprawling city at seventy-nine square miles. With so much land to grow toward inside the city, suburbanization did not really become significant until after the factories that were the "arsenal of democracy" went up in farm fields outside the city limits. Meanwhile, in the middle of the war, Detroit erupted in a race riot. Inequality in jobs, housing, and education were established patterns, but the black population had been growing and spreading rapidly. The 1943 riot signaled changes to come. Now, issues over race were more openly discussed; charges of racism in the Church and in its schools became more common. Mooney began to urge parish integration in the 1950s and his successor, Cardinal John Dearden (1959-1980) was even more insistent in calling for civil rights and social justice.[45] Resistant Catholics angrily responded that it was easy for the cardinal to be all for integration; he had no children in the parish school.

Like their parents before them, Catholic families weighed their options. Fewer of their children would grow up identifying themselves as "from Holy Trinity" or "from St. Stanislaus" deep in Detroit. Postwar, Cold War prosperity brought new freeways and new cars to drive to new or relocated jobs where new housing was going up nearby. A physical move could substitute for occupational mobility in a region so defined by the demands of manufacturers. Catholics were part of Detroit's mainstream and they became a significant presence in the suburbs that were already underway before riots in July 1967. In those suburbs, Catholics set about reclaiming pieces from their past.

When they headed out, Detroiters usually moved along a diagonal line whether to a working-, middle-, or upper-class community. Westsiders sifted north, west, or southwest; eastsiders went to the northeast. Regrouped with friends, relatives, or like-minded new neighbors, Catholics copied the churches and schools of their youth and, when they could, took along their familiar sisters. The Felicians or Sisters of St. Joseph staffed east-side, third-generation Polish parish schools in

Warren, Sterling Heights, and Harper Woods. IHMs, School Sisters of Notre Dame, or Dominicans staffed schools in the new third-generation Irish and German parishes, and they were the congregations most often invited to the "assimilated," upper-class parishes in places like Bloomfield Hills and Grosse Pointe. To supplement their ranks, sisters hired lay teachers they had once taught.

Children sitting in parochial school classrooms in the 1950s and 1960s would be adults in a post-Vatican II Church. Some would grow up to march against open housing or to rage at Dearden when he sold churches to clear a neighborhood for a new General Motors automated plant. Some would sit on interfaith and interracial parish councils. Theirs would be choices made in the most segregated metropolitan region in the nation where, finally, not one Catholic parish high school remained inside the city limits of Detroit.

NOTES

1. *Detroit Catholic Vindicator*, April 30, 1853. Founded within a month of the 1853 Detroit elections, the weekly paper was written and published by Richard R. Elliott with several other Irish Catholics who stated their chief aim: the "necessity of vindicating Catholic rights in regard to Public Schools." It ceased publication after four years.

2. *Detroit Weekly Tribune*, May 3, 1853, 6.

3. Sister M. Rosalita [Kelly], *Education in Detroit Prior to 1850* (Lansing: Michigan Historical Commission, 1928), 135, citing *Michigan Territory: Laws*, I: 879.

4. *Documents: Journal of the House of Representatives of the State of Michigan at the Annual Session of 1843* (Detroit: Ellis and Briggs, 1843), doc. no. 10, 51.

5. Ronald P. Formisano, *The Birth of Mass Political Parties, Michigan, 1827-1861* (Princeton: Princeton University Press), 197, 141-143.

6. Charles R. Starring and James R. Knauss, *The Michigan Search for Educational Standards* (Lansing: Michigan Historical Commission, 1969), 57-58.

7. Ira Mayhew, *Popular Education for the Use of Parents and Teachers, and for Young Persons of Both Sexes* (New York: Harper and Brothers, 1850), 210-211.

8. *Documents: Senate and House of Representatives of Michigan, 1853*, 222.

9. Ibid., document no. 20.

10. Ibid., document no. 6.

11. A Catholic Layman [R.R. Elliott], "The Roman Catholics in Detroit," *Michigan Pioneer and Historical Collections* 13 (1888): 444-450.

12. Richard R. Elliott, MSS, vol. 7 (of 27), describing his father's decision to send his children for schooling at Most Holy Trinity in the 1840s, Burton Historical Collection, Detroit Public Library.

13. *Detroit Weekly Tribune*, May 3, 1853, 6.

14. *The Second Annual Report of the Michigan Bureau of Labor and Industrial Statistics* (Lansing: State Printer, February 1, 1884), 62, citing 1884 statistics.

15. Sisters, Servants of the Immaculate Heart of Mary, *Building Sisterhood: A Feminist History* (Syracuse: Syracuse University Press, 1997), 54.

16. For a perceptive discussion of Rousseau's educational ideas, see Joan Roland Martin, *Reclaiming a Conversation, the Ideal of the Educated Woman* (New Haven: Yale University Press, 1985). Information on the St. Andre System is well cataloged in the Archives of the Sisters, Servants of the Immaculate Heart of Mary, Monroe (SSIHM). See for example, Folder no. 3 and Folder no. 5, St. Andre System box.

17. Assignments are based on my calculations from IHM Sister Personal Files for Most Holy Trinity 1867-1903 staff records; St. Vincent staff records, 1913-1929; and staff records for the German parish of St. Joseph, 1862-1929, Archives, SSIHM.

18. James W. Sanders, *The Education of an Urban Minority* (New York: Oxford University Press, 1977), 59-60.

19. This apparently was basic to their curriculum from the 1850s and still the case when Mother Caroline died in 1892.

20. "The Hundredth Anniversary of the Arrival in Detroit of the First Organized Immigration from Germany" (small paperbound booklet based on letters, interviews, and articles from the *Detroit News* and the *Detroit Abend Post,* covering the years between 1830 and 1930), Michigan Historical Collections, Bentley Historical Library, University of Michigan; Sister M. Rosalita [Kelly], *No Greater Service: The History of the Congregation of the Sisters, Servants of the Immaculate Heart of Mary, Monroe, Michigan, 1845-1945* (Detroit: Congregation of the Sisters, Servants of the Immaculate Heart of Mary, 1948), which includes a handwritten chart from the First Annual School Report MS.

21. *Michigan Catholic*, December 25, 1884, reprinting Pastoral Letter of the Archbishops and Bishops to the Clergy and Laity.

22. "Account Books" for 1886-1887 and 1887-1900, Most Holy Trinity parish files, Archives of the Archdiocese of Detroit (AAD).

23. Lawrence D. Orton, *Polish Detroit and the Kolasinski Affair* (Detroit: Wayne State University Press, 1981), 17-18, discusses problems with this parish name. Initially, it was to be St. Adalbert (Sw. Wojciech), a saint revered by Prussian and Kashubian Poles. But it was recorded by the Press and Borgess as Albert or Albertus, an entirely different saint.

24. Calculated from "Account Books," Item 39, 1894-1916, AAD.

25. See Sister Mary Remigia Napolska, "The Polish Immigrant in Detroit to 1914," *Annals of the Polish R.C. Union Archives and Museum* 10 (1945-1946).

26. Borgess opened the short-lived St. Francis Seminary in Monroe in 1886 to serve as a preparatory seminary and secondary school. At the time, Detroit was still sending boys out of state to study for the priesthood, heavily funded by the diocese. See Leslie Tentler, *Seasons of Grace: A History of the Archdiocese of Detroit* (Detroit: Wayne State University, 1990), 50-51.

27. The best analysis of this issue is found in Leslie Tentler, "Who is the Church? Conflict in a Polish Immigrant Parish in Late-Nineteenth-Century Detroit," *Comparative Studies in Society and History* 25 (April 1983): 241-276. Thorough discussions are also in Orton, *Kolasinski Affair;* Napolska, "Polish Immigrant in Detroit," *Annals*; and Eduard Adam Skendzel, *The Kolasinski Story* (Grand Rapids: Littleshield Press, 1979).

28. Josephine Marie Peplinski, SSJ-TOSF, *A Fitting Response: The History of the Sisters of St. Joseph of the Third Order of St. Francis*, 2 vols. (South Bend: The Sisters of St. Joseph of the Third Order of St. Francis, 1982, 1992), 1:111, 1:86-87.

29. *Pamietnik Ztotego Jubileuszu, Parafil Najstodszego Serca Marii Panny, 1890-1940,* 27 (Sweetest Heart Golden Jubilee Book), Michigan Historical Collections, Bentley Library, University of Michigan; Peplinski, *A Fitting Response*, 1:164.

30. Sister Mary Jeremiah Studniewska, *The Educational Work of the Felician Sisters*

of the Province of Detroit in the United States, 1874-1948 (Livonia, MI: The Felician Sisters, 1962), 48-49.

31. Andrew Untener, "The Old Grad Remembers When," in Holy Cross School thirty-year homecoming booklet (1906-1936), Holy Cross parish, file 4.13, AAD; this booklet lists graduates. For a general discussion of the community, see Malvina Hauk Abonyi and James A. Anderson, *Hungarians of Detroit, Peopling of Michigan Series* (Detroit: Wayne State University Press, 1977). For a discussion of the Dominicans, see Sister Mary Philip Ryan, O.P., *The Alien Corn: The Early Years of the Sisters of Saint Dominic, Adrian, Michigan* (St. Charles, IL: Jones Wood Press, 1967).

32. A School Sister of Notre Dame [Sister Dympna], *Mother Caroline and the School Sisters of Notre Dame in North America*, 2 vols. (St. Louis: Woodward and Tiernan, 1928), 2:197; *The Official Catholic Directory*, 1917 and 1925. The directory, a serial, is known variously as Sadliers' *Catholic Directory, Almanac and Ordo*, Hoffmann's *Catholic Directory, and Almanac and Clergy List*. Hereafter cited as *Catholic Directory*.

33. *Detroit News*, May 23, 1973, 15-E.

34. Silas Farmer, *History of Detroit and Wayne County and Early Michigan*, 2 vols., 3rd ed. (1884, reprint, Detroit: Gale Research, 1969), 1:749; Daniel Putnam, *The Development of Primary and Secondary Education in Michigan* (Ann Arbor: George Wahr, 1904), 90, citing the superintendent of public education in 1872 who complained about lack of public support and opposition, even from "men of character and standing."

35. James A. Burns, "The Condition of Catholic Secondary Education in the United States," *National Catholic Association Bulletin* 2 (Nov. 1915): 416. This listing shows only seven parish schools, failing to include the German parishes of St. Joseph and St. Boniface.

36. Sister Mary Tullia Domain, C.S.S.F., "Mother Mary Angela Truszkowska, Foundress of the Felician Sisters," *Polish American Studies* 10 (July-December 1953): 82; Sister Mary Janice Ziolkowski, C.S.S.F., *The Felician Sisters of Livonia, Michigan* (Detroit: Harlo Press, 1984), 281-319.

37. See P. Douglas Keller, S.J., et al. *The Second Hundred Years: The University of Detroit High School and a Chronicle of the First Hundred Years, 1877-1977* (Detroit: University of Detroit High School, 1977), 21, 20; *Catholic Directory*, 1925, 355. Also, Herman J. Muller, S.J., *The University of Detroit, 1877-1977: A Centennial History* (Detroit: University of Detroit, 1976).

38. De La Salle High School student records, classes of 1917 and 1918, in principal's office at De La Salle Collegiate High School, Warren, Michigan. This is the successor school to St. Joseph's Commercial. Brother Angelus Gabriel, F.S.C., *The Christian Brothers in the United States, 1848-1948: A Century of Catholic Education* (New York: D. X. McMullen, 1948), 356-357.

39. Senate Judiciary Committee, Hearings on Charges of Illegal Practices of Justice, 66th Cong., March 1921, U.S. Congressional Hearings, 41st-73d Congress, 1869-1934, 169:709-723, cited Wilma Wood Henrickson, *Detroit Perspectives, Crossroads and Turning Points* (Detroit: Wayne State University Press, 1991), 304-314.

40. Timothy Pies, "Historical and Contemporary Analyses of the Financing of Lutheran and Catholic Education in Michigan's Saginaw Valley" (PhD diss., University of Michigan, 1983), 82-83. Their slogan, "Whose Is the Child?" was taken from a tract written by a professor at Concordia Seminary in St. Louis and was used in Oregon and similar campaigns.

41. According to the *Detroit Free Press*, November 4, 1920, I, 3, Wayne County went against the amendment by a vote of 179,186 to 94,542. Extensive information about the Catholic campaign is archived in the Anti-Parochial School Amendment Collection, Archives, SSIHM.

42. *Eighty-fourth Annual Report of the Superintendent of Public Instruction* (Lansing: Wynkoop, Hallenbeck, Crawford, 1922), 11-20, describes the history of the fund, dating from the Northwest Ordinance and made operational by constitutional provisions in 1837 and 1850.

43. By state law every school district received a per-capita payment from the Primary School Interest Fund for all children of school age in the district, regardless of whether they attended public, private, or parochial school. In July preceding the academic year of 1920-21, the state allocated $10.64 per child. Detroit public schools received $1,446,436.61 but enrolled 139,019 children in grades K-12 that year, as discussed in *Eighty-Fourth Annual Report of the Superintendent of Public Instruction,* 66-67, 62.

44. A year later, the U.S. Supreme Court settled the issue in *Pierce v. Society of Sisters*, a case originating with an Oregon vote to require public schools; the high court ruled that parents had the right to send children to nonpublic schools.

45. See Tentler, *Seasons of Grace*, 508-514.

Windy City Catholicism:
Catholic Education in Chicago

Ellen Skerrett

Forty years before the Third Plenary Council in Baltimore (1884) mandated parochial elementary schools to ensure the survival of the Catholic Church in America, Chicago's first bishop, William J. Quarter, was already making "no little plans" for Catholic education. His first public act when he arrived in the frontier town on the shores of Lake Michigan on Sunday, May 5, 1844, was to preach in St. Mary's Church, at the southwest corner of Wabash Avenue and Madison Street. In his diary, Quarter omitted any reference to his sermon that day, focusing instead on the future, observing that there is "a lot in the rear of the church, where a free school for the poor children of the congregation may in course of time be erected."[1]

While Quarter could not have predicted that Chicago's parochial school system would become the largest in the nation by the 1890s and rank third among public schools by 1965, his experience as a parish priest in New York City contributed to his resolve that Catholic schools had a vital role to play in urban life. Born in Kings County (Offaly) Ireland, in 1806, he had received a classical education in Tullamore, first with a retired Presbyterian clergyman and then at the academy conducted by John and Thomas Fitzgerald. Determined to become a priest in America, he emigrated at the age of sixteen and was accepted at St. Mary's College in Emmitsburg, Maryland, where he taught Greek and Latin until his ordination in 1829. Recruited to New York by Bishop John DuBois, Quarter found himself in the forefront of the parochial school movement. The need was great: in 1830, only five schools existed to serve nearly seven thousand Catholic students. In 1833, he persuaded the Sisters of Charity to open a free school in St. Mary's parish along with their "select school," and before long nearly six hundred students were enrolled.[2]

So strong was Quarter's belief in Catholic education that twenty-nine days after arriving in Chicago, he opened a college with two professors and six students. In between his travels through the diocese, which included the entire state of Illinois, Quarter succeeded in having the legislature pass a bill incorporating "the University of St. Mary of the Lake" as the first institution of higher learning in Chicago. But how to finance this ambitious undertaking and complete the cathedral? After all, Chicago's Catholics accounted for about 2,000 of the city's 7,590 residents, but most were of modest means. The spring of 1845 found Quarter back in New York where Bishop John Hughes "not very cheerfully" granted him permission to raise funds for Chicago's Catholic college and seminary. Heading the list, with a contribution of $350, was his former parish of St. Mary's on Grand Street.[3]

The new Greek Revival cathedral of St. Mary's was dedicated on October 5, 1845, and Quarter took pride in the fact that its steeple "[is] the first and only spire, as yet, in the city of Chicago." However, in the bishop's view, the fact that the "faithful of every nationality gather in one and the same church" was not cause for celebration because it prevented "special religious instructions for the German children and people in their own language." In 1846, Quarter instituted a policy that would have far reaching consequences for the structure of the Catholic Church and especially for Catholic education in Chicago: he organized two German parishes, one north and one south of the Chicago River, and St. Patrick parish to serve the famine Irish whose numbers were rapidly increasing. This pragmatic solution to the problem of ethnicity became a distinguishing feature of Chicago Catholicism and was embraced by Quarter's successors up until the episcopacy of George W. Mundelein (1916-1939).[4]

Contemporary accounts confirm that the arrival of six Sisters of Mercy from Pittsburgh in October 1846 marked the real beginnings of parochial education in Chicago. The *Chicago Daily Democrat* hailed them as "the choicest of blessings for our city," noting that in addition to teaching, they "also visit the sick and distressed." Quarter had been so insistent on securing the commitment of the Sisters of Mercy that he met their boat from Ireland when it docked in New York in December 1843, months before he ever set foot in his new diocese.[5]

Although more than two years passed before twenty-four-year-old Agatha O'Brien and her colleagues joined him, once in Chicago they wasted little time in outfitting the old frame church of St. Mary as a free school for girls and opening a select school known as St. Francis Xavier. At the time of Quarter's death in 1848, the Sisters of Mercy enrolled more than two hundred girls and taught Sunday school in three parishes, and they soon expanded their mission to include the city's only hospital. By 1852, Chicago Catholics supported twelve schools, including male and female schools in the German parishes of St. Peter and St. Joseph, and a grammar school for boys conducted by professors from the University of St. Mary of the Lake.[6]

Chicago's public schools shared equally inauspicious beginnings with their Catholic counterparts. In 1833, Eliza Chappel opened an "infant school" in a log cabin on Water Street that served children living near Fort Dearborn. Classes subsequently were held in the First Presbyterian church, the Baptist church, and in other makeshift quarters until a new school was constructed in 1844 on Madison Street, just west of where St. Mary's Cathedral was nearing completion.[7]

Throughout the 1850s, the *Chicago Tribune* regularly reported on the growth of the city's public schools and denounced efforts of Catholics to secure a share of public funds. Although the newspaper regarded parochial schooling as inferior, it warned Chicagoans that the distribution of public monies "would be fatal to our present Public School system." Unlike New York, Chicago Catholics never did receive state funds for their schools and without adequate revenues from the diocese, the burden of providing education fell primarily on the shoulders of religious orders, including the Sisters of Mercy, the Jesuits (1857); the Religious of the Sacred Heart (1858); the Redemptorists (1860); the Benedictine Sisters (1861); the School Sisters of Notre Dame (1862); and the Sisters of Charity of the Blessed Virgin Mary (1867).[8]

A major reason why bishops welcomed transnational religious orders is that they could draw on their community's resources to supply teachers and raise funds. Throughout the nineteenth century, Chicago's immigrant population continued to grow, with no end in sight. In inviting Arnold J. Damen, S.J., to Chicago, Bishop Anthony O'Regan acknowledged that he could not "do a better work for religion, for the diocese or for my own soul than by establishing here a house of your

Society [of Jesus]." But he pulled no punches when it came to financial support, explaining that "I have no [resources] . . . we are in debt [and must] erect a hospital, two Asylums, a House of Refuge and a House of Mercy" in addition to schools, rectories, and a cemetery.[9]

Damen's bold plans in 1857 to build a church, college, and free school in Holy Family parish signaled the expansion of Catholic education on an unprecedented scale and set off alarms in the editorial offices of the *Chicago Tribune*. The dynamic Jesuit preacher from St. Louis had already gained public attention for attracting thousands of Chicagoans to a three-week mission and prominent Catholics supported his vision of creating a college that would eventually rival Georgetown. *The Tribune* understood clearly that a Jesuit foundation in Chicago would have profound consequences for Catholic education and asserted its right to warn residents about Damen's "dangerous" and "unworthy" project. The newspaper "beg[ged] Protestants to think twice before they aid in any way the founding of Jesuit institutions in this city," explaining that: "We do this, not in a spirit of intolerance, but [because] the Society of Jesus is the most virulent and relentless enemy of the Protestant faith and Democratic government." *The Tribune* was right to be concerned about the Holland-born immigrant who came to be known as Chicago's "Jesuit Hercules." Damen immediately opened free schools for the children of Irish immigrants who were "pouring in fast" to Holy Family parish and, despite the Depression of 1857, he began construction on a massive Gothic church. Little wonder that the dedication in 1860 received national coverage: at the time, the walls of St. Patrick's Cathedral on Fifth Avenue in New York City had only risen eighteen feet.[10]

In 1860, when Mother Margaret Gallwey of the Religious of the Sacred Heart (RSCJ) decided to move her community's convent academy from the North Side to Holy Family parish, she hired Chicago's most prominent architect, John Van Osdel, to design an imposing structure on Taylor Street. Historians have not paid much attention to nuns as real estate developers, but contemporary accounts confirm that the RSCJ's spacious grounds were "an attractive adornment to the city." Damen was especially grateful to the sisters because their academy enrolled the daughters of Chicago's elite, Protestant as well as Catholic. Moreover, in 1861, at their own expense, the RSCJs taught hundreds of poor girls in Holy Family, "which would cost [the parish] $1,000 a year."[11]

But even more teachers were needed. In inviting the Sisters of Charity of the Blessed Virgin Mary (BVM) to Chicago, Damen stressed that,

"We now have 1,000 boys in our school, and we should have as many girls." The BVMs apparently heeded his advice to send "good teachers, so as to make a good impression, for the first impression is generally the lasting one." Among the young girls who greeted Sister Agatha Hurley and her group of eight sisters on their arrival in Holy Family parish was Mary Kane, who had emigrated from Carrigaholt, County Clare, Ireland in 1865 when she was ten. Accorded the high honor of carrying the altar stone for the sisters' chapel, Kane became a pupil in the sisters' school and in 1870 she joined the BVM order, the first of 196 young women from Holy Family parish to take the veil during the next fifty years.[12]

The investment made by talented young women such as Kane paid dividends for the BVM order and for Catholic education in Chicago. Elected head of her community in 1919, Mother Isabella Kane was directly involved in opening thirty-three new schools in the Midwest and California, including Chicago's Immaculata High School (1922) and the Art Deco skyscraper known as Mundelein College (1930).[13]

That Chicago's Catholic schools compared favorably with public institutions was no accident. Like their German colleagues in the Redemptorist parish of St. Michael and the Benedictine parish of St. Joseph and the Sisters of Mercy in St. Mary parish, the Jesuits of Holy Family invested scarce resources in building modern classrooms. While Chicago's Irish immigrants had more familiarity with the English language than their German and Bohemian neighbors, their formal schooling varied widely. In the 1860s, some national schools in Ireland were little more than thatched huts with mud floors and as late as the 1880s, teachers in "the bogs, mountains & wilds of West Kerry" found themselves surrounded by Gaelic-speaking children for whom English was a foreign language. The challenge, as Damen saw it, was to provide no excuse for parishioners to send their sons and daughters to the public schools where readings from the King James version of the Bible were still part of the curriculum. When classrooms in the original frame church of Holy Family were destroyed by fire in 1864, for example, the Jesuit pastor hired Augustus Bauer to design a four-story brick building with spacious halls that were used for concerts, dramatic productions, and the constant round of fundraising events.[14]

Although not mentioning Holy Family by name, the *Tribune* was aware that it was superior to the nearby Foster Public School, where the pupil-teacher ratio of 80 to 1 made individual contact impossible.

Affectionately known as the "Brothers school" in honor of Andrew O'Neill, S.J., and his brother, Thomas O'Neill, S.J., the new school on Morgan Street with its lay faculty annually enrolled twelve hundred boys. While most of the graduates left school between sixth and eighth grade to go to work, a fortunate few continued on with their education at St. Ignatius College. Opened on September 5, 1870, the impressive brick structure east of Holy Family Church was built on the grand scale "so as to compete with the Protestant colleges and public schools that are like palaces."[15]

As contemporary press accounts made clear, Catholic schools had become an integral part of parish life by the time of the Great Fire of 1871. The inferno that allegedly began in the rear of the O'Leary barn on DeKoven Street crossed the river and destroyed Chicago's downtown and much of its north side, where many of the city's Germans had settled. St. Michael's on North Avenue was described as the "most imposing ruins" in Chicago because the fire had "left the massive walls, abutments, towers, and long windows intact." However, in contrast to many of the city's Protestant churches and Jewish synagogues that relocated to newer residential districts, Catholic parishes not only stayed put but they enlarged their parochial complexes. For example, the Germans of St. Michael rebuilt their church and within a few years doubled the size of the parochial school to accommodate the sixteen hundred students enrolled under the direction of the School Sisters of Notre Dame and the Brothers of Mary. The Irish of St. Patrick's reinvested in their neighborhood by constructing a high school for boys and one for girls. Both institutions quickly gained reputations for preparing students for office employment in downtown skyscrapers as well as for the teaching profession. In 1875, the *Western Tablet* reported that 15,099 children in Chicago attended Catholic schools staffed by "ten religious orders and a large number of lay teachers," but noted that "thousands of Catholic children in the city attend no school, or attend the Public schools."[16]

In St. John parish on the city's south side, Irish-born Father John Waldron refused to build a permanent stone church until the needs of the schoolchildren were met. In a poignant sermon in 1875 that was reprinted in newspapers across the country and in Ireland, the pastor explained the reasons "why half the children of Chicago are not in any school." Canvassing his parish, he asked a young boy, "Why don't you go, Michael?" and was told, "Because I've got no boots." Waldron exhorted the "thrifty and prosperous" among St. John's five hundred families to "give them the boots first, and then we can get them to the books afterward." However, within a few years, the nearby railroads that provided employment for poor Irish laborers began to encroach on the neighborhood. Ironically, at a time when enrollments in their academies and parish schools were booming, the Sisters of Mercy and the Christian Brothers found themselves facing fewer and fewer children at St. John's and the school was closed in the 1890s.[17]

Did the investment in Catholic parishes and schools make sense? John Lancaster Spalding, the widely respected bishop of Peoria, Illinois, reflected prevailing American attitudes about urban life when he declared in 1880 that "[no] good has come of this crowding of the people in the cities, either to themselves or the Church." He disparaged the creation of parishes "of fifteen and twenty thousand souls [which] made the erection of fine and showy churches possible," arguing that "half a dozen churches serve the purpose of an episcopal city as well as a hundred."[18]

At the time Patrick A. Feehan was appointed to head the new archdiocese in 1880, an astonishing thirty-two of Chicago's forty parishes supported schools. Although the proliferation of national parishes based on language did not ensure uniform development, much less uniformity, they remained a pragmatic, albeit complicated, solution to the thorny problem of ethnic identity. However, keeping pace with the city's rapid development was a continuing challenge: in 1890, Chicago covered 178 square miles of territory and its population of one million doubled by 1910.[19]

That the Catholic Church was hardly a monolith became abundantly clear in 1874, when Father Joseph Barzynski, C.R., arrived in the city as pastor of St. Stanislaus Kostka, the "mother parish" of Chicago's Polonia. For nearly twenty years, the Resurrectionist priest battled against nationalists in nearby Holy Trinity Church and peace did not return until Cardinal Francis Satolli intervened in 1893.[20]

Chicago newspapers, both English and Polish, chronicled the fight but rarely, if ever, mentioned the ongoing contribution to education made by vowed women religious. Yet at the height of the controversy in St. Stanislaus parish, the School Sisters of Notre Dame were teaching 1,350 girls while nine lay teachers instructed 1,176 boys. That the sisters who were predominantly of German birth and descent made such headway in the city's most important Polish parish raises significant questions about the relationship between Catholic and ethnic identity. For example, even after the Polish order known as the Sisters of Nazareth opened Holy Trinity School in 1894, enrollment at St. Stanislaus Kostka continued to increase, with nearly 4,500 children in attendance by 1908.[21]

By the late 1880s, Catholic—and Lutheran—parochial schools had become more than a familiar part of Chicago's urban landscape. Increasingly they were viewed as a threat to the public schools. In addition to concerns about the teaching of the German language, reformers decried the willingness of clergymen to sign letters of recommendation for eleven- and twelve-year-olds attesting that they had completed their education. Nativists had inveighed against a separate school system in Chicago since the 1850s and had thwarted Catholic efforts to secure a fair share of the state's educational funds. While some Protestants hailed the 1875 decision of the Chicago Board of Education to end compulsory Bible reading in the public schools as "drop[ping] the impertinent and unjust rule into the dead past, where it belongs," others expressed outrage, claiming that it was "a concession to the growing power of the Romish Church." Arthur Mitchell, pastor of the prominent First Presbyterian Church, asserted that the government had a right to include the King James version of the Bible in the schools because it aided "the making of good citizens."[22]

The debate was still raging in 1889 when Richard Edwards, Illinois State Superintendent of Education, spearheaded efforts to revise existing laws on compulsory education. "An act concerning the education of children," approved by the Illinois Legislature and signed into law by Governor Joseph W. Fifer on May 24, 1889, ignited a firestorm of controversy. Popularly known as the Edwards Law, it required children between the ages of seven and fourteen to attend a public day school for at least sixteen weeks each year or their parents or guardian would be fined "a sum not less than one nor more than twenty dollars." The law stated that private schools would be exempt from the legislation only if they were approved by local school boards. In addition to mandating state control of parochial schools, the Edwards Law stipulated that English was to be the only medium of instruction.[23]

In opposing the Edwards Law, Chicago Catholics took a very public stance on the issue of parochial schools, joining forces with German Lutherans to defend the constitutional right of parents to provide their children with a Christian education. Moreover, Catholics used the

twenty-fifth anniversary of Archbishop Feehan's episcopacy to dem-
onstrate their opposition, to showcase their ethnic and racial diversity, and to prove their loyalty as Americans. Even the *Chicago Tribune*,
which routinely criticized the Church and its school system, was forced
to concede that the torchlight procession of thirty thousand lay men
past the Auditorium Theater on October 29, 1890, overshadowed "the
biggest political parade of any Presidential year."[24]

The fight to abolish the Edwards Law had far-reaching results,
religiously and politically. Illinois' four Catholic bishops, including
Feehan, issued a joint pastoral that linked freedom of worship with
freedom of education, denouncing the legislation as "a violation of our
constitutional rights." Without mentioning the decree of the Third Plenary Council of Baltimore, the pastoral took to task Catholic priests
who neglected their schools, noting that, "In building, maintaining and
perfecting our Catholic schools we are doing the most beneficent work
American citizens can do." Not only did the Edwards Law prompt the
launch of a weekly Catholic newspaper, *The New World*, in 1892, but
for the first time in forty years, Illinois voters elected a Democratic governor, John Peter Altgeld, a German-born immigrant from Chicago's
north side.[25]

Shortly after the repeal of the Edwards Law, Chicago Catholics
again claimed the public spotlight with their enthusiastic participation
in the Catholic Schools Exhibit at the World's Fair of 1893. On display
was the signed work of students from across the nation, intended to lay
to rest worries that Catholic schools were un-American and/or inferior to public schools. As the samples sent from the German parochial
school of St. Francis Assisi on the west side make clear, young women
enjoyed a command of geography, math, and literature, and they were
also familiar with the kinds of letter writing needed to advance in the
business world. Occupying a place of honor was a seven-foot marble
statue of Archbishop Feehan, "the Protector of Our Schools," who had
defended the rights of Catholics to build and maintain parochial institutions.[26]

Much of the growth and development of Catholic education in Chicago continued to be women's work. In addition to encouraging young
women and men to pursue their education beyond elementary school,
sisters identified promising vocations, thereby ensuring a steady supply
of teachers and parish priests. As early as the 1890s, the BVMs in Holy
Family parish were making plans for a central high school that would

draw girls from parishes on the south, west, and north sides. St. Mary's, the first of its kind in the nation when it opened in 1899, compiled a remarkable record of success in preparing students to pass the rigorous entrance exam to the Chicago Normal College so they could become teachers in the public schools. During Archbishop James E. Quigley's tenure as head of the diocese (1903-1915), school superintendent Ella Flagg Young endorsed efforts to impose a quota system to limit the number of young Catholic women matriculating at the teachers' college. Quigley and the archdiocesan newspaper fought back, reminding Chicagoans of the success of Catholic candidates as well as the Catholic Church's critical role in educating more than one hundred thousand children annually.[27]

Over the years, reformers associated with Jane Addams's pioneering Hull-House settlement on Halsted Street had harbored reservations about the ability of Catholic schools to train immigrants for American citizenship, but not Unitarian minister Jenkin Lloyd Jones, founder of the Abraham Lincoln Center in Chicago. During the forty-fifth annual meeting of the Free Religious Association of America in Boston in 1912, he came to the spirited defense of Irish Catholic schoolteachers in the nation's public schools. Alarmed at "the growing church aggressiveness" of Roman Catholics who sought "a division of public educational funds," speaker after speaker decried the Church's political aspirations and its interference in education. Yet when Jones rose to speak, he expressed surprise and dismay at the attitude of prominent Protestant clergy and civic leaders. He informed them that he was not scared by the fact that "perhaps eighty percent of the lower grammar-grade teachers [in Chicago's public schools] are Catholic." On the contrary, Jones praised these women for teaching immigrant children "the love of liberty, the joy of democracy, the pride of Abraham Lincoln and George Washington." Moreover, he asserted that there was no reason for worry because the Catholic Church in Chicago "is helping to digest, more effectually than any other machinery I know of, the great mass of foreign children that come out of undemocratic homes and have inherited undemocratic ideas."[28]

William J. Bogan, who was unanimously elected superintendent of schools in 1928, knew from experience that the city needed good parochial as well as public schools. Born on Mackinac Island in Michigan in 1870, he arrived in Chicago at the time of the World's Fair and quickly rose through the ranks, from teacher to principal. Bogan championed vacation schools, evening schools, and the use of public schools as social centers, and he collaborated with Progressive reformers such as Mary McDowell to create small parks in densely populated urban neighborhoods. His years as principal of Lane Technical High School deepened his concern for the "forgotten 90%" of Chicago public school students who did not plan on attending college, and he supported the expansion of junior high schools as a way of keeping students enrolled beyond freshman year. In 1926, an estimated thirty-seven of every one hundred public school students dropped out after ninth grade.[29]

Like so many of his Catholic colleagues who taught in public schools at the turn of the twentieth century, Bogan understood the challenges facing the children of immigrants, especially those whose parents had been born in Italy. In addition to his work in the classroom, on Sundays he taught catechism at Holy Guardian Angel Church on Forquer Street, just around the corner from Hull-House. A unique collaboration between alumnae of the Convent of the Sacred Heart and 125 Catholic teachers in the public schools, the Italian mission was organized in 1899 and by 1903 its Sunday school numbered 1,433 students. Bogan also served as chairman of the executive committee of the Madonna Center Settlement and worked to raise funds for a parochial school. As the *New World* explained in 1915, the need was great because more than two thousand Italian children lived in the neighborhood in close proximity to "four avowedly proselytizing missions."[30]

Throughout the nineteenth century in Chicago, diverse ethnic groups had embraced the philosophy that, "The future of the Catholic church is locked up in the school that stands beside the church." But Quigley made it official policy by endorsing the concept of the combination church and school. These brick structures, generally two stories and basement, ensured that Catholic education would be part of parish life right from the start. As pastors soon discovered, elementary schools attracted new families and actually helped to speed up the process of building a permanent church.[31]

Novelist James T. Farrell (1904-1979) grew up in St. Anselm's on the south side, one of the "mile square" parishes that came to be a distinguishing feature of Chicago Catholicism in the early twentieth century. As Marvin Ruel Schafer argued in 1929, parish boundaries led to a "sense of social unity," and Catholic schools acted as a "unifying and organizing agency" in neighborhoods. In Farrell's case, the parish school also promoted upward social mobility.[32]

Born to an Irish Catholic teamster who had difficulty making ends meet as his family increased in size, Farrell grew up with his maternal grandmother who lived in one of the new "steam heat" apartments located just west of Washington Park. Transferring from Corpus Christi School in 1915, Farrell enrolled at St. Anselm's and his aunts and uncles paid his seventy-five cent monthly tuition, soon to be raised to one dollar. With a student body of four hundred, St. Anselm's was the tenth school in the city of Chicago to be staffed by the Sisters of Providence from St. Mary of the Woods, Indiana, an order of nuns recognized for their teaching skill. Indeed, Farrell credited his beginnings as a writer to Sister Mary Magdalene (Margaret Miller), who not only read and praised his twenty-page essay on Andrew Jackson, but also cleaned up his exercise books so that he might receive a Palmer Method certificate.[33]

In the opening chapter of his blockbuster novel *Young Lonigan*, Farrell vividly brings to life "the chalk-smelling room ... with its forty or fifty squirming kids" and the parish hall where he received his diploma. At a time when many Catholic boys went directly to work, Farrell's teacher encouraged him to enroll at St. Cyril College (later Mount Carmel High School) in nearby Woodlawn where he received first or second honors in "English, elocution, history, Latin, French, algebra, and Christian doctrine" and wrote his first published story. In part because of the small size of his high school—there were only thirty graduates in the 1923 senior class—he was able to play basketball, football, and baseball and serve as athletic editor of the school magazine. Although Farrell left the Catholicism of his youth behind when he moved to New York after attending the University of Chicago, in later years he acknowledged his gratitude to his eighth grade teacher at St. Anselm and to the Carmelites, especially Albert Dolan, "who graded fairly, praised what he considered good, and tried to stimulate literary activity among the better pupils."[34]

Thanks to the ambitious plans of George W. Mundelein who became archbishop in 1916, Chicago's reputation as a Catholic city deepened. In addition to encouraging the construction of beautiful churches and spacious schools such as Quigley Preparatory Seminary, he moved quickly to unify the parochial school curriculum so that children of different ethnic and racial backgrounds would share a common identity as American Catholics. While standardized textbooks played a role, so too did Mundelein's policy that English be the primary language of instruction. That some Polish women religious were not yet fully bilingual only added to the urgency of the directive. Mundelein sought to avoid ethnic clashes by appointing three pastors—one German, one Irish, and one Polish—as supervisors of parish schools; one sister from each of the fifty religious orders in Chicago was named a community superior. As James Sanders notes, this system provided sisters with "a structured means of communicating with one another for the first time [in the history of the diocese]."[35]

Bringing in a new religious community to teach school in a local parish was a venerable tradition in the Chicago diocese dating back to the 1860s. The arrival of six Sisters of the Blessed Sacrament at St. Monica School in 1912 marked a turning point for the city's only African American parish. Back in 1891, Father Augustine Tolton, the first African American priest in the United States, had sought financial help from Mother Katharine Drexel of Philadelphia. As Suellen Hoy has documented, Mother Katharine responded generously and before his untimely death in 1897, Tolton acknowledged that she stood alone in the history of the Church in America in offering "her treasury for the sole benefit of the Colored and Indians." Because she covered the expenses of the sisters, no tuition was charged in the early years and the school flourished.[36]

In 1917, Archbishop Mundelein assigned St. Monica parish to the care of the Divine Word Fathers and exhorted the "three or four hundred colored Catholic families in this city to . . . build up St. Monica's, clear it of debt, make it attractive, equip the school." Although the archbishop's decision to exclude whites from the church at 36th and Dearborn was protested by some African Americans, including the *Defender* newspaper, Mundelein's hope that "the number of its schoolchildren [would] increase . . . month after month" did come true. As a result of conversions, school enrollment grew so large that in the mid-1920s, Mundelein merged St. Monica's with nearby St. Elizabeth parish and established the city's first high school for African American Catholics. By 1933, the Blessed Sacrament Sisters had expanded their mission in Chicago's "Black Belt" to include St. Anselm School and they were joined in this educational work by the Franciscan Sisters from Dubuque who taught more than six hundred African American students at Corpus Christi School.[37]

Like their counterparts who served black Catholic students on the south side, the Sisters of the Third Order of St. Francis of Mary

Immaculate opened their doors wide, first to Italians, and then to Mexican newcomers. Convent annals confirm that the sisters were well-aware of the decline of St. Francis of Assisi parish as German-American families moved away to "more pleasant parts of the city," but they believed that their school had been "saved for a great and holy task...a future of great usefulness." In 1917, the pastor, Father Charles Epstein, canvassed the neighborhood, visiting Italian families and explaining "the cause of Catholic education." Invitations to enroll made it clear that the school was free and that parents did not need any transfer papers for their children who attended nearby public schools such as Dante, Goodrich, and Foster. Archbishop Mundelein vigorously supported this endeavor and lent financial support so that the sisters could serve a free lunch to their Italian pupils.[38]

Chicago's visibility as a Catholic city increased during 1926 as preparations were underway for the Twenty-Eighth International Eucharistic Congress. While the daily newspapers, understandably, focused on the cardinals and bishops who arrived from throughout the world, Monsignor C. J. Quille admitted that it was the "Good Sisters" who ensured the Congress's success as "a Monument to the City of Chicago." In the months preceding the event in Soldier Field, Catholic sisters trained sixty thousand children to sing the Mass of the Angels. Aside from their value as music lessons, these rehearsals brought together children of different ethnic backgrounds, allowing them to cross parish boundaries and experience places unfamiliar or beyond their reach economically. The Franciscans at St. Francis of Assisi School, for example, accompanied their Italian and Mexican students to the nearby Irish parishes of Holy Family and Sacred Heart for practices and took them by streetcar to the new Cubs' baseball park on Addison Street on May 20, 1926. Sister Augustine Werckmann, O.S.F., described it as a "Red Letter Day for all school children north of 18th Street," and confided in the convent annals that the manager praised the children "for their orderly behavior in coming to and leaving the park," declaring that they were "the most orderly crowd of children ever seated in the Grand Stands."[39]

One of the showplaces of Catholic Chicago in 1926 was Leo High School, on 79th Street near Halsted Street. Located in close proximity to street car lines and the Englewood "L," this new Catholic central high school drew young men from parishes throughout the south side. For years the *New World* had exhorted parents that, "If you decide against a higher education for your child, you are practically condemning him to a life of servitude, at starvation wages." Responding to this challenge, the predominantly Irish parish of St. Leo funded the school which was staffed by the Irish Christian Brothers. The choice resonated with many parishioners whose fathers and grandfathers had attended Edmund Rice's schools in Ireland, known for their strict teaching and discipline. Leo opened in September 1926 and more than five thousand spectators turned out to witness the dedication of the cream-colored brick building with its swimming pool and gymnasium and the twelve hundred-seat chapel which served overflow crowds at Sunday Mass.[40]

Although Leo's enrollment of 530 students was only one fifth that of nearby Calumet High School, which also opened in 1926, the Christian Brothers' school quickly developed a reputation as a football powerhouse. The gridiron game had grown in popularity among the sons and grandsons of Catholic immigrants who cheered on local Chicago teams as well as the "Fighting Irish" of Notre Dame who played in Soldier Field while their new stadium in South Bend was under construction. On October 13, 1928, for example, Notre Dame defeated Navy 7-0 before "the biggest crowd in football history" in America's largest venue. Aspiring Leo athletes battled fierce competition from St. Mel, Mount Carmel, and St. Rita to win the 1934 Catholic league championship and the right to play the public school winner in Soldier Field. Fifty thousand fans turned out to watch the match between Lindblom and Leo, among them Mayor Edward J. Kelly, and school board president James B. McCahey, both of whom were Catholic. And fans at home listened to Bob Elson's play-by-play description of the game over WGN radio. Lindblom won 6-0 but the "Fighting Irish" of Leo did not return empty handed: Mayor Kelly presented each member of the team with individual gold football watch charms. Proclaiming the game the "greatest ever played in Chicago," the Mayor also pointed out that the "great spectacle" on the lakefront had generated forty thousand dollars for destitute children in the midst of the Great Depression.[41]

Throughout the 1920s, Catholic elementary and parochial school building had kept pace with the expanding city. Chicago's population of more than three million in 1930 included significant numbers of foreign-born Poles, Italians, Jews, Lithuanians, Greeks, Slovaks, Slovenes, and Mexicans, along with American-born men and women of Irish, German, and French descent, and African Americans who had come to the city as part of the "Great Migration" from the South. Catholic families who moved away from industrial areas near the steel mills, stockyards, and factories found familiar institutions—schools and churches—in the developing "Bungalow Belts" at the city's edge. Although acknowledging the decline in birthrate as a result of the Depression, in 1933, schools superintendent Monsignor D. F. Cunningham, reported that 136,683 students were enrolled in 254 Catholic elementary schools in the city and that 15,632 young men and women attended 40 secondary schools. While Catholic high school enrollment had experienced a small increase, he observed that "a far greater number of our graduates entered the public high schools this year than ever before." The reason? Cunningham surmised that because students could not find work after eighth grade, they had continued on to high school.[42]

Mundelein's belief and pride in Catholic schools was undeniable. During a special anniversary Mass in his boyhood parish of St. Nicholas in New York in May 1933, he credited German Catholics "for the splendid parochial school system in this country . . . that has no equal anywhere in this world." And he informed his audience that, "In my own diocese, 225,000 children are in Catholic schools . . . not one of them closed, filled to the roof with children of all ages, every teacher at her post, at a time when our costly State school system is threatened with dire collapse and decay." Indeed, Chicago public school teachers had received no paychecks since January 1933, and Superintendent Bogan was searching for ways to cut expenses and stem the $6 million dollar deficit. Left unspoken by Mundelein was the sacrifice Catholic sisters were making to keep diocesan schools open. Already living on poverty wages, elementary school sisters received letters from pastors informing them that because of the Depression, their annual salary of $200 would be cut to $150.[43]

Catholic children attending parochial schools in Chicago in the mid-1930s encountered something very different than earlier generations: textbooks that aimed to communicate "a clearer understanding of their faith" than conventional "catechetical instruction." Father John A. O'Brien, director of the Newman Foundation at the University of Illinois, created the *Cathedral Basic Readers* series published by Scott Foresman and Company in 1932. In addition to introducing children to myths and fables, tales of the outdoors, and famous historical figures, the elementary readers featured men, women, and children who embodied the ideals of Pope Pius XI's encyclical on Catholic action and who in their "everyday life walked in the footsteps of Christ." Chicago's Catholic schools also led the way with an innovative religion series written by the brother-sister team of Father Alexander P. Schorsch, C.M., dean of the Graduate School of DePaul University, and Sister M. Dolores Schorsch, O.S.B., a diocesan supervisor. With their emphasis on religious literacy as well as character formation, the texts acknowledged the intellectual and emotional abilities of children to follow "Christ's own words and actions" and acquire virtuous habits. Far ahead of its time, the series cautioned teachers never to tell a child that he was committing a mortal sin since "he will seldom have sufficient knowledge of the malice of the deed." Moreover, teachers should never admonish students whose families failed to observe Sunday Mass and Friday abstinence but should instead lead the child "sweetly ... to both practices without any aspersions being cast on his parents." Later known as the *Jesu-Maria Course in Religion*, the Schorsch series was adopted by many dioceses in the United States and used by catechists in London, British West Indies, New Zealand, and Australia.[44]

That Chicago parishes such as St. Gregory the Great were able to build parochial schools during the Depression was regarded as a sign of faith in the future of the Church and the city. Since its founding in 1904, the predominantly German parish had constructed a monumental complex including a brick school, convent, rectory, and an English Gothic church, completed in 1926. When Mundelein arrived in the parish to bless the sixteen-room grammar and high school building at 1677 W. Bryn Mawr Avenue on May 23, 1937, the event took on heightened significance. Not only was this the "600th religious structure" completed during his tenure as archbishop of Chicago, but the dedication came just days after Mundelein's famous speech in which he denounced Adolph Hitler as "an Austrian paperhanger and a poor one at that" and called attention to the German government's suppression of religious schools.[45]

When Samuel Alphonsus Stritch arrived in Chicago in March 1940 to head the Chicago archdiocese, he was astounded to find a crowd of two hundred thousand waiting to catch a glimpse of him en route from Union Station to Holy Name Cathedral. With a record population of 3,396,808, Chicago had become "one of the great cities of the world," and as the new archbishop quickly discovered, its network of Catholic churches, schools, hospitals, and charitable institutions continued to shape urban life. In a letter to Sister Justitia Coffey, B.V.M., president of Mundelein College, Stritch acknowledged that "what prosperity the Church enjoys in the United States has come out of Catholic schools," and he went further, emphasizing that "our devoted Sisters have done more than bishops, priests, and laity for our schools." That commitment would be sorely tested during the post World War II era as the institutional Church responded to the "Baby Boom" and dramatic demographic changes in the city and suburbs.[46]

While thousands of Catholic families moved to the suburbs after World War II, a similar migration had taken place within Chicago itself, from older parishes to newer residential neighborhoods at the city's edge. Far from declining in importance, the demand for Catholic schools intensified and prompted a multi-million dollar building boom. At St. Francis Borgia parish, formed in 1949 on the far northwest side of Chicago, for example, construction on a $490,000 school began in July 1951 and classes opened in September 1952 for nearly seven hundred students. Significantly, the new Catholic school was welcomed by local residents because it relieved overcrowding at nearby public schools which were then operating on double shifts. The ten Sisters of Providence who formed the faculty of St. Francis Borgia lived in what the *Chicago Tribune* called "special quarters on the school's second floor" until a convent was constructed in 1954, bringing the total number of classrooms to sixteen.[47]

Already by the early 1950s, however, there were signs that Catholic vowed religious orders were unable to provide the number of teachers necessary for elementary and high schools. In 1952, a record 250,000 students enrolled in the diocese's 384 elementary schools, 88 high schools, and 6 colleges and universities, an increase of 7,500 over the previous year. At St. Walter parish on the far south side of Chicago, Catholics succeeded in building a church and school in 1954, over the objection of Protestant neighbors. But only four classrooms opened the following year because of unprecedented demands on the Sisters of St. Dominic from Springfield, Illinois. Since their first foundation in Chicago in 1910 in St. Edward and Our Lady of Grace parishes, the Springfield Dominicans had expanded to include five more grammar schools in the archdiocese and in 1955 they began the daunting task of establishing Marian Catholic, a coeducational high school in suburban Chicago Heights.[48]

As a result of the "baby boom" of the late 1940s and early 1950s, Catholic school enrollment skyrocketed. Every fall, Cunningham, the superintendent of schools, would announce a record number that would be eclipsed the following year. Yet, for many Catholic Chicagoans, the lure of new suburban subdivisions could not compete with "the old neighborhood" whose stores, saloons, churches, schools, and parks were within walking distance and were well-served by public transportation. At Our Lady of the Angels, for example, 983 children had attended classes in the parish's two brick school buildings during the Depression. Although the construction of a new church in 1941 and a convent in 1952 freed up more space for classrooms, in 1955, 1,526 children of Italian, Irish, and Polish descent were enrolled. And Our Lady of the Angels was far from unique: in that year, 40 of the city's 266 Catholic parochial schools boasted enrollments between 1,000 and 1,900 students.[49]

On December 1, 1958, flames from a fire that began near the base of a stairwell in the north wing of Our Lady of the Angels School at 909 N. Avers Avenue quickly spread to the second floor where 329 students were finishing up their lessons for the day. Some children survived by climbing up onto their classroom's high window sills and jumping twenty-five feet below, but others died or were injured while making the leap. Overcome by smoke, many children suffocated while still seated at their desks. As Suellen Hoy recounts, the tragedy that killed ninety children and three BVM sisters left a parish and a city "Stunned With Sorrow." The 1910 brick school building with its wood interior was like many then in use throughout the nation, lacking fire doors, an alarm system, and sprinklers. Noting that Chicago's school system, "both public and parochial, has almost a thousand buildings and hundreds of thousands of pupils," the Cook County Coroner's Jury made thirty-one fire recommendations.[50]

Archdiocesan officials moved quickly to ensure the safety of its students and immediately closed several parochial schools, including St. Joseph's at 13th and Loomis Street which had been built in Holy Family parish in 1875. Since 1933, the modest brick structure had served as chapel and school for African American children in the Jesuit parish. The Polish Sisters of the Holy Family of Nazareth regarded the opportunity to teach at St. Joseph's as "a high honor," and for the next twenty-five years members of their community lived in the building as well. Although the new fire-resistant Holy Family School, dedicated in 1962, was integrated peacefully, the neighborhood's Italian-American population continued to decline as homes and businesses were razed to make way for the new Chicago campus of the University of Illinois.[51]

While there never had been a golden age of Chicago Catholicism with sufficient funds to ensure that all children could attend parochial schools, by the 1950s nearly every parish in the city supported an elementary school. Maintained through voluntary contributions and the poverty wages of vowed women religious, Catholic schools had become such a familiar part of the fabric of urban life that they were no longer regarded as dangerous to American society, much less unique. Yet in the experience of thousands of Chicago families, it was the parochial school, as much as the parish church, which provided structure and continuity in neighborhoods. Slum clearance, urban renewal, and rapid racial change profoundly threatened this investment in Catholic communal life. Without directly mentioning the construction of new suburban churches and schools, Cardinal Stritch reminded Chicago priests in 1952 that, "As things are going now, we are building a new archdiocese on the perimeter of Chicago." Still, he expressed confidence that "Our great city . . . and many of our fine neighborhoods can be saved," and he urged them to regard neighborhood conservation as a pastoral duty as well as a civic responsibility.[52]

In Chicago's "Back of the Yards" neighborhood, immortalized by Upton Sinclair in his novel *The Jungle*, Catholic parishes embarked on a program of expansion, building new parochial schools, convents, social centers, and gymnasiums. One of the city's most densely populated Catholic neighborhoods, in 1952, it boasted six Catholic elementary schools with an enrollment of 4,698 students and 626 students in two parish high schools. This Catholic reinvestment was part of a larger plan by the Back of the Yards Neighborhood Council to renew the neighborhood's housing stock and prevent illegal conversions that signaled "the first shadows of a slum." Founded in 1940 by Saul Alinsky and Joe Meegan with support from the Archdiocese of Chicago and the C.I.O. United Packinghouse Workers, the Back of the Yards Neighborhood Council was known nationally for its success in unionizing the stockyards. Although the grassroots organization failed in persuading savings and loan institutions to finance substantial new construction, its "fix up" campaigns were embraced by homeowners who chose to live in a neighborhood with deep Catholic traditions.[53]

The single greatest challenge facing the Archdiocese of Chicago when Albert Gregory Meyer succeeded Stritch in 1958 was race. Since the 1930s and 1940s, groups such as the Chicago Inter-Student

Catholic Action (CISCA) and the Catholic Interracial Council (CIC) had challenged the color line in Chicago Catholic schools and hospitals. Motivated by the theological concept of the Mystical Body of Christ which "emphasized the unity of Catholics through the Eucharist," increasing numbers of young men and women, together with Catholic priests and sisters, worked to end segregation in public and private institutions. In 1953, for example, seven hundred students representing seventy-five of the diocese's eighty-five high schools gathered for the first High School Interracial Study Day at St. Malachy High School on the west side where they discussed the morality of racial discrimination and the "practical application of interracial justice."[54]

In keeping with their historic role as agents of upward social mobility, Chicago's Catholic high schools became contested spaces after World War II as African American parents sought admission for their sons and daughters. In 1953, nearly a year before the Supreme Court decision desegregating public schools, the Ladies of Loretto announced their intention to accept "Negro as well as white students" in their academy in the Woodlawn neighborhood. Few superiors of Catholic schools had been as brave as Mother Edwardine Partridge who refused to implement a quota system. According to Steven Avella, in the late 1950s only a handful of Catholic secondary schools welcomed African American students in significant numbers. Schools located in neighborhoods undergoing racial succession found it increasingly difficult to attract white students. Indeed, in the spring of 1960, rumors flew on the south side that the Catholic School Board would establish "rigid boundaries" in an effort to force white students from local elementary schools to enroll in Mercy High School. Founded by the Sisters of Mercy in 1924 at 8131 S. Prairie Avenue, the school had flourished until the surrounding neighborhood had changed, block-by-block, from white to black.[54]

During a clergy conference at Resurrection parish on the west side in September 1960, Archbishop Meyer made clear his stand on race, informing every pastor that he was forbidden "to reject from his school any Catholic Negro child, whose parents, be they Catholic or non-Catholic [lived] within the parish boundaries." As historic as Quarter's policy in 1846 of establishing parishes based on language, Meyer's decision would lead to profound changes in the Catholic school system. Not only did he expect pastors of parish high schools and superiors and principals of secondary schools "to accept all Catholic applicants

without regard to race or color," but he reminded his priests that "it is
a terrible thing—a scandal—for a parent or teacher to lead an innocent
child into the evil of racial prejudice." Meyer's statement, finally published in January 1961, garnered headlines in the local papers, leaving
no question that pastors were to "assume the mantle of leadership and
ensure that all our Catholics of the Negro race are integrated into the
complete life of the church."[56]

Ironically, the one group that had been most closely associated
with the growth and development and survival of the city's parochial
schools—Catholic sisters—were conspicuously absent from the historic meeting in Resurrection parish. Nevertheless, they remained on
the front lines in classrooms throughout Chicago as dramatic racial
and ethnic and economic change continued to alter the city's parish
schools. At a time when Catholics throughout the nation began to debate in earnest Mary Perkins Ryan's question, "Are Parochial Schools
the Answer?" Chicagoans continued to vote "Yes." Since the nineteenth
century, thousands of vowed women religious devoted their lives and
their talents to building a school system that profoundly affected the
lives of the poor and middle-class alike—and shaped Chicago in the
process. By any measure, the extent of their commitment was extraordinary: in 1965, 271 of Chicago's 284 parishes still operated elementary
schools and 48 of them enrolled more than one thousand students each
year. That parish histories rarely mention these sisters by name is a
triple loss, for Catholic history, women's history, and urban history.[57]

NOTES

1. For Daniel H. Burnham's famous line about Chicago, "Make No Little Plans,"
see Charles H. Moore, *Daniel H. Burnham: Architect Planner of Cities* 2 (Boston and
New York: Houghton Mifflin Company, 1921), 147; Quote from Bishop Quarter's diary,
in James J. McGovern, *Souvenir of the Silver Jubilee in the Episcopacy of His Grace The
Most Rev. Patrick Augustine Feehan, Archbishop of Chicago, 1890* (Chicago: privately
printed, 1891), 64.

2. At the 1890 celebration for Archbishop Feehan, Vicar General D. M. J. Dowling
claimed that, "We have comparatively the largest parochial school attendance of any
diocese in our land." *Chicago Tribune*, October 30, 1890; John E. McGirr, *Life of the Rt.
Rev. Wm. Quarter, D.D.* (n.d.; repr., Des Plaines, Illinois: St. Mary's Training School
Press, 1920); Timothy Walch, *Parish School: American Catholic Parochial Education
From Colonial Times to the Present* (Washington, DC: National Catholic Educational
Association, 2003), 19.

3. McGovern, *Souvenir of the Silver Jubilee*, 66, 69, 74; *J. W. Norris General Directory and Business Advertiser of the City of Chicago For the Year 1844* (Chicago: Ellis &
Fergus Printers, 1844), 68, 76.

4. *Chicago Daily Democrat*, October 15, 1845; McGovern, *Souvenir of the Silver Jubilee*, 69; Quarter to Archbishop of Vienna, December 20, 1845, translated and quoted in Rev. Francis J. Epstein, "History in the Annals of the Leopoldine Association," *Illinois Catholic Historical Review* 1, no. 2 (October 1918): 231. On the dynamics of diocesan leadership in Chicago, see Timothy Walch, *The Diverse Origins of American Catholic Education: Chicago, Milwaukee and the Nation* (New York: Garland Publishing, 1988), 76-87; 191-199.

5. Chicago Daily Democrat, December 23, 1847. See also Suellen Hoy, "Walking Nuns: Chicago's Irish Sisters of Mercy," in *At the Crossroads: Old Saint Patrick's and the Chicago Irish*, ed. Ellen Skerrett (Chicago: Loyola Press, 1997), 39-51.

6. A Sister of Mercy, "The Sisters of Mercy: Chicago's Pioneer Nurses and Teachers, 1846-1921," *Illinois Catholic Historical Review* 3, no. 4 (April 1921): 342-343, 346; Gilbert J. Garraghan, *The Catholic Church in Chicago, 1673-1871* (Chicago: Loyola Press, 1921), 118; McGovern, *Souvenir of the Silver Jubilee*, 161-163.

7. For an account of Chicago's early public schools, see Alfred T. Andreas, "Educational Department," *History of Chicago, from the Earliest Period to the Present Time* (Chicago: A. T. Andreas Co., 1884-1886), 1:204-220.

8. "Chicago Free Schools," *Chicago Tribune*, April 21, 1858; "State Schools and the Alternative," *Chicago Tribune*, May 12, 1853.

9. O'Regan to Damen quoted in Gilbert J. Garraghan, S.J., *The Jesuits of the Middle West* (New York: America Press, 1938), 3:396.

10. *Chicago Daily Democratic Press*, May 19, 1857; *Chicago Tribune*, May 25, 1857; *Daily Chicago Times*, August 23, 1857; Ellen Skerrett, *Born in Chicago: A History of Chicago's Jesuit University* (Chicago: Loyola Press, 2008), 3-45; James W. Sheahan, "Church of the Holy Family," in Otto Jevne and Peter M. Almini, *Chicago Illustrated* (Chicago: Jevne & Almini, 1866); Katherine Burton, *The Dream Lives Forever: The Story of St. Patrick's Cathedral* (Dublin: Clonmore and Reynolds, 1962), 35-39.

11. *Chicago Tribune*, July 17, 1860; Arnold Damen, S.J. to Peter Beckx, S.J., September 25, 1861, quoted in Joseph P. Conroy, *Arnold Damen, S.J.: A Chapter in the Making of Chicago* (New York: Benzinger Brothers, 1930), 21.

12. Brother Thomas Mulkerins, S.J., *Holy Family Parish Chicago: Priests and People* (Chicago: Universal Press, 1923), 423, 480-485.

13. Ellen Skerrett, "The Irish of Chicago's Hull-House Neighborhood," in *New Perspectives on the Irish Diaspora*, ed. Charles Fanning (Carbondale: Southern Illinois University Press, 2000), 198-209; Skerrett, *Born in Chicago*, 24, 142-44.

14. Michael Coleman, "'Eyes Big As Bowls With Fear and Wonder': Children's Responses to the Irish National Schools, 1850-1922," *Proceedings of the Royal Irish Academy* 98C (1998), 185; "Bible-Reading in the Public Schools," *Chicago Tribune*, October 5, 1875; Mulkerins, *Holy Family Parish Chicago*, 357.

15. "Our Public Schools," *Chicago Tribune*, October 17, 1865; "Our Common Schools," *Chicago Tribune*, October 20, 1865; Ferdinand Coosemans, S.J. to Peter Beckx, S.J., February 20, 1868, quoted in Skerrett, *Born in Chicago*, 26. St. Ignatius College, the forerunner of Loyola University Chicago, is now known as St. Ignatius College Prep, 1076 W. Roosevelt Road.

16. "The Churches: Rebuilding St. Michael's Catholic Church," *Chicago Tribune*, June 1, 1873; "St. Michael's School," *Chicago Tribune*, September 30, 1881; Hoy, *At the Crossroads*, 32, 34; "Catholicity in Chicago," *Western Tablet*, February 6, 1875.

17. "More Waldrons Wanted," *Chicago Times*, October 3, 1875, reprinted in the *Western Catholic*, September 15, 1877; Harry C. Koenig, ed., *A History of the Parishes of the Archdiocese of Chicago* (Chicago: Archdiocese of Chicago, 1980), 2:1657.

18. J. L. Spalding, *The Religious Mission of the Irish People* (New York: Catholic Publication Society, 1880), 114, 116.

19. Parish and school statistics computed from *Sadlier's Catholic Directory for the Year of Our Lord 1879* (New York: D. J. Sadlier & Co., 1879); Bessie L. Pierce, *A History of Chicago, 1871-1893* (New York: Alfred A. Knopf, 1957), 334.

20. Joseph J. Parot, *Polish Catholics in Chicago, 1850-1920* (DeKalb: Northern Illinois University Press, 1981); Koenig, *A History of the Parishes*, 2:890.

21. McGovern, *Souvenir of the Silver Jubilee*, 252; Koenig, *A History of the Parishes*, 2:891. See also Rima Lunin Schultz, "Sister M. Theresa Dudzik," in *Women Building Chicago, 1790-1990* (Bloomington: Indiana University Press, 2001), 232-235.

22. Florence Kelley, "The Working Boy," *American Journal of Sociology* 2, no. 3 (November 1896): 363; [Puritan Stock], "Let it Stand," *Chicago Tribune*, October 2, 1875; "Bible-reading in the Public Schools," *Chicago Tribune*, October 5, 1875; "The Chicago Presbytery," *Chicago Tribune*, October 5, 1875.

23. For a discussion of the Edwards Law, see Charles Shanabruch, *Chicago's Catholics: The Evolution of an American Identity* (Notre Dame: University of Notre Dame Press, 1981) and James W. Sanders, *The Education of an Urban Minority: Catholics in Chicago, 1833-1965* (New York and Oxford: Oxford University Press, 1977).

24. "Music, Pomp, and Glory," *Chicago Tribune*, October 30, 1890; "Testified Their Love," *Chicago Tribune*, October 31, 1890.

25. "To the Clergy and Catholic people of the Ecclesiastical Province of Chicago," 1892 pastoral, Feehan Folder 9, Archdiocese of Chicago's Joseph Cardinal Bernardin Archives & Records Center, Chicago, IL.

26. I am indebted to Sister Marian Voelker, O.S.F., archivist for the Sisters of St. Francis of Mary Immaculate, Joliet, Illinois, for sharing rare archival documents, including the St. Francis Girls' School, *World's Fair Exhibit or Geography, Letter-Writing and Translation Grade VI* (Chicago, 1893); "For the Catholic Exhibit," *Chicago Tribune*, February 7, 1893.

27. Skerrett, *Born in Chicago*, 55-56; "The Case in a Nutshell," *New World*, February 20, 1904. For a discussion of the Teachers' College, see Charles Fanning, Ellen Skerrett, and John Corrigan, *Nineteenth Century Chicago Irish: A Social and Political Portrait* (Chicago: Center for Urban Policy Loyola University Chicago, 1980), 28-30.

28. In a report about schools in the Nineteenth Ward written for the Illinois Woman's Alliance, Corinne S. Brown and Florence Kelley asserted that, "Experience has shown that wherever the public schools have been sufficient in number that private ones have only flourished spasmodically," *Jane Addams Papers*, ed. Mary Lynn Bryan, et al. Microfilm reel 54:006. According to Jane Addams's biographer Allan F. Davis, "The Hull House reformers never learned to accept a Catholic school as a possible alternative to a public school," *American Heroine: The Life and Legend of Jane Addams* (New York: Oxford University Press, 1973), 121-122. James H. West, "Business Meeting," May 23, 1912, in *Proceedings Free Religious Association Forty-Fifth Annual Meeting* (Boston: Free Religious Association, 1912), 20; "Remarks of Jenkin Lloyd Jones," *Proceedings*, 91-99.

29. "7,000 in Vacation Schools," *Chicago Tribune*, July 9, 1907; "Tells How Boys Are Trained for Plumbing Trade," *Chicago Tribune*, July 18, 1926; "Trustees Elect Bogan to Post McAndrews Lost," *Chicago Tribune*, June 28, 1928; "Bogan, Head of Schools, Dies," *Chicago Tribune*, March 25, 1936.

30. According to her memoir, Mary Agnes Amberg decided to continue her mother's work at Guardian Angel Mission after a long conversation with William J. Bogan. Mary Agnes Amberg, *Madonna Center: Pioneer Catholic Social Settlement* (Chicago: Loyola

Press, 1976); Kate Gertrude Prindiville, "Italy in Chicago," *Catholic World* (July 1903): 452-461; "Catholics Work for Children in Little Italy," *New World*, October 8, 1915.

31. Quote from Los Angeles Bishop Thomas J. Conaty's funeral sermon for Rev. Hugh McGuire of St. James parish, Chicago, New World, September 2, 1911.

32. "One of the New Parishes," *New World*, July 24, 1909; Charles Fanning and Ellen Skerrett, "James T. Farrell and Washington Park: The Novel as Social History," *Chicago History* (Summer 1979): 80-91; Marvin R. Shafer, "The Catholic Church in Chicago, Its Growth and Administration" (PhD diss., University of Chicago, 1929), 70.

33. St. Anselm tuition records, 1915-1920, Sisters of Providence Archives, St. Mary of the Woods, Indiana. I am grateful to Suellen Hoy for sharing biographical information on Margaret Miller, Sister Mary Magdalen, S.P. According to an account in the Sisters of Providence Archives, "Sister Mary Magdalen taught, usually the higher grades. As a boys' teacher most of her life, she was very successful. Her artistic taste was evident in her always neat and attractive classroom. Sister ministered in Indiana and Illinois with the longest periods spent at Our Lady of Sorrows and St. Anselm's in Chicago." Ron Ebest, "The Irish Catholic Schooling of James T. Farrell, 1914-1923," *Eire-Ireland* 30, no. 4 (Winter 1996): 21.

34. James T. Farrell, *Studs Lonigan* (1932, 1934, 1935; repr. Urbana: University of Illinois Press, 1993), 5; *Oriflamme: The St. Cyril High School Yearbook* (Chicago: St. Cyril College, 1923); James T. Farrell, "My Beginnings as a Writer," in *Reflections at Fifty and Other Essays* (New York: Vanguard Press, 1954), 156-163.

35. George W. Mundelein, "Address in Reply to the Welcome of the Laity of the Archdiocese, Delivered in the Auditorium, Chicago, February 13, 1916," in *Two Crowded Years* (Chicago: Extension Press, 1918), 49; Sanders, *The Education of an Urban Minority*, 150.

36. Suellen Hoy, *Good Hearts: Catholic Sisters in Chicago's Past* (Urbana: University of Illinois Press, 2006), 88. For photographs of Father Tolton, St. Monica's, and Mother Katharine Drexel see Hoy's article, "Ministering Hope to Chicago," *Chicago History* (Fall 2002): 4-7.

37. George W. Mundelein to Very Rev. J. A. Burgmer, S.V.D., October 26, 1917 in *Two Crowded Years,* 291-300; "'Jim Crow' School," *Chicago Defender*, March 29, 1913; "St. Monica's Church Again the Scene of Discrimination," *Chicago Defender*, November 17, 1917; Hoy, *Good Hearts*, 92.

38. *Annals of St. Francis from 1917-1919*, Archives, Sisters of St. Francis of Mary Immaculate; "Dear Friend," letter signed by Rev. Charles Epstein, Rev. John Wagener, and Rev. Francis Mueller; August 25, 1917 letter signed by Epstein and Wagener.

39. Sister Augustine Werckmann, O.S.F., November 21, 1926 and May 20, 1926, *Annals of St. Francis*. See especially Jill Thomas Grannan, "Here Comes Everybody: The 28th International Eucharistic Congress," *Chicago History* (Spring 2009): 20-45.

40. "That Boy or Girl of Yours," *New World*, August 6, 1915; "500 [sic] Attend Impressive Leo Dedication," *Southtown Economist*, November 4, 1926.

41. "Start of Fall Term Opens Several New School Buildings," *Southtown Economist*, September 9, 1926; "Biggest Crowd in Football History Sees Notre Dame Defeat Navy," *Chicago Tribune*, October 14, 1928; Charles Bartlett, "Fighting Irish Label Merited by Leo Eleven," *Chicago Tribune*, November 29, 1934; "Music Aplenty Assured at Prep Football Final," *Chicago Tribune*, November 30, 1934; "Today's Features," *Chicago Tribune*, December 1, 1934; "Leo-Lindblom Game Raises Fund of $40,000," *Chicago Tribune*, December 6, 1934.

42. Archdiocesan School Board, *Annual Report of the Catholic Schools, 1933-34*, 19-21; *Annual Report, 1930-31*, 7.

43. George W. Mundelein address at St. Nicholas Church, New York, May 1933, Archdiocese of Chicago's Joseph Cardinal Bernardin Archives & Records Center, Chicago; Philip Kinsley, "Bogan Has New School Plan," *Chicago Tribune*, July 22, 1933; Letter from pastor of St. Francis of Assisi Church to Mother General, March 17, 1933. According to the Archdiocesan School Board *Annual Report*, leading the network of Catholic schools in the city of Chicago in 1933 were the Sisters of Mercy with 27 schools; BVMs (23); Sisters of the Third Order of St. Francis of Mary Immaculate (15); Sisters of the Holy Family of Nazareth (15); Sisters of Providence (14); Felicians (14); School Sisters of Notre Dame (14); Adrian Dominicans (13); School Sisters of St. Francis (13); Sisters of St. Casimir (10); and Sinsinawa Dominicans (10).

44. *Annual Report, 1933-34*, 8, 23; Rev. John A. O'Brien, *Cathedral Basic Readers Book Five* (Chicago: Scott, Foresman and Company, 1932), 160; Rev. Alexander P. Schorsch, C.M., and Sister M. Dolores Schorsch, O.S.B., *A Course in Religion for the Elementary Schools, Teacher's Guidebook Book Four, Jesus the High Priest* (Chicago: Archdiocese of Chicago School Board, 1934), 25-28; Albert J. Schorsch, III, *Schorsch Family Centenary, October 22, 1995* (Chicago: rev. 2008). In 1953, Sister Dolores Schorsch completed her PhD thesis, "John Dewey's Philosophy of Education in Relation to Inquiry as Method and Process," Loyola University, 1953.

45. "Cardinal Opens School; His 600th Building in City," *Chicago Tribune*, May 24, 1937; Thomas M. Keefe, "The Mundelein Affair: A Reappraisal," *Records of the American Catholic Historical Society of Philadelphia* 89, no. 1-4 (March-December 1978): 74-75, includes the text of Cardinal Mundelein's speech on May 18, 1937.

46. "My Aim Is To Be A Good Pastor, Says New Bishop," *Chicago Daily News*, March 6, 1940; Charles Leavelle, "Enthrone New Archbishop in Pageant Today," *Chicago Tribune*, March 7, 1940; Clem Lane, "New Archbishop Enthroned," *Chicago Daily News*, March 7, 1940; Samuel A. Stritch to "My dear Sister Mary Justina [sic]," September 1, 1941, Gannon Center Women's Leadership Archives, Loyola University Chicago.

47. "Canty School Bulges Under Roster Strain," *Chicago Tribune*, March 4, 1951; "Ground Broken on Far N.W. Side Parish School," *Chicago Tribune*, July 22, 1951; "Celebrate New Church School With Carnival," *Chicago Tribune*, July 27, 1952; Koenig, *A History of the Parishes,* 1:290.

48. "Await Record Enrollment in Archdiocese," *Chicago Tribune*, August 21, 1955; Koenig, *A History of the Parishes,* 1:243, 688; 2:1074; Marian Catholic High School, http://www.marianchs.com/about_MCHS/history/history.html

49. Koenig, *A History of the Parishes,* 1:670-672; "Information Concerning Parishes in Chicago," *New World*, December 19, 1930: 27; *Official Catholic Directory for the Year 1955* (New York: P.J. Kenedy & Sons, 1955), 33-39.

50. Hoy, "Stunned With Sorrow," *Chicago History* (Summer 2004): 4-25; "Findings and Recommendations of the Cook County Coroner's Jury, Our Lady of the Angels School Fire, Chicago, Illinois, Presented at the Thirty-First Annual Fire Department Instructors Conference, Memphis, Tennessee, Feb. 24-27, 1959," http://www.olafire.com/Coroner.asp

51. Hoy, *Good Hearts*, 93-94. For more on the African American community in Holy Family parish see *The Miracle on Roosevelt Road: A Collection of Memories* (Chicago: Ellidon Publication, 2009).

52. Samuel Alphonsus Stritch, "Neighborhood Conservation: Housing as a Pastoral Problem," *Catholic Charities Review* 37, no. 2 (February 1953): 33-35; Stritch to Rev. Daniel M. Cantwell, November 8, 1952, Cantwell Papers, Box 9, Chicago History Museum.

53. "The Future of the Back of the Yards," July 2, 1953, Chicago History Museum;

Thomas J. Jablonsky, *Pride in the Jungle: Community and Everyday Life in Back of the Yards Chicago* (Baltimore: Johns Hopkins University Press, 1993); *Official Catholic Directory*, 1952.

54. Hoy, *Good Hearts*, 110-111; Rev. Daniel M. Cantwell, "Catholics and Prejudice," *Voice of St. Jude* (July 1952); Donald J. Thorman, "A Colorful Day," *Voice of St. Jude* (February 1954).

55. Hoy, *Good Hearts*, 103-124; Steven M. Avella, *This Confident Church: Catholic Leadership and Life in Chicago, 1940-1965* (Notre Dame: University of Notre Dame Press, 1992), 304; William Gleason, "Girls' Schools Test Integration," *Chicago American*, June 28, 1960. See especially George V. Fornero, "The Expansion and Decline of Enrollment and Facilities of Secondary Schools in the Archdiocese of Chicago, 1955-1980: A Historical Study" (PhD diss., Loyola University, 1990).

56. The three main speakers at the Clergy Conference held September 20-21, 1960, at Resurrection Auditorium, Chicago, were Rev. Joseph G. Richards, Rev. Patrick T. Curran, and Rev. Rollins E. Lambert, the first African American priest ordained for the Chicago diocese in 1949. For background material on the conference, including "The Apostolate to the Negro in Chicago," and draft statements for Cardinal Meyer, see the Cantwell Papers, Box 8 Folder 2, Chicago History Museum. According to a letter sent along with an 11-page mss. to Cardinal Meyer, August 19, 1960, Cantwell states that "Monsignor McManus, Monsignor Egan, and I to some degree worked this out together." For coverage of Cardinal Meyer's statement on race see David Meade, "Integration Ordered By Cardinal Meyer," *Chicago Daily News*, January 20, 1961, and "Meyer Orders End to Racial Bias in Church," *Chicago Tribune*, January 21, 1961.

57. Mary Perkins Ryan, *Are Parochial Schools the Answer?* (New York: Guild Press, 1963). Statistics compiled from *Official Catholic Directory*, 1965. In 1967, former Catholic Interracial Council leader Rev. Daniel M. Cantwell, pastor of the African American parish of St. Clotilde, captured the changing attitudes toward parochial schools when he commented on "the sympathy directed toward me by my friends who feel I am trapped into running a parochial school. However one feels about parochial schools, it is a fact that the people of our parish want nothing so much as the best possible school for their children. It is my hope and dream that our school in Chatham will attain an excellence which will attract white families to integrate in reverse and to come back for the sake of the education of their children." Matthew Ahmann and Margaret Roach, ed., *The Church and the Urban Racial Crisis* (Techny, IL: Divine Word Publications, 1967).

Part Three
Catholic Education on the Borderland

"From their humble beginnings through the tumultuous years of the nineteenth century...up to the devastation of Hurricane Katrina, Catholic schools in New Orleans have adapted to the educational needs and socioeconomic trends of New Orleans society. In the process, they have, at varying moments, both challenged and reinforced the critical divisions and inequalities of New Orleans society."
— Justin D. Poché

"The development of San Antonio's Catholic schools largely mirrors the development of the Mexican American community in that city and represents in many ways the history of Catholic Texas. While other Catholic ethnic groups certainly influenced the city's educational life, even the educational and faith development of those groups cannot be fully understood absent the influence of the Mexican American community."
— Steve Neiheisel

"Establishing parish schools [in Los Angeles] was never simple but there would be new challenges to maintain and improve the schools that previous generations built at great sacrifice.... A vast network of Catholic schools had been envisioned and planned for Los Angeles by its past leaders. Subsequent generations would need to discern their role in sustaining this legacy and advancing its educational mission."
— Michael P. Caruso

"The Catholic schools in San Francisco entered the twenty-first century in a situation very similar to their beginning—they served a largely immigrant community, they struggled with finances, they competed with public schools, and now public charter schools, for students. And though the number of vowed religious has dwindled dramatically, Catholic schools remain staffed by committed teachers. The fundamental task remains the same: to pass the faith on to a new generation and to promote the Catholic leaders of the future."
— Jeffrey M. Burns

Crescent City Catholicism:
Catholic Education in New Orleans

Justin D. Poché

In 1727, six Ursuline nuns arrived in New Orleans to educate young women of the struggling settlement. The founding of the Ursulines' school inaugurated a nearly three-hundred-year Catholic education system that remains at the center of the Crescent City's religious, social, and political formation. It was a natural task for the pioneering Ursulines. The society originated in 1544 as a lay religious movement for young unmarried women seeking new paths of spiritual and social fulfillment through voluntary chastity and acts of mercy and education among the poor and sick. Their founder, Angela Merici, instructed teachers to treat all students as their own daughters, "having each and every one engraved on your mind and heart, not only their names but also their situation and character and every detail about them."[1] When the Compagnie de Sainte-Ursule formally organized amid the social and political struggles of Reformation France in the 1640s, it concentrated its apostolic mission upon the education of young women in all corners of society. Combining scholarly discipline, intense piety, and charity, an Ursuline education championed Catholic orthodoxy even as it challenged the social hierarchies of seventeenth century Europe. "They trained young daughters of the court sycophants as best they could, not indeed to depreciate ceremony, provided right authority were its center, but to value all human dignity only proportionately with the Divine."[2]

Ursulines carried this vision to the New World. The school in New Orleans nurtured a distinctive female piety that often shunned the

social and racial boundaries of early colonial society. Serving communities of slave and free, black and white, the school generated the
highest literacy rates among the European colonies of the New World.
It also forged an active Afro-Creole Catholic community that used
the Church to build community ties and maintain social influence
through the early nineteenth century.[3] But the expansion of the antebellum plantation economy and the rise of Anglo-American social
and political dominance ultimately supplanted the fluid structures of
social leadership that Ursuline education specifically, and Creole society generally, had engendered through the colonial era. Through the
second half of the century, as the Church expanded to meet the needs
of the booming European Catholic immigrant population, it adapted
to Anglo-American racial customs. While Catholics of African descent
continued to build upon the original Ursuline vision through private
educational ventures, the order itself, alongside other newly arrived religious congregations, largely abandoned work with the slave and free
black communities. After the Civil War, the Catholic Church's development of a segregated, biracial education system helped entrench Jim
Crow within New Orleans for the next seventy years.

As the Ursulines adapted to the changing social, political, and cultural climate of New Orleans through the nineteenth century, it embodied critical tensions that have shaped the establishment, expansion,
and reorganization of Catholic education in the Crescent City into the
present day. From their humble beginnings through the tumultuous
years of the nineteenth century, the rise of Jim Crow segregation and
its decline in the civil rights era, and the social and economic conflicts
leading up to the devastation of Hurricane Katrina, Catholic schools
have struggled to adapt the Catholic Church's evolving spiritual, social,
and intellectual mission to the city's increasingly complex educational
and social needs. In the process they have, at varying moments, both
defined and defied racial and economic boundaries. Their struggle
continues to shape the ways citizens and the Church as a whole understand and respond to the ongoing divisions and inequalities of modern
New Orleans.

The Capuchin Sons of St. Francis arrived in the Louisiana territory
in 1722 and formed the first formal school for religious instruction in
New Orleans in 1725. Armed with reports of the colony's deplorable
spiritual condition, Capuchins envisioned a school and missionary
endeavor to implant the faith among the sons of the colony. An adjoining

school for Indians, they hoped, would create future missionaries in un-
settled regions of the Louisiana territory. Yet little support came from
the governing Company of the Indies. After two failed attempts to revive it, the school closed after 1740.[4] Apathy from the community and
a bitter rivalry between the Capuchins and the Jesuits over missionary
control also ensured that more than eighty years would pass before
another boys' Catholic school arrived in the Crescent City. Prosperous
colonists preferred to hire private tutors or send their sons to Europe
for formal education.[5] Efforts to create a girls' Catholic school in these
early years were more successful.

Since New Orleans' daughters faced more social constraints, parents and officials sought a girls' school that might also bring more social and moral stability to the colony. The local head of the Church,
Ignace de Beaubois, picked the Ursulines for the task. Ever mindful of
their call to offer education to all souls, the nuns set up both a boarding
school for colonists and a day school for "Negresses and Indian girls."
The Ursulines maintained strict order and intense piety within the convent. Paradoxically, historian Emily Clark argues, the maintenance of
monastic discipline and a hierarchy based upon moral and spiritual—
as opposed to economic and social—wealth within the convent walls
created a space that "resolutely welcomed women of all races, classes,
and nationalities through the end of the colonial period."[6] The influence of the convent school grew during the Spanish period in New
Orleans from 1767 to 1803. By the early 1800s, the Ursuline convent
had established enough social power to frustrate colonial and church
leaders bent on establishing a more rigid social structure defined by
Anglo-American hierarchies of race and gender.

During the early "American period" from the 1803 Louisiana Purchase to the middle of the nineteenth century, New Orleans emerged
as a major commercial hub for the early republic. Ethnic tensions between the French-speaking Creole population and Anglo-American
newcomers combined with inadequate resources amid rapid social and
economic growth to paralyze the development of public schooling. In
the meantime, Catholic leadership failed to meet demands for a larger
educational system. During this so-called "dark period" in Louisiana
Catholic history, private school ventures provided general instruction for the city's youth, but public education did not take root until the 1850s with the establishment of night classes for working-class
immigrants.[7]

In the wake of these challenges Archbishop Antoine Blanc (1835-1860) sensed an opportunity. As early as the 1830s, Irish and German immigrants had begun transforming the ethnic geography of New Orleans.[8] By 1850, over 20,000 of the city's 116,000 residents were Irish, while over 11,000 were German-born Catholics who demanded the growth of the institutional Church to meet their needs.[9] In 1854 alone, the archdiocese established fourteen parishes. Responding to the larger Church's demands that the Catholic faithful take care of their own, Redemptorists, Christian Brothers, Jesuits, and Congregation of Holy Cross all arrived in New Orleans to build a Catholic school system to compete with public schools. In addition to schools for boys, the Sisters of Saint Joseph, School Sisters of Notre Dame, Holy Family Sisters, Sisters of Mount Carmel, and the Sisters of the Good Shepherd all staffed schools for the growing immigrant church in New Orleans.

In 1848, Father Edward Sorin, founder of the newly established University of Notre Dame in Indiana, sent five brothers of the Congregation of Holy Cross (CSC) and four sisters of the Marianites of Holy Cross to New Orleans to revive the floundering orphanage of St. Mary's which had been founded in 1835. Despite early struggles, the Congregation persisted in sending Holy Cross priests to New Orleans. Due in large part to the Yellow Fever epidemic of the 1850s, more than fifteen hundred orphans resided at St. Mary's in 1859. That year, Father Patrick Sheil, CSC, sought to secure the orphanage for the CSC's by acquiring a piece of property in present-day Ninth Ward. When Sheil passed away, the Congregation decided to transform the institution into a formal school. In 1890, Holy Cross College was formally chartered by the state. In 1903, French Sisters of the Presentation arrived and would staff the school for the next fifty years.[10]

After establishing houses and schools in other parts of Louisiana, the Sisters of the Sacred Heart finally took up the Ursuline model in 1867 when they created an academy for girls. Like the Ursulines, the Sacred Heart Sisters could offer free education for lower class girls by establishing a boarding school for elite women. Their tuitions subsidized the day school. The congregation's main school opened in 1887 on St. Charles Avenue and enjoyed the patronage of second generation Irish Catholics as well as Creole elite. The school became a significant landmark in Uptown attracting second and third generation New Orleans Catholics through the early twentieth century. Over time, however, impoverished students, who had attended the free school, began attending parochial schools in the surrounding areas.[11]

The establishment of a true parochial system in the late nineteenth century resembled not only the settlement patterns but also the ethnic rivalries that defined Catholic development in other U.S. cities, particularly in the Northeast and Midwest. Irish, German, and later Italian parishes emerged within mere blocks of one another, competing to place their mark on the urban religious landscape. In 1833, the Irish erected St. Patrick's, the second Catholic church in New Orleans. Its pastor, James Ignatius Mullon, built a parish school and an orphanage at St. Patrick's. In 1852, the Irish built St. Alphonsus Church and School directly across the street from the German parish of St. Mary's Assumption. Its priest, the Redemptorist Father John B. Duffy, also constructed a school for the parish.[12] Yet despite the increasing prominence of Irish Catholicism and political life throughout nineteenth century urban America, New Orleans Catholicism did not witness the same type of "Hibernization" seen elsewhere. Irish priests struggled to establish a presence despite the dearth of a truly native-born clergy. As many early twentieth century Church historians were quick to point out, wrangling between the deeply rooted Creole culture and Northern European newcomers had kept the city from nurturing a deferential style among the laity that defined Catholicism elsewhere.[13]

Nonetheless, in the decades following the Civil War, the Church aggressively recruited German Catholics in building the institutional Church in New Orleans. Despite the toll of Yellow Fever in the 1850s, the German-born population in New Orleans increased to nearly twenty thousand by 1860. The epidemic prompted the German Redemptorist priests to establish St. Joseph's German Orphan Asylum in 1854. In 1858, Archbishop Antoine Blanc and the Redemptorist Fathers convinced the School Sisters of Notre Dame to staff St. Mary's Assumption School, the city's first true parochial school, in 1858.[14] In the 1870s, the Church invited the Benedictine Sisters to staff schools at Holy Trinity (1870), St. Boniface (1872), and Mater Dolorosa (1874). In 1873, the Sisters of Christian Charity arrived to staff the school at St. Henry's in Uptown New Orleans.[15]

But if one ethnic group did define a unique New Orleans Catholic style at the turn of the century, it was the Italian population that began migrating as early as 1820. After the Civil War, waves of immigration, largely from Sicily, made them the largest white-ethnic minority in New Orleans. By 1903, an estimated sixteen thousand Italian immigrants resided in the city, up from twelve thousand a decade earlier. When anti-Italian violence gripped the city in 1891, Archbishop Francis Janssens sought to organize the Italian Catholic community. Mother Francis Xavier Cabrini agreed to supply the archbishop with three Missionary Sisters of the Sacred Heart. In 1900, sixteen sisters staffed the school of the Parrochia Italiana on Conti Street. In 1910, the same number instructed over seven hundred students at St. Mary's Italian on Chartres Street, the site of the old Ursuline convent.[16]

By the turn of the century, the rapid growth and increasingly multiethnic character of New Orleans Catholicism demanded a more structured school system. In 1884, the Third Plenary Council of American Bishops in Baltimore had called for an extensive parochial system to spread the faith and protect Catholics from the corrosive effects of public education. In the process the Council called for the establishment of separate black parishes to protect the "Negro Apostolate" in the face of white racism. In New Orleans, the task fell to Janssens, who had arrived in 1890 to "Americanize" the Church and bring the former French colony into line with the Council's mandates. But the rapid growth in the Crescent City did not come without significant cost to the historic identity of New Orleans Catholicism. Despite the efforts of Creole and black activists to prevent separate churches and schools, the Catholic school system played a major role in the birth and survival of Jim Crow in New Orleans. As W.E.B. DuBois would argue for American society as a whole, the major problem facing Catholic schooling in New Orleans well through the next century was indeed "a problem of the color line."[17]

Prior to the Civil War, public schools had denied the city's nearly fifteen thousand slaves access to education. But private efforts to maintain Catholic education for blacks produced some important opportunities for African Americans both before and after the war. Early Union occupation of the city made New Orleans a laboratory for a "revolutionary" experiment. Between 1862 and 1877, its officials and African American activists established the country's first and only truly integrated public school system. Many of these activists came from the Marie Couvent School. Founded in the late 1840s through a bequest from a free African woman to the Catholic Church, Couvent and a handful of other private Catholic establishments reached out to the city's free black population. Operated entirely by black lay personnel, the school nurtured a black leadership class that took an active role in the reconstruction and became for many "the nursery for revolution in Louisiana."[18]

The St. Claude Street School for girls of color, founded by a former Ursuline in 1832 and staffed through the 1890s by the Sisters of Mount Carmel, also produced several African American female leaders. Products of the school founded the nation's second order of African American women religious, the Sisters of the Holy Family. Under the direction of Henriette Delille, the Holy Family Sisters took up the Ursulines' flagging mission among free black and slave communities in New Orleans. Blending Ursuline piety with a tradition of religious activism emerging in nineteenth century France, the congregation established several schools through the end of the nineteenth century.[19] Often falling outside of the purview of the local hierarchy, these schools cultivated a black Catholic leadership that would lay the foundation for resistance to segregation at the turn of the century.

Despite efforts to segregate black Catholic education since the 1840s, the separation of black and white in parochial schools did not become systematic until the 1890s.[20] In 1877, the public schools in New Orleans resegregated, leaving African Americans with only a handful of dilapidated school buildings. Cutbacks continued through the 1880s when the board closed the entire system for the second semester of the school year. According to historian John B. Alberts, in the same years, several white religious orders began abandoning their commitment to black education. In 1888, for example, St. Mary's Italian closed its black school. A decade later, the Carmelites turned their Ecole St. Claude over to the Sisters of the Holy Family. Viewing the conditions of public schools and responding to rising pressures from whites, the Catholic Church sensed an opportunity to adapt a "national parish" system to the needs of African Americans in the city. Allowing German, Irish, Italian, Polish, and other ethnic Catholics to practice faith and nurture distinctive Catholic traditions among "their own" communities throughout the urban north, the "national parish" offered a model for leaders seeking to separate African American and Afro-Creole Catholics from the growing "white" church.

Archbishop Francis Janssens presided over the project. Arriving in 1890 as the first non-French prelate of the archdiocese, Janssens reasoned that the prevailing currents of discrimination within the Church would drive blacks to Protestant congregations. Central to his efforts was the creation of a separate school system for black children. Within

Protestant schools and colleges "many become very careless and a few are lost to the faith," he argued. A separate Catholic school system "is our special hope & reliance for the future."[21] Janssens urged donations for black schools and encouraged clergymen to set up classrooms in the rear of churches for instruction. According to historian James Bennett, the archbishop's interest in parochial education became an important building block to the larger segregation of New Orleans Catholicism.[22] In 1895, the archdiocese opened St. Katherine's Church, a parish exclusively for Catholics of color. Opposition to the move from black and Creole Catholics revealed the strength of black political organization in the waning years of the nineteenth century. A decade of struggle nonetheless exhausted their resources as the archdiocese continued to push for a separate black Catholic system.

In 1905 Archbishop James Blenk revived the program by mandating that every parish have a parochial school connected to it, paid for by the parishioners of the church.[23] While new white schools thrived under the new system, it discriminated against lower-income black parishes. In response, Blenk enlisted the support of local orders to create a "national parish" that could draw African Americans from throughout the city to the school. In 1907, St. Katherine's established the first black Catholic parish school in New Orleans. For the next fifty years, black Catholics learned, prayed, and struggled in the shadows of a burgeoning white church. Catholic parochial schools became an essential function of what became known as the "Negro Apostolate," the term given to direct efforts by clergymen and vowed women religious newly arriving in the South to maintain the faith among Louisiana's black Catholics. Two religious orders—the male Society of St. Joseph (the Josephites) and the Sisters of the Blessed Sacrament founded by Katharine Drexel in 1891—administered the new apostolate, staffing schools and overtaking leadership roles in places once occupied by the black laity. When a hurricane destroyed the Couvent School in 1915, resources from Drexel's Sisters of the Blessed Sacrament reestablished it as St. Louis School. But in order to receive funds, the black laity had to relinquish control to white sisters. By 1917, the school enrolled six hundred children. This number doubled over the next ten years.[24]

Black Catholics criticized the schools' inculcation of deferential manners and customs in the face of white discrimination. Sisters confronted with complaints about whites' treatment of blacks in Mass instructed teachers to remind students that it is their duty, and they love the Mass, and are therefore not concerned about other people. . . . Where children say that white Catholic boys and girls make fun of them—is it not best to remind them that young people are mischievous and make fun of one another because they like to do it, regardless of color.[25]

The teacher, it added, must "distract their attention by asking them to name some of the many wonderful things God has done for them, and God alone matters."[26] According to one youth coming of age in the system, blacks came to accept these rituals of segregation as they would any rite within the church. After all, "we didn't go to church, to make a statement or protest."[27]

Yet despite frequent lessons in racial humility imparted to black Catholic children throughout the early twentieth century, black Catholic schools did not remain simply tools of racial control. As with the Ursuline school and lay-run schools of previous generations, African American schools in the first half of the twentieth century appropriated Catholic rituals and resources to assert their social and political power in the face of white oppression. Through the second quarter of the twentieth century, these schools helped nurture a culture of resistance that, while often subtle, generated a rights consciousness that fueled later efforts to secure legal and social rights. Xavier University, founded by Katharine Drexel as the nation's only black Catholic University, sent lay women to educate children in schools throughout Louisiana. "No opportunity for the improvement of the minds of the children, of living conditions, in the neighborhood are lost upon these teachers."[28] Xavier Preparatory High School also nurtured a rights consciousness among girls through these decades. By the World War II era, alumni of these Catholic schools began sensing the opportunity to mount more direct challenges to the economic and political discrimination in the South. Led by civil rights attorney A.P. Tureaud, black Catholics mounted registration drives in parishes throughout southern Louisiana, actively engaging clergymen in their efforts to promote political literacy.[29]

World War II became a critical turning point not only in black political activism, but also in the demographic transformation of the city. War-related industry drew poor black farmers to cities throughout the country. In New Orleans, the new urban population put pressure on the city's housing and educational system. In response to the increasing educational needs of the city, Archbishop Joseph Francis Rummel inaugurated the Youth Progress Program to build new Catholic high schools and expand existing ones. In 1948, the archdiocese established the white high school, De La Salle, under the direction of the Christian Brothers. Edward Casserly, Superior of the Josephites, also seized the opportunity to establish a school "to provide clerical and lay black leadership both within the Church and within the secular community."[30] In 1951, St. Augustine's High School became the first school exclusively for males in the Crescent City. The school sought to cultivate a strong male leadership class in the Crescent City. In 1957, the school challenged a state law forbidding blacks and whites from performing on the same stage in a program.

The first decades of St. Augustine's history encapsulated the most tumultuous period in the history of Catholic schooling in New Orleans. Over the course of his long career, Rummel had gained a reputation as an advocate for the city's African American population. Along with a handful of priests and active laity through the 1940s and 1950s, Rummel sought to bring Catholic social ethics into contact with local business and industry. In 1947, he established a labor school at Loyola University to bring management and unions together in discussion of Catholic social teaching.

By the early 1950s, Catholic labor activists turned their attention to the critical question of segregation in Catholic churches and schools. As early as 1949, Rummel had challenged the segregation of religious services, cancelling a Holy Hour service in City Park because of the city's exclusion of blacks from the facility. In 1953, he issued a statement calling for the removal of "colored" signs from pews throughout the archdiocese.[31] White segregationists largely ignored these threats until the 1954 *Brown v. Board of Education* decision mobilized leadership on both sides of the school issue. Immediately, the state government moved to denounce the court decision and erect a wall of legislation designed to stall public school integration indefinitely. At the local level, prominent white Catholics organized several groups to exert pressure on local pastors and the archdiocese. In February of 1956, Rummel responded to these challenges, declaring racial segregation to be "morally wrong and sinful because it is a denial of the unity and solidarity of the human race."[32]

The statement did not make any definitive plans for the desegregation of Catholic schools. But with roughly 40 percent of New Orleans children in the parochial system, for most Catholics it was at least as significant as *Brown*. For many, the statement placed South Louisianans on the forefront of racial justice in the Deep South. With Rummel's pastoral letter, *Time* magazine lauded New Orleans as "the first major city in the Deep South to become officially committed to integration on any sizeable scale." *The Nation* declared New Orleans to be a leader in the achievement of racial justice. "Here there is even a chance to balk the forces that have prevailed in Georgia, South Carolina and Mississippi. There is even a change that a new Southern 'tradition'—one of decency in human relations—may be born here."[33]

Yet despite these hopeful voices, practical concerns and grassroots opposition stifled Catholic school integration until 1962, a full two years after the public schools desegregated. For Rummel, practical concerns prevented early action. The schools were already overcrowded. In New Orleans alone, parochial school attendance, which constituted almost half of the city's total school attendance in 1953-54, rose by more than two thousand students from the previous term.[34] Mounting grassroots opposition to desegregation overshadowed these basic complications. At the forefront, the famous political broker Leander Perez flaunted his religious credentials to undermine Rummel's authority and draw the Catholic faithful into the local Citizens' Council movement. "I am a Catholic, although not an Archbishop Catholic," he declared to one council rally. "They call me a 'mother at the knee Catholic' because I understand what it taught because I learned it at my mother's knee."[35]

At the school level, groups such as "Parents and Friends of Catholic School Children" issued statements denouncing the clergy's abuse of authority. The organization denounced the Church's "clandestine conspiracy" to integrate schools, "the gory details of which have purposely been withheld from the laity." The group demanded that the people in the pews, "once they have been informed, set and determine their own objectives."[36] At Jesuit High School, the Blue Jays Parents' Club introduced a resolution that separate facilities were "entirely adequate" and that integration would inevitably lower the school's scholastic standards "because of the disparity that exists between the races in the area of health, morality and culture." Parents' clubs at St. Francis Xavier in Metairie and Holy Name of Mary in Algiers took similar actions. When the principal of Jesuit, Claude J. Stallworth, S.J., ruled the group out of order, between seventy-five and one hundred parents stormed out of the meeting, claiming that discussion "was unfairly stopped" after the resolution had been circulated among nine hundred club members over the previous months. "This is an organized movement," Stallworth warned.[37]

Local organizations under Perez and private citizens generated enough resistance to cause repeated delays in the integration order. Between 1956 and 1960, racial tensions surfaced at parishes throughout the city. Across the river at a parish in Marrero, several students from Xavier Preparatory High School incited a riot when they formed a local action committee and occupied the front row of the church one Sunday morning. A few weeks later, several whites severely beat several black parishioners after the priest's sermon chided the students for attempting to publicize their story.[38] The incident set the stage for the violent opposition to public school integration only months later.

When the federal courts attempted to introduce four black children into two formerly all-white schools, the resulting violence cast a dim light on both civic and religious leadership in New Orleans. As the Catholic schools stood by, progressives from across the country lashed out at the seeming apathy of the church in New Orleans. "The key to the whole racial problem here seems to be in the hands of the Catholic Church," one school teacher lamented in the wake of the 1960 New Orleans School Crisis, "and the inability to turn that key is a particularly poignant one."[39] Rummel's declining health in the years leading up to the incident exacerbated a crisis of confidence among black Catholics and progressive white laity. Jesuit interracialist John LaFarge denounced this "total capitulation of the Church to a militant laity."[40]

In the wake of the storm over public school integration, a group of black and white laity organized the Catholic Commission on Human Relations in March 1961. The group aimed to break the bottleneck of resistance to parochial school integration created not only by Southern whites, but also by Rummel's own unwillingness to move. Several members had been activists in the Save Our Schools campaign, designed to keep public schools open amid legislative turmoil leading to the school crisis. Leaders directed much of the organization's efforts toward the hierarchy. By 1962, with the assistance of the newly appointed auxiliary bishop, John Cody, the organization created enough lay cooperation for the archdiocese to issue the integration order. Shortly thereafter, Rummel excommunicated Leander Perez and two other segregationists who publicly defied the order. For most, it remained merely a symbolic gesture as officials braced for the opening day of school. When, on September 4, sixty African Americans desegregated twenty parochial schools in the city, pickets arrived at several parishes but remained largely scattered. Most parishes weathered the storm, leaving school officials satisfied that it was only a matter of time before school attendance returned to normal. "Quiet seems to prevail Deo Gratias!" the St. Rose principal reported on Sept 7. [41]

As token integration settled into both public and Catholic systems throughout New Orleans, Catholics began to ponder their long-term effect, particularly as white citizens and the state government found new ways to resist desegregation. In 1964, one reporter observed the continued state of segregated Catholic education:

> Not only are school accommodations separate; they are far from equal. A typical white elementary parochial school, St. James Major, has 26 teachers for 783 students, a ratio of 1 to 30. An equally typical Negro parochial school, Holy Ghost, has 15 teachers for a student body of 746, a ratio of 1 to 50. [42]

The state launched a tuition assistance program to support students attending private non-sectarian schools. The legislation encouraged groups like the Parents and Friends of Catholic School Children to continue urging parents to cut off support to the Catholic school system. The group's paper, the *Catholic Warrior*, demanded an exodus into "white flight" schools. "Why not apply for grant in aid and go to a private white school. Don't be a sucker all your life." [43] By 1964, state tuition assistance had channeled roughly 6,000 students from integrated New Orleans schools—about half of that from Catholic schools—into newly erected private schools. In Louisiana as a whole, 10,136 students attending fifty-eight private schools were to receive $3.5 million that year. The amount exceeded state allocations per pupil to city schools in New Orleans. [44]

Problems with Grant-in-Aid and the slow pace of integration augmented a rising crisis of confidence within African American circles. Non-Catholic activists challenged not only the Church's commitment to racial desegregation but also the wisdom of interracialism itself. What did desegregation mean in a city increasingly faced with the rapidly expanding poverty rates and an acute housing shortage? "The Church universal has said many beautiful things about these problems," one Urban League spokesperson chided. "The Pope has written erudite encyclicals on the subject, but WHAT HAS THE LOCAL CHURCH DONE TO DO AWAY WITH SEGREGATION, POVERTY, ILLITERACY, POOR POLITICS?" [45] Many black Catholics echoed these charges. Abandoning the integrationist principles of early civil rights reformers, they denounced diocesan plans to close black schools and send students to the more equipped white schools.

Their efforts to maintain historically black schools revealed the extent to which black parishes and schools offered a source of racial pride and political consciousness. In 1959, several students from Xavier Preparatory School staged a sit-in at a local Catholic church. Preceding the famous Greensboro, North Carolina, sit-ins a year later, their efforts gained national attention and sparked a riot at the church that challenged the archdiocese's commitment to racial justice. In 1965, St. Augustine High School became the symbol of black Catholic empowerment when it launched a lawsuit for membership in the Louisiana High School Athletic Association. The school's famous "Purple Knights" became advocates of a black educational system that was, according to one *Time* reporter, "separate and superior" in its education of Catholic youth. Students from black parochial schools across the diocese engaged in sit-ins and demonstrations. In doing so, they drew upon a centuries-long tradition of black lay activism that, they hoped, would carry them through the challenges of the next decades.[46]

As both Catholic and non-Catholic activists challenged the wisdom of integrationism, Catholic school officials responded by reforming curricula to meet the new moral and spiritual mandates of the Second Vatican Council. Convened in 1962, the council called upon the local church to cultivate a more socially engaged faith among Catholics. At the local level, schools enacted programs designed to promote interracial understanding. Course syllabi reveal the efforts of lay and vowed religious teachers to break down traditional barriers of understanding. But while many activists and government officials continued to score the Church for its failures, whites bristled at this new "social morality" being taught in schools. As one local historian observed of the programs at Sacred Heart,

> The emphasis is on religious humanism and on the teaching of social justice rather than on the inculcation of tenets of faith.... As are all Catholics, the children are still exposed to notions of guilt, but the guilt emanates theoretically from social rather than personal fault.[47]

As such divisions indicate, long before the floodwaters of Hurricane Katrina engulfed New Orleans in August of 2005, storms raged over the future of education in New Orleans. At the heart of the storm was the relationship between the Catholic schools and the declining public system. In the 1960-61 school term, blacks made up roughly 58 percent of the public school population. Through a decade in which the total population of the city declined by thirty thousand, African Americans eventually made up 70 percent of enrollment. A survey conducted by an independent research firm revealed what it called a crisis in confidence in the "atmosphere" of schools. The report concluded that integration was "the most compelling reason for whites to move elsewhere."[48] Despite efforts to avoid becoming an escape valve for whites fleeing integration, reports out of New Orleans concluded that race-related events contributed to an abnormal rise in Catholic school attendance when compared nationally. Indeed, one report concluded, despite the decline of Catholic school attendance in other parts of the country, Louisiana Catholic schools witnessed sizeable increases through the end of the decade.[49]

As with most American cities, "white flight" placed pressure on Catholic churches and schools to respond to the shifting racial and economic geography of New Orleans. A combination of racial fear and the lure of suburban tract homes and modern conveniences drained urban centers where churches anchored communities for generations and threatened the long fought-for diversity of Catholic schools. The burden of suturing a rapidly diverging social and religious community in New Orleans fell to Archbishop Philip Hannan, who succeeded Cody in 1965. As white ethnic Catholics moved to new developments north and west of New Orleans, they insisted the Church accompany them. In 1962 Archbishop Cody oversaw the construction of brand new churches and schools in the growing predominantly white areas of the Lake Pontchartrain shore and Jefferson Parish. Many integrationists feared Catholic schools offering a "haven" for whites fleeing integration. During his tenure, Hannan publicly fought this trend by proposing busing programs for the outlying schools. Nonetheless, by 1968, the eleven new schools had a total enrollment of 6,261 students with no blacks. By 1971, only four blacks attended these schools.[50]

The contribution of Catholic schools to the continued segregation of New Orleans became a central question for school officials for the next twenty years. Throughout the 1970s and 1980s, white flight and economic decline in the inner city devastated the city's largely poor black population. As public schools declined, these transformations raised significant questions about the responsibility of Catholic education to the larger community.

In 2005, Hurricane Katrina threw the economic and social segregation of New Orleans into sharp relief. In the wake of the storm, Catholics rallied to ensure the survival of their parish communities. As important sources of civic and religious identity, parishes and schools remain cultural anchors that will play a major role as the city rebuilds itself over the coming years. Just like the original Ursuline missionaries who waded through the swampland to establish a vibrant Catholic community in the unlikeliest of settlements, the educational vision they helped create will continue to challenge New Orleanians as they come to a renewed understanding of their common identity and aspirations in the years to come.

NOTES

1. Saint Angela Merici, *Rule, Counsels, Testament*, quoted in Joan Marie Aycock, "The Ursuline School in New Orleans, 1727-1771," in *Cross, Crozier, and Crucible: A Volume Celebrating the Bicentennial of a Catholic Diocese in Louisiana*, ed. Glenn R. Conrad (New Orleans: Archdiocese of New Orleans, 1993), 210.

2. Sister M. Monica, *Angela Merici and Her Teaching Idea, 1474-1540* (New York: Longmans, Green and Co., 1927), 390. See also Aycock, "The Ursuline School in New Orleans," 216; Elizabeth Rapley, *The Dévotes: Women and Church in Seventeenth-Century France* (Montreal & Kingstoon: McGill-Queens University Press, 1990), 48-49.

3. Emily Clark, *Masterless Mistresses: The New Orleans Ursulines and the Development of a New World Society, 1724-1834* (Chapel Hill: University of North Carolina Press, 2007), 3, 113-121.

4. Claude L. Vogel, O.M., *The Capuchins in French Louisiana, 1722-1766* (New York: J.F. Wagner, 1928), 25.

5. Roger Baudier, *The Catholic Church in Louisiana* (New Orleans: A.W. Hyatt, 1939), 76-77.

6. Clark, *Masterless Mistresses*, 61.

7. Martin Luther Riley, "The Development of Education in Louisiana Prior to Statehood," *Louisiana Historical Quarterly* 19 (1936): 595-634.

8. Donald E. Devore and Joseph Logsdon, *Crescent City Schools: Public Education in New Orleans, 1841-1991* (Lafayette, LA: Center for Louisiana Studies, 1991), 25-31.

9. Richard Campanella, *Geographies of New Orleans: Urban Fabrics Before the Storm* (Lafayette, LA: Center for Louisiana Studies, 2006), 239, 244, 248.

10. Baudier, *Catholic Church in Louisiana*, 398. George Klawitter, C.S.C., *Boys to Men: Holy Cross School in New Orleans* (Prospect, KY: Harmony House, 1999), 76-90.

11. Sally K. Reeves, "The Society of the Sacred Heart in New Orleans," in Conrad, *Cross, Crozier, and Crucible*, 220-221.

12. Ibid., 58.

13. See Michael Doorley, "Irish Catholics and French Creoles: Ethnic Struggles within the Catholic Church in New Orleans, 1835-1920," *Catholic Historical Review* 87 (2001): 34-54.

14. Baudier, *Catholic Church in Louisiana*, 399.

15. Earl F. Niehaus, "Catholic Ethnics in Nineteenth-Century Louisiana," in Conrad,

Cross, Crozier, and Crucible, 54.

16. Campanella, *Geographies of New Orleans*, 321; Baudier, *Catholic Church in Louisiana*, 489; Niehaus, "Catholic Ethnics in Nineteenth-Century Louisiana," 66.

17. W.E.B. Dubois, *The Souls of Black Folk* (1903; New York: Bantam, 1989), 10.

18. Devore and Logsdon, *Crescent City Schools*, 42-43; James B. Bennett, *Religion and the Rise of Jim Crow in New Orleans* (Princeton, NJ: Princeton University Press, 2005), 218-219.

19. Sister Mary Bernard Deggs, *No Cross, No Crown: Black Nuns in Nineteenth-Century New Orleans*, ed. Virginia Meacham Gould and Charles E. Nolan (Bloomington: Indiana University Press, 2001), *xxx, xxxiv*, 23. Originally penned beginning in 1894, Deggs' history of the Sisters of the Holy Family offers an important firsthand account of the sisters' struggles within a white dominated church to establish an informal system of Catholic education for blacks. Clark, *Masterless Mistresses*, 256-57; See also Emily Clark and Virginia Meacham Gould, "The Feminine Face of Afro-Catholicism in New Orleans, 1727-1852," *William and Mary Quarterly* 59 (2002): 409-448; Cyprian Davis, *The History of Black Catholics in the United States* (New York: Crossroad, 1993), 106-109.

20. John B. Alberts, "Black Catholic Schools: The Josephite Parishes of New Orleans during the Jim Crow Era," *U.S. Catholic Historian* 12 (1994): 80; James B. Bennett, *Religion and the Rise of Jim Crow* (Princeton, NJ: Princeton University Press, 2006); See also Dolores Egger Labbé, *Jim Crow Comes to Church: The Establishment of Segregated Parishes in South Louisiana* (Lafayette: University of Southwestern Louisiana, 1971).

21. Janssens quoted in Bennett, *Religion and the Rise of Jim Crow*, 171.

22. Ibid., 172.

23. Dominican College, located Uptown on the corner of St. Charles Avenue and Broadway opened in 1905, Alberts, "Black Catholic Schools," 85.

24. Bennett, *Religion and the Rise of Jim Crow*, 218-220.

25. Minutes of the "Holy Ghost Catechetical Guide, Semi-Annual Meeting," April 21, 1940, *Annals of the Sisters of the Blessed Sacrament* 30 (1940): 120, Archives of the Sisters of the Blessed Sacrament, Bensalem, Pennsylvania (SBSA).

26. Ibid.

27. Joseph Verrett interview by Jim Bennett, 27 August 1998, transcript in Josephite Fathers Archives, Baltimore, MD.

28. "Impressions of Mother M. Mercedes on Her Visitation of Louisiana, 1938," Box 6, Folder 7, Mother M. Mercedes Correspondence, SBSA.

29. See Justin Poché, "Religion, Race, and Rights in Catholic Louisiana, 1938-1970" (PhD diss., University of Notre Dame, 2007), 54-61.

30. Matthew J. O'Rourke, *Between Law and Hope: St. Augustine High School, New Orleans, Louisiana* (New Orleans: St. Augustine School, 2003), 1; Roger Baudier, "Extensive Colored Work," in Episcopal Jubilee Supplement, *Catholic Action of the South*, March 14, 1953.

31. *Pittsburgh Courier*, December 15, 1949. Joseph Francis Rummel, "Blessed Are the Peacemakers," Pastoral to the Clergy, Religious and Laity, Archdiocese of New Orleans, March 15, 1953, Pastoral Letters Files, Archives of the Archdiocese of New Orleans (AANO).

32. Joseph Francis Rummel, "The Morality of Racial Segregation," February 16, 1956, Pastoral Letters Files, AANO.

33. *Time* 67:80 (March 5, 1956); Alfred Maund, "New Orleans Knows Better," *New Republic*, February 11, 1956.

34. *Southern School News*, October 1, 1954.

35. "Remarks by Leander Perez at Citizens Council Meeting, March 30, 1962," copy in Box 84, Folder 4, Louis J. Twomey Papers, Loyola University of New Orleans.

36. Parents and Friends of Catholic School Children, "You Should Learn and Know the Truth about the Future of Your Children," Volume I, undated copy in Box 84, Folder 2, Louis J. Twomey Papers, Loyola University of New Orleans.

37. *Times Picayune*, January 11, 1956; December 4, 1955; and December 17, 1955.

38. *Louisiana Weekly*, March 14, 1959.

39. Anonymous, "The Scandal of New Orleans," *Commonweal* (February 3, 1961): 475.

40. John LaFarge, S.J., "American Catholics and the Negro," *Social Order* 12 (April 1962): 156.

41. "Supervisors' School Attendance Reports," School Desegregation Files, AANO.

42. John Beecher, "New Orleans: Magnolia Ghetto," *Ramparts* 3, no. 4 (December 1964): 45.

43. *The Catholic Warrior* 1, no. 4 (1963), in Vertical Files, Louisiana Collection, Tulane University Special Collections.

44. "Ten Years in Review," *Southern School News*, May 1964; See also *Times Picayune*, March 23, 1963, reporting that 5,923 children in Orleans and Jefferson Parish received aid, a significant portion of the 6,250 for the entire eighteen parish region. The paper also reported that 183 African Americans were receiving grants to remain in "Negro schools."

45. Urban League of Greater New Orleans, "Facing the Facts of the Racial Relations Dilemma In New Orleans, Louisiana, 1964," Copy in Giles A. Hubert Papers, Amistad Research Center, Tulane University.

46. "Separate and Superior," *Time*, January 1, 1965; Beecher, "New Orleans: Magnolia Ghetto," 45.

47. Reeves, "The Society of the Sacred Heart in New Orleans," 231.

48. F. Guillory, "New Orleans Schools Ten Years Later," *America* 125 (August 21, 1971), 93-95.

49. Donald A. Erickson and John D. Donovan, *The Three R's of Nonpublic Education in Louisiana: Race, Religion, and Region, A Report to the President's Commission on School Finance* (Washington, DC: President's Commission on School Finance, 1972).

50. Ibid., 88-92.

Latino City Catholicism:
Catholic Education in San Antonio

Steve Neiheisel

The development of San Antonio's Catholic schools largely mirrors the development of the Mexican American community in that city and represents in many ways the history of Catholic Texas. While other Catholic ethnic groups such as the Germans, Irish, Poles, and Czechs certainly had a significant presence in San Antonio and influenced the city's educational life, even the educational and faith development of those groups cannot be fully understood absent the influence of the Mexican American community. From its humble beginnings as a mostly rural diocese, the archdiocese has grown in step with the city. Currently the nation's twenty-sixth largest Catholic diocese within America's twenty-ninth largest metropolitan area, San Antonio is a multicultural diocese with a strong and predominant Mexican American character.

The Hispanic Catholic roots of San Antonio are old and deep compared to the European Catholic roots of industrial Midwestern cities and one cannot divorce or compartmentalize the urban development of San Antonio from the growth of Catholicism. Until the beginning of the nineteenth century, except for the Indian tribes, all history in San Antonio was Catholic history, and the entire story of settlement and growth is intimately connected with the Church. The Church played a significant role in creating and maintaining civic cohesion from the city's beginning as a remote outpost of the Spanish Empire.

In 1718, when Catholics first arrived in the area that was to become San Antonio, the landscape was a vast wilderness with low rolling hills, stands of oak trees, and vast tracks of grass interrupted by the occasional cactus. The beginning of San Antonio's urban society grew out of the initial labor of Catholic settlers, soldiers, missionaries, and native Indians organized around a system of missions and forts.

San Antonio was established as a strategic outpost of the Spanish Empire[1] to defend against encroachment by the French.[2] To make the area more hospitable to settlement, the Spanish government sent in Franciscan missionaries, accompanied by a small number of Spanish troops, to establish a chain of missions along el Camino real or King's Highway. In addition, the Spanish built presidios or forts to protect the missions, the first being San Antonio de Bexar.

The missions were less than successful; they were expensive to operate and failed to convert more than a small percentage of the residents. Some of the Indians were serious converts, but early Anglo-American settlers accepted conversion as a type of social contract, to provide economic opportunity as well as physical protection from Apache and Comanche raiders.[3] In addition, support for the missions was dependent on the health of church-state relations in Mexico, often tossed and turned according to the shifting political winds between Old Spain and the new world.

On February 14, 1729, the King of Spain ordered four hundred Catholic families to emigrate from the Canary Islands to San Antonio. Fourteen families arrived the next year with land grants from the king and the city of San Antonio became official.[4] Those families organized the first city government in Texas in 1731, establishing the Villa de San Fernando, later to become San Antonio.[5]

The Catholic presence in San Antonio was firmly established in 1738 with the founding of San Fernando Cathedral to serve these Canary Island families. San Fernando is the site of the oldest parish church in Texas[6] and remains today the oldest continuously operating Roman Catholic cathedral in the United States.

The first urban development was the creation of the "villa," or Spanish colonial town. The blueprint of the town was formally dictated by the "law of the Indies" which stipulated the proper placement of church and government structures situated on a town square. This law symbolized in stone the interlocking relationship between church and state. These two institutions would go on to guide the development of each other and of the city of San Antonio.[7] For example, from colonial times until Mexican independence in 1821, the town council would not only handle secular matters, it also would organize religious festivals as well.[8]

By the 1770s, San Antonio de Bexar had a population of two thousand and officially became the capital of Spanish Texas.[9] Because San Antonio de Bexar was far from the populated areas of Mexico, its residents adopted the values of independent frontiersmen and this outpost spirit was to last well into the twentieth century.[10] This frontier mentality, with its sense of individualism, struggle, and impoverishment, had a significant impact on the later development of San Antonio's Catholic schools.

From the early colonial settlement by Franciscan missionaries and Spanish soldiers, through Texas independence from Mexico in 1836, the economic, political, and social power structure of San Antonio was dominated by "Tejanos," Texas-born Spanish/Mexican Catholic citizens. The character of civic culture was such that it would have been difficult for the foreign observer to recognize a distinct line between civic and church affairs. Had this power structure continued, the development of San Antonio's Catholic schools might have taken a different trajectory. With Catholic Tejanos as the power elite, San Antonio's Catholic schools benefited both economically and socially and perhaps developed earlier and more prominently than similar schools in other cities.

After Texas won its independence from Mexico in 1836, Anglo-Americans in San Antonio, those who had lived in the area for a generation as well as those newly and eagerly arrived and many nominally Catholic, established and energetically practiced their native Protestant faith. They quickly became the dominant political and economic class in San Antonio and usurped the dominant power of the deeply-rooted Tejanos. So anti-Catholic were Anglo-American Protestants in the 1830s and 1840s that only one functioning Catholic parish remained in Texas during that decade: San Fernando Cathedral in San Antonio.[11]

After Texas joined the United States in 1845, Anglo-American and European immigration to San Antonio increased dramatically, further altering the balance of economic and political power until the late twentieth century, as Mexican Americans lost an increasing number of their land holdings and shifted, as an ethnic population, primarily to the laboring class.[12] Gone was the dominant civic power of Tejano Catholics, the largest Catholic ethnic group in San Antonio. This loss of political and economic power would later have an arresting effect on the contours of development among San Antonio Catholic schools.

In 1847, Pope Pius IX established the Diocese of Galveston to administer all of Catholic Texas, and San Antonio reverted to little more
than a frontier village, showing little evidence of the spiritual heritage of
the early Franciscan missionaries.[13] The maintenance of religious cohesion became difficult in the rough frontier environment and never quite
regained the institutional prominence that was so common during the
Spanish colonial period. The backward slide of Catholicism in San Antonio and in Texas generally made organization of the diocese difficult.[14]

San Antonio became a separate diocese in 1874.[15] By that time,
Catholic history in Texas was more than three hundred fifty years old.[16]
In 1874, the entire state of Texas had one bishop, eighty-three priests
and less than one hundred thousand Catholics.[17] When Anthony Pellicer, the first bishop of San Antonio (1874-1880), arrived in the city
at the end of 1874, the population was still predominantly Spanish-
speaking[18] although the preponderance of political and economic power was held by Anglo Protestants. The development of the San Antonio
diocese and the nascent development of Catholic schools followed the
distinctive urban development pattern of the city itself.

San Antonio's Catholic diocesan and urban development was different from the urbanized northern dioceses of the Midwest and East
Coast in five fundamental ways. First, far from America's political and
economic center of gravity, San Antonio was not a major port for the
arrival of European Catholic immigrants. It did not experience the ex-
plosive urban growth that other American cities did in the nineteenth
century and therefore the growth of its Catholic population was relatively modest—a small but steady addition to the existing mix of Mexican American Catholics, Anglo Protestants, and a smattering of Catholic Germans, Irish, Poles, and Czechs. San Antonio missed out on the
national waves of Catholic immigration in the early nineteenth century
which could have diversified and deepened the Catholic presence in
San Antonio. Thus despite its relatively ancient Catholic lineage, the
city of San Antonio as an American Catholic city was bypassed by newer Catholic communities in Cincinnati and Chicago.

Second and related, San Antonio industrialized late, remaining a
small economic backwater and therefore not a magnet for large-scale
European Catholic immigration until World War II, when increased
military spending at Fort Sam Houston and the development of three
major U.S. Air Force bases attracted some immigration from Northern
states. San Antonio missed out on the industrial boom which would

have quickly brought immigrant Catholics and their children into the middle and professional classes. The relatively slow economic development of San Antonio had a destabilizing effect on the development of its Catholic schools.

Third, the lack of urban density meant a lack of urban conflict as ethnic groups and religious denominations could remain separated by geographic as well as class distances. This created distinct identities and isolation among Catholic groups. Lack of diocesan solidarity and a common Catholic identity would impair the development of a cohesive Catholic school system.

Fourth, the need for rapid Americanization by Mexican Americans was not as strong in San Antonio as it was for the Catholic immigrant groups in other American cities. Due to border proximity, Mexican Americans remained more easily connected, physically as well as culturally, to their homeland. Therefore, they did not need to relinquish cultural ties to Mexico as did European immigrants living in industrializing cities of America far from their homelands.[19]

A resident of San Antonio could survive not only socially, but economically, speaking Spanish and expressing cultural affinities. For diocesan development, this meant that Mexican American parishes and schools would deflect attempts by bishops to Americanize them and Mexican American cultural influences would shape liturgical as well as parish community life. The Mexican American Catholic schools did not need to serve a function of either assimilation or preservation.[20] They existed within a cultural milieu as recognizable to newly arrived Mexicans as to later generation Mexican Americans. This only served to heighten the sense of separateness between Mexican Catholics and European Catholics, who Americanized more rapidly.

Fifth, the entire diocese had a "Mexican" air to it yet Mexican Americans remained, for a very long period, *de facto* second-class citizens.[21] The civic and economic power structure of San Antonio was, and remained through the mid-twentieth century, Anglo Protestant. Yet, because of its early history, San Antonio remained culturally Mexican. Perhaps no where else in America did the communitarian values of both the Catholic Church and Mexican American culture clash more readily with the Anglo American value of individualism. This created a clear separation between Catholics and Protestants and provided a hint of "foreignness" to the local Catholic Church in the eyes of the Protestant power elite.

This "Mexican air" was refreshed during and after the Mexican Revolution of 1917. San Antonio's first archbishop, Arthur J. Drossaerts, inherited a diocese that became a haven for those persecuted for religious reasons in Mexico. It was a highly "anticlericalismo" revolution[22] and therefore those who fled to San Antonio did so as ardent supporters of the Church. While on the one hand this new influx of Mexican immigrants expanded and refreshed the ranks of San Antonio Catholics, it further enhanced the idea of the Catholic Church in San Antonio, in part, as "foreign" and therefore made difficult it becoming part of the civic power structure.

In general, therefore, the character of the diocese from its inception until the mid-twentieth century was culturally Mexican, largely rural, with a small urban core dominated by a ranching and a small trade economy.[23] The city lacked an industrial economy that could move large numbers of immigrants into the middle and professional classes. The diocese served a disproportionate population of economically and politically marginalized Mexican American citizens and constantly arriving Mexican immigrants. These factors were to have profound and lasting effects on the development of San Antonio Catholic schools.

One could summarize the historical relationship between San Antonio Catholic bishops and Catholic schools to the mid-twentieth century as "benign distance." Bishops generally cared about the children and about the schools but gave them inconsistent attention, counting the schools as only one of many equally important administrative and pastoral responsibilities and never a priority. Not one bishop ever attempted to establish a legacy as "Bishop Educator."

On the frontier, schooling was not held in high regard among the population in general, so there was little demand from parishioners for a sophisticated Catholic school system.[24] Just enough education to be a good rancher or craftsman was all that was required. In addition, the San Antonio diocese was not led by bishops who were trained as professional educators.[25] Therefore, their view of the purposes of the educational enterprise was limited to maintenance of Catholics in the flock along with the Americanization of immigrant children.

In 1845, Jean Marie Odin, then the vicar apostolic for the Republic of Texas and later the first bishop of Galveston, talked of organizing a school system in his vast diocese, hoping to use the historic Alamo building for the first school. In 1851, he traveled to Bordeaux, France, to meet with Father George Joseph Caillet, the superior general of the

Society of Mary, to request that four teaching brothers be sent to San Antonio to start a school, which they did in 1852.[26] He also gathered six Oblate Fathers, a lay brother, four Sisters of the Incarnate Word and of the Blessed Sacrament,[27] two Ursuline nuns, and eighteen seminarians, all destined to work in San Antonio diocesan schools.[28]

Odin saw the establishment of St. Mary's Institute in 1852 as a bulwark against Protestantization of his Catholic flock, especially among Mexican Americans.[29] Odin also saw the parish schools as a way "to regenerate the poor Mexican population."[30] Thus, the schools were seen by the bishop more as a way to preserve Catholicism than as an instrument for social or economic advancement among his Catholic flock. Protestant influence in public school education specifically, and in San Antonio society generally, was very powerful. Odin and subsequent bishops developed a fortress mentality to protect the flock.[31]

Significant to the development of Catholic schools in San Antonio was the cooperation and missionary zeal, especially to the poor, of several religious orders. In addition to the Society of Mary (Marianists), other religious orders also were recruited to this frontier town. For example, the first Catholic school in San Antonio was an Ursuline Academy for girls founded in 1851.[32] But in general, it was difficult to attract religious communities to San Antonio because of the poor conditions, low vocations, and inadequate support from the diocese itself.[33] That is why most of the religious orders that did establish schools in San Antonio had as their primary calling a mission to the poor.

The third bishop of San Antonio, John A. Forest, was supportive and responsive to the 1884 mandate of the Third Plenary Council of Baltimore calling for a school in every parish. At the same time, he understood the economic limitations of San Antonio. It was during Forest's administration at the turn of the twentieth century that San Antonio witnessed a continuous development of the Church as evidenced by the growth of parishes. The more affluent of these parishes were able to build and maintain schools, including those in the outlying German, Polish, and Czech communities of New Braunfels, Selma, Panna Maria, and St. Hedwig.[34]

The fifth bishop and first archbishop of San Antonio, Drossaerts defended Catholic schools as "the strongest bulwark of our American institutions ... the first act of enlightened patriotism" because Catholic schools do moral formation which makes for better citizens.[35] He was an advocate of parochial schools long before becoming bishop[36] as he envisioned that another purpose of schools was to develop lay leadership for the community, especially the Mexican American community, since most of the priests serving in the parishes were European and therefore culturally separated from the local population.[37]

Despite his interest in Catholic schools, Drossaerts was wary of the political and economic divisions between European Catholics and Mexican Catholics.[38] This apprehension stunted the development of a united and cohesive Catholic school system. In the end, Drossaerts attempted to walk the fine line between educating the poorer Mexican American Catholic population with unrestricted diocesan funds, without putting any demand on the more affluent European Catholics whose parish schools were financially independent.

Like earlier San Antonio bishops, Drossaerts worried about Protestant inroads into his Mexican flock. He wrote in 1928:

> Look at the tremendous efforts of our enemies. Every sect in America seems to have a special delight in having a church in our Mexican district in the city of San Antonio.... Everything possible is being done to wean away our Mexicans from the Faith of their Fathers.[39]

And again in 1937:

> Nothing is more needed among the 100,000 Mexicans of this city than free parochial schools and plenty of them. . . . The result of their going to the public schools is only too evident in the religious indifference and very loose morals of our Mexican youth. If things are let to drift as in the past, we will lose half of our Mexican population for the faith.[40]

Apparently there was some success on the part of the diocese efforts as Protestant congregations never attracted a large proportion of Mexican Americans in San Antonio.[41]

Catholic bishops had to negotiate the culture of Protestant social dominance in San Antonio. Although San Antonio's population was predominantly Catholic, it was a Protestant city in terms of economic and political power by the 1850s.[42] In the matter of education, a relationship of convenience was established between Anglo-American Protestants and the Catholic Church. Protestants, who dominated the public schools, did not want the Spanish language or Mexican American culture as influences in the "public" schools, so they supported the development of Catholic schools as a way of diluting the Mexican influence in public education. Not surprisingly, there was no hostility on the part of the Protestant power elite toward the development of Catholic schools. The situation was quite the opposite.

The real threat to the Protestant power elite was the entrenched poverty of the majority of Catholics in San Antonio. Poverty, at least among the Mexican Catholic population, prevented many parents from sending their children to Catholic schools. For that reason, Archbishop Robert Lucey, the second archbishop of San Antonio, questioned the strategic importance of schools in the building of the diocese.[43] It did not seem to be a cost-effective measure to establish schools when so many parishioners were in need of life essentials. Parish schools would be a burden on limited financial resources that could and should be used on other diocesan programs. Lucey was an ardent advocate for the poor, mostly Mexican Americans, in San Antonio,[44] and not at all sure that Catholic schools were a good way to promote their welfare, relying more on the Confraternity of Christian Doctrine (CCD) programs for faith formation.

Until 1957, the largest and "best" Catholic high schools in San Antonio were private, not parochial.[45] Religious orders could establish schools in San Antonio, operate them with some independence from the diocese, develop an excellent academic reputation for the area, and attract Anglo Protestant as well as affluent American Catholic students. Tuition and endowments paid the bills.

The parochial schools were left to students from lower income families and received only limited support from the bishops of San Antonio. It was not until 1955 that the bishops involved themselves directly in encouraging high schools with Lucey building three diocesan high schools for boys during his tenure.[46]

Each bishop had his own leadership style in overseeing the schools. Drossaerts, for example, was permissive and employed a policy of benign neglect. Lucey had a similar policy, but was more concerned about his authority and the public image of the parochial schools.[47] He was less concerned about academic achievement and would not interfere with a school unless there was a public crisis.[48] Francis Furey inherited a troubled diocese in 1969 and was forced to close many schools. He had, appropriately, a non-inflammatory style.[49] Until the mid-1970s, the financial viability of each Catholic school was left to individual parishes—a concern for pastors, not the bishop.[50]

Little is known of the educational legacy of the first three bishops: Anthony Pellicer, John Neraz, and John Forest. The growth in school enrollments was significant, but due to poor record keeping, little is known of the substance of the education or the role of the bishops. The fourth bishop, John W. Shaw, saw the number of parochial schools increase by 95 percent, from thirty-six schools in 1909 to seventy in 1919. This achievement far outpaced the national increase during the same period which was less than 21 percent. Shaw's ability to build so many new schools was related to his predecessor's (Forrest) acquisition of land upon which to build them. Drossaerts maintained Shaw's building scheme, even in spite of the Great Depression.[51]

Lucey was perhaps the greatest builder of San Antonio Catholic schools. However, he was more interested in the growth of CCD programs than he was in supporting parish schools.[52] Lucey, in part, benefited from the affluent economic times after World War II and received credit for educational growth that was fostered by parents and pastors.

Furey inherited a local school crisis that emerged in many dioceses in the 1960s. Following Vatican II, many Catholics questioned the importance of Catholic schools. In fact, thousands of teaching sisters and brothers across the nation questioned whether education was the best use of their time in service to the Church.[53]

In addition, there were a number of other factors that eroded the health of the Catholic schools in San Antonio. Public schools had improved in quality. Many Catholics had moved to suburban developments where there were no Catholic schools. Some Catholic parents did not perceive that the outcome of Catholic school education was any better than public school education. Added to these concerns was the simple economic fact that the cost of Catholic education increased due to lack of religious staffing, and parishioners without children no longer wanted to subsidize Catholic schools. In this unstable environment, Furey did not open any new parochial schools while closing twelve.[54]

In summary, each bishop tried to fill the Catholic schools and establish more of them[55] but no bishop of San Antonio through the late twentieth century made education a priority or legacy. Catholic schooling was one among many responsibilities of the San Antonio bishops. They cared, were generally supportive, intervened in crises, but did not look at the schools as integral to the role of the Church. They were independent satellites of the Church.

All bishops missed opportunities to sell the schools to Catholic parents. Economic poverty among the dominant Catholic group,

Mexican Americans, was always an obstacle to growth. Overall, the bishops provided minimal leadership and took a bottom-up or subsidiarity approach when it came to school management, leaving it to pastors and parish members whether or not to support a school. It was an administrative checking-off attitude more than the strategic nurturing of a school system.

This policy of benign neglect meant that the development of parish schools in San Antonio was based primarily upon local parish demand and support with relatively little administrative or financial support from the archdiocese. This policy also fostered the development of ethnic parishes. The story of immigrant Catholic groups in San Antonio is one of early cohesiveness and commitment to preserving culture with enough assimilation to do business, not unlike immigrant Catholic groups across America.

European Catholic communities in San Antonio were relatively small in number compared to the number of Mexican Catholics, yet because of their relative affluence they demanded and were able to organize and construct parishes and schools shortly after their arrival. Each of the major European immigrant groups—Germans, Irish, Poles, and Czechs—wanted to develop at least one parish school in order to preserve their culture and to develop cultural leaders. Catholicism was an integral part of their ethnic identity.

German immigrants came to the San Antonio area with specific trade skills. They were artisans and craftsmen and ranchers. Many moved into the political power structure as mayors and city councilmen. Germans had the economic power to support parish schools not only in San Antonio but in the rural areas like Fredericksburg, New Braunfels, and Castroville.[56]

Like the Germans, the Poles came to the San Antonio area with craft skills and enough economic power to establish a significant middle-class presence in the city. Some settled in San Antonio proper but the heartland of the Polish community was in the rural area to the east of the city. Immaculate Conception, the school established in Panna Maria, Texas, in 1868, became the center of all the Polish missions in Texas.[57]

While the nineteenth century was a period of parish development for European immigrants in San Antonio, the development of Mexican parishes was stagnant due to a lack of funds.[58] The development of the Mexican church also was hampered by the relative lack of supporting church structures in Mexico after independence from Spain. Due to a lack of Mexican priests, pastors in the Mexican churches in San Antonio were predominantly European, creating a tension between the institutional Church leaders and the Mexican parishioners in the pews. San Fernando Cathedral, for example, was the cultural heart of San Antonio and predominantly Mexican. It became a focal point of Mexican resistance to Anglo-American domination.[59] San Antonio bishops, to a significant degree, centered their attention on European immigrant Catholics who were economically prosperous and often brought their own clergy.[60]

The eventual development of Mexican parishes and schools, especially on the city's west side, took place after "The Great Migration" from 1910 and 1930. Increasing numbers of Mexicans moved north across the border to escape the social instability of the Mexican Revolution. These increased numbers made San Antonio, at least culturally, a Mexican American Catholic city. The well-being of the Catholic Church in San Antonio in general became more dependent on Mexicans. This growth also led a fearful Anglo community to establish restrictive covenants to keep Mexicans on the west side and prevent integration of the north side. Racial discrimination within the community led Drossaerts to establish separate churches and schools for Mexican Catholics.[61]

Ethnic groups in San Antonio were left to their own devices in establishing and funding parochial schools. For the more affluent immigrant groups like Germans and Poles, the building of schools was possible at a relatively early stage of settlement. For Mexican Catholics on the other hand, support from vowed religious orders and bishops was required to overcome both financial obstacles as well as obstacles emanating from racial discrimination.

The San Antonio Catholic educational experience can best be understood through an analysis of the rise, fall, and resurgence of the Mexican Catholic community. Indeed, that history is what makes the San Antonio Catholic educational experience so distinctive. As historian David Badillo writes: "San Antonio defined a regional pattern of Catholicism differing greatly from that of other areas of the country where the United States immigrant church held long established mechanisms for assimilating foreigners."[62] The San Antonio Catholic schools, especially on the west and south sides, have been able to maintain strong Mexican cultural ties.

Despite being firmly entrenched in a church-state power sharing structure during colonial times, the loss of economic and political power for Tejanos after Texas independence relegated the Mexican
Catholic community to a second-class position within San Antonio society. This decline lasted well into the late twentieth century.[63] Mexican
American Catholic identity remained strong, in part, due to discrimination against them.[64]

Despite San Antonio being one of the oldest cities in the United
States, assimilation into the English-speaking cultural American mainstream has been and continues to be slow in developing.[65] Geographic
proximity to Mexico allowed for a constant and relatively easy flow of
people and culture across borders and refreshed the ethnic identity of
the San Antonio Mexican American population.

For the schools, this has provided a strong and consistent Mexican
ethnic influence within the school communities. This is best expressed
in the celebration of particular feast days, like that of Our Lady of Guadalupe, as well as ethnic-based liturgical and devotional expressions.
This Mexican Catholic cultural expression pervades all of the Catholic
schools in the region to some degree, even those with larger Anglo
student populations.

Education on the Southwest frontier did not receive the early attention and recognized value that it did in the industrializing cities of the
East and Midwest. Education in San Antonio was valued just enough to
meet the needs of a ranching-based economy that did not provide expanded opportunities for professionals or other highly educated individuals. Therefore, despite its status as one of America's oldest cities, it
was not until after World War II that education—public and private—
became a priority in San Antonio.

San Antonio came late to professionalizing the Catholic schools.
An inactive parish school board, stocked with priests until 1963, and
no school board records kept prior to 1960 were indicative of the low
priority given to education.[66] These conditions, along with a *laisse faire*
leadership style on the part of most bishops, never made the assertive
development of a Catholic school system a priority. That, in turn, contributed to the arrested development of San Antonio Catholic schools,
which developed much later than Catholic schools in younger American cities.

The entrenched poverty of a significant part of the Mexican Catholic community, the largest ethnic group of Catholics in San Antonio,

was a persistent obstacle throughout the history of the development of Catholic schools. Tuition-based education made it extremely difficult for a majority of Catholic families to afford private or parochial schooling.

At the beginning of the twenty-first century, there is a small but strong resurgence in the spirit of Catholic school education in San Antonio, fueled in part by the rising economic affluence and civic prominence of Mexican Americans. Archbishop Jose Gomez has made the assertive development of Catholic schools, including the building of new elementary and high schools, a strategic priority and may create for himself a legacy as San Antonio's first "Bishop Educator."

NOTES

1. Joseph W. Schmitz, S.M., "The Beginnings of the Society of Mary in Texas, 1852-1866" *Mid-America* 25, no. 1 (1943): 3.

2. H.W. Brands, *Lone Star Nation* (New York: Doubleday, 2004), 34.

3. Ibid.

4. P.F. Parisot and C.J. Smith, *History of the Catholic Church in the Diocese of San Antonio* (San Antonio: Carrico & Bowen, 1897), 17.

5. Rev. M.J. Gilbert, ed., *Diamond Jubilee, 1874-1949, Archdiocese of San Antonio* (San Antonio: Archdiocese of San Antonio, 1949), 2.

6. David Badillo, "Between Alienation and Ethnicity: The Evolution of Mexican-American Catholicism in San Antonio," *Journal of American Ethnic History* 16, no. 4 (1997): 62.

7. Ibid.

8. Timothy M. Matovina, *Tejano Religion and Ethnicity: San Antonio, 1821-1860* (Austin: University of Texas Press, 1995), 6.

9. Brands, *Lone Star Nation*, 34.

10. Ibid., 21.

11. James Talmadge Moore, *Through Fire and Flood: The Catholic Church in Frontier Texas, 1836-1900* (College Station: Texas A&M Press, 1992), 3.

12. Matovina, *Tejano Religion and Ethnicity*, 52.

13. Schmitz, "The Beginnings of the Society," 3.

14. Ibid., 4.

15. Parisot and Smith, *History of the Catholic Church*, 2.

16. Gilbert, *Diamond Jubilee, xi.*

17. Ibid., 33.

18. Ibid.

19. Robert. B. O'Connor, *The Bishop as Educator: Episcopal Attitudes and Actions Toward Catholic Schooling in the Archdiocese of San Antonio, Texas, 1875-1979* (Ann Arbor: University Microfilms International, 1990), 18-19.

20. Ibid., 20.

21. Ibid.

22. Ibid., 184.

23. Committee, San Antonio Bicentennial Heritage, *San Antonio in the Eighteenth*

Century (San Antonio: Clarke Printing, 1976), 91.

24. O'Connor, *The Bishop as Educator*, 21.

25. Ibid., 37.

26. Schmitz, "The Beginnings of the Society," 5-6.

27. Sister Mary Helena Finck, *The Congregation of the Sisters of Charity of the Incarnate Word of San Antonio, Texas* (Washington, DC: The Catholic University of America, 1925), 23.

28. Schmitz, "The Beginnings of the Society," 6.

29. Matovina, *Tejano Religion and Ethnicity*, 67.

30. Ibid.

31. O'Connor, *The Bishop as Educator*, 35, 38, 39.

32. Ibid., 49.

33. Ibid., 240.

34. Gilbert, *Diamond Jubilee*, 129-130.

35. O'Connor, *The Bishop as Educator*, 44.

36. Ibid., 105.

37. Ibid., 47.

38. Badillo, "Between Alienation and Ethnicity," 71.

39. Bishop Drossaerts, letter to Fr. Romero, May 7, 1928.

40. Bishop Drossaerts, letter to William O'Brian, July 10, 1937.

41. Matovino, *Tejano Religion and Ethnicity*, 80.

42. Badillo, "Between Alienation and Ethnicity," 64.

43. O'Connor, *The Bishop as Educator*, 40-41.

44. Jay P. Dolan and Gilberto M. Hinojosa, eds., *Mexican Americans and the Catholic Church, 1900-1965* (Notre Dame: University of Notre Dame Press, 1994), 115.

45. O'Connor, *The Bishop as Educator*, 109.

46. Ibid., 111.

47. Ibid., 179.

48. Ibid., 181.

49. Ibid., 182.

50. Ibid., 252.

51. Ibid., 299, 301.

52. Ibid., 302.

53. Ibid., 309.

54. Ibid., 304.

55. Ibid., 150.

56. Gilbert, *Diamond Jubilee*, 53.

57. Ibid., 31.

58. Badillo, "Between Alienation and Ethnicity," 64.

59. Motavino, *Tejano Religion and Ethnicity*, 89.

60. Dolan and Hinojosa, *Mexican Americans and the Catholic Church*, 78.

61. Badillo, "Between Alienation and Ethnicity," 70.

62. Ibid., 78.

63. Matovino, *Tejano Religion and Ethnicity*, 85.

64. Dolan and Hinojosa, *Mexican Americans and the Catholic Church*, 82.

65. Matovino, *Tejano Religion and Ethnicity*, ix.

66. O'Connor, *The Bishop as Educator*, 216.

Mission City Catholicism:
Catholic Education in Los Angeles

Michael P. Caruso, S.J.

L os Angeles and its environs evoke images of sunshine, palm trees, beaches, the entertainment industry, along with alluring leisure and vacation destinations. Though the state is composed of substantial agricultural areas, beautiful forests, and vast desert lands, the name of the state prompts images that are often more representative of the southern coastal areas rather than the expansively diverse inland and northern regions.

Among the many California cultural icons such as Hollywood and Disneyland, there is also its rich Catholic history. This distinctive Catholic legacy is irreversibly manifested in its cities' names like Santa Monica, San Fernando, San Gabriel, and Santa Barbara. Many of these cities in what was once called Alta California, or roughly, the current boundaries of the state, began as mission stations founded by eighteenth century Franciscans under the leadership of Blessed Junipero Serra who began his California ministry in 1768.[1]

These missions were a continuation of the project begun earlier by the Jesuits in the length of the peninsula of Baja California.[2] The Franciscans and their lay colleagues established the colonial missions as centers for catechetical, vocational, and agricultural education, as well as foundations for imparting liturgical and musical training.[3]

Though the missions, their purpose, and administration have come under intense scholarly debate in recent years, even to the point of questioning what was once thought to be the saintly character of

Serra himself, these institutions provided the symbolic establishment of the Catholic faith with their catechetical and educational charter at the very founding of the city of Los Angeles.[4] The educational thrust of these missions was aimed primarily at Native Americans and those California Catholics who were native Mexicans, as well as the small Spanish immigrant population.[5]

Of education in this period, Governor Fernando Domengo Sepulveda wrote:

> They learned very little in those days, schools were few, books rare, and the pursuits of the people required not a very extensive book-learning. When any writing was needed, they could easily apply to the few who were the depositaries of legal form or epistolary ability.[6]

This languid educational pace was remarkable when compared to other more seismic movements around the globe. Among critical world events at the time of the emergence of Los Angeles, were the Enlightenment, the French Revolution, and the rise of Napoleon. On the eastern shores of North America, the Articles of Confederation, the first working draft of a constitutional government, had been adopted by all thirteen states (March 1, 1781).

It was also at that time that the Spanish governor established the "El Pueblo de Nuestra Señora la Reina de los Angeles del Río de Porciúncula" on September 14, 1781, on a site suggested by Father Juan Crespi. This was not a mission station, but a settlement founded from the nearby San Gabriel Mission. Los Angeles passed from Spain to Mexico in 1821, and at the end of the Mexican American War (1846-1848), Alta California passed into formal United States jurisdiction under the terms of the Treaty of Guadalupe Hidalgo.

Francisco Garcia Diego y Moreno served as the first bishop of the newly erected diocese of the two Californias (Alta and Baja). He took up residence at the Mission in Santa Barbara and is credited with establishing a seminary there with five students.[7] Though the Gold Rush in the north was drawing many people westward, this influx of people did not have a dramatic impact on southern California. Schools closed as quickly as they started. The missions and presidios had offered the only reliable education which was primarily catechetical, agricultural, and vocational, but this situation was about to change with the advent of a new political identity.

California was admitted to the Union as the thirty-first state in 1850. With the arrival of a new legal system and political culture, many Spanish-speaking citizens and Native Americans lost their land and holdings.[8] The following year, the Picpus Fathers started a school in the Plaza of Los Angeles, but like many other early educational enterprises, this school was fleeting and this missionary group set sail for a ministry in Oceania.[9] Most educational initiatives were sporadic. Schools needed stability, commitment, and continuity; these traits arrived with the advent of new and responsible leadership. In 1859, during the episcopacy of the Spanish-born Vincentian, Thaddeus Amat, the Diocese of Monterey-Los Angeles was established and addressing the needs of evangelization through Catholic schools was begun in earnest.[10]

Amat had been a missionary in the Midwestern United States before his appointment as the bishop of the Diocese of Monterey (1853), a vast diocese that stretched from Santa Cruz in the north to the Mexican border in the south. Amat recruited European priests, sisters, and brothers to the United States to labor in the West.

One of Amat's first acts was to enlist the Daughters of Charity from Emmitsburg, Maryland.[11] This group of sisters sailed to Panama, crossed land by railcar, and continued sailing to San Francisco; the Daughters arrived in late 1855. After a few weeks of rest, five sisters under the leadership of Sister Scholastica Logsden, set sail again for Los Angeles and landed in San Pedro Harbor on January 6, 1856. Traveling twenty-eight miles by horse-drawn carriage to the center of Los Angeles, they promptly opened an orphanage and school for girls; known as "the Institución Caritativa, an 'asylum' modeled on similar worldwide institutions of the Sisters."[12]

The sisters became the face of the Catholic Church to those of other faiths, especially through their social welfare and health care services which were offered to everyone.[13] The orphanage, for example, was an apostolate that drew widespread civic support.[14] These sisters were of European and American origins and provided a link with the church in Europe and the Hispanic culture of Spain and Mexico, while also building a bridge to the emerging Anglo and English-speaking culture in the city. Amat also invited the Sisters of Immaculate Heart of Mary from Olot, Spain, to the diocese; in 1871, ten Immaculate Heart of Mary Sisters arrived in Los Angeles.[15] Under Amat's leadership, St. Vincent's College was established in 1865 and staffed by the Vincentian Fathers.[16]

Several factors contributed to the growth of Southern California. With "the inauguration of transcontinental railroads (1885), the discovery of oil (1891), and the development of the citrus industry, the population of the city and diocese grew rapidly and the Church's progress was marked."[17] These expansions coincided with the Third Plenary Council of Baltimore in 1884, which admonished pastors to establish Catholic parochial schools. Spanish-born prelate, Francis Mora, succeeded Amat. The Sisters of St. Joseph of Carondelet and the Sisters of the Holy Names arrived during his episcopacy and established their first schools. Mora advanced the Church through the establishment of a newspaper, *The Tidings,* in 1895 and strengthened his people against anti-Catholic bigotry.

Mora also confronted the mischief of the American Protective Association (APA). The APA continued the anti-Catholic bigotry of the Know-Nothing Party after the Civil War, in the later part of the nineteenth century.[18] The economic depression of 1893 and the rise of Irish political machines in major cities of the East and Midwest fueled the APA campaign to check the influence and advancement of Catholics.

Again, the prompt response of bishops like Mora and his coadjutor bishop, George Montgomery, to the educational decrees of the Third Plenary Council of Baltimore accounted for some of their difficulties with the APA.[19] Bishops Mora and Montgomery countered much of the APA's work with public talks that explained the fundamentals of Catholicism. Montgomery oversaw the creation of seventeen new parishes and eighteen elementary schools. The close of the nineteenth century and opening of the twentieth century brought a change of leadership with the arrival of Irish-born Bishop Thomas J. Conaty.

Chief among Conaty's strategies was to establish the first educational plan for the diocese, a plan that offered educational opportunities from kindergarten through college. In his first year, he selected a group of priests to serve as a "Board of Examiners" whose foremost responsibility was to "advise him on educational matters, to inspect the schools, and to report on the quality of the teaching observed."[20] The first teachers' meeting was held on August 20, 1903, with representatives from Anaheim, Los Angeles, Oxnard, Pasadena, Redlands, San Diego, Santa Monica, and Alhambra.

As a result of this renewed organization, the role of various religious communities expanded; among the orders taking up the cause were the Dominican Sisters of Mission San Jose, Sisters of the Holy

Names, Sisters of the Immaculate Heart of Mary, Sisters of St. Joseph of Carondelet, the Religious Sisters of Mercy (Burlingame), and the Ursulines. Subsequent to this pivotal convocation, summer sessions were held annually for the training of all teachers, both religious and lay. Conaty also established central diocesan high schools like those in Philadelphia.[21]

Conaty himself was a great educator and brought a tremendous zeal for establishing schools.[22] He had served as the rector of The Catholic University of America from 1886 to 1903 when he was named bishop of Monterey-Los Angeles. Conaty assisted the Sisters of St. Joseph of Carondelet in establishing a provincial house in the diocese, and he invited St. Francis Xavier Cabrini (1850-1917) to establish a school for Italian immigrants.

National parishes and schools, however, were more the exception than the rule in Los Angeles. In contrast to large cities in the East and Midwest, there was never a strong emphasis in Los Angeles upon establishing national parishes despite the respectable influx of Croatians, Italians, Poles, and the French.[23] There were ethnic enclaves and neighborhoods throughout the region, but these neighborhoods were not always clearly defined, nor could they be compared to the cohesive neighborhoods of Eastern cities.

Under Conaty the diocese also maintained a school at Banning for Native American children as well as two other such schools.[24] Overall, during the early years of the twentieth century, under Conaty's leadership there were a total of twenty-nine parish schools, not counting the academies.[25] Following Conaty's death in 1915, the post of bishop of the diocese remained vacant for two years due to a lack of willing and able episcopal candidates. Finally, Monsignor John J. Cantwell accepted the mission in 1917.

Born in Ireland, Cantwell had enrolled in a missionary seminary and was ordained a priest for the Archdiocese of San Francisco. His episcopal leadership spanned the end of World War I, and the Great Depression and continued to the end of World War II. Among the highlights of that era was the phenomenal growth of Southern California at this time with the development of the motion picture industry. In addition, Southern California witnessed: "advertising, agricultural expansion, petroleum discoveries, hydro-electric power development, a deep-water harbor at San Pedro, climatic advantages, readily accessible land, good highways, and ... the war industries."[26]

As the population of the state continued to grow, the Catholic ministerial demands became more pressing in the various cities. The response to these needs was the separation and creation of new dioceses. On December 3, 1936, the Vatican established the Archdiocese of Los Angeles and the Diocese of San Diego.[27]

Like his predecessors, Cantwell showed great solicitude for the Native Americans of California as well as for the Mexican immigrants who were fleeing anti-Catholic persecutions of the on-going Mexican Revolution. He particularly encouraged the Confraternity of Christian Doctrine (CCD) to provide spiritual support to these two groups.[28]

Cantwell was particularly aware of the growing needs of Hispanic Catholics and mandated that seminarians study Spanish as well as the history and culture of Mexico, Spain, and South America.[29] He recognized that all Catholic children were not enrolled in Catholic schools and so he became a strong and early advocate of the CCD movement.[30]

In 1901, Mary Workman organized a group of women to provide catechesis, home economic education, and assistance to immigrants in the Brownson Settlement House located near the Cathedral of St. Vibiana. This and other catechetical centers became the nascent organizations for many Catholic schools and parishes.[31] Cantwell's stress upon education had a civic dimension when he noted that "in making Catholics better Catholics we shall make them better citizens."[32]

Like other bishops across the country, Cantwell encouraged Catholics to be demonstrative in expressing their patriotism. He encouraged his flock to be active participants in the democratic process and to confront unjust political forces that hampered the development of Catholic schools.

In the early days of California, public financing was provided to private educational initiatives, many run by churches, because there were few public schools. However, in 1879 California adopted its version of the Blaine Amendment which denied public funds to church schools.[33] While the wording was aimed at all religious schools, the Catholic Church suffered the most because it had the largest number of schools.[34]

Many Catholic schools across the country suffered from the Blaine Amendment, but only California required religious denominations to pay property taxes on their schools. "In 1913, the California Legislature had passed a constitutional amendment to exempt schools of collegiate grade from taxation."[35] This measure was approved by voters and set into motion several legislative battles to overturn what Catholics believed to be an unjust tax.

During Cantwell's thirty years of leadership (1917-1947) Catholic schools in Los Angeles experienced phenomenal growth.[36] His educational philosophy toward people of every race, class, and creed may be summarized in a desire he expressed at the founding of Cathedral High School in 1925: "I want every high school boy in our diocese to feel that school is a place not for the rich, not for the poor nor any other class in particular, rather it is a place for all boys to be educated, to be trained for true citizenship."[37]

Cantwell was suceeded by James Francis McIntyre, who became a tireless promoter of Catholic schools and an administrative visionary for the ever-growing Catholic population. Consecrated a cardinal in 1953, MacIntyre led the archdiocese during the post-World War II era which saw the population grow through migration to Los Angeles, and the arrival of the Baby Boom generation of the 1950s and 1960s.

Perhaps most pressing was an ardent desire for available desks in Catholic schools. McIntyre rolled up his sleeves and organized one of the most astonishing expansions of Catholic schools ever imagined.

> Shortly after arriving in Los Angeles, Archbishop J. Francis A. McIntyre asked the director of Catholic Schools to compile a survey about the present and future needs of the archdiocese. The statistics were disheartening. Catholic high schools enrolled 10,246 students, but turned away another 41,754. There were only slots for 20% of the Catholic high school youngsters, the rest had to go elsewhere. The picture in the grammar schools was even more alarming. By filling classrooms, 48,608 students were accomodated, but another 52,392 were denied a Catholic education. The survey also indicated that exisiting schools, both elementary and high, were very unequally distributed geographically. The population in certain suburban areas trebled almost overnight and Catholic school facilities, if there were any at all, were unable to keep pace with the increased number of children wanting a Catholic education.[38]

As a layman, McIntyre had worked in an investment house in New York. He understood finances, and this expertise served him well as he executed his vast educational plan. With the help of his staff, he developed his plan which anticipated growth and development throughout the archdiocese by purchasing land in addition to the building program he inaugurated in February 1949.

The newly established Youth Education Fund was directed by Monsignor Martin McNicholas; its paramount charge was a door-to-door solicitation of pledges. This vast campaign set an amazing standard which many organizations envy, but few are able to replicate: the total cost of operational expenses was 2 percent of the entire yield; pastors were able to retain between 5 and 10 percent of their parishes' contribution.[39]

The press, especially the archdiocesan paper, *The Tidings,* gave wide coverage to education and provided ongoing updates to new school projects. Beginning in 1949, parishes were urged to raise funds for new schools and many had teams with precise instructions for making their calls.[40] The collected pledges exceeded all projections. At the end of this campaign, which netted $2,805,630, an annual collection was established for educational purposes.

As the years unfolded, however, the archdiocese continued to be exasperated by the lack of available schools and desks, so subsquently, more extraordinary drives were launched, with each one more successful than its predecessor.

> Auxiliary Bishop Timothy Manning told a friend that there were sixty-one Catholic high schools in the archdiocese, with an enrollment of 32,706. At the same time, there were 253 elementary schools offering classes for 129,406 youngsters. Easily an equal number of students were attending one or another of the many programs being offered by the Confraternity of Christian Doctrine for public school youngsters.
>
> In 1963, the statistics were stated a bit differently by a writer who said that to care for the influx of 1,000 Catholics weekly into the area, "the Archdiocese of Los Angeles for the past 15 years has been establishing a new parish every sixty-six days and building a new school every twenty-six days." Two years later, the school enrollment had increased from 52,000 in 1948 to 192,000 with the erection of over 200 schools.[41]

Along with these schools came many uninteresting cookie-cutter churches with bland aesthetics that were hastily fabricated to dot the sprawling landscape of Los Angeles.

In the 1950s, McIntyre was waging another financial battle which would draw upon his organizational strategies and skills of persuasion, while testing his sometimes irascible nature: the reversal of the tax levied upon private schools in California. While Catholic schools across the country were endlessly campaigning to obtain funding from the government to finance schools in varying ways, the obverse was true in California; the state was drawing funds from the Catholic Church via a property tax on private schools.[42] A tax exemption to Catholic schools was available in every state except California.[43] History attests that whenever antagonism to the public funding for Catholic schools arises, anti-Catholic sentiment, if not overtly apparent, is often part of the subtext.[44]

In 1879, the California State Constitution was amended to indicate that schools not under public direction could not receive any monies. It further decreed that any properties not exempt under law would be subject to property taxes.[45] In 1913, the California legislature passed an exemption from taxes for colleges or universities, but left the tax on elementary and secondary schools. The Catholic Church in California had to pay taxes on all of its Catholic elementary and secondary school properties.

Cantwell's contributions and efforts to change this law were defeated twice due to the influence of the Ku Klux Klan. The first effort in 1925 was to permit an exemption to some secondary schools; it was approved by both houses and signed by the governor, but was defeated by the electorate in November. Cantwell felt the Catholic vote might have been stronger had the measure included the grammar schools.[46]

In 1933, a proposed amendment was placed on the ballot to exempt any private, non-profit school from taxation. *The Los Angeles Times* argued:

> No other state taxes private non-profit schools and we believe that California should not. Certainly the taxpayers who are now relieved of the cost of educating 100,000 children will vote yes on No. 4 if they let their pocketbooks decide. Others will vote yes as a matter of justice.[47]

The resolution failed and the law would remain in place for another two decades. In those lean years of the Great Depression, voters were reluctant to approve tax exemptions. Perhaps people acting out of fear reasoned that it was better to pick the pockets of organized religion, lest their own property be further taxed to pay for public schools. That the measure was closely associated with the Catholic Church naturally elicited strong opposition from groups historically mistrustful of Catholicism and its institutions.[48] McIntyre inherited the tax, but he was determined to change the law.

McIntyre was often described as stubborn or obstinate, but others claimed that he was single-minded or unwavering. In the case of

seeking tax relief for the schools, he was unflinching and indomita-
ble. For nearly the entire decade of the 1950s, McIntyre waged an uphill battle to change the property tax on Catholic schools. In 1950, he
sought a reduction in the property assessment from the Los Angeles
Board of Supervisors. The appeal was denied, even though McIntyre
claimed that the Catholic schools of Los Angeles County were saving
the taxpayers $15 million annually. One local council of the Knights
of Columbus urged McIntyre to counter the board's narrow-minded
position by closing all Catholic schools until a satisfactory remedy was
reached.[49] Cooler heads prevailed.

Another attempt to remedy the tax was introduced in the California State Assembly in 1951. Approved by both houses of the state
legistlature and signed by Governor Earl Warren, the new law granted
tax exemption to non-profit organizations whose property was used
solely for "religious, hospital, scientific, or charitable purposes."[50] If not
contested within ninety days from passage, the law would have gone
into effect, but it was ruled unconstitutional by the State's Legislative
Counsel and the Attorney General's Office.

The California Taxpayers Alliance opposed the new law and McIntyre was convinced that this group and its campaign was a front for
the Scottish Rite Masons and the National Education Association,
two organizations that historically opposed aid of any kind to private
schools.[51]

But McIntyre would not give up. This defeat triggered a carefully
calculated campaign by McIntyre that would rival any military conquest.
He replicated the successful strategies to raise money for an "education
fund" to prove to the people of California that the tax was unjust.

Working with all the Catholic bishops and numerous private school
educators in California, but particularly with Archbishop John J. Mitty
of San Francisco, McIntyre spearheaded a steering committee known
as the Committee for Justice in Education. The purpose of the committee was to fight for their common cause in support of private and parochial education. To make this more than a "Catholic cause," MacIntyre
saw that the committee membership was overwhelminingly Protestant.
The cardinal was not above the use of leverage and he used his position
to make personal calls on influential people from Alexander Stoddard,
the Superintendent of Los Angeles City School District to many civic,
fraternal, and religious leaders.[52] With pamphlets, talks, and door-to-
door campaigning, McIntyre was indefatigable.[53] He was adamant and

clearly presented the facts, through the press and every other means of communication.

Because of this ubiquitous effort to educate voters, a new law passed on November 4, 1952, but this was not the end of the struggle. Judges in Alameda County ruled the passage of the law unconstitutional, and the case was contested in the Supreme Court of California. In 1956, the high court chose not to hear it since there were not substantial questions involved.

In 1957, a group organized under the title Californians for Public Schools, gathered signatures and placed the matter before voters one more time in an effort to overturn the exemption for private schools. On November 4, 1958, after numerous twists and turns, the cardinal saw a victory for Catholic education.[54] Catholic school properties would no longer be subject to taxation.

But McIntyre was not in Los Angeles to celebrate this victory. He had been called to Rome for the election of a new pope. On October 28, the conclave of cardinals elected the avuncular Angelo Roncalli as Pope John XXIII whose subsequent convocation of Vatican II introduced sweeping changes into the Church.[55]

One change led to a mêlée that Andrew Greeley cited as "one of the greatest tragedies in the history of American Catholicism."[56] The controversy emerged when McIntyre tangled with the Sisters of the Immaculate Heart of Mary (IHM). Vastly different ecclesiologies and contrary interpretations of Vatican II, combined with the renewal of religious life, erupted in a battle drawing passionate bias from all ideological sides.[57]

The IHM Sisters had prospered in California from their early days as a missionary order from Olot, Spain. In 1924, the communinity established canonical autonomy apart from Spain. By acquiring pontifical jurisdiction, they were not a diocesan order.[58] Vocations grew along with the number of their educational commitments and by 1963 there were six hundred members.[59] The IHM Sisters staffed about 10 percent of the archdiocesan schools; they were known, respected, and loved as excellent educators. Adjacent to their Motherhouse in Hollywood stood Immaculate Heart College and Immaculate Heart High School.

Like all other religious communities, the IHM Sisters engaged the call of Vatican II to renew their order.[60] Just as many communities of the time, there were enormous pressures to supply teachers for the burgeoning Catholic schools, even if this meant sending sisters with little or no formal training from the novitiates to the schools.[61] The IHM Sisters sought to remedy this responsibility and other educational pressures when they adopted a decree on education that included measures to reduce class sizes, empower principals, and to have adequately prepared teachers working at financially sound schools.[62]

Implicit in these measures of the community's ninth General Chapter in 1967, were demands that McIntyre saw as a threat to the school system he was building. He was not pleased with the decrees and ideals that were coming from this traditionally reliable pipeline of excellent teachers.[63] McIntyre wanted these decrees to be abrogated and saw them as an ultimatum, which if enacted, would have withdrawn the sisters from the schools where the conditions were not met. At this time there were 197 IHM Sisters teaching in twenty-eight grade schools and eight high schools in the archdiocese. The sisters claimed that they had been "fired" by McIntyre, but they were willing to discuss the decrees and/or the timetable.[64] The sisters did not see their decrees as an ultimatum, but as a set of ideals which they were determined to implement.[65]

Not an enthusiast for the reforms of Vatican II, McIntyre was anxious about the manner in which religious were conducting renewal and the direction it was moving.[66] He was particularly vexed by the decision of the order to abandon the religious habit and work in apostolates other than schools—actions he saw as a dangerous secularization.[67] Furthermore, he was concerned about the influence of feminism which many congregations were embracing and simultaneously setting them at odds with Church leadership.[68]

As McIntyre intervened in the renewal process, the conflict received widespread coverage in the national press with ample moralizing, support, and apologetics for both sides. Petitions from every imaginable corner appeared. Some voices supported McIntyre as the champion of tradition, while others pronounced the sisters as prophets of a new church. Ultimately, the dispute moved toward a resolution after official Vatican visitations to the community in 1968.[69] Two years later, *Time* magazine noted that

> About 315 of 380 nuns decided to follow their president, Sister Anita Caspary in asking for dispensations from church vows. The request will be granted. Rather than disband, they plan to form an independent secular organization devoted to "the service of man in the spirit of the Gospel."[70]

At this time the schools were still heavily dependent upon religious sisters as a labor force. McIntyre was able to secure the services of other communities to cover those schools affected by the IHM departures.

As many women were leaving religious life across the country and from this order,[71] each IHM Sister was asked with which of the two organizations she sought affiliation, if any at all. In the end, an ecumenical association known as the Immaculate Heart Community was founded under the leadership of Anita Caspary.[72] "They formed an alternative 'community without walls' with married couples and male members, a syneisactic model of life that was promptly condemned by the hierarchy."[73] There were fifty sisters who chose not to follow the new directives and renewed the congregation under the name Sisters of the Immaculate Heart of Mary, following a shared interpretation with McIntyre of Vatican II's renewal for religious life.[74]

Historians are still evaluating this highly divisive event. Were McIntyre's demands of the IHM Sisters a prescient alarm for all orders of sisters? Did the cardinal's obstinence precipitate the disintegration of vowed religious life in California and mark the beginning of the end of sisters teaching in the schools?[75] Why did McIntyre intercede with this order's renewal when many other communities were conducting similar projects? Or, if left alone, would the IHM Sisters have gone the evolutionary route of many large religious orders rather than the revolutionary action they chose?[76] In either scenario, these events clouded the educational legacy and labors of all who were involved. It also served as a harbinger for the dissappearance of teaching sisters in Los Angeles and across the country.[77]

When Cardinal McIntyre retired in 1970 there were 275 parochial and private elementary schools with 117,797 students, and 71 diocesan and private high schools with 39,710 students in the Archdiocese of Los Angeles.[78] Succeeding generations of Angelinos would see the "past as prologue" with recurring themes from the history of Southern California. Recalling California's growth from the Spanish conquest, Gold Rush, and post-World War II years, the population of Los Angeles continued to swell, as people from all over the world migrated to make the "City of Angels" their home. In fact, the three-county Archdiocese of Los Angeles became the largest diocese in the United States.

Echoing its early history, Spanish was on ascendency as a vital language. Catholic schools faced challenges with this growth. The decline in the number of vowed religious available and willing to staff the schools, gave rise to lay leaders and teachers who had always been essential to the educational mission and would attain even greater responsibilities in the coming decades.

Establishing parish schools was never simple but there would be new challenges to maintain and improve the schools that previous generations built at great sacrifice. Along with advancing the mission of Catholic schools came the challenge of keeping tuition costs within reach of the poor and middle classes. Each generation is presented with unique projects, problems, and obstacles, while simultaneously blessed with the skills, vision, and inventiveness of men and women to meet their appointment with destiny. A vast network of Catholic schools had been envisioned and planned for Los Angeles by its past leaders. Subsequent generations would need to discern their role in sustaining this legacy and advancing its educational mission.

NOTES

1. John Tracy Ellis, *American Catholicism* (Chicago: The University of Chicago Press, 1969), 1-40.

2. William Bangert, *A History of the Society of Jesus* (St. Louis, MO: Institute of Jesuit Sources, 1986).

3. Harold A. Buetow, *Of Singular Benefit: The Story of Catholic Education in the United States* (New York: The Macmillan Company, 1970), 11-13.

4. James A. Sandos, "Junípero Serra's Canonization and the Historical Record," *The American Historical Review* 93, no. 5 (December 1988): 1253-1269.

5. Francis Weber, *California's Reluctant Prelate: The Life and Times of Right Reverend Thaddeus Amat, C.M.* (Los Angeles: Dawson Book Shop, 1964), 137.

6. William E. North, "Catholic Education in Southern California" (PhD diss., The Catholic University of America, 1936), 39; Sepulveda, *Historical Memoirs*, MS, 34, quoted by Hubert Howe Bancroft, *A History of California* (San Francisco: The History Publishing Co., 1890), 5:643.

7. Ibid., 80.

8. Michael E. Engh, *Frontier Faiths: Church, Temple, and Synogogue in Los Angeles, 1846-1888* (Albuquerque: University of New Mexico Press, 1992), 165-186.

9. North, "Catholic Education in Southern California," 123. The Picpus Fathers draw this name from the street of their headquarters in Paris. The order's name is the Congregation of the Sacred Hearts of Jesus and Mary. One of their better known members was Blessed Damian de Veuster who ministered to the lepers on the Hawaiian island of Molokai.

10. The establishment and division of archdioceses and dioceses follows this chronology: 1840 Diocese of the Two Californias (what is today the entire state of California and Baja California); 1848 Diocese of Monterey; 1853 Archdiocese of San Francisco; 1859 Diocese of Monterey-Los Angeles; 1922 Diocese of Los Angeles-San Diego; 1936 Archdiocese of Los Angeles and Diocese of San Diego; 1976 Diocese of Orange.

11. Engh, *Frontier Faiths*, 75.

12. Ibid., 145.

13. Ibid., 141. Engh maintained that "This blue-robed band proved to be the most flexible and adaptive Roman Catholic personnel in the pueblo. Invited to found a school and orphanage, the nuns later undertook hospital nursing, disaster relief, job placement for women, parish catechism instruction, fundraising for Catholic causes, and care of smallpox victims. Because of the nuns' far greater numbers, range of ministries, and contacts with the broader community, they contended more directly than most priests with local pastoral problems."

14. Ibid., 159.

15. Anita Caspary, *Witness to Integrity: The Crisis of the Immaculate Heart Community of California* (Collegeville, MN: The Liturgical Press, 2003); S.C. Fedewa, "L.A. to Keep Schools; Woos 'Approved' Nuns," *The National Catholic Reporter*, January 31, 1968; Francis Weber, *His Emminence of Los Angeles: James Francis Cardinal McIntyre*, 2 vols (Mission Hills, CA: St. Francis Historical Society, 1997); Francis Weber, *A History of the Archdiocese of Los Angeles and its Precursor Jurisdictions in Southern California 1840-2007* (Strasbourg: Éditions du Signe, 2006). Later, the Immaculate Heart of Mary community would provide an extensive workforce of educators, and then overnight, after an infamous clash with James Francis Cardinal McIntyre, the order was devastated.

16. St. Vincent's College closed in 1911, and the Jesuits opened Los Angeles College that same year. The name would change to Loyola College, then Loyola University, and eventually Loyola Marymount University, when it joined with the Religious of the Sacred Heart of Mary who had established Marymount College in 1932. Shortly before the Loyola and Marymount merger in 1973, the Sisters of St. Joseph of Orange had joined the Marymount Sisters as partners. The Sisters of St. Joseph of Carondelet established Mount St. Mary's College for women in 1925. The Immaculate Heart of Mary Sisters opened Immaculate Heart of Mary College 1916, but it closed in 1982.

17. T. Manning, "Archdiocese of Los Angeles," in *New Catholic Encyclopedia*, 2nd ed. (Washington, DC: The Catholic University of America, 2002), 1:790-791.

18. John Tracy Ellis, *Documents of American Catholic History* (Chicago: H. Regnery, 1967), 2:483-485.

19. J. L. Morrison, "American Protective Association," in *New Catholic Encyclopedia*, 2nd ed. (Washington, DC: The Catholic University of America, 2002), 1:352-353.

20. Archdiocese of Los Angeles, "History of the Schools in the Archdiocese of Los Angeles," http://www.la-archdiocese.org/learning/schools/about/history.html

21. James T. Fisher, *Communion of Immigrants: A History of Catholics in America* (New York: Oxford University Press, 2000), 87-91; Francis Weber, *Thomas James Conaty: Pastor-Educator-Bishop* (Los Angeles: Westernlore Press, 1969), 31.

22. Ibid., 47.

23. Weber, *John Joseph Cantwell: His Excellency of Los Angeles* (Hong Kong: Cathay Press Limited, 1971), 125.

24. Manning, "Archdiocese of Los Angeles," 791.

25. Ibid.

26. Weber, *John Joseph Cantwell*, 125.

27. Ibid., 80. In a radio broadcast from St. Vibiana's Cathedral, Archbishop John T. McNicholas, O.P., of Cincinnati observed the following in paying tribute to Cantwell as a proponent of Catholic schools: "In furthering Catholic education, no fewer than sixty-six parochial schools have been built through your efforts. Since 1917, your first year as Bishop, the nine thousand pupils in all the Catholic schools in the larger Diocese of Monterey-Los Angeles, have increased to no fewer than 28,641, who now receive daily instruction in what, until recently, was the Diocese of Los Angeles-San Diego."

28. Manning, "Archdiocese of Los Angeles," 791.

29. Weber, *John Joseph Cantwell*, 116.

30. Timothy, M. Dolan, *Some Seed Fell on Good Ground: The Life of Edwin V. O'Hara* (Washington, DC: The Catholic University of American Press, 1992), 128. "In what was to become one of the most vibrant programs, John J. Cantwell, bishop of Los Angeles, started the confraternity in 1922."

31. Michael Engh, "From the City of the Angels to Parishes of San Antonio: Catholic Organization, Women Activists, and Racial Intersections, 1900-50," in *Catholicism in the American West: A Rosary of Hidden Voices*, ed. Roberto R. Trevino and Richard Francaviglia (Arlington, TX: Texas A& M University Press, 2007), 42-71.

32. Weber, *John Joseph Cantwell*, 105.

33. David Kirkpatrick, "The Pain of the Blaine (Amendments) is on the Wane," *Vermonters for Better Education* (August 2003), http://www.schoolreport.com/schoolreport/articles/blaine2_08_03.htm

34. California State Constitution, "Blaine Amendments: California," *Blaine Amendments* (2008), http://www.blaineamendments.org/Intro/whatis.html

35. Weber, *John Joseph Cantwell*, 155-160.

36. Ibid., 163. As Weber observed: "The three colleges, thirty-four secondary and seventy-two primary schools inaugurated during Cantwell's episcopate in an area twice reduced in its geographical extention, to say nothing of the new facilities provided for already existing institutions, are a measure of the concern exhibited by the Irish-born prelate for the furtherance of Catholic educational opportunities."

37. Ibid., 162.

38. Weber, *James Francis Cardinal McIntyre*, 249-250.

39. Ibid., 251.

40. Ibid., 251-252. "When visiting the potential donors, team members were given ten procedural directives: a. That they are the representatives of the Archbishop, b. That they be courteous and ready to listen even though at times it be a trying experience, c. They will ALWAYS act as official solicitors, and, therefore, do not accept any hospitality or DISCUSS what their neighbors on the block gave, d. If the anticipated amount is not given, then try to get something. A man may not be able to give a hundred dollars; he may be able to give ten. Ten dollars is better than nothing, e. If the party wants to make special arrangements, he should make them right there, f. Always get signature on the subscription blank, g. Don't leave the house without definitely 'clinching' the call, h. Try, if at all possible, to get a 'down payment' – no matter how small, i. Explain the fact that they will be notified when the payments on their pledges are due, j. Returns and reports on each call MUST BE MADE every night."

41. Weber, *James Francis Cardinal McIntyre*, 284-285. "Over the years, Cardinal McIntyre received many honors, awards and citations, but none meant more to him than the two which recognized his work on behalf of Catholic schools (the first was an honorary doctorate in 1953 from the University of Notre Dame and the other was a scroll of commendation from Mayor Sam Yorty and the City Council of Los Angeles in 1965)."

42. Timothy Walch, *Parish School: American Catholic Parochial Education from Colonial Times to the Present* (New York: Crossroad, 1996), 159.

43. "Catholic Schools and Public Money," *Yale Law Journal* 50, no. 5 (March 1941): 917-927, 922.

44. Engh, *Frontier Faiths*, 75; prior to 1855 private and parochial schools received public funds. "Antipathy toward foreigners and Roman Catholics in the state emerged in the Know-Nothing movement and crystallized in two actions in 1855, affecting public education. That May, the California legislature prohibited public financing of sectarian education, and the state Bureau of Public Instruction curtailed the practice

of public instruction in the Spanish language."

45. Weber, *James Francis Cardinal McIntyre*, 120.

46. Weber, *John Joseph Cantwell*, 156-157.

47. *Los Angeles Times*, May 14, 1933.

48. Weber, *John Joseph Cantwell*, 158-159.

49. Weber, *James Francis Cardinal McIntyre*, 120-121.

50. Ibid., 124.

51. Ibid., 125.

52. Ibid., 127.

53. Ibid., 132. He commanded four unwavering principles in moving this issue ahead against growing and widespread opposition from the Scottish Rite Masons: "1. All statements had to be factually and objectively accurate; 2. There could be no real or implied threats, reprisals or boycotts for those holding opposing views; 3. The language used should be simple and persuasive, but always friendly, kind, and courteous; 4. The 'Catholic' involvement should be downplayed. This was an issue of 'justice' not 'religion.'"

54. Ibid., 137-144. This final campaign was characterized by bigotry and scare tactics. McIntrye actually interceded with Masonic leadership and their friends in hope of addressing any misunderstandings or fears about the intent and substance of the exemption, but this did not yield the desired result. McIntyre drafted a personal letter which outlined his case and was sent to thousands of people. He solicited and received supportive endorsements of important politicians and civic leaders. In addition, the press throughout the state sounded a tone of exasperation with detractors of the exemption. On November 4, 1958, Proposition 16 went down in defeat by a 2 to 1 margin. One handbill noted: "attempts to secure exemption of taxes was only an introduction or prologue to the sure demands of private and parochial schools. 'Before long, they will be demanding free books, free lunches, free transportation and rally a share of the tax dollar for capital expenditures and operating costs for their private and parochial schools,'" Leon Whitsell brochure (n.d.).

55. Mary Ewens, "Women in the Convent," in *American Catholic Women: A Historical Experience*, ed. Karen Kennelly (New York: Macmillan, 1989), 17-47.

56. Andrew Greeley, *The Catholic Voice*, March 27, 1968.

57. Ellis, *American Catholicism*, 232-235.

58. Caspary, *Witness to Integrity*, 17-18. "Ignoring Bishop Cantwell's desire to have juridical authority over the new community, the Vatican granted the new institute pontifical status. This rank in Catholic orders of women historically has meant that the community designated 'pontifical institute' was assigned a cardinal-protector in Rome to defend the sisters against possible encroachment of their rights by anyone, including the local hierarchy. The new order was now to be called 'The California Institute of the Sisters of the Most Holy and Immaculate Heart of the Blessed Virgin Mary,' and its members were asked to modify their habit slightly to distinguish them from the original group."

59. Ibid., 18.

60. John J. Fialka, *Sisters: Catholic Nuns and the Making of America* (New York: St. Martin's Press, 2003), 213-225.

61. Kevina Keating and Mary Peter Traviss, *Pioneer Mentoring in Teacher Preparation: From the Voices of Women Religious* (St. Cloud, MN: North Star Press of St. Cloud, 2001). An excellent description of the pressures to supply teaching sisters is provided in this ethnography. The book illustrates that while many sisters went directly from their initial training at the motherhouse to a teaching position without benefit of formal teaching certification, the sisters benefited from an informal system of mentoring

with resident experts.

62. Caspary, *Witness to Integrity*, 225-262.

63. Weber, *James Francis Cardinal McIntyre*, 421. The measures read: "a) Reasonable class sizes (ideally between thirty-five and forty); b) Full time principals with authority to exercise responsibilities as administrator, supervisor, initiator (of new programs) and communicator with the pastor, parishioners, school staff, students and her professional peers; c) Sufficient financial resources to facilitate the employment of a full staff of adequately prepared teaching personnel and to provide for instructional materials, adequate maintenance and clerical assistance."

64. Ibid., 437.

65. Ewens, "Women in the Convent," 43.

66. "The Immaculate Heart Rebels," *Time*, February 16, 1970.

67. Robert Kugelmann, "An Encounter Between Pshychology and Religion: Humanistic Psychology and the Immaculate Heart of Mary Nuns," *Journal of the History of the Behavioral Sciences* 41, no. 4 (Fall 2005): 347-365. The IHM Sisters engaged Carl Rogers and William Coulson from the Western Behavioral Science Institute to conduct encounter groups as an ongoing exercise in renewal with results that have been fiercely debated. Their philosophical views questioned obedience and governance in Catholicism and religious life as an unhealthy and authoritarian imposition which stunted personal growth and integration.

68. Ann Carey, *Sisters in Crisis: The Tragic Unraveling of Women's Religious Communities* (Huntington, IN: Our Sunday Visitor Publishing, 1997), 197.

69. Weber, *James Francis Cardinal McIntyre*, 429-430.

70. "The Immaculate Heart Rebels," *Time*, February 16, 1970. The exact numbers of departures, transfers, and associations are difficult to calculate. Caspary, *Witness to Integrity*, 210, noted: "The most publicized separation was certainly that between those who had objected to the new decrees, and indeed to the renewal plans in general. This group, now directly responsible to Sister Eileen, had fifty followers, while the group who professed loyalty to the decrees of renewal had about three hundred fifty members, a number having left the community altogether or relocated to another religious community by the end of 1969."

71. Jay P. Dolan, *The American Catholic Experience: A History from Colonial Times to the Present* (Garden City: Doubleday, 1985), 438.

72. Caspary, *Witness to Integrity*, 210. Three hundred fifty IHM members joined the new organization; later it welcomed men, as well as single and married persons, *Immaculate Heart Community* (March 21, 2009), http://www.immaculateheartcommunity.org/communitydb/index.php?option=com_frontpage&Itemid=1

73. Jo Ann Kay McNamara, *Sisters in Arms: Catholic Nuns through Two Millennia* (Cambridge: Harvard University Press, 1996), 640-641. The author observed that "Communities of this sort are probably not destined for institutional longevity, but there is no reason to dismiss an apostolate that springs up in answer to a need, dissolves, and reshapes itself as circumstances require."

74. "The Immaculate Heart Rebels," *Time*, February 16, 1970.

75. Carey, *Sisters in Crisis*, 184-191.

76. Caspary, *Witness to Integrity*, 45-53.

77. Michael P. Caruso, "Teaching Sisters: Triumph, Trial, and Legacy," Loyola Marymount University, 2009.

78. *The Official Catholic Directory* (New York: P.J. Kenedy and Sons, 2008), 440.

Bay City Catholicism:
Catholic Education in San Francisco

Jeffrey M. Burns

As late as 1846, San Francisco was a tiny port community of less than a thousand residents located in Mexico's northernmost province. In 1834, Mexico had begun closing the extensive mission system in California and by the time the United States took over San Francisco in late 1846, not much was happening in the city.

Then in 1848, James Marshall discovered gold at Sutter's Mill, north of Sacramento, and set off an international gold rush that thoroughly transformed San Francisco and California. In Carey McWilliams' apt phrase, San Francisco became a city where "the lights went on all at once," and became what historian Gunther Barth referred to as an "instant city."[1] Thousands of goldseekers streamed through San Francisco on their way to the gold country in the Sierra Nevada; many eventually returning to settle in San Francisco. The result was a very cosmopolitan city.

By 1850, 50 percent of the city was foreign born, and by 1880 San Francisco had a higher percentage of foreign-born residents than any city in the United States. Equally significant, San Francisco had a highly mobile population with only one in ten staying through the city's first three decades.[2] San Francisco was relatively isolated from the rest of the United States until 1861 when it was connected with the transcontinental telegraph and in 1869 when the transcontinental railway was completed.

The development of the Catholic Church in San Francisco followed the city's urban development. Even though Mission San Francisco was closed by the Mexican government in 1834, it continued to operate as a parish church, and popularly came to be known as "Mission Dolores." In 1849, the first non-mission parish, St. Francis, was established in North Beach, followed by St. Patrick in 1851 in the South of Market area. The growing community required a resident bishop, so in 1850, Joseph Sadoc Alemany, O.P., was appointed the first bishop of Monterey; he quickly understood San Francisco was the more important city. In 1853, San Francisco was made an archdiocese with Alemany its first archbishop.[3]

Catholic schools were begun at once. By 1851, the bishop had established three schools with 220 students: St. Francis and St. Patrick's for boys, and St. Patrick's for girls. In 1852, Mission Dolores began a school. The schools were staffed by lay teachers and clergy. From their inception, Catholic schools were plagued by problems of finance and personnel. Alemany had few priests and vowed women religious at his disposal to staff the school system.

Nonetheless, in his pioneer diocese, Alemany stressed the importance of developing good schools. In 1851, seeking funds, he wrote the Society for the Propagation of the Faith in Paris, "Good schools and colleges are of the utmost importance," but he lamented, "to build churches and schools is exceedingly expensive."[4]

Alemany also actively recruited orders of vowed religious men and women. Before coming to San Francisco, he recruited the Dominican Sisters from Belgium who accompanied him to California in 1850. They eventually became the Dominican Sisters of San Rafael and served in a number of schools including St. Rose Academy, founded in 1862. In 1851, he secured the services of the Sisters of Notre Dame de Namur who came by way of Oregon, opened Notre Dame Academy in San Jose, and later staffed several San Francisco schools as well. In 1852, the Daughters of Charity from Emmitsburg, Maryland, arrived and quickly opened St. Vincent's School as well as staffed the Catholic orphanage in the city.

Not content, Alemany sent Father Hugh Gallagher to Ireland to obtain more sisters. Gallagher succeeded: in 1854 the Sisters of the Presentation and the Sisters of Mercy came to San Francisco. The Presentation Sisters became the premier teaching order, teaching one third of Catholic school children in the city by 1870. They opened their first school in North Beach in 1855. The "Mercies," as they were called, opened St. Mary's Hospital but did not open their first school until 1871.

Alemany also recruited male religious including the Jesuits who opened Santa Clara College in 1851 and St. Ignatius College in 1855, which later was renamed the University of San Francisco. Alemany later came to believe St. Ignatius was too narrowly focused, so he began his own college, St. Mary's, in 1863 and in 1868 the Christian Brothers came to staff the college.[5] (It must be remembered that a "college" in the nineteenth century maintained a grade school, high school, and college divisions.)

In the first several years of the city's history there was a struggle to determine if Catholic schools could receive public funding. In 1851, as the San Francisco common school system began to develop, Catholic schools were included in the distribution of public money. However, this did not last long. In 1852, funds were withheld from denominational schools.

Alemany protested, arguing, "The will of the people throughout the whole Republic, is obviously to give such assurance and stability to education, as to have by law its doors thrown open to every child, to guaranty to all a school-house and a teacher."[6] As such, denominational schools should be funded. The state superintendent agreed, and in 1853 three Catholic schools received public funds.

This too was not to last. Already the anti-Catholic and anti-immigrant "Know-Nothing" Party—"Los ignorantes" as the Californios called them—was growing in power. In 1855, the Know Nothings won the state governorship. The same year, they split the city's board of education with the Democrats and succeeded in requiring that the sisters staffing the Catholic schools pass a certification exam and attend a Saturday morning normal school class. The sisters argued that they were cloistered and so could not attend the exam or the school. As a result, Catholic schools could not be certified and thus lost funding.[7] The era of public funding of Catholic schools had come to an end. The following year Bible reading and daily prayers were removed from the public school curriculum, though standard textbooks used in public schools regularly used Bible stories.

Despite the loss of public funds, Catholic schools continued to develop. In large part, school development rested on the commitment of vowed women religious, whose practical poverty enabled the schools to remain tuition free or to rely on voluntary tuition. Three types of school sponsorship developed by the 1870s: (1) schools sponsored by religious orders such as the Presentation Sisters; (2) schools sponsored by parishes; and (3) schools sponsored by the archdiocese such as Sacred Heart College founded in 1874.

By the twentieth century the vast majority of grade schools were parish sponsored, placing them on a firmer financial footing. Fundraising became a regular part of Catholic school and parish life—bazaars, fairs, raffles, card parties, lectures, dinners, and later, Bingo were ever present. The working-class composition of the faithful in San Francisco made the rapid expansion of schools difficult. Even so, by 1870, more than ten Catholic schools were in operation with about five thousand students.

Despite this success, Catholic enrollment was declining in relation to the public schools. As such, Catholic schools felt compelled to keep up with the public school curriculum in order to attract students. Mother Teresa Comerford, superior of the Presentation Sisters affirmed this, writing in 1874, "The system of public education being now matured with a very high standard of education, we are obliged to embrace the same sciences in our teaching in order to compete with them."[8] Historian Lawrence Scrivani put it this way:

> In the 1870s, the public schools introduced sciences to their curriculum. Catholic schools without them felt obligated to add them. . . . Thus the pattern was set that would remain for the future. . . . Relatively well-funded public schools would set the standards and Catholic schools would struggle to find some way to keep up so as to remain credible alternatives.[9]

By 1869, Catholic schools were using the same textbooks as public schools, except for religion, and taught most of the same subjects. Catholics even added business courses and commercial schools to their secondary schools.

Religion, of course, retained a central place in the Catholic schools and was the prime reason for their existence. Religion was generally presented in a catechism format. After 1888 the *Baltimore Catechism*, commissioned by the Baltimore Council, would be employed, though its use would be altered in San Francisco.

Nonetheless, schools were concerned with much else. The Presentation Sisters' guide book instructed the teachers, that "although much time must be employed in teaching the poor children to read, write, and work . . . Christian doctrine, decency, cleanliness and correctness of manner, are the chief and necessary points to be attended to."[10] And though the public schools were seen as the great Americanizing institutions, Catholic schools soon adopted the same outlook. By 1920, the archbishop of San Francisco could assert, "There is no adequate system of education equal to the system of the Catholic Church in America, to reach at once the ideals of our American State, the ideals of American citizenship, the ideals of perfect living and thinking."[11]

Despite the large immigrant population, San Francisco did not mirror the Catholic Church in the East; national parishes, and thus national parish schools, did not develop to the extent they did in the urban east. National parishes did develop, but on a much smaller scale. By 1925, there were three Italian parishes, two German parishes, two French parishes, and one for the Spanish-speaking, the Maltese, and the Slavonians. Mission parishes had also been established for the Chinese and Japanese.

The establishment of national parish schools reflected patterns seen in the East. Germans were most aggressive in establishing parish schools: St. Boniface German parish established a school the same year it was founded, 1860, and the second German parish, St. Anthony, began a school within a year of its foundation, 1893 and 1894 respectively.

The Italians took more time: the premier Italian parish in the city, Saints Peter and Paul founded in 1884, did not have a school until 1924, in part because the Presentation Sisters operated a school within its boundaries, though the school was not Italian. The other two Italian parishes started their schools well after their founding: Corpus Christi, founded in 1898, started its school in 1927, and Immaculate Conception, founded in 1912, waited until 1957 to begin its school.

The French parish Notre Dame des Victories founded in 1856, did not have a school until 1924, though the second French parish, Jeanne D'arc, began a school the year of its founding, 1922. The Maltese parish, founded in 1915, did not have a school until 1956. The Spanish and Slavonian parishes had no schools at all.

A mission school for the Chinese was established in the 1880s but it did not last long. Another was established in 1921, St. Mary's Chinese School, which continues to operate to the present day. Morning Star School for the Japanese was established in 1930, and though it had a difficult time during World War II with the internment of the Japanese, it survived until the 1980s.

The male and female vowed religious communities that staffed the schools were largely immigrants themselves, but for the most part they did not serve their own immigrant populations exclusively. The Jesuits were Italian; the Christian Brothers were French and Irish. The Presentations and Mercies were Irish, the Notre Dame, French; the Mission San Jose Dominicans, German, and the Daughters of Charity had an American foundation. Only the Mission San Jose Dominicans served their own immigrant community at St. Boniface and St. Anthony German parishes. On the other hand, their Immaculate Conception Academy in the Mission District served a mixed community. Interestingly, the only order of vowed women religious indigenous to the Archdiocese of San Francisco, the Holy Family Sisters founded in 1872, did not work in the Catholic schools; rather their primary ministries were to provide day care to the children of working parents, and catechetical instruction to students who did not attend Catholic schools.

In 1884, Alemany retired and turned the archdiocese over to Archbishop Patrick W. Riordan. By this time San Francisco had developed into the leading commercial city on the West coast and was the center of the region's finance, trade, culture, and intellectual life. Large scale immigration from Italy peaked during the first two decades of the twentieth century, and San Francisco maintained its status as an immigrant city. In 1906, San Francisco was rocked by a devastating earthquake and fire which wiped out the city's downtown and financial districts. The city would rebuild, but it never regained its status as the premier city on the West coast—that honor went to Los Angeles.

Coming from the East, Riordan was a strong advocate of parochial education and he was disappointed with the condition in which he found San Francisco's Catholic schools. More than four fifths of Catholic children in the city were enrolled in public schools. This was unacceptable to Riordan, who lamented that Catholic children in public schools suffered an "inevitable impairment of faith and morals."[12]

Though Riordan was critical of Alemany's efforts, Alemany had done as well as could be expected with limited resources. As early as 1854, Alemany issued an order that, "The pastor shall endeavor, as far as possible, to have schools for boys and girls."[13] Thirty years later, Riordan issued the same order, this time supported by the recently concluded Baltimore Council which had legislated that each Catholic parish have a school within two years unless excused by the local bishop.

Despite this, Riordan's program was not embraced by all pastors. The reality of too few teaching orders coupled with the financial burden placed on largely working-class parishes, led to a less than enthusiastic response on the part of some pastors. One advisor noted, the archbishop "has much opposition on the school question . . . from the older prominent priests."[14]

Nonetheless, Riordan forged on, welcoming new orders of teaching sisters and encouraging new schools. Within five years, the Catholic school population had nearly doubled to eight thousand students. In 1893, anxious to display the success of his Catholic schools, Riordan encouraged San Francisco's participation in the Catholic Educational Exhibit held in conjunction with the World's Columbian Exposition in Chicago. San Francisco sent the third largest exhibition of any diocese in the United States.[15]

Riordan also confronted what he perceived as a continuing anti-Catholic bias in the public schools. Indeed, many non-Catholics continued to perceive the Catholic schools as "unpatriotic and foreign."[16] In 1894, Riordan sought to have the San Francisco School Board remove a textbook being used in the public schools, which he considered anti-Catholic. The offending text was Philip V. N. Myers' *Outlines of Medieval and Modern History*, published by Ginn and Company.

The archbishop's overture ignited a vigorous response from nativists who attacked the prelate's meddling in public schools.[17] John Quincy Adams Henry, pastor of the First Baptist Church, railed against the archbishop and raised the traditional complaints against Catholic schools. He published a pamphlet entitled, "Rome's Red Hand in the Public Schools," in which he quoted Pope Pius IX as saying, "The Romish Church has a right to interfere with the discipline of the public schools and the choice of teachers."[18]

Rising up to defend the archbishop was a young priest from Ireland who would come to play a major role in San Francisco's Catholic schools, Father Peter C. Yorke. Yorke employed a slashing, take-no-prisoners style of rhetoric that viciously flayed his opponents. His tactics were unsuccessful; the school board decided that the textbook would remain, but that teachers were permitted to omit the offending passages in their presentation of the textbooks. Yorke railed against the decision arguing that the California state constitution insisted that sectarianism be absent from the public school.

Though Yorke was defeated, it was just the first encounter of what became a major controversy with the anti-Catholic American Protective Association (APA) which raged between 1894 and 1896. As editor of the archdiocesan newspaper, *The San Francisco Monitor*,

Yorke became the leading Catholic spokesperson for the Catholic community in general and the archdiocese in particular. As legend would come to relate the story, Yorke "vanquished" the APA and established himself as a major figure in the history of the archdiocese.[19]

Equally important to the history of Catholic schools in San Francisco was the development of Catholic teachers' institutes in the 1890s which were intended to improve the quality of the teaching in Catholic schools. The first teachers' institute was inspired by a Catholic school teacher who had attended a summer school program in Plattsburg, New York. She allegedly remarked to a Sister of Mercy, "Oh, how I wish we could have a convention of our Catholic teachers here."[20]

The idea began to be discussed and received major support from the Presentation Sisters, who hosted a planning meeting at their convent. All the major teaching orders in the city eventually signed on to the project. From September 20 to 22, 1894, between 120 to 150 people attended the first Catholic Teachers' Institute at the Presentation Convent. It claimed to be "the first Archdiocesan Convention of Catholic Teachers ever held in America."[21]

There is no evident way to dispute such a claim. In any case, it was a significant gathering featuring ten different orders of vowed women religious in attendance. The institute included workshops on the various courses such as "Elementary Science," "Object Teaching," "Literature," "Penmanship," "Practical Arithmetic," and others. Religion was also addressed with presentations on teaching the Old and New Testaments, and the highlight of the institute, the Reverend Peter C. Yorke on the "Teaching of Religion." All workshops were led by vowed women religious or priests of the archdiocese. One session, entitled "Uniform Grading in Parochial Schools" by a Sister of Mercy, reflected the reality that the Catholic schools were not unified in content, approach, curriculum, or grading. One of the outcomes of these institutes was to create a greater uniformity among Catholic schools within the archdiocese, though this did not come easily.[22]

The institutes met each year until 1899, and their programs reflected a growing professionalism among Catholic school teachers in San Francisco. The second convention featured lay men and women—not just religious—presenting workshops. The third through fifth years featured speakers from the great secular universities, including Stanford University and the University of California among others. Scripture, liturgy, and religion remained the preserve of the clergy, but the presence of secular scholars indicated the seriousness of the endeavor.

It is not clear why the institutes faded away in the early 1900s, but several significant achievements had been accomplished. Committees were established to explore the possibilities of a uniform grading system, a uniform syllabus, uniform textbooks, and other common concerns. Collaboration between the various religious orders did result in greater uniformity, but the fact that orders had begun to collaborate was a major step forward.

Most significantly, the institute attendees, particularly the teaching sisters, expressed their dissatisfaction with the *Baltimore Catechism*. They believed the "Baltimore Catechism too difficult for young children."[23] A committee of seven sisters was formed under Yorke's leadership to create a "simple book of religious instruction which could be easily understood by the youngest children and which would be so well illustrated as to attract them."[24]

Over the next decade, Yorke developed five *Textbooks of Religion*, that presented the material in "graduated form."[25] Additionally Yorke used Scripture, liturgy, devotional materials, and paintings to make the layouts more attractive. Yorke tested the materials on Catholic school classes before they were published. The books were accepted by the San Francisco Catholic schools and became the standards of religious education in the archdiocese for several decades. Interestingly, the catechetical world would be transformed once again in the late 1950s and early 1960s by Sister Maria de la Cruz Aymes, H.H.S., and her landmark *On Our Way Series* published by Sadlier. Aymes worked for the archdiocese's school department.

In 1906, San Francisco was hit by a devastating earthquake that damaged many schools and churches in the city. The church in San Francisco committed itself to rebuilding all of its institutions, and schools were kept going. In one memorable photo, the Sisters of the Presentation are seen teaching their students amid the ruins of their school.

As San Francisco struggled to rebuild itself, the archdiocese received its third archbishop. In 1914, Riordan died, and in early 1915, Auxiliary Bishop Edward J. Hanna was elevated to the archbishopric. Hanna continued Riordan's dedication to Catholic schools. A highly educated seminary professor himself, Hanna emphasized the importance of the Catholic school. He observed early in his episcopate, "Since the time the Pastoral Office in this archdiocese was committed to our charge, nothing has been closer to our heart than the education of our Catholic children."[26] That commitment remained a hallmark of Hanna's episcopate. Under his tenure the Catholic schools in San Francisco were successfully systematized for the first time. In addition, from 1915 to 1935, the number of students in Catholic schools nearly doubled.

Hanna's most important contribution was the centralization and systemization of Catholic schools in the archdiocese. This was in conjunction with a general centralization of Catholic life evident in the creation of the archdiocesan Catholic Charities and other central diocesan offices such as building and finance. Hanna appointed the first archdiocesan superintendent of Catholic schools in 1915, shortly after he had become archbishop. Father Ralph Hunt was assigned the task of "examining, systematizing and co-coordinating the program of instruction in our Elementary and Grammar schools."[27]

To assist Hunt, Hanna formed a scholastic council consisting of all the orders of men and women vowed religious engaged in teaching in the archdiocese: two orders of men (the Brothers of Mary and the Christian Brothers), and twelve orders of women. Together the council worked toward creating a uniform curriculum. In 1922, the council produced a *Course of Study for the Elementary and Grammar Grades* published by the school office and approved by Hanna. The course of study provided standardized courses in "Reading, Language, Grammar and Composition, Spelling, Arithmetic, History and Geography" for grades one through eight.

The council asserted that "these courses should be obligatory in the Parish Schools of the Archdiocese."[28] Hanna "commanded" that all teachers under his jurisdiction follow the course outline, but "requested" that pastors and superiors of religious communities "co-operate" with the program. This indicated the standardization of courses still depended on the good will of pastors and religious. A list of approved textbooks was also provided. A "Course of Study in Religion" was developed with the *Baltimore Catechism,* the required textbook. Yorke's *Textbooks of Religion* were "strongly recommended."[29] A uniform system of textbooks would be in place by 1926.

Hanna also revived the Catholic teachers' institute in 1916 with Dr. Edward Pace of The Catholic University of America providing a week-long series of lectures. By 1918, this was transformed into a four-week summer school program for teachers, directed by Pace and employing professors from The Catholic University of America. By 1929, the program was operating out of Dominican College in San Rafael, and in 1931 it officially became an extension of The Catholic University of America, offering college credit and giving Catholic school teachers an opportunity for post-graduate study.[30]

In 1925, Father James McHugh replaced Hunt as superintendent, and McHugh was replaced in 1929 by Father James Long. In 1929, a school board consisting of seven priests was established for the first time to assist the superintendent in directing the schools.

One last initiative of Hanna's was the "Catholic Educational Fund" (CEF) established in 1922. Though established ostensibly to raise funds for the construction of a new minor seminary, Hanna's advisors suggested making a broader pitch for Catholic education that would appeal to a broader audience. Hanna set three goals for the CEF: (1) to enhance St. Patrick's Seminary, the major seminary for the archdiocese; (2) to build St. Joseph's Minor Seminary; and (3) to erect a normal school to better prepare Catholic school teachers.

The fund drive did not meet with overwhelming success, but Hanna did manage to construct the Minor Seminary which was dedicated in 1924.[31] As the CEF implied, one of the major goals of the Catholic school system was to promote vocations to the diocesan priesthood and to the sisterhood. And for the first six decades of the twentieth century Catholic schools did provide a steady stream of candidates to the seminaries and novitiates.

The final years of Hanna's episcopacy were beset by the economic troubles brought on by the Great Depression. Hanna, never known for his financial acumen, received a coadjutor archbishop in 1932, John J. Mitty from New York. In 1935, Mitty took over as archbishop and set about placing the archdiocese on a firm financial basis. Catholic schools did not regress during the Depression. Surprisingly, enrollments held as Catholics, like other Americans, struggled to make it through the difficult economic times.

Following World War II, the archdiocese and Bay Area enjoyed a boom period of economic and material prosperity. Catholic San Franciscans finally were lodged firmly in the middle class; the church was no longer predominantly working class. The suburban areas of what then constituted the archdiocese especially in San Mateo, Alameda, Contra Costa, and Santa Clara counties witnessed a population boom that resulted in the building of many new parishes and schools.

Construction seemed to be underway everywhere.

The city of San Francisco prospered as well and Catholic schools boomed. Well over 21,000 students were enrolled in Catholic elementary schools by 1960, up from 12,028 in 1940.[32] Though only two new parishes were established in San Francisco during the post-war years, nine new parish schools were established. The two new parishes founded in 1950—St. Stephen and St. Thomas More—opened schools quickly, in 1952 and 1954 respectively.

More surprisingly, long established parishes also erected schools for the first time. For example, St. Michael's parish, founded in 1898, dedicated its school in 1951. By 1960, forty-four of the city's fifty-four parishes had functioning schools. The Baltimore Council mandate that every parish have a school had virtually been accomplished.

High school expansion was equally impressive in the post war years. During the 1910s and 1920s the typical Catholic high school was an extension of the parish grade school. Only three high schools in the city were not attached to a grade school or parish—St. Ignatius, Sacred Heart, and Presentation. By 1960, the number of high schools had declined in the city, but the overall enrollment increased. In the archdiocese, the number of high school students increased by 145 percent in the period from 1945 to 1965.[33] Only seven of the sixteen high schools were attached to parishes, and that number continued to decline in the 1960s.[34] Two new non-parochial high schools were established—Riordan in 1949 and Mercy in 1952. More than seven thousand students were enrolled in the city's Catholic high schools as of 1960.

Many consider the period from 1945 to 1960 to be the golden age of Catholic education in San Francisco. Enrollment reached an all-time high as new schools were being built and old ones expanded. The high morale in school circles reflected that which permeated the rest of the archdiocese and the church in the United States in the 1950s. Scrivani concludes,

A heady ambiance permeated Catholic education. The archdiocesan school office took great pride in the conspicuous material improvements in Catholic education. Similarly, the teaching orders exuded confidence in their swelling numbers, and growing professionalism. Catholic schools were achieving a respectable showing relative to the public schools and a growing respect from the normative culture. A clear horizon offered a seemingly endless expansion of the prevailing pattern.[35]

Unfortunately, this did not turn out to be the case.

With so much expansion, financial strains continued to confront Catholic education. One source of relief was an attempt to achieve tax-free status for Catholic schools. As of 1950, California remained the only state in the Union to tax religious schools. In California, ballot initiatives had been put forth in 1926, and again in 1933, to make denominational schools tax-free. Both initiatives were defeated.

In 1952, church leaders made another attempt, and succeeded in having a proposition ending the tax placed on the California ballot. San Francisco rallied to support the initiative. The campaign, however, resurfaced the old anti-Catholic bogeys, not surprising given the success of Paul Blanshard's *American Freedom and Catholic Power* (1949). Catholic schools were accused of undermining the public schools, of undermining American democracy, of being too foreign and intending to install the pope over all Californians.

Nonetheless the ballot initiative passed and Catholic schools became tax-free. Undeterred, the proposition's opponents, led by the Scottish Rite Masons, contested the proposition in the courts until the Supreme Court finally upheld the proposition in 1956. A new initiative qualified for the 1958 election intending to reestablish the tax. Again, anti-Catholicism reared its ugly head. One advertisement read simply, "California Should Not Pay Taxes to a Foreign Religious Dictator." Despite the Catholic baiting, the initiative was defeated by a wide margin, and Catholic schools remained tax-free.[36]

The church in San Francisco entered the 1960s with great promise. School enrollments continued to soar. In 1961, the Catholic school department was largely responsible for the overwhelming success of Father Patrick Peyton's Rosary Crusade which had succeeded in gathering more than half a million people to pray the rosary in Golden Gate Park. In 1962, the opening of the Second Vatican Council promised continued progress. The death of Mitty in 1961 caused some pain, but the appointment of the popular Archbishop Joseph McGucken assured San Francisco Catholics that everything would be all right.

What a difference a decade makes. By the end of the 1960s, both the Church and the city were in disarray. San Francisco became renowned for its political protests and for the counterculture anchored in the city's Haight Ashbury District. Catholic schools found themselves in a precarious position and experienced their first significant declines in their history.

The problems were not all a result of the 1960s. On one level, Catholic schools were a victim of their own success. The rapid expansion of schools in the post-war era had made impossible personnel demands. There simply were not enough vowed religious to staff the schools. This would have been the case even if convents had remained full. But one of the most startling effects of the 1960s was the exodus of so many sisters from the convents. In addition, fewer young women entered the novitiates. On top of this, many sisters who remained in the convent left the teaching profession in search of more meaningful, often social justice oriented ministries. As a result, Catholic schools had to depend more and more on lay teachers.

Lay teachers had always been a part of Catholic education, but by 1970 they were becoming the core. In 1935, the ratio of religious to lay teachers in the Catholic schools of San Francisco was 50 to 1. By 1968, it was 1 to 1.[37] By the 1970s there were more lay teachers than religious in most schools.

This shift had at least two major effects. First, a tremendous financial strain was placed on the school system as lay teachers had to be paid a living wage. The single greatest increase in parish budgets was the transfer to a lay faculty. As a result, tuitions jumped noticeably. In 1970, for example, Mercy High School doubled its tuition. The same year, Notre Dame des Victoires High School closed, unable to afford the current cost of Catholic education. This story was repeated often over the course of the next four decades. Indicative of the new order, in 1971 archdiocesan high school teachers went on strike to secure recognition of their union and better pay. Second, lay teachers with families could not be expected to have the same devotion to school as sisters and brothers for whom the school was their only ministry and concern.

Though school enrollments remained high through the mid-1960s, they did not last. Between 1969 and 1973, for example, Catholic school enrollment declined by 12 percent. Catholic schools began to look for government assistance to supplement the loss of tuition income. In 1967, thirteen San Francisco schools participated in the government's Title I programs by providing remedial services and materials to qualified students. Many schools became involved in Head Start, Upward Bound, and other Great Society programs.

The biggest change in Catholic schools was their changing ethnic composition. By the mid-1960s significant numbers of Mexican and

Central American immigrants had settled in the Mission District and began to attend Catholic schools. This presaged the future: by 2000 more minority students were attending Catholic schools than the traditional white students of European heritage.

The Catholic schools in San Francisco entered the twenty-first century in a situation very similar to their beginning—they served a largely immigrant community, they struggled with finances, and they competed with public schools, and new public charter schools, for students. And though the number of vowed religious has dwindled dramatically, Catholic schools remain staffed by committed teachers. The fundamental task remains the same: to pass the faith on to a new generation and to promote the Catholic leaders of the future.

NOTES

1. Carey McWilliams and Gunther Barth, quoted in Robert W. Cherny and William Issel, *San Francisco: Presidio, Port, and Pacific Metropolis* (San Francisco: Boyd and Fraser, 1981), 9.

2. Ibid., 10.

3. For the history of the Archdiocese of San Francisco, see Jeffrey M. Burns, *History of the Archdiocese of San Francisco*, Volumes 1-3 (Strasbourg, France: Editions du Signe, 1999-2001).

4. Quoted in John J. McGloin, *California's First Archbishop: The Life of Joseph Sadoc Alemany, OP, 1814-1888* (New York: Herder and Herder, 1966), 126.

5. See Ronald E. Isetti, F.S.C., *Called to the Pacific: A History of the Christian Brothers of the San Francisco District, 1868-1944* (Moraga: St. Mary's College, 1979), 3-5.

6. Quoted in Catherine Ann Curry, P.B.V.M., "Shaping Young San Franciscans: Public and Catholic Schools in San Francisco, 1851-1906," (PhD diss., Graduate Theological Union, Berkeley, CA), 24.

7. Ibid., 23-29.

8. Quoted in Ibid., 67.

9. Brother Lawrence Scrivani, S.M., "Catholic Schools in the Archdiocese of San Francisco," in Jeffrey M. Burns, ed., *Catholic San Francisco: Sesquicentennial Essays* (Menlo Park: Archives of the Archdiocese of San Francisco, 2005), 229.

10. Quoted in Curry, "Shaping Young San Franciscans," 68.

11. Edward J. Hanna quoted in Richard Gribble, C.S.C., *An Archbishop for the People: The Life of Edward J. Hanna* (New York: Paulist Press, 2006), 72.

12. James P. Gaffey, *Citizen of No Mean City: Archbishop Patrick Riordan of San Francisco* (San Francisco: Consortium, 1976), 197.

13. Quoted in Zephyrin Englehardt, O.F.M., *San Francisco or Mission Dolores* (Chicago: Franciscan Herald Press, 1924), 366.

14. Quoted in Gaffey, *Citizen of No Mean City*, 197

15. See Gaffey, *Citizen of No Mean City*, 211.

16. Quoted in Curry, "Shaping Young San Franciscans," 253.

17. See Joseph Brusher, S.J., *Consecrated Thunderbolt: A Life of Father Peter C. Yorke of San Francisco* (Hawthorne, NJ: Joseph Wagner Publishers, 1973), 17-19.

18. Ibid., 17-18.

19. See Jeffrey M. Burns, *A History of the Archdiocese of San Francisco: Glory, Ruin, and Resurrection 1885-1945,* vol. 2 (Strasbourg, France: Editions du Signe, 2000).

20. Quoted in *First Annual Report of Superintendent of Schools, 1915-1916,* 43; Copy in Archives of the Archdiocese of San Francisco (AASF), Menlo Park, CA.

21. Ibid., 44.

22. Ibid.

23. Ibid., 45.

24. Ibid.

25. Peter C. Yorke, *The Fourth Grade: Textbooks of Religion* (San Francisco: The Text Book Publishing Company, 1935, Eighteenth Edition), 3.

26. Quoted in Gribble, *An Archbishop for the People,* 71.

27. Edward J. Hanna, "Mandate of The Most Reverend Archbishop Concerning the Course of Study in Catholic Elementary and Grammar Schools," in *Course of Study for the Elementary and Grammar Grades* (San Francisco: Catholic School Office, 1922), *iii,* AASF.

28. Ibid., *iv.*

29. Sister Mary Ligouri, "Report of the Scholastic Council," in *Course of Study for the Elementary and Grammar Grades* (San Francisco: Catholic School Office, 1922), *v,* AASF.

30. See Brother Lawrence Scrivani, S.M., "Some Trends in the Bay Area Catholic Schools Movement Since 1850," (Unpublished paper presented at The History of Bay Area Catholicism Conference, 1986), AASF.

31. See Gribble, *An Archbishop for the People,* 78-79.

32. "Statistics," School Files, AASF.

33. Scrivani, "Catholic Schools," 233.

34. See Brother T. William Bolts, "Catholic High Schools of San Francisco and the Marianist Tradition," in Burns, *Catholic San Francisco,* 173-180.

35. Scrivani, "Catholic Schools," 234.

36. See Gordon Seeley, "Church-State Conflict and Catholic Schools in California," in Burns, *Catholic San Francisco,* 237-244.

37. Scrivani, "Catholic Schools," 233.

Contributors

JEFFREY M. BURNS has served as the archivist for the Archdiocese of San Francisco since 1983. In addition, he is currently the director of the Academy of American Franciscan History in Berkeley and teaches at the Franciscan School of Theology, St. Patrick's Seminary in Menlo Park, and California State University East Bay in Hayward, California. He is widely published including his *Disturbing the Peace: A History of the Christian Family Movement, 1949-1974* and *Keeping Faith: European and Asian Catholic Immigrants.*

THE REVEREND MICHAEL P. CARUSO, S.J., is an associate professor of education at Loyola Marymount University in Los Angeles, and chairman of the Department of Educational Leadership. He holds a doctorate from the University of San Francisco. His background includes serving in parishes and teaching theology in Jesuit high schools in Missouri and Colorado. He authored fourteen articles for *Catholic Schools in the United States: An Encyclopedia*, published by Greenwood. *Stay with Us Lord: Reflections and Prayers for Educators* was published by NCEA in 2005. He is preparing a manuscript for publication entitled, *Teaching Sisters: Triumph, Trial, and Legacy.* In 2010, Caruso became the thirtieth president of St. Ignatius College Prep in Chicago, Illinois.

ROGER A. FORTIN has been the provost and academic vice president at Xavier University in Cincinnati since 2002 and professor of history at Xavier since 1973. Educated at St. Francis College in Maine, the University of New Hampshire, and Lehigh University, he is the author of several articles and books on a range of historical subjects. His two most recent publications are *Faith and Action: A History of the Catholic Archdiocese of Cincinnati, 1821-1996* and *To See Great Wonders: A History of Xavier University, 1831-2006.*

THOMAS C. HUNT received his Ph.D. in 1971 from the University of Wisconsin-Madison. From 1971 to 1996 he served on the faculty of Virginia Tech University where he received a number of awards for teaching, research, and service. In 1996, he joined the faculty of the University of Dayton where in 2002 he received the University's Alumni Scholarship award. He has authored or edited thirteen books in the last thirteen years, all but one on religion and education. From 1998 to 2008 he served as co-editor of *Catholic Education: A Journal of Inquiry and Practice*, at the time the only refereed journal on Catholic schools in the nation. A professor in the Department of Teacher Education, Hunt is also a Fellow in the Center for Catholic Education.

THE REVEREND RICHARD M. JACOBS, O.S.A., is a professor of educational administration and public administration at Villanova University near Philadelphia. He received his Ph.D. from the University of Tulsa and has published five volumes in the NCEA's "Catholic Educational Leadership" monograph series as well as numerous book chapters and articles in professional journals.

JOHN T. JAMES holds a doctorate in educational administration from the University of Nebraska. He is an associate professor in the Department of Educational Leadership and Higher Education and the director of Catholic Leadership Programs at Saint Louis University. He had thirteen years of experience in education as a Catholic high school teacher, a science department chair, a high school principal, and a president of a K-12 Catholic school system before joining Saint Louis University in 2002. He has published internationally, authored numerous articles, and has contributed to books on Catholic education including the *Encyclopedia of Catholic Education*.

MARIA MAZZENGA is education archivist at the American Catholic History Research Center and University Archives, and adjunct instructor of history at The Catholic University of America in Washington, D.C. She received her Ph.D. in history from The Catholic University of America and is the author of several articles on education in the United States.

STEVE NEIHEISEL is professor and chairman of political science and director of the London Semester Program at Saint Mary's University in San Antonio and visiting professor of public administration at the University of Dayton. He earned the B.A. and M.B.A. degrees from Xavier University in Cincinnati and the Ph.D. from Washington University in St. Louis. In addition to award winning teaching and numerous publications, he actively serves on boards and advisory committees of Catholic schools and colleges.

DAVID O'BRIEN is University Professor of Faith and Culture at the University of Dayton and Loyola Professor of Catholic Studies Emeritus at the College of the Holy Cross. An American historian, he writes on the history and current life of American Catholics.

JUSTIN D. POCHÉ is assistant professor of history and Alexander F. Carson Faculty Fellow in U.S. History at the College of the Holy Cross in Massachusetts. After attending Louisiana State University he received his Ph.D. in history at the University of Notre Dame. He is the author of "The Catholic Citizens' Council: Religion and Massive Resistance in Postwar Louisiana," in a recent issue of the *U.S. Catholic Historian* and is currently revising his manuscript, "Religion, Race, and Rights in Catholic Louisiana, 1938-1970," for publication.

MONSIGNOR THOMAS J. SHELLEY, a priest of the Archdiocese of New York, is professor of Church history at Fordham University. He received his doctorate from The Catholic University of America where his mentor was Monsignor John Tracy Ellis. He is the author of seven books and co-editor of *The Encyclopedia of American Catholic History*. His most recent work is *The Bicentennial History of the Archdiocese of New York, 1808-2008*.

ELLEN SKERRETT, a social historian and independent scholar, is the author of *Born in Chicago: A History of Chicago's Jesuit University*, the first published history of Loyola University. She has written widely about Chicago, its neighborhoods, and its Catholic parishes and institutions. A native of Chicago, she received her B.A. from Rockford College and her M.A. from the University of Chicago's Committee on Social Thought. She served as the primary scholar advisor for the Chicago History Museum's exhibit on Catholic Chicago in 2008-2009, and most recently she co-edited *Chief O'Neill's Sketchy Recollections of an Eventful Life in Chicago* with Mary Lesch.

JOELLEN MCNERGNEY VINYARD grew up in a small Nebraska town where she attended its public school. She received her Ph.D. in urban history from the University of Michigan. She was introduced to the world of Detroit Catholics at Marygrove College where she began her teaching career. Her publications include *The Irish on the Urban Frontier: Nineteenth Century Detroit; For Faith and Fortune: Education of Catholic Immigrants in Detroit, 1905-1925; Michigan: The Great Lakes State;* and *Behind Democracy: Right in the Michigan Grassroots*. She received the outstanding professor award at Marygrove and the outstanding professor and outstanding scholar awards at Eastern Michigan University where she is a professor of history.

TIMOTHY WALCH is director of the Herbert Hoover Presidential Library, one of thirteen such institutions that are part of the National Archives and Records Administration. He also serves as associate editor of the *U.S. Catholic Historian*, the quarterly journal of the U.S. Catholic Historical Society. Educated at the University of Notre Dame and Northwestern University, he is the author or editor of sixteen previous books including *Parish School: American*

Catholic Education from Colonial Times to the Present. The Reverend Andrew M. Greeley refers to *Parish School* as "the best summary review of the history of Catholic education in the last half century."

JOHN J. WHITE is assistant professor of social studies education at the University of Dayton, where he also teaches Irish and Irish American history. Educated at the University of Massachusetts, Boston, and at Boston College, White has published articles on the Marian shrine at Knock and on the development of inquiry-based social studies and history curriculum in the 1960s.

Index

LaVergne, TN USA
30 June 2010

187952LV00004B/6/P